D1154287

DK38
.H42

Nancy Whittier Heer

POLITICS AND HISTORY IN THE SOVIET UNION

INDIANA
PURDUE
LIBRARY
SEP 1974
FORT WAYNE

Copyright © 1971 by
The Massachusetts Institute of Technology

Set in Linotype Baskerville by The Heffernan Press Inc.,
printed and bound in the United States of America by The Colonial Press Inc.

All rights reserved. No part of this book may be reproduced in any form or
by any means, electronic or mechanical, including photocopying, recording,
or by any information storage and retrieval system, without permission in
writing from the publisher.

ISBN 0 262 08 045 1 (hardcover)

Library of Congress catalog card number: 70–128539

DK
38
. H42

For My Parents

To chronicle a revolution can be more difficult and dangerous than to create one. The professional and personal life experience of Soviet historians of the Communist Party of the Soviet Union since the Bolshevik Revolution is often cited to demonstrate the proposition that he who commands the present controls the record of the past. But Soviet historiography also suggests that he who controls the record of the past legitimates his authority to command the present and to define the future.

One of the premises of this book is that historiography functions in any political system to socialize the coming generation, to legitimate political institutions, to perpetuate established mores and mythology, and to rationalize official policies. It is further argued that within the post-Stalin Soviet political system — because of a unique blend of ideological, historical, and political factors — historiography is charged with these functions to an unprecedented degree. The very specific claims of Marxist-Leninist doctrine, in which history is seen as both the decadent past and the glorious march of progress toward communism, place the Soviet historian under special tensions.

The Soviet historian, and particularly the specialist in the Communist Party, is required to perform as scholar, high priest, and political functionary. He is hedged about with a variety of official and socioeconomic or informal mechanisms, designed by the regime to stimulate the scholarly and propagandistic production of historical materials within approved boundaries and, at the same time, to curb undesirable interpretation and any challenge to official hypotheses and doctrines. There is evidence, however, that this very attempt by the party at total control, once terror has been discarded in favor of more subtle methods, is dysfunctional to a marked degree. Party history often becomes the vehicle of revisionist political concepts and unorthodox interpretations, precisely because the regime closes off overt contemporary discussion of political alternatives. The historiography of the party, dealing as it does with the most sensitive political issues, can fruitfully be examined as a subsystem that reveals features of the larger political system in high relief and intensified colar. Part One of this study attempts to delineate and evaluate this subsystem.

Khrushchev's denunciation of Stalin in 1956 cast the party historian in the role of guardian of the new social conscience: he was ordered to write *Hamlet* without Hamlet — to create a new image of the party as an infallible collectivity, to decry Stalin and his policies without discrediting the political system in which he had flourished. Part Two deals with the story of how Soviet historians of the CPSU of varying personal and professional backgrounds and viewpoints interpreted their assignment during the first eleven years after the secret speech, traces the development of group consciousness among them, and suggests a typology of historians.

Part Three focuses on some specific historical issues which raise significant political and theoretical questions. Here I am concerned about what appear to be key ongoing political aspects of the system which are only cryptically discussed in the historical literature: the bases of party legitimacy, the limits of political opposition, the infallibility of the party, the party as an international model for socialist development, the role of the individual leader in a socialist state.

Finally, Part Four confronts Soviet historiography in the guise of Janus. It is argued that this subsystem can be pushed outward in the temporal as well as the spatial dimension, that political history in a monolithic system provides some base for speculation on future political trends.

The present study is based upon a doctoral dissertation prepared for the Department of Government, Harvard University. I owe an enormous debt of gratitude to Professor Merle Fainsod, who guided the dissertation and provided generous counsel later. I am also grateful for the comments of Professors Donald L. M. Blackmer, John Keep, Sanford R. Lieberman, Barrington Moore, Jr., Richard Pipes, and Adam B. Ulam. And to the happy subsystem of the Russian Research Center and its library within Harvard, a heartfelt thank you.

N.W.H.

Cambridge, Massachusetts
May 1970

Every historian is a revolutionary at heart . . . or should be.

Truman Nelson, *The Right of Revolution*

The study of history has never been mere curiosity, a withdrawal into the past for the sake of the past . . . Historical science has been and remains an arena of sharp ideological struggle; it has been and remains a class, party history . . . Our ideological opponents contend that the Party spirit of Soviet historiography is incompatible with objective scientific research . . . [But] the great force of Marxist-Leninist doctrine is that it places in the researcher's hands the only correct and scientific creative method of objective, comprehensive study of social phenomena and processes.

Editorial, "Soviet Historical Science at a New Stage of Development," *Voprosy istorii,* no. 8 (1960).

Marx captured the Hegelian god of history and brought him to earth to reign over a dialectic of modes of production and property relationships. The process of transubstantiation, however, did not destroy the mystical quality of history, which persists in Marxist social theory. The sense of mystery behind Marx's system consists precisely in the ineluctable flow of the dialectic, that life force which brings men — unaware and often unwilling — inevitably to the threshold of communism.

With Marx the ultimate cause or first mover of history becomes any change in the methods of production and exchange; all other factors are derivative. "The mode of production in material life determines the general character of the social, political and spiritual process of life. It is not the consciousness of men that determines their existence, but, on the contrary, their social existence determines their consciousness."[1] Tradition, natural conditions, institutions, and ideas may exert an influence upon events; but they can only modify, accelerate, or retard the process of the historical dialectic. Thus in attempting to understand any phenomenon, the Marxist historian must cut through the superstructure ("the legal, political, religious, aesthetic, or philosophic — in short, ideological — forms") to discern its substance, or economic foundations. These foundations "can be determined with the precision of natural science."[2]

The Marxian thesis that the economic factor is the determining element in all historical situations has generated a rich literature

1. Karl Marx, *A Contribution to the Critique of Political Economy,* in *Basic Writings on Politics and Philosophy — Karl Marx and Frederick Engels,* ed. L. S. Feuer (Garden City: Doubleday, 1959), p. 43.
2. *Ibid.,* p. 44.

of scholarly dispute over the nature and extent of his economic determinism. Already in 1890 Engels wanted to clarify (or revise) the doctrine. Writing to Joseph Bloch he avers:

According to the materialist conception of history, the *ultimately* determining element in history is the production and reproduction of real life . . . The economic situation is the basis, but the various elements of the superstructure — political forms of the class struggle and its results . . . also exercise their influence upon the course of the historical struggles and in many cases preponderate in determining their form.[3]

Whatever the exact parameter of the secondary role accorded to the superstructure, clearly it is the inconsistencies or "contradictions" in material life which propel the Marxian dialectic of historical materialism. The basis of economic causation is always a lack of fit between the material or technological modes of production and the societal relationships imposed upon economic activity. Marx is principally concerned with the phenomenon of British industrialization, which he sees as a classic example of the incongruity of a production relationship (private ownership of factories) made obsolete by new methods of production (communal work) within the factory. The derivative social situation is in acute contradiction with the primal material factors: a revolutionary moment exists. This revolutionary moment is only the most recent in the long line of crises that have propelled human historical experience from one epoch to a higher stage of economic and social development.

At a certain stage of their development the material forces of production in society come into conflict with the existing relations of production, or — what is but a legal expression for the same thing — with the property relations within which they had been at work before. From forms of development of the forces of production these relations turn into their fetters. Then comes the period of social revolution.[4]

The concept of historical movement as progress remains unquestioned by Marx and his followers, whether revisionist or orthodox.

Perhaps the most complex aspect of Marxian historical theory is the problem of the political actor. Marx opens his argument in the *Manifesto of the Communist Party* with the proposition:

3. Engels to Joseph Bloch, London, September 21–22, 1890, in *ibid.*, pp. 397–398.
4. *A Contribution to the Critique of Political Economy*, in *ibid.*, pp. 43–44.

"The history of all hitherto existing society is the history of class struggles." Vital to his argument is the theory of a dominant class within every society, which exploits other classes and creates a repressive state to enforce its economic interest. Economic contradictions are acted out on the social level through the continuous struggle of the repressed class against the ruling class and its tool, the state. On the heels of victory for the oppressed class follows the crystallization of a new pattern of class antagonisms based upon the new economic system, which will in turn culminate in violent class struggle. The historical actor is thus the emergent class, and Marx's revolutionary appeal is so directed.

Historical materialism requires an adaptive human being, and the Marxian man is favored with a plastic nature. Man's ideas, goals, interests, and behavior are class-engendered. The human being is environmentally determined; a man's environment is structured by society and, more particularly, by his class position within society. When it is remembered that for Marx the hidden basis of any society is its system of material production, the argument comes full circle back to the economic factor.

But Marx wants more to change the world than to explain it, and this dichotomizes his view of man and his theory of history. He is apparently caught in a contradiction between economic determinism and revolutionary activism, and this dilemma is displayed most clearly in his treatment of the historical actor. On the one hand, he pictures men as enmeshed in production relationships and political tradition independent of their will. On the other, he attacks Feuerbach for what he sees as his typically German preoccupation with the contemplative, abstract side of philosophy. Marx insists that materialism must be practical activity. Further, "The materialist doctrine that men are products of circumstances and upbringing and that, therefore, changed men are products of other circumstances and changed upbringing, forgets that it is men that change circumstances, and that the educator himself needs educating."[5]

However, the real question for Marx does not consist of choosing between the passivity of historical determinism and revolutionary activism, since he manages to have some of both. Rather his dilemma is one of defining the historical context within which man can meaningfully act. Men do not control their circum-

5. Karl Marx, *Theses on Feuerbach*, in *ibid.*, p. 244.

stances; even their consciousness is determined by their social existence. But history, as noted before, is cunning and possesses a mysterious sense of timing.

No social order ever disappears before all the productive forces for which there is room in it have been developed, and new, higher relations of production never appear before the material conditions of their existence have matured in the womb of the old society. Therefore mankind always takes up only such problems as it can solve, since, looking at the matter more closely, we will always find that the problem itself arises only when the material conditions necessary for its solution already exist or are at least in the process of formation.[6]

Men make their own history, but they do not make it just as they please; they do not make it under circumstances chosen by themselves, but under circumstances directly encountered, given, and transmitted from the past.[7]

From time to time, then, historical conditions are appropriate for class actions, and at these historical moments the emergent class moves decisively in the direction established by the dialectical process.

Marx's concept of the political leader is never fully enunciated in his writings; but it is possible to derive from scattered remarks what might be called a theory of interchangeable leadership. The figure of the individual leader is of incidental importance to Marx, since the leader appears within the economic context and is historically significant only as a class agent. If Napoleon had not appeared, the historical situation would have generated another leader to act his part. Like any other element of the superstructure, the individual leader can act only within the historical situation presented; his power is to modify, accelerate, or retard a single incident pertaining to a necessary outcome.

Even the communists are significant only as "the most advanced and resolute section of the working-class parties of every country . . . which pushes forward all others"; "they do not set up any sectarian principles of their own, by which to shape and mold the proletarian movement."[8] Although the communists possess a clear understanding of the historical process and ultimate class

6. *A Contribution to the Critique of Political Economy,* in *ibid.,* p. 44.
7. Karl Marx, *The Eighteenth Brumaire of Louis Bonaparte,* in *ibid.,* p. 320.
8. Karl Marx and Friedrich Engels, *Manifesto of the Communist Party,* in *ibid.,* p. 20.

goal which is beyond the average member of the class, they have no interests distinct from those of the proletarian class as a whole, no separate and self-conscious identity.

Such, then, is Lenin's heritage of historical theory. But with Lenin's appearance historical determinism becomes activism, because Lenin reads Marx in the imperative voice. Lenin's unique perception is that history is more than the majestic Hegelian force moving the world: history provides the situations within which the revolutionary hero acts. Lenin thus opted fcr the activist Marx, who hoped and worked for revolution in 1848; he personalized Marx's concept of the communist party and identified it with the Bolshevik faction. His choice of Marx the incendiary author of the *Manifesto* and revolutionary organizer over the scholarly Marx was neither sudden nor without ambivalence. The thrust of the Bolshevik argument moved progressively from the anatomical science of revolution to the art of creating the revolution; it paced the worsening crisis as Marx's arguments had in 1848.

Was Lenin's insistence on revolutionary action simply a function of his own temporal position in the history of Russia, that is, a classically Marxist analysis of the leader as the necessary product of his class and time? We will never know whether, had Lenin died in exile, another such leader would have appeared. But class as a determining category in Lenin's case must be dismissed, for he had no hereditary claim as spokesman for the proletariat; his family was of the petty landed gentry. The argument that his activism can be explained entirely by the Russian context must also fail, for other professed Russian Marxists of his day disputed bitterly his vision of the role of the Russian workers as well as his analysis of the historical moment in 1917.

Lenin never set out for the scholar's delight an integrated theory of history. Historical materialism had been invented, and Hegel was standing quite firmly on his head: Lenin saw his task to be that of the Marxist apostle to Russia who would lead the few, convert the masses, and usher in the revolution. Faced with such a role and sensing the approach of the revolutionary moment, the faithful cannot be allowed to remain passive; they must seize history and shake it until it yields its promise. Despite the paucity of his philosophical writing, however, Lenin's interpretation of

Marxism runs deeper than a mere apologia for tactical decisions: his activist concept of history is central to his unique brand of Marxism. Such an argument becomes more plausible when we look at one of Lenin's early works, before the idea of revolution had become completely suffused in the political maneuvers and tactical quarrels of 1917.

Lenin's *What Is To Be Done?*, published in 1902, is more analytical than most of his works and provides an unusually compact selection of statements and assumptions relevant to his concept of history. In trying to define the nature and functions of the nascent Russian social-democratic party, Lenin comments on the uses of history. Because social democracy is "essentially an international movement . . . starting in a young country," it can be successful "only on the condition that it assimilates the experience of other countries." But mere acquaintance with this historical evidence is not sufficient. "A critical attitude is required . . . and ability to subject it to independent tests."[9]

The notable feature in Lenin's historical references is their instrumental quality, which is reminiscent of the Machiavellian utilization of history as a kind of treasure chest of illustrative examples. This does not mean that the two approaches can be equated; indeed they cannot be, except in this shared concept of history as a didactic tool. Machiavelli, of course, lacked that vision of history as progressive development which is essential to Marx and Lenin. The point here is simply that Lenin sees an instrumental side to history which is not present in Marx: historical examples will be consciously used by the leader and the party to move history forward.

In delicate balance with this instrumental facet of Lenin's view of history is his insistence upon the uniqueness of the Russian situation. Because of the severity of autocratic repressions, the Russian worker will have to withstand "trials immeasurably more severe" than those of his German brother. "History has now confronted us with an immediate task which is *more revolutionary than are the immediate tasks* that confront the proletariat of any other country. The fulfillment of this task . . . places the Russian proletariat in the vanguard of the international revolutionary proletariat."[10] Lenin then admonishes the Russian social demo-

9. V. I. Lenin, *What Is To Be Done?* (New York: International Publishers, 1929), p. 28.
10. *Ibid.*, p. 30.

crats to be inspired with the same devoted determination and energy that marked the Russian revolutionists of the seventies (who were most certainly not workers or peasants). In the same context he manages to convey the impression that Engels's designation of the German workers as occupying the leading position among the European proletariat referred to a particular, and long past, episode.[11]

The development of the socialist movement, then, is seen by Lenin as culminating in a particular country, Russia, in which history has cunningly prepared the greatest contradiction of all time. This national fixation is obviously antithetical to Marx's historical theory, which, because it dealt in economic (and therefore transnational) categories, anticipated a general European revolution.

Moreover, Lenin defines the uniqueness of the Russian situation as essentially political. It is the antisocialist laws, the "gloom of autocracy and the domination of the gendarmes," which define the Russian historical moment; according to Marx's criteria, though, Russia was not ripe for revolution because it was insufficiently capitalistic and industrialized. When Lenin discusses the problem of the peasantry, it is almost entirely in political rather than economic terms, reflecting again his determination to elude Marx's pessimistic prognosis for a backward and preponderantly peasant economy.

Lenin's political focus appears most sharply in his quarrels with those Russian Marxists nicknamed the Economists. He denounces their slogan "Politics always obediently follows economics" as a crude vulgarization of economic materialism.[12] Material or economic conditions are not, then, the sole — or even the ultimate — causal factors in history. The Economists' plea of "unfavorable conditions," as justifying the political passivity of most social-democratic groups in Russia during the 1890s, is flayed by Lenin as an untrue and cringing excuse for their own lack of perception and courage. Not the material environment but the leaders' lack

11. Lenin reproduces a passage from Engels's *Peasant War in Germany*, which credits the German workers with two advantages: they belong to the most theoretical nation of Europe, and the Germans were the last to appear in the labor movement. He then concludes: "Engels's words proved prophetic. Within a few years, the German workers were subjected to severe trials in the form of the anti-Socialist laws; but they were fully armed to meet the situation, and succeeded in emerging from it victoriously." Cf. *Ibid.*, pp. 29–30.
12. *Ibid.*, p. 28.

of sufficient training was to blame for the stagnation.[13] Thus Lenin's analysis of this historical situation is a startling reversal of Marx.

Essentially the same argument is made with respect to the current (1902) period: "the principal cause of the present crisis in Russian Social-Democracy is that the *leaders . . . lag behind the spontaneous rising of the masses . . .* The most serious sin we commit is that we *degrade* our political and *our organizational* tasks to the level of immediate, 'palpable,' 'concrete' interests of the every-day economic struggle."[14]

Such statements exhibit more than tactical preferences. They betray a perception new to Marxists: that of historical movement as politically rather than economically engendered. Certainly Lenin believes that every leader moves within a given set of economic conditions, but this assumption had become a truism and even an excuse for inaction by the dull and fearful. Historical events are caused and mastered by the political activities of men who can read the present as well as the past in the light of the Marxist dialectic and who can act artistically as well as scientifically to force the historical moment to fruition. Marx has been politicized.

Central to Lenin's political and activist view of history is his theory of spontaneity and class consciousness. Left to their own devices, that is, acting out of material deprivation alone, the proletariat can achieve only a trade-union consciousness — a purely economic set of demands and program of action.

The history of all countries shows that the working class, exclusively by its own effort, is able to develop only trade-union consciousness, i.e., it may itself realize the necessity for combining in unions, to fight against the employers and to strive to compel the government to pass necessary labor legislation, etc.

The workers can acquire class political consciousness *only from without,* that is, only outside of the economic struggle, outside of the sphere of relations between workers and employers.[15]

The social democrats must bring this consciousness to the workers through political agitation.

As Plekhanov pointed out as early as 1904, Lenin's argument

13. *Ibid.,* p. 35.
14. *Ibid.,* pp. 99–100.
15. *Ibid.,* pp. 32–33, 76.

was non-Marxist because it denied the fundamental Marxist tenets that material conditions determine thought and that objective factors alone — economic necessity — would drive the proletariat to a socialist revolution.[16]

Leopold Haimson's analysis of the development of Bolshevism shows the deep roots in Russian intellectual history of the conflicting concepts of consciousness and spontaneity. These terms came to stand for complex clusters of ideas about rationalism and feeling, economic determinism and voluntarism, which altered their content depending on the times and the individuals. He correctly points out that in the Russian context

even the most deterministic of Russian Marxists, even Plekhanov, had been agreeable to the active supervisory role that Social Democracy would exercise in Russia's transformation; thus it was that most of them had been reconciled to the completely independent political role that Social Democracy would maintain as the sole responsible agent of the historical process . . . even the Revisionists supported the political activities of Social Democracy as positive efforts toward Russia's awakening to political life.[17]

Lenin, however, went beyond this general position to insist that political consciousness and spontaneity are two discrete categories. He rejects Marx's expectation that spontaneous workers' revolts will develop of themselves into a self-conscious class movement. But Lenin does see a relationship in time between spontaneity and consciousness, which he develops in an historical analysis of the widespread strikes of the late 1890s.

this strike movement certainly bore a spontaneous character. But there is a difference between spontaneity and spontaneity. Strikes occurred in Russia in the seventies, and in the sixties . . . accompanied by the "spontaneous" destruction of machinery, etc. Compared with these "revolts" the strikes of the nineties might even be described as "conscious," to such an extent do they mark the progress which the labor movement had made since that period . . . Definite demands were put forward, the time to strike was carefully chosen, known cases and examples in other places were discussed, etc. While the revolts were simply uprisings of the oppressed, the systematic strikes represented the class struggle in

16. G. V. Plekhanov, "The Working Class and the Social Democratic Intelligentsia," *Iskra*, nos. 70–71 (July 25–August 1, 1904); as cited in Leopold Haimson, *The Russian Marxists and the Origins of Bolshevism* (Cambridge: Harvard University Press, 1955), p. 193.
17. *Ibid.*, p. 213.

embryo, but only in embryo . . . the workers were not and could not be conscious of the irreconcilable antagonism of their interests to the whole of the modern political and social system, i.e., it was not yet Social-Democratic consciousness.[18]

By recognizing a temporal rather than a causal relationship between spontaneous worker revolts and class-conscious revolution, Lenin requires conscious political action, which he defines as the exclusive province of a party of professional revolutionists. And a definition of the propelling force of history as not only political but conscious in the Russian context requires the Leninist party and its leader, who go beyond a scientific interpretation of the course of history to shape its course. Both Russian history and its Bolshevik leader are unique; and such a leader can demand the overleaping of stages of history and the conditions for revolution thought essential by Marx. When the subjective factors for revolution present themselves, the god of history "requires" the hero to rewrite the theory of history. Thus Lenin on the eve of revolution in 1917 said: "It would be naive to wait for a 'formal' majority on the side of the Bolsheviks; no revolution ever waits for *this* . . . History will not forgive us if we do not assume power now."[19] "To hesitate is a crime."[20]

Although Lenin has rewritten Marx's theory of history in the active voice, he retains much of the same ambivalence toward history that plagued Marx. The past is evil, oppressive, and rushing toward destruction: it must be repudiated by the revolutionist. Yet the past is literally the passport to the future, and history represents the dynamic process that culminates in communism. This attraction-repulsion syndrome is always subtly at work in Soviet historiography, as symbolized by the early post-Revolution establishment of institutions for the study of history.[21]

18. Lenin, *What Is To Be Done?*, p. 32.
19. N. Lenin, Letter to the Central Committee, the Petrograd and Moscow Committees of the RSDLP, September 25–27, 1917, in *Collected Works of V. I. Lenin* (New York: International Publishers, 1932), XXI, book I, p. 222.
20. N. Lenin, Letter to the Central Committee, Moscow Committee, Petrograd Committee, and Bolshevik Members of the Petrograd and Moscow Soviets, October 16–20, 1917, in *Collected Works of V. I. Lenin*, XXI, book II, p. 69.
21. The Socialist Academy for the Social Sciences was set up under the Marxist historian M. N. Pokrovsky in 1918. The Commission on History of the Party and the October Revolution ("Istpart") was created by a Sovnarkhom decree in April 1920 to collect party documents and memoirs and other materials relating to the October Revolution and the Civil War; and the Red Archives were founded in 1922.

The Central Committee proceeded from the fact that the Party should not be afraid to tell the people the truth.

Historians are dangerous people. They are capable of upsetting everything. They must be directed.

N. S. Khrushchev, 1956

HISTORY AS A POLITICAL SUBSYSTEM 1

Although the role of historiography in the USSR is grounded in Lenin's concepts of history, it has become ever more closely bound up with the concerns of governing. The imminent dream of a socialist state has become reality, and the essential focus of official Soviet historiography has shifted from revolution to controlled change in the service of political stability. Nonetheless, the basic functions performed by history in the Soviet Union have remained remarkably constant since 1918. The changes in historiography since 1956 — however significant and portentous — must in the last analysis be defined as incremental shifts of emphasis, method, and approach which have tended to modify, augment, and dramatize — rather than to overturn — the functions of historiography in the Soviet system.

For purposes of analysis, I shall distinguish here between stated — that is, officially declared — objectives of historiography and those unacknowledged functions that operate by virtue of the very nature of the Soviet political system. These categories may be termed the formal and informal functions of Soviet historiography. It is important to stress that unstated or implicit objectives are not fortuitous or esoteric: these more subtle usages of historical writing are consciously encouraged by the political leadership and are generally recognized by the broad reading public in the USSR as well as by the scholarly community. But such common knowledge does not constitute official acknowledgment. The distinction being made here is that the informal functions are not explicitly and openly described in published articles and books as reasons for writing history.

There are obvious problems in any functional analysis of historiography in the Soviet system. A focus on the political uses of history by the regime by definition is skewed toward an examination of the leadership's intentions and the capacity of a political-cultural factor to contribute to the stability of the system. Dysfunctional and disruptive effects that are unintended or unanticipated tend to fall outside the functional model, and this is of course especially damaging to a study of a controlled but always fluctuating political system. Nonetheless, there are important insights to be gained from such an approach.

The Formal Functions
Repository of tradition and legend. In any society, history functions in part as a repository of public tradition and legend. But

myth building poses special problems for historians in a state born of revolution. The overturn in 1917 repudiated tsarist society and politics *in toto*. True, Stalin reincorporated much of the older Russian tradition into Soviet history, beginning in the mid-1930s, but this nationalist impulse has again been muffled since his death. The tsarist Russian state is now no longer adjudged automatically more advanced than its Central Asian or other neighbors. With the repudiation of some of the more glaring examples of Stalin's Russian nationalism, the focus of heroic legend becomes political, the criteria more complex, and the tasks of evaluating legends more difficult.

Pressure is continuous upon historians, and particularly historians of the Communist Party of the Soviet Union (CPSU) and the Soviet period, to provide examples worthy of emulation, since an important and officially stated function of history is to acquaint Soviet youth with their revolutionary forebears. Khrushchev, the self-made man par excellence, had a well-known and often-articulated horror of softness among the new generation that was growing up in a relatively affluent society, unable to imitate or even to imagine the sacrifices of the early Russian Bolsheviks. Although his successors' style of governance and oratory does not permit such outbursts against the ignorant and selfish youth, there is no evidence that they are any less concerned with the problem of perpetuating this heritage. An article in *Pravda* on the eve of the Twenty-Third Party Congress is typical of many. In it the author, who is head of the Central Committee Department of Propaganda and Agitation for the RSFSR, stresses society's responsibility for bringing up the younger generation, who

did not see with their own eyes the great labor victory of their fathers and mothers, the first people in the world to build a socialist society; they did not see their heroic struggle in the harsh years of the Great Patriotic War . . . It is precisely by the example of the courage and heroism of the grandfathers, fathers and mothers . . . that today's youth is tempered.[1]

Exhorter and agitator. Closely linked with the function of repository of tradition and legend are the conscious, didactic uses of history. "The honorable duty of Soviet scholars is to bring en-

1. M. Khaldiev, "Vospityvat molodezh v dukhe revoliutsionnykh idealov," *Pravda*, November 28, 1965, pp. 2–3.

lightenment to the masses."[2] Stalin's usage of history in this respect was crudely instrumental, as witnessed by his famous formulation of the transmission-belt image. He saw historiography simply as another means of molding public opinion, as the *Short Course* attests.[3]

During the decade 1956–1966 a subtle but significant change took place in the official concept of the didactic function of history. History remains a utilitarian and politically oriented science, but its very utility as a teacher and guide to policy is increasingly seen to be dependent upon higher scholarship, more sophisticated methodology, and more concrete investigations of the past. The following quotations are representative of the new formulation:

History is a political science. But not in that vulgar sense which merely proposes the distortion of historical truth to please a political situation. History is not "politics projected into the past." Soviet historical science has successfully outgrown the subjective posture of the M. N. Pokrovsky school . . . History is inseparably linked with political life, because it helps society delimit the tasks lying before it arising out of the path already trod.[4]

The Party has always stressed that history is a Party science, that scholars should not retreat into their shells, should not dissociate themselves from life and study history for history's sake. History is not politics projected into the past but the study of the past which helps in the framing and implementation of contemporary Party policy. Soviet historians have always been and always will be the Party's worthy helpmeets in the communist education of the working people.[5]

One of the chief reasons for repudiation of the "illustrative method," associated in Soviet writing with the personality cult of Stalin, was its inutility. This method is castigated in one article: "Particular propositions were simply bolstered with individual examples, without inquiry into the extent to which they were typical, or comparison and criticism of sources, and without study of the material in its totality."[6] The rational policymaker requires better historical support than such methods can provide.

2. "Ob ocherednykh zadachakh idealogicheskoi raboty partii," *Pravda*, June 22, 1963, p. 1.
3. *History of the Communist Party of the Soviet Union (Bolsheviks), Short Course* (Toronto: Francis White Publishers, 1939).
4. E. Zhukov, "Istoriia i sovremennost," *Kommunist*, no. 11 (1959), p. 46.
5. M. Nechkina, Iu. Poliakov, and L. Cherepnin, "Nekotorye voprosy istorii sovetskoi istoricheskoi nauki," *Kommunist*, no. 9 (1961), p. 70.
6. *Ibid.*, p. 60.

The view of history as a teaching tool easily generates the analogy of Soviet historians as engaged in the writing of bad Westerns or, at best, somewhat sophisticated morality plays. A theoretical problem then arises: What happens to the morality play itself after all the sinners are reformed? To be sure, the Devil remains as an ultimate evil (Trotsky persists in this guise). But the removal of the class enemy by the completion of the building of socialism has robbed Soviet and party history of its natural pupils and antiheroes. Nonetheless, the pedagogic function is officially understood to be a permanent aspect of Soviet historiography: the analogy of the morality play becomes more relevant because the lessons become spiritual rather than political. One commentator resolves the issue: "In our country, where class and national antagonism is absent, in a country which is led by the great ideas of communism, the didactic function of history is completely directed to the formation and development of the highest, most positive, spirit of man."[7]

The Informal Functions

Legitimation of the system. By chronicling the exploits of the revolutionary founders of the Soviet Union, by showing the obedience of their historical actions to Marxist historical laws, and by developing personal and ideological connections between the founders and contemporary leaders, Soviet historiography performs the implicit function of legitimating the political system. Quite evidently, the seizure of power in 1917 by the Bolsheviks does not in and of itself justify the act of revolution: historical rationalization of the events of 1917 rests on Lenin's correct analysis of the historical situation in Marxist terms and popular support of the Bolsheviks, as well as Lenin's tactical genius. The treatment accorded the October Revolution by various Soviet historians over the last few years is of interest on several counts and will be discussed in some detail later. My concern here is to point out that the history of the year 1917 and the figures of Lenin and the Old Bolsheviks are used to legitimate the Soviet system down to the present day.

The Old Bolsheviks act as living icons, whose very appearance at selected public occasions links the present political leadership

7. Iu. A. Poliakov, "Kommunisticheskoe vospitanie i istoriia," *Voprosy istorii*, no. 7 (1963), p. 3.

with the founders of the system. Lacking a blood line, religious ordination, or popularly elected party leaders, this ideological legitimation is of considerable symbolic importance. Old Bolsheviks also perform the function of validating historical accounts. On occasion, letters from Old Bolsheviks published in a newspaper or journal will point out factual errors or omissions, although such criticism always stops just short of any interpretative analysis of the significance or underlying causes of the events. There are also letters and messages that convey a greeting or stamp of approval to various party, Soviet, or other official meetings. Such communications are almost invariably a group effort, and most convey the impression of being inspired by someone outside the group. However, the prestige of the Old Bolsheviks seems sufficiently imposing to support this kind of exploitation without itself being tarnished.

Since the Twentieth Party Congress, the treatment of the Old Bolsheviks in historical and general writings has become more complete, sophisticated, and scholarly. They emerge from the obscurity to which a jealous Stalin consigned them in the *Short Course* as personalities in their own right, comrades of Lenin. It might be said that they now perform their legitimating function more successfully, as flesh-and-blood heroes. The turning point was announced in a critique of the treatment of Old Bolsheviks by the *Great Soviet Encyclopedia,* published in *Voprosy istorii* in mid-1956.[8] The author of the review decries the reduction in number of articles about early Bolshevik activists in the second edition (published in 1950–1958) as compared to the first (1924–1947), and points out some important omissions and errors of fact which he traces to the desire to exaggerate Stalin's role in the party.[9] In general the Mensheviks receive more publicity than the Old Bolsheviks in the second edition. The reviewer suggests that the editors issue a special volume of the encyclopedia to correct the many mistakes and omissions (this has not been done). But a number of reminiscences and memoirs of Old Bolsheviks did begin to appear in celebration of the fortieth anniversary of the

8. G. M. Denisov, "Ob osveshchenii v Bolshoi Sovetskoi Entsiklopedii deiatel-nosti vydaiushchikhsia bolshevikov," *Voprosy istorii,* no. 5 (1956), pp. 141–145.
9. This policy of denigrating Old Bolsheviks to inflate Stalin has caused some curious phenomena. In volume nine, for example, the article on the Eighth Congress (pp. 223–225) lists those who came out against the Leninist line and omits all Lenin's supporters except Stalin.

October Revolution, and their exploits and contributions continued to be more fully reflected in historical literature in the ensuing decade. Special efforts seem to have been made to publish materials demonstrating the organizational talents of Elena Stasova and Sverdlov and his wife, K. T. Novgorodtseva, which were long ignored to focus on Stalin's cadre building.[10] A special conference of Old Bolsheviks was held in 1962, at the Central Party Archives of the Institute of Marxism-Leninism, to develop a systematic publication schedule for memoirs of the early party workers.[11]

The figure of Lenin in this context of historical legitimation is especially interesting. The resurgence of attention to Lenin developed during the Khrushchev period to the magnitude of a cult. The focus on Lenin was specifically called for by speakers at the Twentieth Party Congress in 1956 and bears a clear relationship to the denigration of Stalin: Lenin was exalted during the post-1956 period to heights previously reserved only for Stalin, and this adulation was designed to serve a specific political function, namely, the eradication of Stalin's historical and theoretical preeminence and the destruction of his claim to be Lenin's heir. The way was cleared for the buildup of the party as Lenin's legitimate successor. By means of such a theory of the CPSU as the repository of Leninism, Lenin's legacy could be passed without direct personal contact with Lenin himself to leaders of the new generations. The party thus provides the mechanism for a papal succession, replacing apostolic succession.

Lenin functions in contemporary Soviet historiography simultaneously as an actual historical figure, as a deity whose utterances are sacred, and as a historian. These functions are for the most part performed discretely, and the literature shows subtle modulations in tone when treating Lenin in these several guises. For example, a straightforward descriptive style — albeit more adulatory than that accorded other political personalities — is employed by the historian who is relating an anecdote or describing

10. See "Iz perepiski E. D. Stasovoi i K. T. Novgorodtsevoi (Sverdlovoi) (Mart-Dekabr 918)," *Voprosy istorii*, no. 10 (1956), pp. 85–101; K. T. Sverdlova, "Deiatelnost Ia. M. Sverdlova v 1917," *Voprosy istorii*, no. 6 (1956), pp. 3–15; and F. I. Drabkina, "Vserossiiskoe soveshchanie bolshevikov v marte 1917," *Voprosy istorii*, no. 9 (1956), pp. 3–16.
11. "Ob uchastii starykh bolshevikov v rabote zhurnala," *Voprosy istorii KPSS*, no. 2 (1963), pp. 155–156.

any particular aspect of Lenin's leadership. As standards of historical research in general have improved, there have been efforts on the part of at least some historians of the party to apply scholarly methods of research to materials on Lenin's activities. In an article on the methodology of historical references, a leading historian of the CPSU reports with evident satisfaction: "There have also been several achievements in the development of the youngest area of Soviet source-work — regarding the sources on history of the CPSU." He then commends several journal articles in *Voprosy istorii KPSS* which are concerned with the problems of validation of specific works of Lenin and the usage of reminiscences of Lenin as historical sources.[12]

Forty years after Lenin's death new documents and writings are still being discovered, and a continuing stream of anthologies of his work is being published, many of which are oriented toward specific problems of theory or tactics.[13] When Lenin is invoked as an authority on a point of doctrine or of tactics for general application, it is Lenin's writings that are consulted. In such cases, the citation is made to the *Collected Works*, by volume and page; virtually never is there an indication of the specific work referred to, or its date of conception or publication, or the historical situation that evoked such a formulation. In short, in the case of doctrinal reference, any consideration of temporal limitation or qualification is eliminated and Lenin's writings are treated as a religious text. Obviously the *Collected Works* throughout its several editions has enjoyed the advantage of other doctrinal compilations that span a period of many years and varying circumstances: inconsistencies and shifts of emphasis and evaluation in the text allow selective citation to meet the needs of changing situations and to solve a variety of theoretical problems.

The conscious and explicit development of Lenin as a historian of Russia and the early Soviet period, as well as the utilization of his writings as scholarly sources of historical evidence as well

12. G. N. Golikov, "Na perednem krae istoricheskoi nauki," *Voprosy istorii,* no. 11 (1961), p. 37.

13. An example of such a topical collection is one especially relevant to history of the CPSU, titled *V. I. Lenin on the Laws of the Rise and Development of Socialism and Communism,* published in 1960 by the State Political Publishing House. It is described as containing chapters from books, articles, speeches, reports, and documents from the period 1915 through 1923 — all concerning Lenin's views on the party. Such a compilation is obviously designed more as a source-reference handbook for party personnel than as a historical text.

as analysis, is a new phenomenon since 1956.[14] This is again related to the need to set up counterauthorities to many of Stalin's accounts and interpretations in the *Short Course* as well as to the official attempts to encourage more thorough scholarship in the field of party history.

The Commission on History of Historical Science of the Institute of History of the Academy of Sciences, which had remained quite inactive from its creation in 1946, began in 1955 to publish a series of volumes called *Sketches of History of Historical Science in the USSR*. With the appointment of M. V. Nechkina as president in December 1958, the theme of "V. I. Lenin as Historian" began to take on great significance. At a general meeting of the Department of Historical Sciences of the academy in March 1959, Nechkina stated that a central problem for the commission in editing the *Sketches* was the concept and role of Lenin "as the founder of Soviet historical science."[15] The official position of the commission remains to date that Lenin's works are not only an unparalleled source on the October Revolution and other historical events of Lenin's lifetime, but that his assessments of historical figures, trends, and movements are still of fundamental importance and should be followed and emulated by present-day historians.[16]

But this theme was not pressed without opposition within (and, one assumes, among historians outside) the commission. In the account of a commission meeting in 1959, the president reportedly answered "those who objected to the formulation of the theme 'V. I. Lenin as Historian' [by stating] that V. I. Lenin wrote valuable historical works, such as 'The Development of Capitalism in Russia,' 'The Agrarian Question in Russia at the End of the XIX Century,' 'Memories of Hertzen.' "[17] There is, however, no further reference in this account to the "objectors," none of whom, according to the report, spoke at the meeting.

There has been impressive evidence of concern for higher standards of scholarship among Soviet historians since 1956, which contributes to a more sophisticated and subtle utilization of

---

14. As an example of the genre, see Nikolai N. Maslov, *Lenin kak istorik partii* (Lenizdat, 1964).
15. M. I. Assaturova, "Obshchee sobranie otdelniia istoricheskikh nauk," *Voprosy istorii*, no. 6 (1959), p. 161.
16. See Nechkina, Poliakov, and Cherepnin, "Nekotorye voprosy," pp. 58–70.
17. N. A. Koroleva, "V komissii po istorii istoricheskoi nauki pri Institute istorii AN SSSR," *Voprosy istorii*, no. 9 (1959), p. 204.

Lenin's writings than in Stalin's day. Nonetheless, there are still occasional lapses into quotation mongering and simplistic flights to Lenin's authority in the face of unpalatable historical material.[18]

This legitimation of the regime in ideological terms can be expected to continue as a major function of Soviet historiography, especially that of the CPSU. As human memories of 1917 fade and the Old Bolsheviks die, if the leadership's claim to legitimacy is to rest on grounds other than mere utility and efficiency, it will have to depend more heavily upon the writings of Lenin and the history of the party as the one institution that carries Lenin's doctrines into the present. It is not by chance that the emphasis on Lenin and the history of the CPSU demanded at the Twentieth Party Congress coincided with the denigration of the cult of a personal and tyrannical leader and with Khrushchev's efforts to revitalize the party.

Rationalization of policies. Another important function infor-

---

18. A case in point is a critique by G. Golikov, "Ob izuchenii istorii Oktiabrskoi revoliutsii," *Kommunist*, no. 10 (1960), pp. 82–90. The book under review is P. N. Sobolev's *The Poor Peasantry — Ally of the Proletariat in the October Revolution*, published in 1958. The reviewer first praises the author's thorough work and the extensive factual material adduced. However, Sobolev has contradicted Lenin's historical account of the same events by stating that "The proletariat did not acquire the support and sympathy of the majority of the working population [the peasantry] immediately after the victory of the revolution." Lenin, we are reminded, says that on the eve of the October Revolution "The majority of the people followed them [the Bolsheviks]." The reference is to *Collected Works*, vol. 26, p. 6. Sobolev has also raised the problem of the elections to the Constituent Assembly. "Yes," agrees the reviewer, "these elections, held in November 1917, did not give a majority of votes to the Bolsheviks." But Lenin's statement that the Bolsheviks had majority support was based on "objective facts, the existence of a nationwide revolutionary crisis [demonstrated by] the peasant uprisings against the Kerensky government." The argument is made that more facts and better research techniques are not in themselves sufficient to explain historical phenomena without the party outlook. By suggesting that the Bolsheviks had acted in 1917 as agents of the minority, Sobolev calls in doubt the legitimacy of the October Revolution and the basic authority of the party. This particular instance seems to evince a misunderstanding and underestimation on the part of a historian as to the sacredness of the identification of the Bolsheviks as leaders of the majority, at the head of the masses. Also, he was apparently the quite innocent victim of a change of the official line. When he was working on his book — presumably in 1956 and 1957 — the great emphasis on the alliance of the Bolsheviks with all the working peasantry, which was soon to be a key theme in historiography, was not yet clearly apparent. Although unusual in the period under review, this bald usage of Lenin's writings to counter historical evidence, and the absence of dissent or commentary following upon it, indicate that sacred writ is still a powerful weapon of last resort.

mally performed by Soviet historiography is the rationalization of official policies and programs, both past and present. Under the rubric of Marxist-Leninist historical theory, errors of timing, miscalculations, and inconsistencies of programs and policies ranging from the trivial to the disastrous — all may be explained and justified by the skillful historian as necessary to the march toward communism.

Quite clearly the true picture of the collectivization of agriculture qualifies as a national tragedy; during Stalin's lifetime it was relegated to the Orwellian memory hole. And when in 1956 historians were ordered to incorporate this event into Soviet history for the first time, they were confronted with a most difficult test of their skill. To rationalize collectivization — to tell the truth without defaming or "blackening" the entire Soviet system, as they were directed — is considerably more complex than treating the issue of concentration camps, or of World War II defense strategy, or of Stalin himself. This is precisely because the matter of agrarian policy always hits close to the ideological bone; because discussion of any economic policy of this scope involves technical niceties and nasty doctrinal problems such as the relationship of industrialization to agricultural production and technology; and because the political decisions regarding collectivization obviously and intimately concerned the whole system. It is difficult to conjure up a more perilous enterprise from the point of view of the party historian than an attempt to explain collectivization as rational, necessary, and beneficial. But it was undertaken, despite the risks, with a certain enthusiasm. To date, rewriting the story of collectivization constitutes a major and continuing project, and probably it provides the best possible illustration of Soviet historiography acting in its rationalizing capacity.

This endeavor represents more than a reordering of events to conform to later and more rational policies. It provides a good example of the reading back into history of a contemporary institutional model. The CPSU of 1930 is portrayed as if it were the ideal form toward which Khrushchev was driving in 1959: that of a dedicated, responsible apparat which was in close touch with the masses and could be encouraged to take the initiative at all levels. Stalin is shown as having been quickly curbed by the decisive action of "the leaders of local Party organizations" and "the leaders of a number of territorial and regional Party organizations" acting with some members of the Politburo. Thus historiography can rationalize not only policies and events but political institutions as well.

Barometer of the political climate. Significant changes have taken place since 1956 in the methodology and scope of historical research and writing in the USSR. However, the ideological rhetoric as well as the practice of the craft make it clear that historiography must continue to reflect party consciousness by focusing on class conflict and casting analysis in Marxist-Leninist semantics. As long as historiography remains formally within the political arena, fulfilling a didactic function and responsive to some kind of overt political control — however subtle and sophisticated — it will perform the informal functions of sensing the political climate and signaling shifts in the wind.

It is well established that historiography as well as literary criticism and belles lettres developed a cryptic Aesopian language in the tsarist period for just such purposes and for the conveyance of proscribed ideas. For a number of reasons, the frequency and intensity of this kind of covert communication are now much diminished and modified in comparison with the good old days of tsarist inefficiency. It is not only that the modern Soviet state has developed more effective methods of supervision over scholarship, aided by technological advances; the decisive factor is undoubtedly the doctrinal thrust of communism, which sees in heresy not just the threat of physical insubordination but the seeds of destruction of an entire ideological system.

Because of more effective controls, especially over history designed for mass consumption — popular texts in mass editions, encyclopedias, handbooks for party workers, official pronouncements and speeches, articles in the central newspapers — the history of the party and state acts as a repository of the current official position on historical events, movements, and individuals. A substantive alteration or even a changed nuance of expression thus performs the twin informal functions of recording and foreshadowing changes of personnel or policy.

The historical record must be continually revised to display attractively and credibly the achievements of the current political leadership and to link those leaders with successful policies of the past; otherwise historiography cannot perform its didactic function. But Soviet history can also display a premonitory quality, suggesting forthcoming political maneuvers and modifications or dramatic reversals of policy. Khrushchev's ominous remark concerning the need for further investigation of Kirov's murder in his secret speech at the Twentieth Party Congress is a case in point: "It must be asserted that to this day the circumstances surrounding Kirov's murder hide many things which are inexplicable and mysterious and demand a most careful examination."[19] This suggestion for further historical research was duly reflected in official histories of the CPSU. A textual comparison of the several chronicles of Kirov's murder in the *Short Course* and the first and second editions of the 1959 *History* is useful in this connection.

Speeches were also made at the Seventeenth Congress by the Trotskyites Zinoviev and Kamenev, who lashed themselves extravagantly for their mistakes . . . However, the Party did not yet know or suspect that while these gentry were making their cloying speeches at the congress they were hatching a villainous plot against the life of S. M. Kirov.
On December 1, 1934, S. M. Kirov was foully murdered in the Smolny, in Leningrad, by a shot from a revolver.
The assassin was caught red-handed and turned out to be a member of a secret counter-revolutionary group made up of members of an anti-Soviet group of Zinovievites in Leningrad.
S. M. Kirov was loved by the Party and the working class, and his murder stirred the people profoundly, sending a wave of wrath and deep sorrow through the country . . .
As it later transpired, the murder of Comrade Kirov was the work of this united Trotsky-Bukharin gang.
Even then, in 1935, it had become clear that the Zinoviev group was a camouflaged Whiteguard organization whose members fully deserved to be treated as Whiteguards.
A year later it became known that the actual, real and direct organizers of the murder of Kirov were Trotsky, Zinoviev, Kamenev and their accomplices, and that they had also made preparations for the assassination of other members of the Central Committee.
(*Short Course*, pp. 325, 326, 327.)

The Party came to its [Seventeenth] Congress solidly united. There were no opposition groups at the Congress. Zinoviev, Kamenev, Bukharin, Rykov, Tomsky and other former oppositionists, who had been defeated ideologically by the Party, made

19. *Current Soviet Policies — II,* Leo Gruliow, ed. (New York: Frederick A. Praeger, 1957), p. 176.

repentant speeches, extolling the achievements of the Party. But the Congress delegates did not believe in the sincerity of their statements, since they did not back the formal admission of their mistakes and formal agreements with the Party's general line by practical work . . .

On December 1, 1934, S. M. Kirov, an outstanding leader of the CP and the Soviet State, was foully murdered in the Smolny, Leningrad, by a revolver shot. The assassin, who was caught red-handed, turned out to be an embittered renegade. He was full of hatred for the CP leaders, who were firmly implementing the Party's general line aiming at the victory of Socialism in the U.S.S.R. He had been connected with some of the former members of the Zinoviev anti-Party group. He was a Party member, held a Party card and had used it as a cover for his heinous crime.

The assassination of Kirov showed that the Party card could be used as a screen for infamous anti-Soviet acts. It was indispensable to safeguard the Party against the penetration of alien elements . . .

(History of the Communist Party of the Soviet Union, 1960, pp. 491, 492.)

The Party came to its [Seventeenth] Congress solidly united. There were no opposition groups in it. Zinoviev, Kamenev, Bukharin, Rykov, Tomsky — former leaders of opposition groups — made repentant speeches at the Congress and acknowledged the achievements of the Party . . . [Paragraph on the Stalin cult follows here.]

The Party and the whole Soviet people took legitimate pride in their achievements . . . But their joy was marred by a sad event which took place at the end of 1934.

On December 1, 1934, S. M. Kirov, an outstanding leader of the CP and the Soviet state, a member of the Political Bureau, Sec'y of the CC and Sec'y of the Leningrad Regional Committee of the C.P.S.U.(B.), was foully murdered in the Smolny, Leningrad, by a revolver shot. His death was a heavy loss for the Party and the people.

The assassin, who was caught red-handed, was full of hostility towards and hatred for the Party and its leaders who were firmly implementing the Leninist general line aiming at the victory of socialism in the U.S.S.R. An embittered renegade who had once already been expelled from the Party, he had used his Party membership card as a cover to commit his heinous crime. It was a premeditated crime whose circumstances are still being investigated, as N. S. Khrushchev announced at the Twenty-Second Congress of the C.P.S.U.

The assassination of Kirov had a most adverse effect on the life of the Party and the state. It was committed under the personality cult. Stalin seized upon it to begin dealing summarily with people who did not suit him. Numerous arrests ensued. This was the beginning of wholesale repressive measures and the most flagrant violations of socialist legality.

It was in those conditions that the verification and exchange of Party documents were carried out.
(*History of the Communist Party of the Soviet Union*, 2nd ed., 1962, pp. 486, 487.)

These passages provide a striking example of the multilayered texture of Soviet historical revision. The passages from the *Short Course* itself illustrate this dramatic step-by-step discovery of the true murderers, as the circle widens from the assassin, to the Leningrad group of Zinovievites, to an enormous White Guard organization with centers in Moscow and Leningrad inspired by Trotsky and led by Zinoviev, Bukharin, and Kamenev. There is likewise a progressive quality to the disappearance of the White Guard organization and the involvement of Trotsky, Bukharin, and Zinoviev in the assassination. In the first edition of the new history text, suspicion clings to these unrepentant figures, and it is pointed out that the assassin had been connected with them in the past. But in the later edition, personal embitterment is suggested as motivation for the murder, and the White Guard conspiracy explanation disappears entirely. By ruling out the Zinovievites as the organizers and referring to the continuing investigation, the new account obviously opens the door to further revelations in future editions.

Another ominous signal is given in the explicit connection made between the Kirov murder and the purges. Khrushchev's secret speech established 1934 as the critical year in Stalin's political life, the point at which he developed the personality cult and began to display his "sickly and suspicious" qualities. Now we are told that it was precisely the Kirov affair which provided the excuse for the onset of the purges of party members. Certainly the nature of guilt that falls upon associates of Kirov's killer is thus enormously increased, and the portents for anyone so designated in the future are dismal. Again we are reduced to speculation as to whether Khrushchev had some individual or group in mind for this assignment. We may be sure, however, that such ruminations have not been confined to academic historians of the CPSU.

There is a further dimension to this function of history as recorder and foreshadower of political events, which is bound up with the symbolic overtones clustering around any major Soviet political figure. The revision of the historical evaluation of Stalin is, of course, the outstanding example of history as a system of cryptic political signals.[20] Because Stalin was dramatically associated in the popular mind with a unique program and style of leadership, the reappraisal of his personal characteristics and career inevitably were understood — by the public as well as the political elite — to be a rejection of his politics and a sign of coming changes. In the continuing — and sometimes daily — development of stages of revision of Stalin's image in official speeches and the public media, shifts in policy and methods of political control are thus being covertly debated.

It is therefore possible for the Soviet or foreign observer, by constant evaluation of the historical treatment of Stalin, to test quite accurately the status of policies associated with Stalin and to sense probable changes. Just such a barometric reading was apparently made by the twenty-five noted scientists, writers, and artists who reportedly signed a letter to First Secretary Brezhnev in early February 1966. Anticipating a build-up toward some kind of official partial rehabilitation of Stalin at the forthcoming Twenty-Third Party Congress and worried about the implications of the Siniavsky-Daniel trial then going on, they decided to petition Brezhnev directly. This highly unusual petition has never been published or even referred to in the Soviet press, but "informed sources" in Moscow reported that it was an appeal "against any gesture to elevate Stalin's status and against any slowdown in the movement away from Stalinist totalitarian techniques that was begun by Nikita S. Khrushchev.[21] Their intent was apparently to try to deter historical reappraisal not only because they felt that such a rehabilitation was unjustified but also because it would symbolize and support a resurgence of Stalin's methods.

In the same manner, Trotsky, Bukharin, Zinoviev, and Rykov are inseparably bound up with heretical policy platforms, which remain beyond the pale of political discussion. Any genuine rehabilitation of such men is unlikely, because it would in fact acknowledge the existence of their policy positions as real alter-

20. The particular problem of the image of Stalin and the more general dilemma of historical leadership will be discussed in Chapter Nine.
21. Peter Grose, "25 Soviet Intellectuals Oppose Any Elevation of Stalin's Status," *New York Times*, March 21, 1966, p. 2.

natives and would be generally interpreted as an official opening of debate.

Ideological and theoretical discussion. For much the same reasons that Soviet historiography acts incidentally as a political weathercock, it also performs a function regarding questions of Marxist-Leninist theory. There is a significant distinction between these functions, however. In contrast with the signaling of political change, there has been a marked alteration since the Twentieth Party Congress in the way in which history points to theoretical issues.

Whereas during Stalin's regime history furnished the occasion only for ideological declamation, the post-1956 reorientation of historiography requires some effort at description and analysis of ideological heresies beyond simple vilification. A brief glance at the treatment accorded Trotsky since 1956 shows how the new history, when it deals with a symbolic historical figure or episode, is also implicitly discussing theoretical problems.

The opening move was made by Khrushchev: it is difficult to imagine the initiative on such a sensitive subject arising elsewhere than in the top political leadership. As an example of the kind of improved scholarship he wished to encourage, he said: "At present, after a sufficiently long historical period, we can speak about the fight with the Trotskyites with complete calm and can analyze this matter with sufficient objectivity. After all, around Trotsky were people whose origin cannot by any means be traced to bourgeois society."[22] This remark hints at a desire to move the battle against Trotsky from the arena of personal feud, political maneuver, and treachery to a more ideological plane, as well as to reject the dismissal of Trotsky and his followers as class enemies purely by virtue of birth.

The matter of reexamining Trotsky's place in Soviet history is so perilous that little has been done outside the relatively secure confines of authorized party texts. Further, it must be emphasized that the changes are quite subtle and more of tone than of substance. The 1959 edition of the party history fails to link Trotsky with direct plots against Soviet leaders as did the *Short Course*. This edition and the second edition of 1962 progressively modify the *Short Course* in terms of the designs imputed to Trotsky: although his policy recommendations remain evil and useless, his ultimate motivation is not the reestablishment

22. Khrushchev's secret speech, *Current Soviet Policies — II*, p. 174.

of capitalism and the defeat of Soviet power. Rather, the implication is that Trotsky's views were mistaken methods toward a good end, and the formula is that his proposals had to be defeated because they "in the end, would have led to the restoration of capitalism."[23] The violently abusive descriptive phrases are no longer invariably a part of any mention of Trotsky, and his policies are described in somewhat more straightforward and detailed fashion.

Since Khrushchev's removal there has been some evidence of pressure for a more objective picture of Trotsky, not because his ideas are alleged to be worth considering but because the summary and unrealistic treatment accorded him indirectly reflects badly on Lenin and the early party workers. The most forceful demand was cast in the form of a film critique in the Defense Ministry newspaper, *Krasnaia zvezda*. The critic's complaint was that Trotsky, Kerensky, and others are presented as "dummies" and "cardboard enemies." Trotsky, who actually was "an experienced, strong demagogue in real life," is shown in such an "elementary and cheap fashion that it is quite incomprehensible how such a man could have confused anyone for even a moment."[24] If this kind of argument is pursued, more thorough explanations of his proposals will inevitably be necessary as well as more skillful theoretical counterarguments.

A quite similar process has taken place with respect to the Right Opposition. Bukharin, Tomsky, and Rykov have progressed from traitors and plotters against Lenin and the Soviet state, who had to be destroyed, to honestly mistaken anti-Leninists who repented and were no longer a threat after the Seventeenth Party Congress in 1934.[25] These revisions were not only connected with the reappraisal of Stalin and a more believable ordering of events, but also represented an implicit discussion of such problems in Marxist-Leninist theory as the role of lower party organizations in agricultural policy, the nature of the Leninist union of proletariat and peasantry, the role of the peasantry in building socialism, and the concept of the USSR as the model for other states building socialism.

Political weapon. Because historical writing provides clues to the

23. *History of the Communist Party of the Soviet Union*, p. 381; *ibid.*, 2nd ed., p. 379.
24. V. Bushin, "Zaria revoliutsii," *Krasnaia zvezda*, November 3, 1965, p. 3.
25. *History of the Communist Party of the Soviet Union*, 2nd ed., p. 486.

current political hierarchy and policies, the historical treatment of any political figure — or any policy that can be correctly or incorrectly identified with him — becomes a weapon in the hands of the dominant faction or individual. Stalin rewrote history clearly for self-adulatory purposes: the *Short Course* depicts the political stage as strangely depopulated except for the gigantic figure of a single hero. Further, the absent actors had been not only pushed off stage but identified as traitors unworthy of their parts.

In Khrushchev's revisions, the whole process is changed. With the exit of the blood purge and terror, historical revision becomes a more activist political weapon that is put to use by Khrushchev at an earlier stage in his attempted consolidation of personal power. Stalin's *Short Course* accurately portrayed his absolute monopoly of power after the fact, in the late 1930s; but Khrushchev's style of historical rewriting was revelatory and designed to force the pace of events. Even if for the sake of argument we adopt the questionable premise that Khrushchev would have liked to eliminate physically his political rivals, political reality denied him this choice. It became much more necessary, and enormously more difficult, to discredit them while they were still on the scene. Faced with this dilemma, Khrushchev relied heavily on his own special brand of historical morality play; and under his hand party history became a very sophisticated weapon indeed. Unfortunately, however, it is also true that the more advanced the weapon, the greater the need for safeguards to protect the user.

The Special Function of Party History
Soviet historiography of the CPSU is both inextricably intertwined with and yet distinguishable from the general historiography of the Soviet period. It is obviously impossible to delineate separate terrains because in the Soviet system the CPSU has been the single agent of government and the prime mover in social, intellectual, and cultural spheres. Thus an attempt to impose the Western scholarly concept of the history of political parties as a separate field of the discipline would be artificial and counterproductive. The history of the CPSU both contains and is contained by the record of all the years after 1917.

Paradoxically, however, the CPSU is set apart from other elements in the historiography of the Soviet period by its unique, semimystical status as the chosen instrument of history and the vanguard of the leading socialist country. Moreover, the history of the party operates as a powerful educational tool, providing the illustrative facts that prove the doctrine. Party history is often defined in Soviet literature as the union of theory with practice, the acting out of the official concept of the party. "The history of the CPSU is living Marxism-Leninism in action, fulfilling the connection of the theory of scientific communism with the practice of communist construction in the USSR."[26] Therefore, party history performs to an even higher degree and with greater efficiency than general history the several formal or stated functions of Soviet historiography noted above. Party history is understood by the public to be more authoritative than other branches of history, since it recounts the exploits and policies of an infallible institution. Despite grudging Soviet recognition of the different paths to socialism that may be taken by various states, the CPSU still maintains that it is the model for other socialist parties. Historians of the party are adjured to show "the organic link between the history of the CPSU and the history of the world Communist movement."[27]

The need for continuous revision to bring the past into accord with current political reality is especially great with respect to party history, since its subject matter is exclusively and obviously political. And, happily for the party leadership, because it can maintain tighter control over the actions and records of the party than over the broader society, party history is more susceptible to manipulation and revision than more general historical works. Many of the relevant documents are apparently still inaccessible even to trusted historians high in the party — at least to the extent that they cannot be utilized as source material. This situation makes possible the revelation of new documents, memoirs, and interpretations at any time. Further, as the Kirov case shows, important political events have either taken place in secret or been successfully suppressed or falsified from the moment of occurrence.

But party historians are not only concerned with events and

26. B. N. Ponomarev, "Istoricheskii opyt KPSS — na sluzhbu kommunisticheskomu stroitelstvu," *Voprosy istorii KPSS*, no. 4 (1960), p. 36.
27. Editorial, "Postanovlenie TsK KPSS 'O zadachakh partiinoi propagandy v sovremennykh usloviiakh' i istoricheskaia nauka," *Voprosy istorii*, no. 6 (1960), p. 4. Also, "Postanovlenie TsK KPSS: O zadachakh partiinoi propagandy v sovremennykh usloviiakh," *Pravda*, January 10, 1960, pp. 1–2.

personalities. The chronicle of the CPSU must be periodically altered to maintain consistency and factual support for the current official image or theory of the party. Thus the appearance in Soviet historical literature of works showing the CPSU as a mass movement throughout its history and stressing the temporary status of the dictatorship of the proletariat, follows the development of Khrushchev's theory of the "party of all the people." The following examples can be readily duplicated.

It is important to show how the party at all stages strengthened its links with the broad popular masses, teaching the masses and being taught by them, rallied the people around its slogans and achieved success, actively supported each manifestation of creative initiative in the struggle for the revolutionary transformation of society, for the victory of socialism and communism.[28]

In the merciless struggle against the bourgeoisie and its agents the party of Lenin enlisted the majority of the working class, attracted to its side millions of workers. V. I. Lenin wrote on the eve of October that "the bolsheviks speak . . . as the representatives of the interests of all the people . . ."
But from all this the fact remains that the process of development of the CPSU into the party of the whole people encompasses its entire history, even including the struggle under conditions of capitalism. In the pre-October period this process proceeded in two basic directions: first, along the line of attracting to its side the majority of the working class and all laboring people . . . Second, along the line of gradually transforming the party into a mass party, with a broad network of party cells in enterprises, with strong connecting links with all legal societies and organizations, which made it possible for the bolsheviks to work among the masses under the difficult conditions of the autocracy.
The second stage of development of the Communist Party and Soviet society was completed at the XXII Congress of the CPSU. "The chief result of the activity of the party and the people"— emphasized N. S. Krushchev at the Congress—"is the full and final victory of socialism in the USSR." For this reason the long heroic struggle was necessary, so that the CPSU from the party of the working class became the party of all the people. This process was concluded with the full and final victory of socialism in the USSR and the reorientation of the country to the large-scale building of communism, with the transformation of the

28. D. Kukin, V. Selinskaia, and N. Shatagin, "O nauchnoi razrabotke istorii KPSS," *Kommunist*, no. 16 (1960), p. 23.

government of the dictatorship of the proletariat into a government of all the people.[29]

In this way Khrushchev's theory of the party was read back into the earliest stages of the Bolshevik history to become its conscious goal from the beginning.

29. G. I. Shitarev, "Partiia vsego naroda," *Voprosy istorii*, no. 6 (1963), pp. 7, 8, 9.

Although several Western scholars have concerned themselves with Soviet institutional structures in relation to historians during the post-Stalin years, their interest has been either more specialized or somewhat peripheral to the present undertaking.[1] An analysis of political historiography as a subsystem of the Soviet system requires investigation and speculation on institutional inputs or supports as well as demands. It is appropriate at this juncture to discuss those features of the Soviet system which operate as spurs as well as curbs or controls on the historian specializing in the CPSU. The efforts here will be synthetic rather than descriptive, since virtually all of the several institutional bodies have been carefully observed by Western scholars in other contexts. The aim is to build upon their specific observations as well as classic studies of the Soviet system in its entirety, rather than to present a detailed portrayal of the relevant bureaucracy *de novo*.

The Institutional Framework

The institutional frame within which the Soviet historian works is an elaborate structure that governs his professional activity and indeed his entire life style to a far greater extent than in pluralist democracies or traditionalist autocracies. As we shall see, this formal structure is reinforced and further complicated by the informal context.

Let me first trace out the network of administrative bodies that hedges in the Soviet scholar of the CPSU. As in other phases of activity in the USSR, the individual is subject to twin chains of

1. Black's essay on "History and Politics in the Soviet Union," which presents a brief analysis of the mechanics of official control over historians, specifically excludes from its purview "the party historians, who have in fact been relatively few in number, [and who] devote themselves primarily to revolutionary and party history" (Cyril E. Black, ed. *Rewriting Russian History*, 2nd rev. ed. [New York: Vintage Books, 1962], p. 23). Similarly, Shteppa's excellent study, which is itself more historical than analytical or synthetic, carries the story only up to 1957 (Konstantin F. Shteppa, *Russian Historians and the Soviet State* [New Brunswick: Rutgers University Press, 1962]). A later volume edited by John Keep — and especially those essays by S. V. Utechin and George Katkov — contains valuable material on the organization of archives and historical research (*Contemporary History in the Soviet Mirror* [New York: Frederick A. Praeger, 1964]). A more general work on the Soviet publishing industry and its bureaucracy provides a good outline of the censorship and editing processes as they pertain to historical as well as other scholarship (Boris I. Gorokhoff, *Publishing in the USSR* [Washington: Indiana University Publications, Council on Library Resources, 1959]). Lowell Tilletts' *The Great Friendship* is a study of the Soviet historiography of non-Russian nationalities (Chapel Hill: University of North Carolina Press, 1969).

2 THE STRUCTURE OF SOVIET HISTORIOGRAPHY

command, the dual and roughly parallel hierarchies of party and state. But the Soviet historian who studies the CPSU is, from the moment he begins his specialization, in a unique category. As "party historian" he is by definition both a party member of considerable standing and a historian. Although all persons who constitute the Soviet managerial, artistic, and intellectual elite can be perceived as partaking of this uneasy party-professional duality, it is easy to see that some activities present more difficulty than others in terms of conflicts of interest and loyalty. In such a spectrum, the party historian would be found at the weakest edge, because the regime sets for him intangible and ill-defined norms while providing him only explosive materials and dangerous tools. By virtue of his job description he is eternally condemned to write exclusively on the most politically sensitive topics; yet he is required to be active politically and to set the pace for other historians as well as for lesser members of the teaching and propaganda hierarchies. Avenues of escape open to the ballet dancer, the fiction writer, or factory manager are denied him. In short, he is adjured by the regime to be simultaneously a scholar and a politician.

State structures. Ultimately, of course, the historical profession is subject to the published and unpublished decrees of the Central Committee and the Council of Ministers. Policy may also be set on historical issues by pronouncements of individual political leaders. In terms of the state bureaucracy, the Soviet chronicler of the CPSU, like any historian, is responsible to a bewildering array of agencies subordinate to the USSR Council of Ministers. Depending on whether he is concerned with domestic or foreign policy, he must apply to the Main Archive Administration of the Ministry of Internal Affairs or the Archive Administration of the Ministry of Foreign Affairs and be governed by their regulations on the use and publication of documentary materials.[2]

Historians, as well as all academic and scientific personnel, are also subject to regulations and administrative decisions of the State Committee for Coordination of Scientific Research, which is directly responsible to the Council of Ministers at the all-union level. Under a Central Committee and Council of Ministers decree of May 18, 1962, this committee was given increased

2. For a description of the archives and rules for publication, see George Katkov, "Soviet Historical Sources in the Post-Stalin Era," *Contemporary History in the Soviet Mirror,* pp. 130–154.

authority to supervise the training and assignment of personnel.

In common with other Soviet writings, the works of historians are controlled by official government censorship, performed under the aegis of the Main Administration for Guarding Military and State Secrets in Publications, familiarly if not affectionately known in the Soviet Union as Glavlit. This is an all-union administration, directly responsible to the USSR Council of Ministers, with subordinate republican bodies and representatives down to the publishing-house level.[3] Since the summer of 1956, the censorship code has apparently been somewhat relaxed, so that "speeches by government leaders, official statements, proceedings of the Supreme Soviet, administrative documents of various types, dictionaries, and texts of classical writers" are exempt.[4] This modification has had no apparent effect upon historiography, however, and even so highly authoritative a publisher as the Higher Party School of the Central Committee is subject to censorship of its historical teaching materials.[5]

A separate bureaucracy operates with regard to the teaching of history outside the party schools. The USSR Ministry of Higher Specialized and Secondary Education has administrative control over all universities, correspondence divisions, institutes, and technicums — in short, over all teachers, textbooks, teaching aids, and curricula in all branches of history above the elementary level (which is administered by republican ministries). The operative branches of concern here are the Department of Social Studies and its Section on Party History, which act as funnels to lower educational agencies with regard to new departures in research and teaching. Checking and setting pedagogical standards as well as selecting research topics for special attention is done by a separate and elite Scientific-Technical Council attached to the ministry. This council apparently is comprised of researchers and writers in contradistinction to the pedagogical and administrative cadres who generally staff the ministry. Its duties have been described in a Soviet source as follows:

In connection with the developing of scientific-research work in

3. See Gorokhoff, *Publishing in the USSR,* chap. 6, for a description of the censorship process.
4. *Ibid.,* p. 81.
5. For example, see *Uchenye zapiski,* Department of History of the CPSU, Higher Party School, 5th ed. (Moscow: "Thought" Publishing House, 1966), which bears the censor's stamp on its title page.

higher educational institutions more tasks accrue to the Scientific-Technical Council of the Ministry of Higher Education of the U.S.S.R., where are gathered leading specialists of Moscow and the periphery. It must play a directive role in organizing scientific-research work of departments of Party history, in choice of basic directions of development of Party-historical science, in lending active aid to strong local departments.[6]

In a very real sense the history faculties of universities — and especially the prestigious ones — must be considered as entities distinct from the Ministry of Higher Education. That is to say, each university or institute itself creates a unique atmosphere and imposes somewhat diverse incentives or curbs upon its own researchers, professors, and students. It is difficult to go beyond this general observation without a detailed study of the various history faculties and departments of history of the CPSU. However, the sources clearly reveal that — despite a centralized bureaucracy for higher education — recognizable diversity in quality of faculty and students, research orientation and topics of interest, professional morale, and even extent of revisionist tendencies persist among institutions. Thus the pressures upon historians vary depending upon the characteristics of their university administrations and departments, which may well be quite distinct from those imposed by the central ministry.

Similarly, the USSR Academy of Sciences with its republican affiliates cannot be considered simply as an arm of the Council of Ministers. The backgrounds, outside relationships, and institutional affiliations of its members are too diverse for this to be true. It is likewise an oversimplification to pass off the academy as "the principal agency of party supervision" over historiography, because "the Party . . . has firm control over all aspects of the academy's work."[7] Certainly the CPSU has units at the various levels of the academy, as in all research and academic institutions; but Soviet sources show that such an organizational arrangement does not necessarily guarantee monolithic interpretation of party directives on party history, especially when those pronouncements are vague and incomplete.

The pertinent units of the academy are the Department of Social Sciences and its Section on Historical Sciences. There is in addi-

6. A. A. Zemskov and I. G. Mitrafanov, "O nekotorykh voprosakh nauchno-issledovatelskoi raboty v vuzakh po istorii KPSS," *Voprosy istorii KPSS*, no. 6 (1958), p. 222.
7. Black, *Rewriting Russian History*, pp. 16, 17.

tion a separate research body, the Institute of History. Since 1956 both the Section on Historical Sciences and the Institute of History have responded to a tendency toward narrower specialization among Soviet historians, which has in turn resulted from the greatly improved and multiplied source materials, by creating interspecialization and interdisciplinary scholarly groups called, respectively, scientific councils and study groups. These are designed not only to foster exchange of knowledge but also to encourage more generalizing and collaborative work, presumably at the expense of technical monographs.

Despite the similarity in organization and partial duplication of functions, the Academy of Sciences and the Ministry of Higher Education are completely separate bureaucracies, with the academy's historians enjoying considerably higher status than those attached to the ministry. The fact that the academy, the ministry, and some of the larger universities maintain their own publishing houses and journals accentuates their structural independence from one another.

Party structures. Parallel to and intersecting the several state bureaucracies is the enormous machinery of the CPSU, which attempts to control the historical profession by coopting its leading scholars into membership and by training promising young apparatchiki in history. The incidence of party membership and activism among historians of the CPSU is markedly higher than among historians with other specialties; and this remains the case even though they no longer are recruited almost exclusively from the ranks of the more ambitious propagandists in the Agitprop apparat. For instance, Pospelov reports proudly on the beneficial effects on historians of the party who are exposed regularly to close contact with the workers:

At the present time departments of history of the CPSU are working out entirely new, more effective forms of linking theory with practice. Regular appearances are being organized at meetings of departments, scholarly councils and theoretical conferences of higher educational institutions, of engineering-technical workers and production innovators, members of brigades of communist labor of the leading social organizations. The strengthening of links with production helps the teachers of Party history to gather rich factual materials which are helpful in raising the caliber of lectures and seminars, improving their educational work among students.[8]

8. Speech of P. N. Pospelov, *Vsesoiuznoe soveshchanie o merakh uluchsheniia*

Even within the CPSU bureaucracy, there are several bodies that concern themselves with historiography and an even greater number that are given some responsibility for checking them and each other with respect to the history of the CPSU. The fact that most of these agencies are directly subordinate to the Central Committee indicates the importance attached to their work. It should not be forgotten that the Central Committee itself — by means of its resolutions, announcements, and such documents as slogans and theses on the occasion of anniversaries and holidays — is continually engaged in the writing and rewriting of the history of the party.

The Institute of Marxism-Leninism of the Central Committee is probably the single most important of the relevant party agencies. It represents the latest successor to Lenin's original Commission on the History of the Party and the October Revolution, which was set up on August 20, 1920. As early as December 1921 the party archives were transferred into custody of the Central Committee; on March 26, 1929, a single central archive was established as part of the Lenin Institute; and the Central Committee in 1931 merged the Lenin Institute (which concentrated on party history and Leninism) with the Institute of Marx and Engels (which was charged with Marxist theory) to combine the study of Marxism-Leninism with that of the history of the CPSU. But the Central Party Archive of the Institute of Marxism-Leninism evidently never did gain control of all of the regional party archives; much of the more original research on party history since 1956 has in fact utilized documents held in provincial areas.

After 1956, as party history became less of a black art, more historians were allowed to utilize the archives and to write on an increasingly scholarly level. And this process has made the whole enterprise of documentary preservation, classification, and retrieval enormously complex. The Institute of Marxism-Leninism has had to recruit employees of a higher calibre, to train its archive staff in new techniques, and to set up for the first time a systematized and public set of regulations.[9] The 1966 "Regulations for the Preservation and Treatment of Archive Materials in Party, Komsomol Organs, and Primary Organizations" provide

podgotovki nauchno-pedagogicheskikh kadrov po istoricheskim naukam (Moscow: "Science" Publishing House, 1964), p. 207.
9. "O sokhrannosti i obrabotke arkhivnykh dokumentov," Partiinaia zhizn, no. 15 (1966), p. 49.

that documentary materials should be kept for five years by central committees and Komsomol organizations at the union republican, areal, and regional levels; for three years at the district and city levels; and for two years by primary party organizations. Documents of "scientific and practical significance" must be transferred for registration and permanent preservation in the Central Party Archive under a single classification system.[10]

The renascence of historiography of the CPSU after 1956 has radically transformed the tasks of the Institute of Marxism-Leninism's Sector on History of the CPSU to the point where the old methods and staff are recognized to be inadequate. At the December 1962 all-union meeting of historians a representative of the institute confided:

In the near future there will be created in the institute a group or sector for direction of the work of affiliates and those scientific organizations which work on questions of history of the Party. It is necessary to create also a council for coordination, where directors of affiliates of the Institute of Marxism-Leninism and important research organizations should come, and where Party-history themes could be developed.[11]

Such a coordinating body has indeed been constituted: the All-Union Council on Coordination of Scientific Research on History of the CPSU now represents the apex of an entire new hierarchy consisting of coordinating councils in all union republics. A report of the All-Union Council's plenum in December 1965 listed the following achievements:

(1) The union-republican councils have increased the linkages of the institutes of party history run by city and regional party committees with departments and teachers at higher educational institutions. One of the chief concerns of the Institute of Marxism-Leninism has obviously been not only the lack of communication between these party-controlled local institutes and their academic counterparts but also between the local party functionaries in these institutes and their superiors at the Moscow institute. No mention is made, however, of progress in the latter sphere.

(2) Some councils give regular help to doctoral candidates on dissertations. Thus the councils are evidently designed partly to

10. *Ibid.*
11. Speech of B. S. Telpukhovsky, *Vsesoiuznoe soveshchanie*, p. 277.

compensate for the inadequate academic background of many of the older teachers of party history.

(3) Many councils have held scientific conferences on a variety of special topics and areas of research.

(4) The All-Union Council has worked out the main lines of a draft plan for research in the most critical fields of party history. The necessity for developing this plan confirms other indications that the plans worked out by the Institute of History and the Section on Social Sciences of the Academy of Sciences and the various publishing houses have proved inadequate to establish and maintain a genuinely centralized control over research.[12]

The Central Committee's choice of the Institute of Marxism-Leninism to take general responsibility for the six-volume *History of the Communist Party of the Soviet Union* indicates the institute's preeminent position. This project has as a matter of fact further enhanced its prestige and authority, since it requires the cooperation of the institute's own affiliates, institutes of the Academy of Sciences and especially the Institute of History, other research centers and many higher educational institutions, and party and state archives and libraries.

Although the Institute of Marxism-Leninism may be seen as performing most archival, research, coordinating, and supervisory functions on the party side, the education of party historians is conducted within the CPSU primarily by the Academy of Social Sciences of the Central Committee. The academy's Department of CPSU History grants a doctorate, as do the departments of philosophy, political economy, history of the USSR, modern history, and theory of literature and art. It is apparent that the official pressure for better-trained historians has had an impact even here: since 1956 the entrance requirements have been stiffened somewhat (a forty- to fifty-page essay must now be submitted in addition to the entrance examinations), but the need for cadres has caused the course to be reduced from four to three years and the maximum age at entrance to be lowered from forty to thirty-five years.[13]

There are in addition several party organs that bear responsi-

12. "Vo vsesoiuznom sovete po koordinatsii nauchnoi razrabotki istorii KPSS," *Voprosy istorii KPSS*, no. 2 (1966), pp. 153–155.
13. "Ot Akademii obshchestvennykh nauk pri TsK KPSS," *Kommunist*, no. 1 (1956), p. 128; and "Ob ocherednom prieme v Akademiiu obshchestvennykh nauk pri TsK KPSS," *Pravda*, March 21, 1964, p. 4.

bility for historiography as part of a more general supervision of the ideological sphere. The Commission on Ideology, set up by Khrushchev under the Central Committee and presumably still in existence, is a group of high-level functionaries charged with eliminating inconsistencies of interpretation and phraseology and exposing revisionist errors in Soviet publications. The Society for the Dissemination of Political and Scientific Knowledge, also responsible to the Central Committee, operates at a lower level, propagating officially approved historical and other information to the population by way of meetings, pamphlets, and the like.

Two departments of the Secretariat are considerably more important in terms of establishing party policy on specific issues of doctrine — including, of course, historical matters — and with regard to the regular supervision of scholarly, cultural, and ideological activities: the departments of Agitation and Propaganda and of Culture and Science. There is obviously considerable overlapping and sharing of functions and responsibilities between them. Of the two, the Department of Agitation and Propaganda is specifically charged with ideological work and its mass dissemination, and is divided into two sections that are responsible for the supervision of culture and science and of literature and art. According to a member of the department, its principal weapon is the press.[14]

A glance at the internal structure of the Department of Culture and Science makes clear its duplication of Agitprop and suggests that in fact it may operate at a higher or policy-making level, although it is not above Agitprop in formal or hierarchical terms. The Culture and Science Department is composed of two sections on culture and on science and schools. The Science Section — which is relevant for this discussion — is in turn divided into four subsections, each with a chairman and two vice-chairmen: natural sciences, social sciences, universities and higher educational institutions, and secondary schools. Visiting Italian communists were told that the subsection on the social sciences consists of six functionaries, one of whom is an historian. The subsection was described as concerned not only with general super-

14. *Problemi e realtà dell' URSS* (Rome: Editori Riuniti, 1958), p. 60. The following discussion of the Culture and Science Department is also based on material presented in this report of Italian Communist Party leaders on their trip to the Soviet Union in the summer of 1957 (pp. 71–83).

vision of these disciplines but with the direction of the various institutes of the USSR Academy of Sciences, including of course the Institute of History. Further, "The subsection participates in the elaboration of decisions of the Central Committee and assists the scientific institutes of the Party organization in implementation of the decisions of the XX Congress."[15]

In order to illustrate the active policymaking functions of the Science Section, a member of the section referred to the 1956 replacements on the *Voprosy istorii* editorial board.

Our own department is not limited simply to keeping the Central Committee informed on developments in the cultural debate but also takes part in working out the projects and decisions of the Secretariat and the Central Committee. For example, the decision about *Voprosy istorii* was taken after long discussion inside the Secretariat of the Central Committee which was based on a project drawn up by the department. To draw up the project we invited at the start the comrades from the editorial board of the review to the department. Next, in January [1957], we held a bigger meeting, convened by our department, and the propaganda department, at which [there] participated not only the editorial board of the review, but also the president and vice-president of the Academy of Sciences and representatives from the Academy of Sciences. For two days we had eight- to nine-hour discussions. At the next meeting of the Secretariat, the editors of the review, the comrades of the propaganda department and our department, and finally Comrades Pospelov and Suslov all spoke. After this debate, the decision to change the editorial board of the review was approved.[16]

It is apparent from this account that the Culture and Science Department (spurred on, most probably, by the social-science subsection) took the initiative in reviewing the problem and preparing the case against the dissident editors. The effective decision was evidently taken at the Secretariat level.

A graphic overview of the party and state bureaucratic systems described is presented in the accompanying figure. This chart does not show all of the party organizations within each university department, research institute, and state agency, which set their policies. It should be observed, however, that methods and sanctions differ somewhat in academic institutes. In the institutes of interest here, the party organization defers in some

15. *Ibid.*, pp. 72–73.
16. *Ibid.*, p. 75, as quoted in Merle Fainsod, *How Russia Is Ruled*, rev. ed. (Cambridge: Harvard University Press, 1963), p. 339.

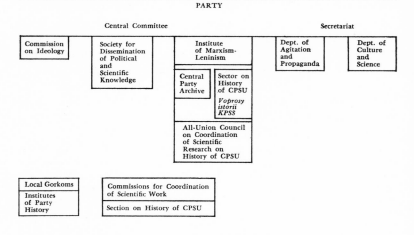

matters to the officers, presumably because in historical or ideological centers such staff members would automatically be of high party rank:

Of course, one institute differs from another. Take, for example, the V. I. Lenin All-Union Electro-Technical Institute and the I. P. Bardin Central Scientific-Research Institute of Ferrous Metallurgy . . . This institute is of an industrial character. The Party Rules of the CPSU have granted the power to control the administrative activities of such an institute inseparably linked with production, to the Party organizations. But there are also institutes of another type, of the so-called academic (theoretical) kind. To them, in particular, belong the institutes of the U.S.S.R. Academy of Sciences and the academies of union republics (for example, the Institute of Chemical Physics, the Institute of State and Law, etc.). Here the Party organizations do not exercise the right of control over administrative activities.[17]

Quite clearly this is a formidable apparatus. It should also be remembered that these institutional arrangements are reinforced by a centralized financial system which — despite the reform inroads of recent years — continues to provide a significant control over journal circulations, publishing plans, numbers and specializations of professors, researchers and graduate students, and

17. "Partorganizatsiia nauchni-issledovatelskogo instituta," *Partiinaia zhizn*, no. 16 (1963), p. 33.

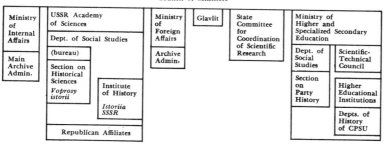

Council of Ministers

Ministry of Internal Affairs	USSR Academy of Sciences			Ministry of Foreign Affairs	Glavlit	State Committee for Coordination of Scientific Research	Ministry of Higher and Specialized Secondary Education	
	Dept. of Social Studies							
Main Archive Admin.	(bureau)			Archive Admin.			Dept. of Social Studies	Scientific-Technical Council
	Section on Historical Sciences						Section on Party History	Higher Educational Institutions
	Voprosy istorii	Institute of History						
		Istoriia SSSR						Depts. of History of CPSU
	Republican Affiliates							

topics for research projects. The special character of the Soviet economic system, with its insistence on planning and its proscription of "parasitism," forces the scholar into an institutional association with a university, research institute, or publishing house; this in turn places him within the elaborate system of official controls over financial rewards, fringe benefits, housing, and research facilities. Moreover, the party leadership holds a tight rein on scholarly exchanges, permission for private foreign travel, and access to foreign literature and books. The fact that these regulations have been relaxed from time to time since 1953 does not obviate the equally apparent periodic clampdowns. The political leadership has overtly insisted on its prerogatives of control in these areas.

Finally we should recall the absence of any kind of permanent professional association of historians in the Soviet union, despite the obvious widespread desire for this among historians and the long-standing unions of writers, scientists, teachers, journalists, and so forth.

Informal Controls

The official fostering of competition and checking of one institutional bureaucracy by another has been well documented by a number of scholars of the Soviet political and economic system.

The same is true of Soviet historiography. Party and government agencies conduct rivalries among themselves and duplicate bodies attached to the other's bureaucratic structure. The political leaders rely on the resulting jealousies and competition for funds and facilities to expose indiscretions and unauthorized historical revisionism at whatever level it occurs. We can see, for instance, an important functionary in party history, B. N. Ponomarev, deliberately take advantage of a traditional rivalry to set provincial and less prestigious historians against their colleagues at some leading universities, in order to spur the latter to greater production:

the departments of Party history at a series of leading higher educational institutions of the country, for example, Leningrad, Kazan, and Odessa universities, still participate only weakly in scholarly work on the history of CPSU . . . Local historians correctly are taking up the question of improving published work in the area of history of the CPSU.[18]

The regime has at its command a wide variety of incentives and curbs — as diverse as material gratification, professional advancement, and social approval or ostracism — which can be and are consciously manipulated to a much greater degree than in a less politically and ideologically centralized society. The leadership also — and this was true to an unprecedented degree during Khrushchev's regime — utilizes both the general public media and the device of mass meetings to publicize some new policy or event such as a party congress. On such an occasion, there may be huge conferences of editors, writers, teachers, historical researchers, ideologists, and other party functionaries — who gather to hear what the congress or new party program means to history, ideology, or pedagogy.

But the chief extrainstitutional means relied upon to curb the historian or any other scholar is the system of multiple roles or interlocking directorates. It operates in essentially the same manner as did certain corporate boards in the United States before the antitrust law was enacted, if one casts the appropriate top Central Committee organs — in this case, the Institute of Marxism-Leninism, the Commission on Ideology, and the All-Union Council on Coordination of Scientific Research on History

18. B. N. Ponomarev, "Istoricheskii opyt KPSS — na sluzhbu kommunistich-eskomu stroitelstvu, "*Voprosy istorii KPSS*, no. 4 (1960), p. 36.

of the CPSU — in the role of the parent or holding company with relation to its subsidiaries.

This aspect of party control can best be demonstrated by reference to the career patterns of a few of the leading historians of the CPSU. Consider the fact that G. D. Obichkin, a frequent contributor to historical journals, was in 1956 simultaneously an editor of *Voprosy istorii* and director of the then Marx-Engels-Lenin-Stalin Institute. He left *Voprosy istorii* to become the first chief editor of *Voprosy istorii KPSS* in February 1957. The career of P. N. Pospelov is also a case in point.[19]

E. I. Bugaev provides another example of this kind of dual responsibility and multiple career. A candidate in historical science, Bugaev received his training at the Chernyshevsky Institute for History, Philosophy and Literature and the Central Committee's Higher Party School, graduating, respectively, in 1940 and 1942. His field of special competence is the CPSU in 1917 and the very early years of Soviet power. In 1956, at the time of his encounter with Burdzhalov, he was at once chief of the Union Republic Sector of the Agitprop Department of the party Secretariat and deputy chief editor of *Partiinaia zhizn*. In 1958 he became a departmental head of the journal *Problemy mira i sotsializma*, was moved in 1960 to *Voprosy istorii KPSS* as successor to Obichkin, and in February 1961 to the editorship of *Partiinaia zhizn*. He was referred to by *Voprosy istorii KPSS* in September 1960 as chief of the Department of History of the CPSU of the Institute of Marxism-Leninism.[20] Bugaev was removed from *Partiinaia zhizn* in early 1966, presumably because of his reputation as a Khrushchev protegé, and it is unclear whether he retains his high post at the Institute of Marxism-Leninism.

By contrast, the background and employment affiliations of Academician I. I. Mints have been rather more oriented to the academic than the party bureaucracy. But Mints possesses the proudest credential of all, that of Old Bolshevik, having joined the party in April 1917. Without doubt, Mints is the most competent and well-known contemporary Soviet historian specializing in the party as well as the October Revolution and the Civil War.

19. See below, Chapter Five.
20. I. M. Filimonova, "K sozdaniiu mnogotomnoi istorii KPSS," *Voprosy istorii KPSS*, no. 5 (1960), p. 229.

His bibliography runs to two hundred items, which include important contributions and editorial responsibilities for such massive works as *History of the Civil War in the U.S.S.R.*, *History of Diplomacy*, and both the textbook and the six-volume *History of the Communist Party of the Soviet Union*. His seventieth birthday in February 1966 occasioned lengthy congratulatory articles in *Istoriia SSSR* (of which he is an editor) and in *Voprosy istorii*,[21] and he was given the Order of Lenin.

Mints spent his early career in the military and party bureaucracies and evidently maintains close connections and a high standing with them. During the Civil War he rose to be military commissar in the First Cossack Cavalry Corps, and in 1923 he was named commissar of the Air Force Academy in Moscow. At that time he began to study part-time in the history department of the Institute of Red Professors and did so well that upon graduation in 1926 he was made head of that department and deputy head of the institute. In 1939 he became a member-correspondent of the Academy of Sciences and, in 1946, a full member.

He successfully weathered some severe criticisms of his work during Stalin's later years and emerged in a position of great influence during the 1950s: in 1958 he became president of the academy's Institute of History and also head of its scientific council on the problem of "History of the Great October Socialist Revolution" which was to direct all research on the subject in preparation for the fiftieth anniversary. His teaching activities have continued all the while: for many years he headed the Department of History of the USSR at the Higher Party School and lectured at Moscow University, going on to be in charge of the departments of History of the USSR at the Potemkin Pedagogical Institute and the Lenin Pedagogical Institute, both in Moscow. Mints's talents and trustworthiness have been rewarded in many ways, among them an amazing number of trips abroad. One of these was a lengthy scholarly exchange visit to the United States, during which he helped "many professors and students" see the "basic errors of those evaluations and views contained in the books of American 'sovietologists.' "[22]

21. "K 70-letiiu so dnia rozhdeniia Akad. I. I. Mintsa," *Istoriia SSSR*, no. 1 (1966), p. 246; A. P. Sheliubsky, "Bolshevik, voin, uchenyi," *Vopsosy istorii*, no. 3 (1966), pp. 167–170.
22. Sheliubsky, "Bolshevik, voin, uchenyi," p. 169.

One of the most intriguing aspects of Mints's career is the smooth manner in which the scholar-functionary duality has been handled by a man with considerable ability in both areas. It seems reasonable to conclude that his staying power through a variety of political regimes is largely due to this particular skill. The anniversary article in *Voprosy istorii* in fact pays tribute to this talent when it notes his great influence on his many students:

I. I. Mints generously shares his knowledge and experience with everyone who turns to him, whether he is a mature scholar or aspirant, school teacher or propagandist . . . I. I. Mints has helped many scholarly collectives to direct their attention to contemporary problems and strengthen the front of practical research having the greatest ideological-political resonance.[23]

In this vein it is mentioned that he was one of the founders of the "Knowledge" propaganda society and currently is its deputy president for Moscow and the RSFSR.

Dysfunctional Aspects of the Control System

It is just short of this point that most analysis of Soviet historiography has traditionally stopped. But there are, if not additional data to present, at least further questions to ask and perhaps some judgments and speculations to be introduced. Certainly, despite the elaborate administrative and informal control mechanism, there exists a growing body of evidence that the machine functions imperfectly and moreover that it has produced some unexpected and dysfunctional results.

Perhaps I should make the most general point first. It is, after all, the absence of terror that most clearly marks off recent years in the Soviet Union from its earlier history. And much of the regime's activity since 1956, as well as the semiofficial and individual actions that these policies have generated, can be seen to be a series of attempts to create new legal, administrative, and social controls that can effectively replace the repudiated Stalinist terror. Some measures have been markedly more successful than others, and quite clearly certain areas lend themselves to the transition more neatly than others.

The social sciences — and particularly political history — are perhaps the most difficult for the regime, since they afford no intrinsic escape from prickly issues and controversial person-

23. *Ibid.*, p. 170.

alities. The regime's problem is not just the disappearance of the ultimate threat; it must contend with the inevitable subjectivity of the materials with which the historian deals and the consequent lack of precision of the directives he is now given. The only safe substitute for terror is to inculcate an individual inhibition to guide the historian's research from its earliest stages — but the conscience is notoriously difficult to inform and impossible to monitor.

Thus the intricate web of institutional bureaucracies continues to be the major control, and it generates — in historiography as in other aspects of Soviet life — its own countermechanisms. The existence of an imperfectly coordinated and to some extent competing multiplicity of research institutes, journals, and publishing houses, manipulated by the party elite, has inevitably induced the formation of those transitory, informal, mutually protective groups known in the Soviet press as "family circles." These groups, which are made to sound decidedly sinister in Soviet accounts, are in the case of historians nothing more than cliques of friends based on old school ties or common institutional or scholarly associations and opinions. Unlike their managerial counterparts in the economic bureaucracy, these circles are not cemented by financial gain; but the currency is equally valuable — access to journal pages to secure publicity for one's viewpoint, professional prestige, and in some cases protection from exposure for shoddy research or even plagiarism.

The most spectacular examples of family circles have been described in the pages of *Voprosy istorii*. By far the most entertaining was the exposure during late 1956 of the little band of admirers of A. F. Moshaisky, "the first in the world to build an airplane." Led by two very energetic historians, N.A. Cheremnikh and I. F. Shepilov, they furbished the thin sources with wrong dates, imagined incidents, mythical witnesses to the first flight, and even passed off a photograph of the hero's son as the hero when they could not find one of the proper generation. All of this was accomplished

Because the authors of these books work in the editorial offices of aviation publications. I. Shepilov is deputy editor of "Air Force Bulletin," and he is also a member of the editorial board of the journal "Wings of the Motherland." His co-author B. Simakov is editor of "Wings of the Motherland," and N. Cheremnikh is chief of the editorial-publishing department of "Air Force Bulletin." Using their official positions, these people support one another, guaranteeing their books laudatory reviews and preventing the publication of critical remarks and works of other authors.[24]

A somewhat different clique apparently existed in 1956 among the revisionist members of the editorial board of *Voprosy istorii*.[25] They were described by a hard-line member of the new board that succeeded them as having "set themselves off from the staffs [of research institutes of the Academy of Sciences] and detached themselves." The ringleader, Burdzhalov, was asserted to have acted on his own, despite the protests of some other members of the board.

Meetings of the editorial board were not called regularly . . . close friends of the editorial staff rather than the most qualified specialists in various fields of knowledge were asked to write articles. [Thus] in time the editors alienated a large number of the most experienced historians and reduced the possibility of receiving highly qualified articles [with] adverse effect on the subject matter and content of materials published.[26]

The fact that the existence of family circles becomes generally known only upon their destruction makes it impossible to go beyond speculation as to their numbers and influence. But remarkably similar cliques of scholars are often formed in more open societies with far fewer centralized directives, wherever there may exist a rift within the profession, a feud with a university administration, or some such stimulus to informal alliances. For this reason — in conjunction with the generally safe assumption that any single incident exposed in the Soviet press can be duplicated many times in actual life — we may assume that the family circle is quite a familiar phenomenon among Soviet historians.

At the level of the individual's confrontation with the bureaucracy, it is a generally observable fact that the more huge and unwieldy the machine, the more it develops multiple points of access and becomes open to the threat of misuse, or possibly manipulation of a rudimentary sort, by the disgruntled or mis-

24. Letter by E. F. Burche and I. E. Mosolov, "Protiv iskazhenii istorii aviatsii," *Voprosy istorii*, no. 6 (1956), p. 128. Also "Obsuzhdenie nekotorykh voprosov istorii aviatsii," *Voprosy istorii*, no. 11 (1956), pp. 207–212.
25. See below, Chapter Three.
26. "Za leninskuiu partiinost v istoricheskoi nauke," *Voprosy istorii*, no. 3 (1957), pp. 17, 18.

chievous. And as the atmosphere has lightened, this has evidently become a common feature of the Soviet bureaucracy, even with respect to touchy aspects of party history. Thus we find that at a meeting to discuss the third volume of the *History of the Communist Party of the Soviet Union*, a crusty Old Bolshevik, determined to remove the halfhearted appraisal of the *Short Course* as having been "useful," does not hesitate to play one party body against another. He tells the chief editor Pospelov — who is responsible to the Institute of Marxism-Leninism — that he has taken his objection to Sergei Trapeznikov, head of the "science department" of the Central Committee, that Trapeznikov shares his views and has "promised to give relevant instructions."[27] At the same meeting a casual remark by Snegov reveals that the presence of the Old Bolsheviks was only by virtue of considerable pressure on the editorial board and maneuvering which included a letter from thirty-four of them "to the four [*sic*] secretaries of the Central Committee and to Comrade Brezhnev."[28]

The Soviet system, as we have seen, is relied upon to limit not only popular discussion of historical topics but also to channel the general direction and pace of the continual revisions. The problem for leaders since Stalin has been one of keeping historical rewriting within approved limits, once official impetus was given to specific and often dramatic changes in party history. Many stratagems have obviously been brought into play for this purpose: Khrushchev's secret speech in 1956, official decrees that further delineated the extent of de-Stalinization, mass meetings of party leaders with historians, editors, and propagandists, and the issuance of a new text on party history. But the structural characteristic that works to direct and contain new departures in historiography is part of the system of elites permeating Soviet society. There is ample evidence of the regime's fostering of a series of stratified levels in party historiography which parallels those found in other political and economic areas: a system of historians and their audiences that graduates downward from leading figures in the Academy of Sciences and the Institute of Marxism-Leninism to the university departments of party history and members of research institutes on CPSU history, to journal

27. "Discussion of the draft third volume of The History of the Communist Party of the Soviet Union," *Survey*, April 1967, p. 163. See Chapter Six, note 43, with regard to this protocol.
28. *Ibid.*, p. 164.

and newspaper editors, secondary-school teachers, and regional propagandists, and finally to the ordinary reader of the mass press. There is a careful effort to limit access by any of the subsidiary categories to historical sources and professional discussions except as funneled to them through the approved hierarchy; and specific kinds of information and research materials are cut off at various levels, according to the special requirements and capabilities as perceived by the party leadership assigned to historiography. Less sophisticated and less trusted readers are progressively more passive and dependent upon those higher on the ladder for their sources as well as interpretive nuances.

Again, the tools available for this manipulation are varied: the continued control of access to the several classes of documents in state and party archives, according to the historian's party and government position; the further complex of regulations defining which of the discovered sources can be published or quoted from or referred to in historical works; the frequency of closed meetings on a variety of topics, to which only certain kinds of historians are invited; the official censorship of all published materials; and even more subtle, the amazing spectrum of types of publications and sizes of editions, which is designed to keep the more exploratory or revisionist research in the hands of a tiny circle of scholars. All of this produces a sophisticated caution among the more creative historians, so that they print and say different things to a variety of audiences.

A remarkably frank explanation of this kind of mental segregation was given to an American historian when he protested that an important memoir had been omitted from a Soviet collection of documents, *The Workers' Movement in Baku in the Years of the First Russian Revolution*. The editors stated that they knew of the document — the memoir of a general who worked for the tsarist secret police, which described a unified Bolshevik-Menshevik meeting in 1904 at which the Bolsheviks resisted the Menshevik pressure for a strike. Further they implied that they recognized it as genuine. But they explained that they had not included it because "It is understood that in a jubilee collection, distributed to the mass of readers, such mistaken views of a tsarist general would have disoriented society and led to confusion regarding the actual state of things."[29]

How effective is this system of vertical or stratified containment?

29. Unpublished letter to E. L. Keenan, Russian Research Center, Harvard

It must be recognized that very special burdens are placed upon it under present conditions of improved access to sources for more historians, the great boom in publications, and the release of many proscribed topics. And there is evidence that the pyramid of elites is not only functioning imperfectly but that it is to some extent dysfunctional, that it can be used other than to serve the party leadership. There have been several known occasions — and undoubtedly more unpublicized one — when a closed meeting called to establish the line for the elite turned into a forum for more independent historians: the December 1962 all-union conference, the meeting in February 1966 to discuss the war novel *22 June 1941,* and the discussion of the third volume of the new party history come to mind. Such instances have a contagious quality.

It is also clear that the manipulation or distortion of the regime's system of elites can run in the other direction. Thus, rather than an unauthorized leakage downward of revisionist ideas until they reach the mass level — as with Burdzhalov's 1956 reappraisal of the Bolsheviks in the spring of 1917, much of which is now quite generally incorporated in popular treatments — a number of historians are upgrading the small-edition scholarly publications into semiprivate or club circulars, which do not fulfill their official function of guiding the lower echelons. Ponomarev's complaint is quite specific:

As to articles in "Works" and "Scholarly Notes" of higher educational institutions, they are published in such small editions and so poorly distributed that they remain in fact inaccessible and unknown to the broad Party atkiv, to those Party cadres for whom they were intended in the first place. Our historical journals and especially the journal "Voprosy istorii KPSS," which should have given scholarly appraisal to these works and introduced the best works to the readers, often avoids their analysis and evaluation.[30]

Not only is there a real problem for the regime in preserving its system of vertical containment, but post-Stalin conditions imperil the elaborate network of barriers designed to effect a topical or horizontal separation between approved and disapproved areas of discussion. The preeminent example, of course, is

University, from A. N. Guliev and M. I. Naidel, Institute of History, Academy of Sciences of Azerbaijan, dated April 25, 1961, p. 4.
30. B. N. Ponomarev, "Istoricheskii opyt KPSS — na sluzhbu kommunisticheskomu stroitelstvu," *Voprosy istorii KPSS*, no. 4 (1960), p. 33.

the spillover of the denunciation of Stalin. One revelation led to another: the date of his alleged criminal insanity could not be kept fixed at 1934, just as it proved impossible to disparage his role in collectivization without opening up the topics of the purges and concentration camps. It is interesting to note that this spillover tendency was recognized by Khrushchev and by his own account was used to argue within the Presidium for delivery of the secret speech.

The danger of leakage into a forbidden area is congenitally present in historiography as riddled with inconsistencies and strange blank spots as that of the CPSU. And the plain accretion of facts and sources during the past fifteen years has strained it even more. Filling in one aspect or declaring another topic to be open for research inevitably jeopardizes related but proscribed matters. Every piece added to the jigsaw puzzle provides clues to the next.

In relation to the dysfunctional aspects of these control mechanisms, the stratagem of the party historian's duality of role deserves special notice. It can be seen that this institutionalized schizophrenia has become more difficult for the individual to sustain since Stalin's death. Whereas during the earlier period the historian of the party always knew that he was a functionary assigned from Agitprop to behave like a historian, today he must experience some confusion and conflict. The reasons have fundamentally to do with the substitution of more subtle and less discernible official guidelines, the drastic lowering of the penalties imposed for error or willful revisionism, the enormous increase in accessible source materials, and — perhaps most important — the improved status and education of historians specializing in the CPSU.

The following figures show a decided trend not only toward more trained historians entering the field, but also toward an increasing proportion of them being educated at universities rather than in party schools.[31] The distribution of a total of 125 candidate dissertations on the history of the CPSU submitted between May 15 and December 31, 1958 is shown in Table 1. Unfortunately, the figures for a later period are not exactly com-

31. "Kandidatskii dissertatsii po istorii KPSS, zashchishchennye s 15 maia po 31 dekabria 1958 goda," *Voprosy istorii KPSS*, no. 2 (1959), pp. 232–236.

Table 1

Universities	69
Pedagogical institutes	15
Military-Political Academy	5
Academy of Social Sciences	29
Institute of Marxism-Leninism	2
Higher Party School	2
Academy of Sciences	1
Affiliates of Academy of Sciences	2
	125

Table 2

Universities	209
Pedagogical institutes	41
Military-Political Academy	2
Academy of Social Sciences	38
Institute of Marxism-Leninism	3
Higher Party School	1
Republican Central Committees' Institutes of Party History	9
Institute of History, Academy of Sciences	2
Affiliates of Academy of Sciences	8
Moscow Institute of Chemical Science	7
	320

parable and cover the period 1964–1965.[32] But the relative proportion of academic to party-trained historians can be seen to have shifted from almost 3:1 to over 5:1 as shown in Table 2.

It would seem that the increasingly academic rather than apparat background of historians of the party, coupled with the official pressure for more respectable methods of research work against the regime's determination to retain control of its own historical image.

The ultimate question remains: Has Soviet historiography of the CPSU reached a point of no return, or is it still possible for

32. "Spiski tem dissertatsii, zashchishchennykh v 1964 i 1965 gg. na soiskanie uchenoi stepeni kandidata istoricheskikh nauk po razdelu 'Istoriia kommunisticheskoi partii sovetskogo soiuza,'" *Voprosy istorii KPSS*, no. 4 (1966), pp. 151–158.

the political leadership to impose a doctrinal text or a compulsory set of interpretations such as those furnished by the *Short Course*? Any new flagrant falsification of history has become virtually impossible, because of more stable political conditions and such official policies as the publication of archival materials, the greater access of historians to foreign sources and documents, higher educational standards for historians of the CPSU, and increased scholarly exchange with the West. Because of the documentation of Stalin's crimes against party cadres, it has been possible — indeed necessary — to rehabilitate almost endless ranks of middle- and low-level party workers. By the same token, sudden and unjustified denigration of individuals has become very much more difficult. Under the conditions of a generally more rational political system, what is published today does, for the first time in the USSR since the early thirties, place some limits on what can be published tomorrow. To the extent that the present leadership perceives de-Stalinization as having set in motion some unsettling and potentially dangerous trends, it can be expected to avoid another such dramatic and wholesale revision of party history. Revision in either direction may be expected to be piecemeal and of relatively modest proportions. In these circumstances, the political leaders' future delineation of approaches to party history is conditioned upon extant interpretations of that history.

Developments since 1956 also have effected net incremental changes within the substantive body of historiography itself — owing largely to the publication for the first time of many important original sources — which cannot easily be swept aside in any future reversal of policy. The denigration of Stalin can be modified, but Stalin can never again become the godlike figure of the 1940s. Topics forbidden before 1953 have been opened to historical and thence to public discussion and have become part of scholarship and general parlance; they can no longer be disposed of by vilification. Party history is not petrified in a *Short Course*; the beginnings of scholarly research and documentation of sources — which were officially initiated in order to achieve more convincing political argumentation, consistency, and international respectability — have accumulated a body of new knowledge and interpretation, which in turn generates a degree of genuine scholarship.

When all of this is said, however, the fact remains that there have been no significant institutional changes of a liberalizing nature. The sphere of competence accorded to historians of the party has been considerably enlarged since 1953, and many historians have interpreted their prerogatives generously. But the state of the discipline — and especially that of party history — is far from autonomous. The most creative developments have been of an informal, interpretive, or extrainstitutional nature.

The introduction of real and dramatic changes in party history, and the growth of liberalizing trends that could no longer be halted or reversed by the political leadership, would have to be preceded by a renunciation of the claim to infallibility by the CPSU. Such a development cannot soon be expected; and it must be assumed that it is still possible for the CPSU, under conditions of international or domestic political crisis, to reinstitute severe controls. As long as such conditions do not pertain and the regime refrains from imposing strong controls, the outlook is encouraging. Continued moderate cyclical swings from more to less liberal policies may be expected. But the improved knowledge and access to sources, accompanied by higher professional standards and increased self-respect, will more and more obviate bald falsification and drastic revisions and generate some momentum toward objective historiography.

Since 1956, in my view, the process of historical writing and rewriting in the USSR has become less of a reflex action and more of a dialogue between historian and politician. This conclusion is, of course, not universally shared by scholars of Soviet historiography. For example, it directly counters the analysis of Konstantin Shteppa, who feels that the post-Stalin "line in Soviet historical science is merely a response to the new turn in the Party line."[33] I agree with Shteppa that Soviet historiography is a microcosm in a macrocosm,[34] an extremely sensitive subsystem that displays the larger political system in high relief. But, precisely because this is true, the assertion that the party is able to maintain rigid control over the writing of history is oversimplified and even inaccurate. We should look more closely now at pertinent events and the relationship between politics and historiography — as system and subsystem — from the Twentieth to the Twenty-Third Party Congress.

33. Shteppa, *Russian Historians and the Soviet State*, p. 371.
34. *Ibid.*, p. 380.

The most important thing has been done. The Twentieth Congress of the CPSU roused our critical thought, and it will not now run amok. Although with zigzags and retreats, Soviet historical science will nonetheless go forward.

E. N. Burdzhalov, remarks at All-Union
Conference of Historians, December 1962

HISTORY AS A POLITICAL RECORD 2

With the Twentieth Party Congress the Soviet Union entered a new historical period. As the first party congress after the death of Stalin, it closed a confused three-year interim of successional struggle and marked the onset of Khrushchev's predominance. From this point onward, although Khrushchev's strength within the elite group continued to vacillate and his rivals pursued their attempts to dislodge him, there could be little further doubt that he was the most equal of the equal and collective leadership.

The Twentieth Congress and its political aftermath have been analyzed by many scholars, and there is no need here to recapitulate that work. On the other hand, any attempt to explore the common ground of politics and historiography in the post-Stalin era must be rooted in this congress. The Twentieth Congress and succeeding developments up through the Twenty-Third Congress in historiography and the larger sphere of general politics will be traced out in this and succeeding chapters with a special and circumscribed purpose: to discover the relationship between politics and history in the contemporary Soviet system.

One of the most important themes discernible in the Twentieth Party Congress is the imposition of stringent duties and standards upon both politics and historiography, as the CPSU was called back to the Leninist path and historians were required by the party leadership to take upon themselves greater initiative and to impose upon themselves higher criteria of scholarship. With official blessing some work was to be repudiated, and much historical writing — especially with regard to the party — would be replaced by studies utilizing newly available documentary material.

The Twentieth Congress is of further interest to us because it was here that Khrushchev had the audacity to claim initiative as the prime spokesman for the future by means of seizing title to the past. His secret speech to the congress is an unparalleled enunciation of the unity of theory and practice — the history of the party merges into party politics. And it is upon his performance as historian of the Stalin period that Khrushchev based the argument for his vision of what Soviet society should become. But, it is also a fact that the method of bold attack on the recorded history of the CPSU and the drastic denigration of Stalin's role ultimately defined the anachronism of such measures.

The Twentieth Party Congress

The report of the Central Committee to the congress, delivered by Khrushchev as First Secretary, occupied eleven pages in *Pravda* of February 15, 1956, and touched on a wide spectrum of topics. His remarks concerning the party are especially significant when taken in juxtaposition with those on party history. The CPSU is presented as the hero of Soviet history, and Khrushchev reminds the congress that the country "owes its tremendous achievements to the correct policy of our Communist Party, to its tireless organizing work."[1] The themes of party unity, party spirit, work with the masses, and collective leadership are all Lenin's principles, and Khrushchev identifies the CPSU with Lenin time and again during his speech.

The Central Committee has been and is guided undeviatingly by Lenin's teaching on the party . . . Underlying the unity of the Communist Party and its leading core is the moral-political unity of the whole of Soviet society and the firm principles of Marxism-Leninism . . . [Lenin] vigorously combatted every attempt of any kind to belittle or weaken the guiding role of the Party in the Soviet state system . . . People enter our Party not for personal advantage, but for the achievement of a great goal — the building of communism . . . To further strengthen Party unity and make the Party organizations more active, it was necessary to restore the norms of Party life worked out by Lenin, which had often been violated in the past. It was of cardinal importance to restore and strengthen in every way Lenin's principle of collective leadership.[2]

Khrushchev then illustrates the party's concern for creativity among the working population and party cadres by citing the Central Committee's efforts to counter the personality cult. The phraseology here is careful:

the Central Committee took measures to explain widely the Marxist-Leninist view of the role of the individual in history. The Central Committee resolutely condemned the cult of the individual as alien to the spirit of Marxism-Leninism and as turning one or another leader into a miracle-working hero, at the same time belittling the role of the Party and the masses and tending to reduce their creative efforts. The spread of the cult of the individual diminished the role of collective leadership in the Party and sometimes led to serious defects in our work . . .

1. *Current Soviet Policies — II*, ed. Leo Gruliow (New York: Frederick A. Praeger, 1957), p. 55.
2. *Ibid.*, pp. 55, 56.

The people, led by the Party, armed with Marxist theory, are a great and invincible force, the creators of a new life, the makers of history![3]

The infallible party and, through it, the masses are thus to reoccupy their creative role usurped by Stalin. Clearly Khrushchev's vision is of rejuvenated party cadres manipulating the state machinery, rather than of activist state, economic, and cultural officials who see themselves only incidentally as party workers. His goal is the active interpenetration at every level of all elements of the socioeconomic system by party organizations.

But the party, he cautions, has had some failures (unspecified) as well as victories, and there is no ground for complacency. The example of the kind of self-criticism that Khrushchev selects to present for emulation is the recent discussion among the leadership of defects in economic development. The homily he elicits is more interesting: "the Central Committee proceeded from the fact that the Party should not be afraid to tell the people the truth about the faults and difficulties besetting our advance. He who fears to admit mistakes and weaknesses is no revolutionary. We need not conceal our shortcomings, for our general line is correct."[4] Such strictures on the party and its place in the Soviet system accurately reflect Khrushchev's philosophy of the CPSU and are the keynote for his later policies. The political record of the ensuing decade represents a conscious attempt to structure the party to fulfill exactly these norms. Further, this concept of the party exists in the historical as well as the political dimension. The heroic quality of the CPSU and the specific characteristics noted in 1956 are developed and stressed to an unprecedented degree in the historiography of the party during the Khrushchev years.

The sole specific comment on historiography in Khrushchev's open report to the congress dealt with the history of the CPSU and was made within the context of questions of ideological work. His concern is exclusively with the didactic function of party history:

During the past seventeen years our propaganda was based mainly on the "History of the Communist Party of the Soviet Union (Short Course)." The glorious history of our party must continue to be one of the most important sources for the educa-

3. *Ibid.*, p. 56.
4. *Ibid.*

tion of our cadres. Therefore, it is essential to produce a popular Marxist textbook on the history of the party, based on historical fact, presenting a scientific generalization of the party's world-historic struggle for communism, and bringing the history up to our day.[5]

The secret speech is by contrast essentially a political document cast in historical language. In Chapter Nine I shall consider the question of Stalin's denigration in historiography and the more general problem of the Soviet political leader as hero or antihero. The focus here is political: not on the "what" of the post-Stalin revision of party history, but on the "why" and "how." It will perhaps be useful to examine the secret speech as we may assume Soviet historians did, in an effort to discern not only substantive information but — more important — the new official guidelines for historiography. Khrushchev stated at the outset that the report would deal not with a thorough evaluation of Stalin but would merely point to the specific problem of how the Stalin cult grew. However, the discussion could not be so circumscribed and necessarily encompassed many more general issues. This obvious fact about the secret speech is interesting to us because it presents in microcosm the ensuing dilemma of the regime with regard to party history.

Khrushchev's central point was that the Stalin cult was an abnormal growth that must be exposed and cured for the health of the party and all of Soviet society. The history of the CPSU is thus given a new temporal ordering: the Leninist period (or golden age) is severely set off from the following years, which Khrushchev subdivides according to Stalin's behavior into the "first period after Lenin's death" — when Stalin still paid attention to Lenin's warnings — and the "last years" — when Stalin's "grave abuse of power . . . caused untold harm to our party."[6] The periodization is in gross terms: Khrushchev specifies that Stalin played a positive role in the party's righteous struggle against the Trotskyites and Right Opportunists. He is more vague with regard to Stalin's fall from Leninism, saying only that "Stalin's willfulness vis-à-vis the Party and its Central Committee became fully evident after the Seventeenth Party Congress, which took place in 1934."[7] Throughout, it must be stressed,

5. *Ibid.*, p. 60.
6. *Ibid.*, p. 173.
7. *Ibid.*, p. 175.

Khrushchev's criterion and sole evident concern is Stalin's actions with regard to party cadres. The implicit theme of theoretical discourse that underlies the repudiation of Stalin's excesses is a reexamination of the identity, purposes, and legitimate tactics of the CPSU.

Khrushchev's method of argument is the dichotomization of Lenin and Stalin. To this end he enters into a lengthy exposition of Lenin's methods of handling dissension, focusing on Lenin's insistence that a distinction be made between party members "who had shown indecision or temporary nonconformity with the Party lines, but whom it was possible to return to the Party path" — who should be patiently educated and persuaded — and "those people who had in fact committed criminal acts against the Soviet system" — against whom the Leninist criteria would allow "extraordinary methods."[8]

Not only is Stalin set apart from Lenin, he is portrayed as increasingly divorced from the party after 1934: Stalin alone bears ultimate guilt for the purges of party cadres, aided by secondary figures such as Yezhov. There was no "exchange of opinions or a Political Bureau decision." What sort of sanction could there be when "Stalin decided everything?"[9] Stalin initiated the mass deportations; fabricated the postwar Leningrad case against Voznesensky, Kuznetsov, and others, at the suggestion of Beria; personally ordered the purge of the Georgian party organization in 1951 and 1952; set up the case against the "doctor plotters." Beria appears in Khrushchev's account as an evil genius as early as 1931, when he received his initial party post by defaming the first secretary of the Transcaucasus Territory Committee to Stalin. It is incidentally noted that Mikoyan and Kaganovich were also present with Stalin at the meeting that chose Beria and deported his rival,[10] providing a hook upon which to hang possible future accusations.

There is a final refinement in the Khrushchev periodization of Stalin's career: he tells us that "after the war the situation became even more complicated. [Stalin's] persecution mania reached unbelievable dimensions . . . He decided everything alone.[11] The

8. *Ibid.*, p. 174.
9. *Ibid.*, p. 179.
10. *Ibid.*, p. 184.
11. *Ibid.*, p. 182.

progressive development of Stalin's isolation and tyranny obviously parallels Khrushchev's own political ascendancy; it is difficult to believe that Khrushchev was unconcerned about establishing his own lack of involvement in Stalin's later policies.

With respect to specific measures to improve Soviet historiography, Khrushchev has little to say. In light of the havoc created in the party's ideological work by the errors of the *Short Course*, which Stalin claimed as his own work in 1938, Khrushchev sees urgent need for a "serious textbook on the history of our party, edited in accordance with scientific Marxist objectivism." Specifically, the historical and artistic accounts of the October Revolution and the Civil War must be revised to restore Lenin to the leading role usurped by Stalin. Also needed are textbooks on the history of Soviet society, the Civil War, and World War II.[12]

Khrushchev's secret speech is thus a pragmatic program for revision of the substance of party history, principally designed to eradicate the Stalin cult and to restore the historical CPSU to a preeminence comparable to the central role it was now to enjoy in Soviet politics. Yet, despite the relatively modest goals, the unintended consequences of the speech were enormous: the customary image called forth by Khrushchev's denigration of Stalin is that of a Pandora's box. Quite clearly his motivation was not a pure concern for historical accuracy; he states that the reasons for rewriting the history of the Stalin years are political and pragmatic — better propaganda and more effective indoctrination of the young generation. But merely to state that his aims were political rather than scholarly begs the question. The evidence suggests that Khrushchev's primary goal was not just the aggrandizement of personal power but rather that he came to his decision out of a complex of motivations: his determination to force the party membership out of its fear-frozen inefficiency, rigidity, and corruption and his feeling that only such a shocking rejection of Stalin and his terror would be sufficient, combined with bitter personal memories of fear and indignity suffered at Stalin's hands.

Doubtless there were also political goals of a more crass nature which Khrushchev could expect to realize. By initiating such dramatic historical revelations he automatically preempted the

12. *Ibid.*, pp. 188, 185–186.

role of original protester against the terror and advocate for the people, and imputed cowardice and lack of concern to those other leaders — notably Molotov, Malenkov, Kaganovich, and Beria — who were ostensibly closer to Stalin than he. Denouncing the cult of the single personal leader would also act to allay fears and deny possible allegations that he was himself building just such a concentration of power and adulation.

For a concern with more technical, methodological problems of historiography, we must refer to the speeches of Mikoyan and Anna Pankratova. Mikoyan's ostensible concern parallels Khrushchev's: the deplorable condition of the party's propaganda requires a more accurate text on party history to replace the *Short Course*.

The Central Committee's report speaks out plainly on the unsatisfactory state of our *propaganda work*. A principal reason for this is that as a rule we still study Marxism-Leninism solely from the "Short Course" on the history of the Party. This is wrong, of course. The theme of our Party's history cannot accommodate in its restricted framework the wealth of ideas of Marxism-Leninism, and this is even more true of the "Short Course." What is needed is special theoretical textbooks, written for comrades at different levels of training. This is the first requirement. Secondly, we cannot be satisfied with the existing "Short Course" on the Party's history, if only because it fails to illuminate the events of almost the last twenty years of our Party's life . . .

Furthermore, if our *historians* were to make a genuine and profound study of the facts and events in the history of our Party in the Soviet period — including those that the "Short Course" deals with — if they were to delve properly into the archives and historical documents, and not only into the back issues of newspapers, they would be able to give a better explanation, from the positions of Leninism, of many of the facts and events dealt with in the "Short Course."[13]

The implication as well as the overt substance of these remarks have proved quite significant for party history. Mikoyan quite clearly is saying that the needs of both propaganda and history would be better served by some differentiation of their functions. This is because the philosophy of Marxism-Leninism simply cannot be adequately discussed when confined to the factual and thematic material contained in any party history text, even a

13. Speech to Congress of A. I. Mikoyan, *Current Soviet Policies — II*, pp. 87–88.

good one. Conversely — and perhaps this reflects Mikoyan's special feelings as an Old Bolshevik — the existing text simply is an inadequate and inaccurate record of events. Further, by suggesting that historians rather than party functionaries be given the task of doing this research under new and more scholarly standards, he provides some possible means for applying a criterion of historical accuracy, albeit within the framework of "positions of Leninism." He castigates the existing work on party and Soviet history as "perhaps the most backward sector" of the ideological sphere.[14]

One other aspect of Mikoyan's speech deserves notice here: his criticism of "some historians" for passing off "complex and contradictory events of the 1918–1920 Civil War" as sabotage by certain party leaders "who were wrongly declared enemies of the people many years after the events described."[15] The main point of this remark is obviously to decry the practice that had become common among historians of the Stalin period of reading back current interpretations and denigrations into earlier events. There is also evident a recommendation — not necessarily confined to study of the Civil War period — that historians be more subtle in their analysis and go beyond the formula of "enemies of the people" to discern "changes in the correlations of class forces." Such an approach obviously requires a more competent group of scholars than had adorned party history for several decades and also better archival resources.

Pankratova, secretary of the Section of Historical Sciences of the Academy of Sciences, chief editor of *Voprosy istorii*, and member of the Central Committee, was entrusted with the more detailed development of this theme of resuscitating party history, and she began by pointing to the complete decay of scholarship in this field:

The task of raising the study of our great Communist Party to truly scientific heights brooks no delay. The influence of the cult of the individual as a brake on progressive science has been especially pronounced in this sphere. And now it cannot but alarm us that almost no serious scientific work is being done on Party history, that the journal on problems of Party history which existed before the war is no longer being published and that there is no scientific center for the study of Party history.

14. *Ibid.*, p. 88.
15. *Ibid.*

Nor is the History Institute of the U.S.S.R. Academy of Sciences working on problems of Party history.[16]

Such pointed references to the absence of "serious scientific work" and a "scientific center" could only signify disgust with the type of work on party history being done under the auspices of the Central Committee at the Marx-Engels-Lenin-Stalin Institute.

But before examining Pankratova's proposals, we should consider the concurrent events in historical circles and attempt to assess the moods of historians on the eve of the Twentieth Party Congress. As Fainsod and Schapiro have shown, there were signs in mid-1955 and early 1956 that some historians were beginning to try to break out of the petrified formulas of the *Short Course* and that these expressions found outlet in the pages of *Voprosy istorii*.[17]

A conference of readers of the journal *Voprosy istorii* in late January 1956 set the stage for the Twentieth Congress in its concern with historiography, and indeed raised issues that were to remain alive throughout the ensuing decade.[18] More than six hundred leading teachers, historians, and historical researchers and archivists from the Moscow area discussed the work of the journal in 1955 and its plans for 1956; and suddenly a conference in the tradition of so many tedious and propagandistic gatherings came to life. The participants listened to a rather quiet report by the chief editor in which she seemed proud of articles published in 1955 that began cautiously to open long-closed topics. She also welcomed a new department for the publication of letters and the expansion of another department to publish articles on historiography. Without making a specific recommendation, Pankratova regretted the lack of specialized journals for modern history, the history of Soviet society, the history of the CPSU, and military history. She was careful to explain why these journals would be valuable: to enable *Voprosy istorii* to concentrate on the fundamental questions.[19]

16. Speech to Twentieth Congress by A. M. Pankratova, *Current Soviet Policies — II*, p. 147.
17. Merle Fainsod, "Historiography and Change," and Leonard Schapiro, "Continuity and Change in the New History of the CPSU," *Contemporary History in the Soviet Mirror*, ed. John Keep (New York: Frederick A. Praeger, 1964), pp. 19–21, 69–70.
18. "Konferentsiia chitatelei zhurnala "Voprosy istorii,'" *Voprosy istorii*, no. 2 (1956), pp. 199–213.
19. *Ibid.*, p. 200.

The assistant editor, E. N. Burdzhalov, was considerably more forthright and did not hedge his arguments. He criticized Soviet work on many sensitive questions, among them collectivization, the 1905 Revolution (treated by most Soviet historians "in such a way that on one side there was tsarism, the liberal bourgeoisie, Essars and Mensheviks, and on the other side — only the Bolsheviks"),[20] the positive activity of the (predominantly Menshevik) Petersburg soviet in defiance of its Menshevik leaders, the struggle against oppositionist groups within the party ("as if in the twenties the party struggled not against antiparty, anti-Leninist currents and groups, but against circles of unmasked spies and wreckers").[21] This is strong talk and must have created a sensation at the meeting, despite Burdzhalov's assertions that the purpose of eradication of "oversimplification, time-serving, vulgarization" in historiography was to enable historians to "battle the bourgeois world view" more effectively.[22] He was clearly troubled by the credibility gap created by the stereotyped treatment of the 1905 and 1917 revolutions and attacked the usual black-and-white accounts.

Other proscribed topics were discussed openly for the first time in many years. Two speakers denigrated the cult of personality surrounding such figures as Ivan IV and certain military leaders who were quite obviously reactionary. It is perhaps suggestive that E. Iu. Barush, who criticized the military-hero cult, was identified as associated with the Central Committee's Marx-Engels-Lenin-Stalin Institute. This was the only critical remark attributed to a historian employed directly by the party; all of the other liberal or revisionary comments were those of historians associated with *Voprosy istorii*, Moscow University, the Chief Archives Administration, or the Institute of History of the Academy of Sciences.

A real altercation developed around the problem of the publication of archival documents, apparently initiated by M. A. Dvoinishnikov of the Marx-Engels-Lenin-Stalin Institute. He wished to register dissatisfaction with the failure of *Voprosy istorii* to "express its own relationship to collections in which were included a large number of police documents and Menshe-

20. *Ibid.*, p. 201.
21. *Ibid.*, p. 202.
22. *Ibid.*, pp. 202, 203.

vik publications." He was also disturbed that the review of a collection of documents concerning the revolutionary movement during 1905 in Irkutsk did not specify that the Irkutsk Party Committee was "composed of Mensheviks."[23] Dvoinishnikov was answered by an archivist who would have elicited Stalin's wrath as an "archive rat": V. A. Kondratev of the Chief Archives Administration defended the integrity of the collection and maintained that the Irkutsk committee's documents must be included. He was not foolhardy enough to define historical veracity as comprehensiveness, however, but rested his case on the ground that the Irkutsk committee was not Menshevik but unified and in fact dominated by its Bolshevik contingent from the end of 1905. "How then can one exclude its documents from the collection?"[24]

Kondratev was answered by M. D. Stuchebnikova, of the Marx-Engels-Lenin-Stalin Institute, who was quite unimpressed by the need for a complete documentary record at the risk of some possible ideological contamination of the reader. She stated flatly: "The publication of Menshevik documents is impermissible if such documents affect Bolshevik influence . . . Our documents are published for a wide circle of readers and by an incorrect choice of published documents we might only confuse them."[25]

Burdzhalov's concluding remarks revealed a sharp dispute with other members of the Institute of History of the Academy of Sciences, in particular A. L. Sidorov, whose policies as chief editor or contributing editor of a number of books and series had been severely criticized in *Voprosy istorii*. Burdzhalov accused the Institute of History and Sidorov of not facing fundamental problems, of misunderstanding the role of *Voprosy istorii*. He denied that feature articles should or did bear a directive quality — but neither should the editorial board be a "letter box." Its obligation is "to enunciate our opinion on the important questions in history."[26] He was disgusted that Sidorov refused to declare himself on the substantive correctness or error of the journal's criticisms of his work.

23. *Ibid.*, p. 205.
24. *Ibid.*, p. 207.
25. *Ibid.*, p. 209.
26. *Ibid.*, p. 212.

Finally, Burdzhalov pressed proposals that had been made for organizing a society of historians and convoking an all-union conference of historians; these and other important matters raised at the readers' conference should be discussed further, he insisted. These remarks apparently were not followed up, and the conference was given a hackneyed conclusion by Pankratova's pontification: "The problems of Soviet historiography are problems of our communist ideology."[27]

The January 1956 *Voprosy istorii* conference is a fascinating prelude to the events under review. One readily observes a nascent professional identification and pride in the historian's craft, some rudimentary concern with methodology and the historian's responsibility for the accuracy of his work. The issues raised and professional concerns voiced — regarding taboo subjects, the use of documents, access to journals for historians with novel theories, the role of the hero in historical materials, questions of professional conferences and organization — all become matters of continuing debate after the Twentieth Party Congress. Further, this discussion adumbrates the split between historians associated with academic and bibliographic or archival institutions and those who work for party institutions. It is already clear, though, that this was not a perfect bifurcation and that institutes and university departments were often internally divided (witness Sidorov of the Academy of Sciences in contrast with its other spokesmen).

It is extremely doubtful that the arguments presented at this conference were originated on the spot; the interchanges have the atmosphere of a continuing dialogue that had developed over the preceding year, largely on the basis of controversial journal articles. If one wonders how these articles appeared in *Voprosy istorii* before the liberalizing directives of the Twentieth Congress, there is no conclusive evidence for any answer. We must look to the general thaw that was beginning to be felt, especially in intellectual and artistic circles, and that was variously interpreted by historians as by the rest of Soviet society. Perhaps the best argument for this interpretation is the disparity of the evaluations by Pankratova and Burdzhalov of what was now possible. Although both obviously were toward the liberal end of the spectrum and were jointly responsible for *Voprosy istorii*'s editorial policy, Pankratova was more cautious — whether by vir-

27. *Ibid.*, p. 213.

tue of temperament, longer experience, or somewhat more privileged information, we cannot know. But the very fact that two
such prominent and responsible historians could have different
judgments of the alternatives open to them and their profession
indicates that policy was already in flux and veering toward a
more relaxed though still undetermined line.

Pursuing its editorial policies of 1955, *Voprosy istorii* continued
to publish pathbreaking articles in the new year; more and more
during the spring and summer of 1956 it became the focal point
and mouthpiece for those historians who wished to reinforce
their new prerogatives. Even a brief resumé of the subjects
treated will indicate the climate being created in the pages of
Voprosy istorii during the months before the Twentieth Party
Congress. One of the chief themes was the reemergence of Soviet
historiography into the world, the participation of Soviet historians in the Tenth International Congress of Historians in
Rome in September 1955, and the increasing concern with historical work done abroad as being, in part at least, serious
scholarship rather than merely bourgeois propaganda. Coupled
with this was a growing preoccupation with the evaluation of
works by prerevolutionary Russian and early Soviet historians.
The editorial of the journal's first 1956 number was devoted to
this topic and clearly demanded a more scholarly appraisal of
such proscribed historians as M. N. Pokrovsky, Kliuchevsky,
Karamzin, Petrushevsky, and Soloviev.[28] These writers could no
longer be dismissed with a few deprecatory remarks, or completely omitted from historiographical studies, nor should French
and German bourgeois historians be treated in completely negative fashion.

During this period there is more evidence of concern for higher
scholarly standards and better research in studies of the Soviet
period — and most particularly of the CPSU. In *Voprosy istorii*,
number 2, 1956, sent to press before the Twentieth Congress
convened, there is an interesting critique of a newly revised
collection of brochures on a series of party congresses and conferences.[29] The revised collection was published in 1955 after a
review article had appeared in *Voprosy istorii*, number 8, for

28. "Ob izuchenii istorii istoricheskoi nauki," *Voprosy istorii*, no. 1 (1956), pp.
3–12.
29. "Broshiury o sezdakh i konferentsiiakh KPSS," *Voprosy istorii*, no. 2
(1956), pp. 124–129.

1953. The originals were issued during the years 1948 to 1952. Although the anonymous reviewer notes a significant improvement in the more detailed statement of Lenin's role as organizer and leader and a generally less schematic presentation, he is critical of the dull and superficial treatment accorded the struggle with the various anti-Leninist groups within the party, as well as the fact that the revised brochures present little new material. The authors

almost never use the rich archival sources, do not bring into scholarly use the significant material hidden in dissertations on history of the CPSU (as is known, the overwhelming majority of dissertations remain unpublished). More than this: the authors of many brochures make little use of protocols or stenographic minutes of Congresses and conferences . . . It would be important to use the memoirs of participants at the Congresses and conferences.[30]

Further, he suggests that the authors have not been able to analyze satisfactorily the debates at the Fifteenth and Sixteenth Conferences because they have not studied the significant material contained in speeches of several participants later purged by Stalin.[31]

It is also worth noting that several articles in this second issue of *Voprosy istorii* for 1956, commemorating the fiftieth anniversary of the 1905 Revolution, emphasized the close ties between the party and the masses in 1905. G. D. Obichkin, director of the party's Marx-Engels-Lenin-Stalin Institute, reportedly stressed that "by directing the activities of the soviets, strike committees, trade unions and other organizations, the Bolsheviks not only taught the masses, but were themselves taught by the masses."[32] This identification of the party with the people and delineation of its use of intermediate organizations was to become a hallmark of party theory as well as party history during the Khrushchev period.

In the context of these developments in historiography, Pankratova's speech to the Twentieth Congress can be seen as demonstrating a new official sanction of criticism of certain aspects of

30. *Ibid.*, p. 128.
31. *Ibid.*, p. 127.
32. "K 50 letiiu pervoi russkoi revoliutsii" [Session of the Marx-Engels-Lenin-Stalin Institute under the Central Committee, CPSU], *Voprosy istorii*, no. 2 (1956), p. 195.

Stalinist historiography and also representing a middle position in the continuing debate among historians over more specific scholarly and philosophical questions. Pankratova's argument for more truthful evaluations and examination of mistakes and shortcomings is marked by the attempt to ward off charges of lack of party spirit or disloyalty. She fortifies her position by quoting Lenin's insistence that all relevant facts be studied in order to avoid suspicion of arbitrary selection, as well as his acknowledgment to the Eighth Congress that "Very often we had to feel our way in the dark [in] undertaking a job no one in the world had ever attempted on such a scale."[33] Soviet historians must cease their glossing over and embellishment, not — and she is careful here — out of any professional calling to present objective truth but because such prettifying prevents party history from exercising its function as the guide of Soviet cadres and foreign socialists.[34]

Despite her caution, however, Pankratova's concern for the historical profession is evident from her strictures against low academic standards, bureaucratization, and lack of scholarly research at the Central Committee's Academy of Social Sciences and the Institute of History of the Academy of Sciences. The cause of historiography would also be served by creation of an all-union society of historians and a separate institute for the study of Soviet history, publication of more journals devoted to specialized aspects of history, and the calling of an all-union conference of historians.

The Twentieth Party Congress was a landmark for both the CPSU and its chroniclers. Many hopeful signals pointed to the invigoration, reorganization, and rededication of the party and its historians toward a more effective and rational fulfillment of their tasks in the Soviet system. Not only was the party to be revitalized and the substance of its history to be reworked at Khrushchev's direction, but at the behest of two authoritative party figures there would be a drastic improvement in historians' methodology and scholarship.

The precise steps to be taken toward these ends were less clearly

33. Lenin, *Works*, XXIX, 132; quoted by Pankratova in *Current Soviet Policies — II*, p. 148.
34. *Ibid.*

set forth. Pankratova suggested that more use be made of Old Bolsheviks' memoirs and suitably reworked studies done by "old [discredited] party historians," presumably M. N. Pokrovsky in particular. Malenkov's derisive references to the exclusive reliance of party historians on the back issues of newspapers foreshadowed the opening of more archives. Nonetheless, the official remarks at the congress provided very flimsy guidelines for historians being asked to adopt a new course. The situation must have been very confusing for people whose experiences under Stalin had trained them to respond quickly to a monolithic and clearly enunciated line. And indeed the record of ensuing years has proved in essence to be a continuing process of clarification, elaboration, and modification of those vague instructions given historians at the Twentieth Congress in 1956.

Revisionism in History and Politics: 1956

However one evaluates the performance of Soviet historians during the ten-year period following the Twentieth Party Congress, the most striking feature is the enormous increase in writing, which parallels developments in literature and the arts. It is as if a dam had been broken. The number of books on historical topics issued in 1957 increased two and a half times over 1956, and the number of copies printed was more than doubled.[35] In 1957 and 1958 alone five new historical journals were founded, of which two deal specifically with party history: *Istoriia SSSR* and *Voprosy istorii KPSS*. And the proliferation of historical journals has continued. Archives have been made more accessible to researchers, the list of historical subjects denied scholars has been significantly shortened, a separate course on party history has been introduced into the curriculum of all higher educational institutions, and the collection, writing, and reissuance of out-of-print memoirs has been encouraged.

This publication explosion automatically makes the investigation of the political-historiographical relationship an enormous undertaking. My discussion must therefore attempt a schematic or analytical — rather than an encyclopedic — account, in an effort to show turning points, reactions, and interactions. The principal sources of such information with regard to historiog-

35. L. V. Danilova and V. P. Danilov, review, "Rewriting Russian History. Soviet Interpretations of Russia's Past," *Istoriia SSSR*, no. 6 (1959), p. 191.

raphy are the issues from January 1956 through December 1966 of *Istoriia SSSR, Voprosy istorii,* and *Voprosy istorii KPSS.* Additional evidence has been obtained from military and literary journals. The political climate, ideological policies, and official decrees and resolutions have been followed through the central press (*Pravda* and *Izvestia*), central periodicals (*Kommunist, Verkhovnogo soveta SSR,* and *Partiinaia zhizn*), occasional issues of some specialized newspapers (notably *Literaturnaia gazeta, Trud, Krasnaia zvezda*), and the party workers' handbook, *Spravochnik partiinogo rabotnika.*

The real question is one of determining the nature and extent of the interrelationship between the political and the historical spheres of Soviet life. Until 1955 this could be quite easily established and documented as a causal or directly reactive relationship: a change in the political stance or ideological line in any area was unequivocally stated and immediately followed by collaborative work by historians. As noted, the situation with regard to party history, in particular, was vastly simplified after 1938 with the emergence of the *Short Course* as a single and unchanging sacred text. The sudden removal of the absolute dictator and the ensuing policy changes in 1954-55 destroyed forever the hackneyed but relatively certain world of the historian. Even before the Twentieth Party Congress members of the profession responded to a sensed indecision and hints of forthcoming changes in various ways, depending on their own individual temperament and experience. And then the congress directly ordered historians into a fever of production while denying them a clear set of directives.

The situation of Soviet historians after the Twentieth Congress was one of disarray and disagreement over what the new policies meant to them professionally. Some were badly confused over the absence of a clear official line on sensitive subjects; others obviously wanted to maintain the old norms and methods even in the face of the possibility of more freedom; still another group was apparently trying to utilize to the fullest the new responsibilities now accorded historians. In the months following the congress, the confusion among historians persisted, but the substantive arguments and professional philosophies became increasingly more cogent and dichotomized.[36]

36. For a detailed chronicle and analysis of the 1956 debate between the

Certainly the political leadership, despite probable elite dissension over many policy matters, was pursuing a liberalizing line in early 1956. The 1934 decrees, setting up secret police administrative boards to try antistate acts outside the court system, were abolished by decree of the Presidium of the Supreme Soviet on April 19, 1956. In April and May a series of decrees eased the rigid restrictions on workers: criminal penalties for tardiness and absenteeism were removed; it became possible legally for workers to change jobs on their own initiative; the old-age pension was increased; a new minimum wage was established as well as a six-hour workday for workers under eighteen. On May 26 a move was made in the direction of economic decentralization with the transfer of certain light-industry, textile, and transport enterprises to the union republics. Moreover, a Central Committee decree of August 17 abolished the post of party organizer in all enterprises and scientific institutions. Replacing the Central Committee's appointee on the local scene would be full-time secretaries of local party organizations. On April 18 the Cominform — symbol and instrument of undisguised Soviet control of foreign communist parties — was liquidated. In May Khrushchev and Bulganin visited Great Britain; and at the beginning of June the appointment of a Khrushchev favorite to replace Molotov as foreign minister not only weakened a troublesome rival but also signaled a more accessible and flexible mood of Soviet diplomacy.

Tangible evidence of officially inspired liberalizing influences at work in historiography could also be seen early in the year. Already before the party congress, on February 7, the USSR Council of Ministers had passed a resolution opening state archives to scholars.[37] *Istoricheskii arkhiv,* the organ of the Institute of History, published an account of work recently done to improve the scholarly reference apparatus, circulation, and classification of archives.[38] However, the editorial indicated an almost

liberal and conservative historians, see Fainsod, "Historiography and Change," *Contemporary History in the Soviet Mirror.*
37. The Chief Archives Administration of the Ministry of the Interior, the Archive Administration of the Ministry of Foreign Affairs, TASS, and all other ministries or departments having archives were specifically directed to prepare for research all prerevolutionary materials and also those materials of the Soviet period not classified secret. They were also ordered to organize systematic publication of schedules of their unclassified resources.
38. "Razvivat obshire opublikovanie dokumentov po istorii sovetskogo obshchestva," *Istoricheskii arkhiv,* no. 1 (1956), pp. 3–8.

complete dearth of documentary publications concerning the period 1921–1941 and the postwar years, so that these periods were those least studied by Soviet historians. Although nowhere was it said that this neglect was the result of official proscription until 1956 of these documents, the editorial did show that the fault was not primarily with the archivists and historians. It pointed out that some publishing houses were still loath "without any good reason" to risk putting out collections of documents on some aspects of Soviet history. One instance cited of such "excessive caution" was of a collection titled "History of the Collectivization of Kursk Province Agriculture," which had been favorably appraised by the Chief Archives Administration and other reviewers but which was nonetheless rejected by the Kursk Province Publishing House.

On this subject, it is interesting that an article published after the congress in a journal of the CPSU was considerably more critical than *Istoricheskii arkhiv* of the "fantastic" impediments placed in the path of researchers who wish to use the archives, the "causeless" restrictions on certain kinds of documents, the absence of catalogues and surveys even of nonsecret collections, the lack of proper storage facilities and modern machines for reproduction of documents.[39] *Partiinaia zhizn* placed responsibility for these and other failings principally and directly upon the USSR Ministry of Internal Affairs' Chief Archives Administration. This same article raised the touchy problem of what treatment should be accorded papers adorned with the signatures of leaders who had become nonpersons. Hitherto, of course, these documents had been suppressed, regardless of the problems created for the historian trying to explain or recount credibly an important episode. This writer felt document collections to be "impoverished" by such omissions, especially when the document in question reflects Soviet policy. His solution was simple and ingenious: publish it as a "collective document," bearing no signatures but merely indicating the originating organization or institution.

With the issuance of the third number of *Voprosy istorii* in April 1956, the full impact of the new liberalism is seen in the writings of the more adventuresome historians. Virtually every item on

39. "Shire ispolzovat dokumentalnye bogatstva arkhivov," *Partiinaia zhizn,* no. 4 (February 1956), pp. 43–46. This issue was sent to press only on March 6.

the content page represents a new departure in Soviet historiography. Two articles are directed toward a new appraisal of national minority areas in the late eighteenth and early nineteenth centuries.[40] Both go a long way toward mitigating the virulent Russian nationalism of the Stalinist era by showing progressive elements in cultures and national movements previously written off as completely backward. They are most interesting to us, however, by virtue of their methodological references. Both reflect careful, documented research in depth and a concern to set out facts that will refute the established trite appraisals. Another pair of articles in the issue, by overturning the official Soviet appraisal of a contemporary of Radischev's as a revolutionary, cast doubt upon the common Soviet practice of attributing glory as well as guilt by association.[41]

If one is to identify a set of demands or a program of the revisionist historians clustering around *Voprosy istorii* in 1956, one need only turn to the editorial in the third number.[42] Many of the ideas and phrases are reminiscent of Burdzhalov's remarks to the readers' conference in January, and he most certainly drafted the editorial; the concepts are no longer tentative, however, and the issues have clearly been much discussed and refined within professional circles. The editorial is too rich to summarize, but the key areas of concern to the revisionists can be identified. First of all, it is important to underline the obvious fact that the history of the CPSU has been chosen by the liberals as their primary target, because of the literally fantastic treatment it had received under Stalin and the mandate of the congress for its rewriting. The editorial points to the many distortions and oversimplifications of party history in Stalin's *Short Course* and then treats specific areas that need scholarly reworking. Plekhanov has been belittled, his great work in developing Russian Marxism examined from the standpoint of his subsequent evolution toward Menshevism; Lenin's opposition to great-power chauvinism and his interpretation of Russian socialism as part of the international workers' movement have been suppressed. Historians must resume

40. A. M. Pikman, "O borbe kavkazskikh gortsev c tsarskimi kolonizatorami," *Voprosy istorii*, no. 3 (1956), pp. 75–84; O. D. Chekhovich, "O nekotorykh voprosakh istorii Srednei Azii XVIII–XIX vekov," *ibid.*, pp. 84–95.
41. K. V. Sivkov and S. V. Paparigopulo, "O vzgliadakh Fedora Krechetova," *ibid.*, pp. 121–128.
42. "XX Sezd KPSS i zadachi issledovaniia istorii partii," *ibid.*, pp. 3–12.

their abandoned study of the October period, give a truthful picture of the situation within the party before Lenin's return as well as the struggle to construct a wide democratic bloc in the period of the bourgeois-democratic revolution, and show the party's other peaceful activities before the July Days.

The party's difficulties, mistakes, and weaknesses must be revealed truthfully. The history of the CPSU can no longer be treated as a "straightforward, constantly ascending process" marred only by the agents of foreign intelligence services: specifically, Trotsky and his followers and the right-wing or nationalist deviationists should be shown to have expressed the interests of the exploiting classes, who were resisting the Bolsheviks. Research must be undertaken on the history of local party organizations, since no scholarly account of the CPSU can be undertaken without first accumulating and generalizing from local experiences. In particular, an effort must be made to overcome the hackneyed treatment of the proletarian revolution in the Ukraine or Central Asia as simply a delayed reflection of the process in the central Russian provinces.

The attitude expressed with regard to the treatment of the Mensheviks is especially interesting:

Instead of describing Menshevism as a trend hostile to Marxism in the workers' movement and showing its evolution [some historians] depict the Mensheviks as accomplices of the Tsarist autocracy and completely pass over the merging of the Bolsheviks with the Mensheviks, which began at the end of 1905. There are comrades who refuse to study the history of joint committees of the RSDLP on the grounds that Mensheviks were members of these committees. But can one delete the very fact of such committees' existence? The task of historians is to explain and not to hush up historical facts.[43]

Special attention should be devoted to establishing truthful accounts of other neglected or distorted periods and aspects of party history: collectivization, the Civil War, the Great Patriotic War. Also, the editorial lays down strictures aimed at better access to historical documents and more professional sourcing of materials: absolutely essential is the release of party records and stenographic minutes of congresses and conferences, which have become "bibliographical rarities." There is a very unsatisfactory state of affairs with regard to the compilation and publication of memoirs, espe-

43. *Ibid.*, p. 7.

cially for the Soviet period. *Voprosy istorii* itself had not paid sufficient attention to researching party history, nor have the university departments.

It is important to note here that the liberals do not suggest that the study of party history be weaned from the control of the CPSU to more scholarly precincts: one can only speculate about whether they in fact would have felt such a move desirable, had they visualized it as a possibility. It seems entirely credible that at this point Burdzhalov and his sympathizers honestly felt that — given the liberalized policy indicated at the Twentieth Congress — they could expect cooperation in a gradual raising of scholarly standards from most historians in their field, whether associated with party institutes or universities or editorial boards of publishing houses. At any rate, the editorial in *Voprosy istorii* argues for the creation of a center to guide the development of party history and expresses the hope that the Central Committee's Institute of Marxism-Leninism (which changed its ponderous title of Marx-Engels-Lenin-Stalin Institute after the Twentieth Congress) with its regional branches will become such a center.

The final thrust of the editorial neatly expresses the revisionists' concept of what the Twentieth Congress demanded, namely, an entirely new approach to historiography: "the cult of the individual cannot be overcome by excluding quotations and crossing out names. What is required is truthful, Marxist interpretation of the historical process and the role of individual persons . . . It must not be regarded as a rush campaign."[44]

Considerable attention has been devoted to this editorial because it constitutes a conscious program of action on the part of the revisionists, acting in good faith to fulfill what they understood as their new prerogative. Many of the proposals had been suggested in at least truncated form before the congress convened. Their originators were doubtless aware of opposition from conservative historians and party theorists; they were also consciously elaborating a program out of a bare outline; yet, unless we credit them with an urge to self-destruction, we must conclude that the revisionists maintained reasonable hopes of success in carrying out their platform. One of the more surprising aspects of a study of the succeeding decade is the considerable extent to which this program has indeed been realized.

44. *Ibid.*, p. 12.

But the platform of the *Voprosy istorii* editorial represented only one of several plausible courses open to historians in 1956. It is an interesting commentary on the complexity of the Soviet political scene during that year and much of 1957 that, well in advance of official curbing of the revisionists, there was evidence of foot dragging among some historians. The initial indications related to some provincial party historians: *Bakinskii rabochii* on March 28 complained that officials of the Institute of History of the Azerbaijan Academy of Sciences — unrestrained by the institute's party organization — had amassed private archives of historical materials which they would not turn over to the central fund for study by other scholars. Moreover, the institute had on that date not yet begun a systematic study of the Twentieth Congress.[45]

In late April there occurs the first published hint of conflict within the party leadership over the denigration of Stalin. On April 22 *Pravda* published two new Lenin manuscripts. Buried in a 1922 letter concerning local party organizations, is the remark:

there are powerful tendencies both in the localities and at the top that are fighting against truthful proclamation and truthful evaluation of local experience. To wash dirty linen in public is feared; the naked truth is feared and dismissed "with no more than a glance," with a superficial wave of the hand.[46]

Pravda can here be interpreted as lending its support to Khrushchev's campaign, an inference that would most probably be shared by alert Soviet historians.

One final indication of the confusion and disagreement during this early phase may be cited. The Defense Ministry's newspaper *Krasnaia zvezda* for May 9 carried an indignant rebuff to the editorial board of the journal *Voennii vestnik*, also published by the ministry. The newspaper expressed surprise and grief over the lead article in the April issue of *Voennii vestnik* as belittling the importance of Soviet victory in World War II by telling of early defeats and defensive battles waged by unprepared and poorly equipped troops. *Krasnaia zvezda* contended that these events were presented in the guise of the struggle against the personality cult: this campaign is important but must not be

45. "Preodolet otstavanie obshchestvennykh naukov," *Bakinskii rabochii*, March 28, 1956, p. 2.
46. "Novye dokumenty V. I. Lenina," *Pravda*, April 22, 1956, p. 1.

allowed to minimize the role of the party and its Central Committee.[47] This quarrel is especially instructive since it occurs not between different adminstrative hierarchies, but rather among editors and historians working for a single ministry, who presumably received the same ideological instructions.

The April issue of *Voprosy istorii*, number 4, was sent to press a month late, and it continued the thrust of the liberals toward more careful scholarship and truthful recounting of fact, especially with regard to the history of the CPSU. Two articles dealt with the Stalin cult — one in the guise of an attack on Thomas Carlyle's political theory and the other in the context of correcting a false history of the social-democratic organization in the Transcaucasus in 1905.[48]

Burdzhalov presented an article clearly drawn to the specifications of the editorial in the previous number, "Concerning the Tactics of the Bolsheviks in March–April 1917."[49] Utilizing archive materials to draw a living and human portrait of this period, Burdzhalov implicitly challenged the long-hallowed account of an omniscient Lenin who encountered no opposition within the party upon his return to Russia.

Smirnov's critique of the state of historiography on the CPSU was equally devastating.[50] Referring to the "scorn" in which auxiliary disciplines — such as source work, archive research, and bibliography — were held by historians of the party, he asked for publication of memoirs and documents of all kinds, as well as university courses, texts, and journal articles that would lead to a unified system of usage and classification of original sources. He demanded that the Institute of Marxism-Leninism perform its legitimate function of selection and publication of party documents; no "useful" (scholarly in distinction to propagandistic) publications have been issued by the institute since 1934. Smirnov reported only one positive item: the Central Committee had pro-

47. "Velikii podvig sovetskogo naroda," *Krasnaia zvezda*, May 9, 1956, p. 2; "Slavnaia godovshchina," *Voennii vestnik*, no. 4 (1956), pp. 2–9.
48. I. N. Nemanov, "Subektivistsko-idealisticheskaia sushchnost vozzrenii T. Karleilia na istoriiu obshchestva," *Voprosy istorii*, no. 4 (1956), pp. 144–155; and G. A. Arutiunov, review of *Listovki Kavkazskogo soiuza RSDLP 1903–1905*, Institute of History of the Party under Central Committee, Georgian Communist Party, *ibid.*, pp. 158–160.
49. E. N. Burdzhalov, "O taktike bolshevikov v marte-aprele 1917," *ibid.*, pp. 38–56.
50. I. S. Smirnov, "Ob istochnikovedenii istorii KPSS," *ibid.*, pp. 194–201.

posed that its Academy of Social Sciences raise the standards imposed on dissertations.

Finally, this fourth number of *Voprosy istorii* included a strong protest against the practice of drastic editing of memoirs of Old Bolsheviks.[51] The author was able to compare 1931 and 1955 editions of one memoir, the earlier one published while the Old Bolshevik was still alive. He specified precisely what kinds of remarks were deleted in 1955 — which amounted to almost half the book. He also was quite forthright in stating why this editing is bad and did not take refuge in pious thoughts about the need to educate the young or guide foreign socialist parties. Nikolaev's concern was quite simply historical truth: "Obviously this practice of publishing memoirs must be decisively stopped. An arbitrary approach to historical sources, distortions and omissions lead to a falsified representation of historical collections and obscure the true picture of the past."[52]

The atmosphere of confusion and muffled debate remained suspended until late June. On June 30 *Kommunist*, number 9, carried several notes dictated by Lenin at the end of 1922 and in January 1923. The introductory text, signed by the Institute of Marxism-Leninism, explained that these documents, including the "Letter to the Congress" that describes Stalin's rudeness and capriciousness, had been read to the Thirteenth Party Congress and also brought to the attention of the Twentieth Congress and later circulated to party organizations. The introduction also stated that these papers were being published by instruction of the Central Committee, but no date for that decision was specified.[53]

It must be argued that the Central Committee's decision to publish the famous "Lenin Testament" was initiated by Khrushchev to maintain the impetus of the campaign against the Stalin cult and to signal the leadership's continuing support for the policies inaugurated at the Twentieth Congress. However, it seems equally evident that the entire Soviet leadership was becoming progressively more concerned to curb the domestic ferment of discussion as well as that within European communist parties and intellec-

51. Ia. T. Nikolaev, "O bestseremonnom obrashchenii s memuarami starykh bolshevikov," *ibid.*, pp. 139–141.
52. *Ibid.*, p. 141.
53. "Neopublikovannye dokumenty V. I. Lenina," *Kommunist*, no. 9 (1956), pp. 15–26.

tual circles. The dispute among the elite group had probably passed beyond the merits of the secret speech itself and was now turning on such matters as the permissible limits of discussion and methods of keeping the denigration of Stalin from infecting other issues and raising related and dangerous questions. The Poznan uprising of June 28 was graphic evidence of the political consequences attendant upon such ideological disputes in Eastern Europe and probably provided the conservatives with a valuable dramatic argument for junking the liberalization.

Quite clearly the entire Soviet leadership could now agree on a real political need for clarifying and containing the attack on the Stalin cult; although for some — later identified by Khrushchev as the antiparty group — this must have represented the minimum acceptable policy. This basic agreement was enunciated in the Central Committee's resolution of June 30 "On Overcoming the Cult of the Individual and Its Consequences," which marks the turning point toward a policy of retrenchment.[54] The stated reasons for the resolution were the slandering campaign of the bourgeois press and the lack of clarity regarding Soviet policy on the cult among "certain of our friends abroad." Surely there was also perceived a domestic need for clarification, especially among historians and other intellectuals.

The resolution of June 30 set out to accomplish several things. It explained the growth of the cult and why Stalin could not be exposed by another leader (the people would not have understood or supported such a move); and showed how the cult could have caused great harm, retarded the growth of socialism, and yet not be intrinsically related to the nature of the Soviet social system (Marxism shows that no individual can have "such superhuman powers as the ability to change the system of a society" and Soviet society is based on public ownership of the means of production). It argued that the fact that the CPSU undertook to correct mistakes connected with the cult demonstrated its strength and unity. And the resolution dropped another clue for the party historian of the immediate post-Stalin period:

After victory [in World War II] the negative consequences of the cult of the individual again made themselves strongly felt.
But immediately after Stalin's death the Leninist core of the

54. "Postanovlenie tsentralnogo komiteta KPSS: O preodolenii kulta lichnosti i ego posledstvii," *Pravda*, July 2, 1956, pp. 1–2.

Central Committee set a course of resolute struggle against the cult of the individual and its grave consequences.

Politics would decide who was to be included in the "Leninist core."

In July, warning signals were displayed in a pair of authoritative articles that criticized the revisionists. In neither case, however, was the tone abusive. The editorial in *Kommunist*[55] reaffirmed much of the new substantive material presented in recent scholarly articles on the party; the complaint was not with new facts but with the lack of theoretical framework or party spirit in explaining these newly published facts. The second warning developed into a sharp attack on Burdzhalov's article on Bolshevik tactics in 1917. The Burdzhalov analysis was termed "one-sided," "incomplete," and negative.[56] The author, Candidate of Historical Sciences Bugaev, could be readily identified as the voice of the party's ideological apparatus, functioning at that time as head of a section of the Agitation and Propaganda Department of the Secretariat and chief editor of the Central Committee's journal *Partiinaia zhizn*. Upon the creation of a specialized journal on party history in late 1956, he would be made its chief editor. And yet these official warnings were not merely ignored but were overtly disputed until the end of the year by the revisionist historians of *Voprosy istorii*.[57]

By way of illustrating the multiple voices crowding the debate in midsummer, we may note the discrepancy in treatment accorded a conference with Leningrad readers held on May 19 and 20 by the editors of *Voprosy istorii*, as reported in *Leningradskaia pravda* on August 5 and in the July issue of *Voprosy istorii*. The Leningrad paper utilized some of Burdzhalov's more inflammatory comments with respect to the need for historical truthfulness as the springboard for a vicious personal attack on Burdzhalov

55. "Za tvorcheskuiu razrabotku istorii KPSS," *Kommunist*, no. 10 (1956), pp. 14–26.
56. E. Bugaev, "Kogda utrachivaetsia nauchnyi podkhod," *Partiinaia zhizn*, no. 14 (1956), pp. 62–72.
57. Fainsod, "Historiography and Change," pp. 23–25. The July issue of *Voprosy istorii* carried an unsigned note "From the Editorial Board" which countered the substantive points in Bugaev's *Partiinaia zhizn* article. And succeeding numbers of *Voprosy istorii* contained a further article by Burdzhalov attacking his "opponents" on the basis of archival sources (no. 8, 1956, pp. 109–114) and a study of the party conference in March 1917 which supported and further developed Burdzhalov's analysis (no. 9, 1956, pp. 3–16).

and a demand for stronger ideological guidance. One hardly recognizes the account in *Voprosy istorii* as of the same conference.[58] Burdzhalov's report is briefly summarized, and the body of the article concerns the animated discussion that took place among fourteen participants. Most comments were from scholars associated with higher educational faculties, institutes of the Academy of Sciences, or archives, and were directed toward the expansion or qualitative improvement of the journal's work. Only one speaker was extensively quoted as being in opposition to these sentiments, T. P. Bondarevskaia of the Institute of Party History under the Leningrad obkom of the CPSU. Several speakers argued against her position.[59]

Manifestly, October marks a dramatic shift in Soviet policy. Khrushchev, accompanied by two of his most critical colleagues on the Presidium, Kaganovich and Molotov, in addition to the more careful Mikoyan, found it necessary to go to Warsaw to discuss "questions of interest" with Gomulka. The Hungarian uprising demonstrated that the new liberalism inaugurated only eight months before had got out of control in Eastern Europe and that the Soviet reaction was reversion to the old pattern of force.

The further unspoken question for the leadership was to what extent the revisionist infection had taken hold of the domestic population — should it and could it now be eradicated, or should an attempt be made to stabilize and contain the discussion with new methods of control? By late autumn 1956 the party leaders were sufficiently nervous about the potentialities for political dissent implicit in the historical debate to try to shut off all discussion of dangerous topics. The uneasiness became more and more apparent with a series of regional conferences of historians held in September, October, and November to prepare for the fortieth anniversary of the October Revolution. The *Voprosy istorii* articles on 1917 and the Revolution had had considerable impact among provincial party historians, although they were generally more cautious than their comrades in the capital cities. The discussion among historians was obviously only

58. "Konferentsiia chitatelei zhurnala 'Voprosy istorii' v Leningrade," *Voprosy istorii*, no. 7 (1956), pp. 184–190.
59. *Voprosy istorii*, no. 8, 1956, carried a strikingly similar account of a readers' conference held in Kiev in June. "Konferentsiia chitatelei zhurnala 'Voprosy istorii' v Kieve," pp. 198–203.

a part of a more generalized phenomenon within the USSR, as evidenced by the flow of questionable literary works, both published and in manuscript, and the heated debates among students.

Thus in late November the regime once more escalated the conflict with the revisionists. Khrushchev personally remonstrated with Moscow youth;[60] Molotov — newly named Minister of State Control — took a vocal and repressive part in a conference on fine arts held by the Ministry of Culture;[61] the press opened fire on the recent flood of nonorthodox fiction and literary criticism. *Pravda* on November 20 published the letter of V. Smirnov, instructor in history of the CPSU at Moscow University, which directly accused *Voprosy istorii* of revising indisputable truths under the guise of carrying out decisions of the Twentieth Party Congress.[62]

The most direct and forceful attack on the journal — and this time Pankratova was held jointly responsible for its failings — came from the *Partiinaia zhizn* editorial in its December issue.[63] *Voprosy istorii* had failed to profit from Bugaev's critique of its embellishment of the Mensheviks and continued to make the same mistakes. Moreover, *Partiinaia zhizn* made the ominous accusation that *Voprosy istorii* was incorrectly claiming to have a monopoly on interpretation of the decisions of the Twentieth Congress in the field of historiography. Certainly this editorial was sufficiently clear and authoritative that it was now no longer possible for the dissidents to take cover in general confusion. A Central Committee decree of January 12, 1957, established the journal *Voprosy istorii KPSS* under the Central Committee's Institute of Marxism-Leninism to break *Voprosy istorii's* monopoly on questions of party history and to be directly responsive to the CPSU.[64]

Revision and Official Restraint: 1957

By early 1957 Khrushchev had apparently bounced back from the Hungarian crisis and was now campaigning for his massive economic reorganization project: the Central Committee plenum held on February 13 and 14 requested proposals by the Central

60. *Pravda*, November 10, 1956, p. 1.
61. *Sovetskaia kultura*, November 20, 1956, p. 2.
62. "Pismo V. Smirnova," *Pravda*, November 20, 1956, p. 2.
63. "O zhurnale 'Voprosy istorii,' " *Partiinaia zhizn*, no. 23 (1956), pp. 71–77.
64. *Spravochnik partiinogo rabotnika*, 1957, p. 372.

Committee and Council of Ministers; on March 30 *Pravda* printed Khrushchev's draft theses, which were adopted by the Supreme Soviet in May. However, the leadership was soon forced to turn its attention once more to the historians, as it became evident during January and February that the reprimands in *Pravda* and *Partiinaia zhizn* were not sufficient to silence their discussions of sensitive topics. A significant number of articles in the first two issues of *Voprosy istorii* for 1957 continued to raise — albeit in a more muted fashion — the kinds of issues now officially declared out of bounds.[65]

The revisionists' determination to study rather than merely castigate the Mensheviks and other oppositionist groups had led to a general contagion, as revealed even in an official organ such as *Izvestiia*. Criticizing a film on the 1905 Revolution, the Old Bolshevik reviewer feels that the characterization of Nicholas II as "overly stupid" is a "serious error." Moreover, "The Mensheviks are not portrayed convincingly enough; they were more serious and dangerous adversaries of the Bolsheviks in those days than the film makes them appear."[66]

With the continuation of such developments, once again, nine months after the supposedly final Central Committee resolution delineating the limits of historical investigation, the regime found it necessary to take further official action. The Central Committee decree of March 7 "On the Journal *Voprosy istorii*" was well designed to do this job, condemning the impermissible errors of the editorial board: with regard to party history, the glossing of the Menshevik position in both the 1905 and 1917 revolutions, the close identification of Zinoviev's and Stalin's positions in the spring of 1917, and the tracing of unified Bolshevik and Menshevik committees in 1917 and early 1918.[67] The March issue of *Kommunist* carried an editorial that essentially restated the resolution.[68]

At last in June, with the delayed publication of *Voprosy istorii*, number 3, the regime's headlong attack on recalcitrant historians

---

65. *Voprosy istorii*, no. 1 (1957), p. 67; A. F. Ilin, "Problemy vtoroi piatiletki sovetskoi promyshlennosti v kandidatskikh dissertatsiiakh," *ibid.*, pp. 185–192; L. A. Iakovlov and V. A. Kondratev, "Novoe v rabote sovetskikh arkhivov," *ibid.*, pp. 192–194.
66. P. Bliaklun, "Film o podvig naroda," *Izvestiia*, January 3, 1957, p. 2.
67. *Spravochnik partiinogo rabotnika*, 1957, pp. 381–382.
68. "Strogo sobliudat leninskii printsip partiinosti v istoricheskoi nauke," *Kommunist*, no. 4 (1957), pp. 17–29.

made an impact. The editorial,[69] written by a new board, hammered at the long list of offensive articles the journal had published since 1955, Burdzhalov's being distinguished as having done the greatest damage. Most disturbing were the articles showing Menshevism and Bolshevism not as "basically opposed political trends, expressing entirely different class interests and pursuing opposite aims, but as similar in order and type." This interpretation was, moreover, alleged to be the "line" of the old editorial board and not merely an indication of inattentiveness or sloppiness in choosing items for publication. The board allegedly had isolated itself from the research and educational institutions that presumably would have guided and corrected its policies; Burdzhalov personally violated principles of collectivity by failing to call regular board meetings and publishing articles over the disagreement and protests of other editors; close friends rather than recognized authorities were asked to write on special subjects, which in turn alienated many experienced historians and reduced the number of articles submitted by them.

This charge of organized and intentional attempts to bypass official policy is new; previous attacks on the revisionists had been couched in terms of mistaken emphasis or interpretation. The accusation that the editorial board "attempts to confuse the harm done by the cult of the individual leader with the entire activity of the Party and the people" is uncomfortably close to a charge of ideological sabotage.

Perhaps even more serious in terms of long-range effect on the historical profession was the official attempt to destroy the nascent concept of scholarship and research as ends in themselves rather than instruments of the political leadership. The authors of the editorial criticize the grave errors permitted to appear in the "Discussion and Debate" department:

the altogether natural right to present contentious academic questions has sometimes been used by the magazine to the detriment of the true interests of scholarship. First of all, in a number of instances problems that in reality are not debatable were raised as contentions. Secondly, the discussions often became an end in themselves, a kind of game that distracted historians' attention from the most important problems of scholarship . . . a Party approach to matters was often lost.[70]

69. "Za leninskuiu partiinost v istoricheskoi nauke," *Voprosy istorii*, no. 3 (1957), pp. 3–19.
70. *Ibid.*, p. 11.

Having thus defined the problem of *Voprosy istorii* as one of willful malfeasance of its board, the political leadership could logically proceed to administrative methods of correction; and indeed this must have seemed at this point the sole feasible corrective method. The appearance of number 3 revealed a dramatic renovation of the editorial board: eight of the previous eleven members, including Burdzhalov, had been replaced. And Chief Editor Pankratova had died a few days after the issue was sent to press. The lead editorial notes that the journal has been removed from the aegis of the Academy of Sciences' Institute of History to that of the academy's Division of Historical Sciences, a development that required a basic reorganization. This was explained as a means of gaining better control by multiplying the journal's supervising agencies: "Whereas before it was connected, and only formally, with one of the scientific institutes, now it has a direct and immediate relationship with the work of all the institutes of the Division of Historical Sciences."[71] It was further specified that from now on, with the appearance of the new specialized journals, *Voprosy istorii* would focus on broad problems and would no longer treat "narrowly specialized problems" (such as, presumably, Bolshevik tactics in the spring of 1917). Finally, the editorial stated that the journal would now actively seek out more provincial contributors instead of continuing the practice of relying largely on members of academic institutions in Moscow (who had proven unreliable).

The remainder of the contents of *Voprosy istorii,* number 3, were case studies in conformity to the new restraints and left no doubt that the new editors had clear instructions to refute the revisionist "line" with corrective formulas as well as the willingness to do so.

The events recounted above help to answer several important questions about the relationship of historiography to politics. The most obvious and basic is: What factors were at work in the dramatic tightening of official policy toward historians? A model that evaluates historiography and historians as puppets of the political leadership, completely subject to the demands of power politics, must obviously be rejected as inaccurate and unhelpful. To say that the writing of history during this period was a direct

71. *Ibid.,* p. 19.

reflection of the political climate and official directives, or that the political leadership bothered to tinker with historiography only when a political crisis appeared imminent or when it had a respite from other and more urgent considerations — this simply does not fit the facts. For one thing, Burdzhalov and other contributors to *Voprosy istorii* in 1955 and early 1956 were not just passively carrying out political instructions: they were interpreting in creative and rather independent ways a very loosely defined and somewhat open-ended policy. The revisionists were proceeding under the real or fancied protection and encouragement of Khrushchev, Mikoyan, Shepilov, and probably others. That patronage seems to have been considerably more real than fancied, while it lasted, although the dissident historians may well have exaggerated its certainty and permanence. At any rate, they almost immediately overextended their prerogatives by linking the Bolsheviks with the Mensheviks in 1905 and 1917, thus casting doubt on the sacred principles of party uniqueness and infallibility.

A more functional model of the historical-political relationship during this period would be one of complex interactions. Thus the dramatic rewriting of party history unveiled in Khrushchev's secret speech set in motion significant developments in historiography as well as in politics. The political and scholarly revisionist trends were intimately interconnected, in the tradition both of Marxist theory (which identifies history as the driving force of politics) and of the Russian intelligentsia (which customarily reads into scholarly writing a political relevance). In this manner scholarly discussions of methodology, sources, the historian's craft, the party's role in the 1905 and 1917 revolutions, all stimulated and at the same time reflected the questioning of Stalin and his policies by political revisionists in Eastern Europe and the USSR. This ferment generated political revolt as well as reforms. Inevitably, the historical derogation of the figure of Stalin not only buttressed official reforms but also raised serious doubts among intellectuals and some others concerning the political system in which he flourished, which could not be explained away by Central Committee resolutions.

Therefore, I suggest the developments in historiography — and especially that relating to the CPSU — as the partial, and perhaps the ultimate, causal factor in the political unrest and uprisings of the year 1956. Party history would in this scheme be viewed as an active political force rather than a purely manipulative instrument of the regime or a political derivative. Historiography in the USSR simultaneously reflects and delineates the political controversy and unrest of this period.

What, then, specifically triggered the sharp policy shift? Again, the conclusion is that it was both political events and scholarly revisionism, in different degrees at various times. It will be remembered that this was a step-by-step process, progressing from warnings to diatribes and administrative measures as the milder methods failed and the political situation worsened. Initial steps were taken at the end of June. The simple bracketing of the Poznan riots on June 28 and the Central Committee resolution on June 30 is tidy and tempting, but not an entirely satisfactory explanation. There is evidence of earlier dissension and uneasiness at the top party level regarding the political aftermath of the secret speech. Most probably, Poznan supplied the proverbial last straw that pushed Khrushchev and the majority of the leadership firmly over to a more conservative position. The harder line in November is much more evidently a reaction to events in Poland and Hungary; but it is significant that, although the political crisis was considerably more severe than in June, the action against dissident historians was minimal and completely verbal. On the other hand, the real crackdown occurred only in March 1957, at a time of relative political tranquility: Khrushchev had survived November and was consolidating his supporters for a massive assault on the economic order. The historians, however, were still in disarray, having continued to debate among themselves in defiance of all warnings. This time organizational measures were taken which could not be ignored. Thus in March the regime's action was a response to the cumulative disruption among historians rather than to a general political crisis.

This attempt to distinguish the causes of the crackdown on historians is not in any way to deny the peculiar extent to which Soviet historiography is politically sensitive or to portray it as a completely independent element in the Soviet system. It represents, instead, an effort to develop an analysis of the relationship of history to politics subtler than one of passivity and manipulation.

Several further generalizations can be made at this juncture. The first is that both the regime and the historians were working out their attitudes, scholarly and policy positions, and actions as they went along. The record of this period is one of indecision and experimentation, whether one examines the pronouncements and policies of the party and its organs or the arguments of the several varieties of liberal and conservative historians. All of them responded to their political milieu in a more direct manner than do historians and politicians in other systems, but their responses were now varied and those reactions themselves helped to create the evolving post-Stalin system.

The obvious test of this theory lies in the years after 1957 and will be deferred to later chapters. We may ask several questions here. Did the measures taken in the winter and spring of 1957 to destroy the revisionists' access to public media effectively and permanently silence them? Could troublesome questions and journal debates be excised from historiography; could the genie of revisionist party history be captured and reconfined to a larger and more comfortable, but escape-proof, container? Or had the rewriting of party history taken on an uncontrollable momentum of its own? These dilemmas of Soviet historiography point to the larger problem for the leadership of maintaining a high degree of political control while relaxing police terror and decentralizing the economic system. Are these areas of policy necessarily interrelated, or can the regime successfully tighten the screws in certain spheres of intellectual and cultural life while continuing to liberalize aspects of economic and social control, as it was attempting to do in 1957? Finally, does a revisionist flood such as occurred in 1956 leave against the dike a residue of accumulated attitudes, methods, and factual material that will remain to raise future tides and leave even higher floodmarks?

Developments in Soviet historiography have shown the year 1956 to be a unique concatenation of events and forces, which created special opportunities and responsibilities for historians. As we have seen, Khrushchev's shock therapy for historians of the CPSU had some unpredicted consequences and had to be modified and in part retracted. The period from June 1957 — when reasonable order was finally restored to Soviet historiography — to the autumn of 1961 can be categorized as one of consolidation, relative stability and continuity of official policies toward historiography, and quiet professional activity among historians. But within this atmosphere of comparative calm some rather remarkable developments took place.

June 1957 — The Twenty-First Congress. If one is concerned with political-historiographical relationships, the affair of the antiparty plot in June 1957 comes instantly to mind.[1] From the perspective of Soviet historians, this crisis has many analogies to Khrushchev's secret speech at the Twentieth Party Congress of the previous year; but there are also some significant differences.

We may observe initially that the abortive attempt to oust Khrushchev occurred in the midst of strenuous political and economic reform on the one hand and, on the other, a drastic tightening of the line and consolidation of controls over the arts, literature, and intellectual expression in general. The professional journals for historians, and especially the new monthly *Voprosy istorii KPSS*, in the spring and summer were full of articles expatiating on the errors of *Voprosy istorii* and developing corrective interpretations.

The announcement of the defeat of the antiparty group, like the secret speech, revealed the malfeasance of former high party leaders and dramatically changed their official status. Another basic similarity is the complex progression of insinuation and revelation which distinguished the derogation of both Stalin and the antiparty group. In the case of the latter, of course, not only were increasingly more serious charges made during the course of ensuing years, but the group itself was expanded on several occasions. Certainly there was again visible in the treatment of the antiparty group, as in the campaign against Stalin's personality

1. For an excellent chronicle and political analysis of the genesis and aftermath of the antiparty crisis, see Roger Pethybridge, *A Key to Soviet Politics* (New York: Frederick A. Praeger, 1962).

4 THE ANTIPARTY PLOT AND STALIN'S GHOST, 1957–1961

cult, Khrushchev's determination to utilize party history to his own ends. In the later case, his rivals in the presidium were initially compared with earlier opposition groups within the party, sometimes in the specific context of the unity resolution at the Tenth Party Congress in 1921, which provided for the expulsion from the CPSU of fractionalists.[2]

But the denigration of the antiparty group is not a mere repetition of de-Stalinization. Most important is the fact that the antiparty group plot did not call forth a massive and self-conscious rewriting of historical works; nor was there any attendant tightening of the official attitudes toward party historians. Moreover, in reiterating the call for party unity, which became a primary topic and slogan in the journals of middle and late 1957, one authoritative article was careful to draw the distinction that whereas the Trotskyites, Right Oppositionists, and other early groups "appeared as representatives of the ideology of the liquidated exploiting classes and petty-bourgeois strata,"[3] under the conditions of socialism the antiparty group "had no social basis in life" since it was completely divorced from the people.[4] Such a caveat is necessary to accord not only with the official doctrine that Soviet society was now classless, but with the new analysis of the early oppositionist groups as representing hostile class interests rather than the intelligence of foreign powers.

Another new feature of the attack on the antiparty group was the subtle linkage of the plot with the recalcitrant historians. This was absent from the secret speech, which implicitly recognized that Soviet historians had been forced agents of Stalin's self-glorification and historical distortions. There were now hints that the revisionist historians centering on *Voprosy istorii* in 1956 were supporters of the early oppositionists. In an editorial written by the new board of *Voprosy istorii* there is a reference to

one of the revisionist tendencies of the present period [which] consists of presenting in modernized guise several pages of historical activities of the Party, distorting their relationship to one's ideological enemies in those or other historical periods. This is manifested first of all in the fact that, contradictions and struggles in the Party being hidden, their actual significance is

2. For example, see the unsigned article, "Leninskaia rezoliutsiia 'O edinstve partii,' " *Partiinaia zhizn*, no. 13 (1957), pp. 55–58.
3. "Edinstvo partii i razvitie kritiki," *Partiinaia zhizn*, no. 21 (1957), p. 51.
4. *Ibid.*, p. 55.

underestimated. In this circumstance the role and activities of ideological enemies of Leninism — the "Economists," Mensheviks, Trotskyites, Bukharinists, bourgeois nationalists, etc. — are embellished.[5]

More interesting here is the juxtaposition of the revisionist historians with Khrushchev's rivals, by the utilization of this passage in the context of a diatribe against the antiparty group. The implication would seem to be that by their embellishing of the early anti-Leninist groups and soft-pedaling of their antagonism to Lenin's tactics, the dissident historians lent intellectual and moral support to the contemporary opposition within the party. Probably this judgment against the revisionist historians — as having compressed history and strengthened the antiparty group by their modified appraisal of the Mensheviks — is not a fictional one in the Soviet context. Given the premise of an infallible and monolithic party, any deviation from the orthodox position at any point in history is seen as condusive to all other splitting activities, and the justification of one is automatically relevant to all. With regard to innerparty factionalism, then, the temporal or chronological criterion vanishes: all history becomes contemporary.

The question now becomes: With what success did Khrushchev's regime move to rescind the unauthorized historical revisions of 1956? Could it, under the pressures of foreign and domestic political turmoil and the added crisis of the attempted antiparty coup, turn back the clock to eradicate Burdzhalov's analysis of 1917 and similar gaucheries? Close examination of Soviet historiography in the latter half of 1957 suggests that the clampdown on historians had not excised the past, that 1956 could be neither recreated nor erased.

The first issue of *Voprosy istorii KPSS*, which appeared in July 1957, carried another rebuttal to Burdzhalov's account of Bolshevik tactics in the spring of 1917.[6] But this is not merely a recapitulation of old arguments: if one compares this effort with Bugaev's earlier attack on Burdzhalov,[7] the changed atmosphere and level

5. "Leninskoe edinstvo partii nesokrushimo," *Voprosy istorii*, no. 5 (1957), p. 12.
6. E. I. Bugaev, "K voprosu o taktike partii v Marte-nachale Aprelia 1917," *Voprosy istorii KPSS*, no. 1 (1957), pp. 13–36.
7. E. I. Bugaev, "Kogda utrachivaetsia nauchnyi podkhod," *Partiinaia zhizn*, no. 14 (1956), pp. 62–72.

of discourse become apparent. The first Bugaev article (published exactly a year earlier, in July 1956) was more rhetorical than scholarly in tone and represented a debate rather than a presentation of analysis or sources that would correct Burdzhalov. Bugaev's July 1957 article relies heavily on source references and attempts to destroy the scholarly credibility of Burdzhalov's argument by casting doubt on his research and evaluation of documents. He is forced by Burdzalov's documentation to argue some points he would rather continue to pass over as assumptions: for example, he must now tacitly admit that there was confusion among local party organizations when the line on support of the soviets changed, while doing his best to show that it was brief, localized, and of no real significance.[8]

Other evidence of this dilemma may be cited. The author of an article in *Kommunist*,[9] which is designed to demolish as "unproven and absurd" Burdzhalov's contention that Stalin upheld the Kamenev position at the April 6, 1917, Central Committee meeting, runs up against the necessity of dealing with the fact "now widely known" (since its republication by Burdzhalov) that Stalin held his anti-Leninist position during the first half of April. His resolution of this obvious contradiction is quite lame. Furthermore, in digging among archive records to trace the course of a series of regional and national party conferences that took place in the spring of 1917, he finds — and passes along to his readers — not only proof of Lenin's final triumph but also evidence of sincere and serious differences of theoretical analysis as well as tactics among party leaders and cadres. In the process of quoting from the arguments of Piatakov, Kamenev, and others who opposed Lenin's position, in an apparent effort to show how their mistaken views were rejected by the party, he exposes their reasoning in unusually detailed and pure form.

There is thus a new type of problem for the historian of the CPSU, which might be categorized as that of creeping archivism: the inexorable and cumulative pressure to take account of existing research, the necessity to speak to the level of scholarly discourse established during the year 1956, even while rebutting its conclusions. In general, we may conclude that although there

8. Bugaev, "K voprosu o taktike partii," pp. 16–17.
9. V. Yevgrafov, "Ot Aprelskikh tezisov k aprelskoi konferentsii," *Kommunist*, no. 7 (1957), pp. 12–26.

was a propaganda campaign beginning in July 1957 to vilify the members of the antiparty group and to tarnish their image, this political crisis produced neither a spasmodic official hardening of the line in party history nor a frantic revision of relevant historiography.

The period under review is characterized by a wave of publication of historical materials. The stabilizing of the general policy and limits of historiography in late 1957 produced a certainty and confidence among editorial boards and publishing houses sufficient to generate a spate of authoritative publications on the party. The new official *History of the Communist Party of the Soviet Union* was serialized by chapters in *Voprosy istorii KPSS* and *Kommunist*. By decision of the Central Committee, "after a lapse of many years" a new Party Workers' Handbook was announced. In July it was officially stated that the monthly *Military-Historical Journal*, which had been suspended in July 1941, would reappear beginning in January 1959. And the repeal by the Central Committee of decrees of 1938 and 1947, which had imposed stringent restrictions that effectively prohibited publishing books on Lenin, allowed publishing houses to pass independent judgment on such works, whether now or previously suppressed. The consent of the Institute of Marxism-Leninism had to be obtained, however, in the case of more evaluative items, such as reminiscences and biographies.[10] In addition, work was being pressed forward on two new courses of lectures on history of the CPSU: one for the humanist higher educational institutions and the other for technical institutes.

A mood of limited discussion and continued exploration seemed to settle over most historians during this period of consolidation.[11] Although no one explicitly supported Burdzhalov's now heinous findings regarding 1917, scholars evidently did not con-

10. N. A. Lomakin, "Nastolnaia kniga partiinogo rabotnika," *Voprosy istorii KPSS*, no. 3 (1958), pp. 205–207.
11. For a survey and critique of literature on regional party history, see E. G. Gimpelson, "Nekotorye voprosy istorii velikoi oktiabrskoi sotsialisticheskoi revoliutsii na mestakh," *Istoriia SSSR*, no. 3 (1958), pp. 221–227. And for a revealing description of one regional meeting of historians, see M. A. Gorlovsky, "Pervaia mezhoblastnaia nauchnaia konferentsiia po istorii Urala," *Voprosy istorii*, no. 6 (1958), pp. 192–195. Materials concerning collectivization of agriculture are discussed in V. I. Kuznetsov and A. P. Proushtein, "Nauchnaia rabota istorikov Rostovskogo gosudarstvennogo universiteta," *Voprosy istorii*, no. 8 (1958), pp. 214–216; and V. A. Ovsiankin and V. V. Fatsobin, "Obsuzhdenie uchebnogo posobiia 'Istoriia SSSR. Epokha sotsializma.' Leningrad, Sverdlovsk, Voronezh," *ibid.*, pp. 207–209.

sider the matter closed or out of bounds. Again we find evidence of the intrinsic problems involved in attempts by even the most loyal and orthodox historians of the party to utilize documentary source materials to prove their point. An article by V. V. Anikeev in the new journal *Voprosy istorii KPSS*[12] openly designed "to prove that the overwhelming majority of [party] organizations during the entire period from February to October [1917] stood firmly on the Leninist position regarding organizational structure," on the basis of some quite elaborate research in party archives concluded that 20 percent of organizations at the oblast and lower levels were unified Bolshevik-Menshevik organizations.[13] Obviously, his figures did show that only a minority of RSDLP organizations in 1917 were joint efforts with the Mensheviks, but in comparison with the uniform insistence prior to 1956 that absolutely no organizational cooperation with the Mensheviks occurred, Anikeev's study was itself a serious revision of the official historiography of 1917.

It should not be forgotten, however, that such attempts at archival confirmation of argumentation shared the stage with more traditional and authoritarian ripostes. An example is the report of M. D. Stuchebnikova, chief of the Section on History of the CPSU of the Institute of Marxism-Leninism, at a conference on the theme of "The CPSU as Inspirer and Organizer of Victory of the Great October Socialist Revolution." We have seen her in a similarly conservative pose at the *Voprosy istorii* readers' conference in January 1956. She flatly reaffirmed the analysis of party tactics in the spring of 1917 as given by Stalin. But it is interesting that she now felt it necessary to claim Stalin's version to be supported by "many documents."[14] Also of note is the fact that other speakers at the meeting, including the deputy chief of the section, were considerably more at pains to document their statements than Stuchebnikova was. No one else referred to Stalin's writings.

It may be argued that, although domestic politics apparently had little relevance for historiography in this period, the threat of revisionism as practiced in Yugoslavia did have a certain impact. Publication of the new draft program of the Communist

12. V. V. Anikeev, "Svedeniia o bolshevistskikh organizatsiiakh s Marta po Dekabr 1917," *Voprosy istorii KPSS*, no. 2 (1958), pp. 126–193.
13. *Ibid.*, p. 127.
14. K. Kh. Khanazarov and V. M. Tsherbok, "V sektore istorii KPSS Instituta marksizma-leninizma," *Voprosy istorii KPSS*, no. 1 (1958), p. 215.

League on Yugoslavia in March 1958 touched off a frantic propaganda campaign in the Soviet press. The effort was directed at what was perceived as a latter-day Bernsteinian theory of evolutionary socialism. This attack found its way into some of the historical journals in the guise of exhortations to historians to show the discredited origins of contemporary revisionism. As historians of the CPSU, they should make use of the example of the defeated oppositionists within the Russian party to prove that contemporary revisionists are neither original in their ideas nor sound in their tactics.[15] In the late spring and early summer two special meetings were held to deal with the problem of contemporary revisionism.[16]

The depiction of these years as marked by consolidation and stabilization should not imply stagnation among historians or complete success of the regime's measures to bring historiography to heel. Obviously Khrushchev's goal was not petrification of historiography in any case, but rather a limited and controlled reinterpretation of party history. Scholarly discussions of sensitive topics continued, albeit in more cautious and muted tones after 1956, archives continued to be opened, and documents were published. And, most important, the impact of the debates and more sophisticated methods of research initiated during 1956 was not quashed by the official crackdown at the end of that year. All during 1958, historians and party ideologists were obsessed by Burdzhalov's findings, and the literature reverberated with both veiled and specific arguments about the Bolsheviks in 1917. The debate over the alleged lack of revolutionary fervor of Stalin and other Bolsheviks before Lenin's return to Russia was, of course, intimately connected with the furious rejection of the Yugoslav contention that "alongside the *revolutionary* socialist transformation there is proceeding also an *evolutionary* process of transformation of capitalism into socialism."[17]

15. Some examples of this kind of argument may be found in the editorial "Za glubokuiu nauchnuiu razrabotku istorii KPSS," *Voprosy istorii KPSS*, no. 4 (1958), p. 20; and in G. Shanshiev, "Velikaia vekha v istorii nashei partii," *Partiinaia zhizn*, no. 14 (1958), p. 26.
16. See V. N. Balazhov, "Sessiia otdelenii obshchestvennykh nauk AN SSSR po borbe s sovremennym revizionizmom," *Voprosy istorii*, no. 7 (1958), pp. 171–190; and A. I. Puliakh, "Neuklonno razoblachat proiski sovremennogo revizionizma," *ibid.*, no. 9 (1958), p. 195.
17. P. Fedoseev, I. Pomelov, and V. Cheprakov, "O proekte programmy Soiuza kommunistov Iugoslavii," *Kommunist*, no. 6 (1958), p. 17.

If we again refer to the attack on Burdzhalov as a touchstone, it is possible to gauge the further development of a more scholarly level of discourse reflecting increased archival research. An article in the December 1958 issue of *Kommunist* illustrates this new departure in Soviet historiography and represents the official party critic as the champion of thorough source work. In the context of reviewing recently published volumes of party protocols and stenographic records,[18] A. Kostin makes the following attack on Burdzhalov:

By deliberately limiting his "research" to narrow chronological bounds, he painted a picture of complete disorder and vacillation in party ranks. Further, contrary to the facts and documents, the author falsified the policies of the Bolsheviks in the period of transition from a bourgeois-democratic revolution to a socialist revolution . . . one of the reasons for such a series of mistakes is ignorance of or ignoring of documents, an incorrect relationship to primary sources. A deep knowledge and use of party documents, in this case the protocols and decisions of the Petrograd City Committee and the Seventh All-Russian Conference of the RSDLP(B), would help correct mistaken assumptions, and reliable sources would shed a deep and objective light on the party history of that time.[19]

Certainly these are new standards for the official ideologist in trusteeship over party historiography. It seems clear, furthermore, that no matter how insincerely or reluctantly developed, such official requirements must necessarily have a powerful and cumulative impact on the quantity and quality of archival research.

The latter part of 1958 saw Khrushchev moving to consolidate his power within the top leadership. By September he felt strong enough to move against Bulganin, forcing him out of the Presidium; in a speech on November 14 he added Bulganin's name to the list of members of the antiparty group, which was duly certified by *Pravda* on November 23. Khrushchev renewed his offensive against the antiparty group at the Central Committee plenum on December 15, 1958, extending their crimes to account for failures in agriculture and forcing a somewhat unsatisfactory confession from Bulganin. At the Twenty-First Congress in Jan-

18. These volumes covered the First and Sixth Party Congresses, and also the Petrograd City Party Conference and the Seventh All-Russian Party Conference held in April 1917.
19. A. Kostin, "Vazhneishii istochnik izucheniia i nauchnoi razrabotki istorii partii," *Kommunist*, no. 18 (1958). p. 118.

uary 1959 Khrushchev and his supporters pressed the attack, culminating in more confessions — from Saburov and Pervukhin — which again did not satisfy the more militant members of the leadership.[20] With regard to the antiparty group at least, the Twenty-First Congress proved indecisive; in fact this failure on the part of Khrushchev to galvanize the party to take punitive action against his enemies — to read them out of the party and its history — remains one of the most persuasive indications of continuing instability within the Presidium during 1958 and 1959.

1959 and the New CPSU History Text. The year following the Twenty-First Congress produced no basic reorientation of Soviet historiography. As in July 1957, the new revelations concerning the antiparty group did not touch off a rewriting program in party history. The boom in publication of history texts and official compilations which began in 1958 was continued. Enough time had now elapsed since the furor of 1956 for the official demands and the general level of scholarly discourse to have become more clear, and for the efforts of large editorial collectives to be processed.

Thus in June the *History of the Communist Party of the Soviet Union* requested by the Twentieth Congress went to press, without, it should be noted, the official sponsorship of the Central Committee which had graced the flyleaf of the *Short Course*. It may be objected that this is an immaterial omission, that the authors who contributed chapters had status within the CPSU and the Academy of Sciences that was tantamount to official sanction. But we still run up against the kind of problem endemic to any attempt at analyzing the post-Stalin system: Is there a point where the symbol becomes reality; when and how does a symbolic change become reified? The very fact that the responsible political leaders felt a scholarly collective authorship preferable to an editorial commission of the Central Committee

20. Pethybridge makes a persuasive argument that the delegates to the Congress were divided into three blocs: those who wanted further action against the group and who — as Khrushchev appointees to the apparat — stood to gain politically, those who wished to consider the matter a closed issue — which included most of the delegates, and a third bloc led by Mikoyan which avoided discussing both the antiparty group and Khrushchev and eventually succeeded in staving off further action against the group. See Roger Pethybridge, *A Key to Soviet Politics,* pp. 166–174.

is of real and not merely symbolic significance. Further, the removal of official authorization automatically broadened the acceptable area of evidence and interpretation.

Of interest in this connection is the fact that the authoritative review of the new text in *Kommunist*, although generally very favorable, does point to some deficiencies. One of the reviewers' specific examples concerns the matter of the Bolsheviks' tactical shift in July 1917 and their abandonment of the slogan "All Power to the Soviets": precisely the problem around which debate had raged spasmodically in the journals since 1956. The authors state their complaint: "For example, the question of the position of the party after the July Days in 1917 is treated in such a way that it remains unclear if it carried on its activities legally or illegally."[21] This vagueness would certainly indicate that the contributing editors themselves were either confused or split over the whole issue of the Bolsheviks in the spring and summer of 1917 — and that their editorial indecision had resulted in mangled and blurred prose. All this despite continued pressure from more conservative historians in the Institute of Marxism-Leninism and elsewhere.

Although later chapters will include rather detailed analyses of specific aspects of the 1959 and 1962 editions of the *History of the Communist Party of the Soviet Union*, it is appropriate here to discuss the Khrushchev *History* in general terms. Of course, the most dramatic aspect of revision is that of the historical Stalin, who is transformed from the demigod of the *Short Course* into a figure of insignificance during 1917, who "at first took up an erroneous position" early in the year of revolution,[22] whose qualifications for leadership were called in question by Lenin's letter to the Thirteenth Party Congress,[23] whose "misappreciation of the strategic situation" contributed to early defeats in World War II,[24] who warned against exaggerations of the role of the individual in history but in practice deviated from this and other Marxist-Leninist propositions and "encouraged the cult

21. A. Berezkin and S. Mezentsev, "Geroicheskaia istoriia Kommunisticheskoi partii Sovetskogo Soiuza," *Kommunist*, no. 10 (1959), p. 65.
22. *History of the Communist Party of the Soviet Union*, B. N. Ponomarev, chief editor (Moscow: Foreign Languages Publishing House, 1960), p. 217.
23. *Ibid.*, p. 387.
24. *Ibid.*, p. 548.

of his own personality,"[25] whose "erroneous thesis" of intensified class struggle as the state strengthened in 1937 "served as a justification for mass repressions against the Party's ideological enemies who had already been routed politically."[26] Although this treatment represents a radical departure from the fawning adulation of the *Short Course* and should not be underestimated, it is important to recognize that the textbook picture of Stalin does not reflect the paranoid tyrant of the secret speech and much of the historical writing thereafter. Stalin is still quite frequently credited with specific speeches, reports, and policy decisions; he "rightly stressed the necessity . . . of keeping a watchful eye on the intrigues of enemies";[27] his famous 1930 article "Dizzy with Success" is praised as having "clarified the Party line on the collective-farm movement and directed the members of the Party towards rectifying the mistakes committed in the process of collectivization";[28] and it is Yezhov and Beria who, "taking advantage of Stalin's personal shortcomings,"[29] bear primary responsibility for the purges. Khrushchev's flamboyant descriptions of Stalin's last years are subsumed into the flat statements that success and praise "turned his head" and that "the cult of personality caused particularly great damage to the leadership of the Party and the State."[30]

Several possible explanations may be advanced for the muddled image of Stalin in the 1959 edition, and probably each has some value. On the political level, there clearly was indecisiveness and confusion among the leadership as to just how much initiative and research on the part of historians was desirable; and opposition to de-Stalinization persisted at all levels of the party hierarchy, despite the defeat of the antiparty group. Equally evidently, there were sharp differences among historians over how Stalin should appear in historiography. The group of well-known authors who prepared the text, each of whom had a long record of politically careful work, would have to be placed toward the conservative or cautious end of a spectrum of historians of the CPSU. And the additional factor of collective authorship worked as a conservative and restraining influence

25. *Ibid.*, p. 512.
26. *Ibid.*, pp. 512–13.
27. *Ibid.*, p. 512.
28. *Ibid.*, p. 450.
29. *Ibid.*, p. 513.
30. *Ibid.*, p. 671.

—this is not peculiar to the Soviet Union—to qualify and dull the impact of any controversial prose. Finally, there is another general phenomenon, which operates most powerfully in the context of a controlled press and official ideology: the dampening impact upon a mass-edition textbook of the editorial process, which modifies new or dramatic interpretations in an effort to guard against future revision and withdrawal from sale.

The sections in the 1959 *History* dealing with the Kirov assassination and the purges, collectivization, World War II, various intraparty oppositionist groups, and the Mensheviks also represent major changes from the *Short Course*. The revised account of the Kirov murder remains incomplete and tentative,[31] but a very subtle link is forged between that killing and the purges. The assassin is no longer "a member of a secret counterrevolutionary group . . . of Zinovievites in Leningrad"[32] but "an embittered renegade" who "held a Party card and had used it as a cover for his heinous crime." The conclusion is clearly drawn: "The assassination of Kirov showed that the Party card could be used as a screen for infamous anti-Soviet acts. It was indispensable to safeguard the Party against the penetration of alien elements."[33] Then follows a description of the verification and exchange of party cards during 1935 and 1936, which is judged as on the whole valuable. The purges are discussed for the first time in Soviet historiography ten pages later, and the analysis is parallel to that of the 1935 expulsions: "Many honest Communists and non-Party people, not guilty of any offense, became victims of these repressions," but Yezhov and Beria were duly punished and the victims exonerated by the Central Committee in 1954 and 1955. Even such serious "mistakes" could not change the system or mar its success.[34] As we shall see, in the 1962 edition this implicit linkage of the Kirov murder to the 1935 membership purge and thence to the bloody purges was made explicit.

The historiography of the Great Patriotic War is beyond the scope of this book, and of course the *Short Course* ended its account of party history in 1937; nonetheless it should be noted that the 1959 *History* dramatically revises previous accounts by

31. See Chapter One.
32. *Short Course*, pp. 325–326.
33. *History of the Communist Party of the Soviet Union*, p. 492.
34. *Ibid.*, p. 513.

downgrading Stalin's role from that of military genius. The significant formulation is as follows: "The Soviet Union won the Great Patriotic War under the leadership of the Communist Party and its Central Committee headed by Stalin. During the war the Central Committee was the military leader of the Party and the people."[35] The only other direct reference to Stalin's wartime leadership is the derogatory commentary on his lack of perception with regard to Nazi intentions.

Not only the purges but the problems raised by collectivization of agriculture now appeared for the first time in official party history: the 1959 *History* describes in some detail the "craft and cunning" of the "anti-Soviet elements" in sabotaging collectivization and the "violations of the Party's policy" by some party organizations.[36] Although the formulations of these problems in the text are not quite so forthright or complex as some journal discussions during the preceding several years, nevertheless collectivization in the 1959 text is a social phenomenon very different indeed from that described in the *Short Course*.

The treatment of Trotsky, the New Opposition (Zinoviev and Kamenev), and the Right Opposition (Bukharin, Rykov, and Tomsky) in the 1959 edition is in terms of political opposition rather than anti-Soviet treachery and sabotage. The Mensheviks and Socialist Revolutionaries receive harsher treatment, having "voluntarily surrendered power to the bourgeoisie."[37] It is interesting that, except for accounts of the June 1957 Central Committee plenum and the Twenty-First Congress, members of the antiparty group are singled out for neither praise nor blame. Perhaps it is because of editorial negligence or indifference that Bulganin and Kirichenko are included in the list of prominent party members who served on military councils during World War II;[38] and Zhukov is included in the long list of "prominent military leaders" of World War II.[39] Otherwise he and the antiparty group are remarkable only for their absence from history.

Further, in general the account is notably depersonalized — with action taken largely by "the Party" or "the Central Committee" — and this phenomenon becomes progressively more acute with time. Thus, until the end of the 1920s (that is,

35. *Ibid.,* p. 602.
36. *Ibid.,* pp. 448–449.
37. *Ibid.,* p. 209.
38. *Ibid.,* p. 555.
39. *Ibid.,* p. 602.

through chapter eleven of the text) the historical stage is populated with heroes and villains; but with the destruction of all opposition a strange silence or the passive voice replaces their strident arguments. Even Stalin, who once filled the scene, is now subdued. The situation changes with the death of Stalin, and in the final two chapters a new solitary hero appears in the person of N. S. Khrushchev. But even Khrushchev is devoid of life, and his presence is distant and formal: on his initiative a policy is taken or a report is authority for action. It could not be said that a Khrushchev cult has replaced the Stalin cult of the *Short Course,* because there is no charismatic appeal. Khrushchev appears as the benevolent, dominating, but impersonal figurehead of the party. This of course could be anticipated from Khrushchev's own denunciation of personal cults.

The almost total absence of other contemporary political leaders, except for a hurried listing of the Presidium and Secretariat in the final chapter,[40] is somehow less expected in view of the great official stress on collective leadership. But we may assume that the authors knew what they were about and that their perception of political realities and of the need for caution was well founded in their long experience as historians of the party.

Here is a brief review of the outstanding and essentially revisionist arguments of the 1959 edition:

(1) Stalin's role was positive until the Seventeenth Congress (January–February 1934); thereafter he made serious mistakes, but they could not alter the socialist nature of the system.

(2) Lenin was the central figure in Soviet and party history, completely overshadowing all others as the "genius theoretician, leader and organizer of the working masses."[41]

(3) The Bolsheviks were *always* completely distinct from the Mensheviks in theory and practice, despite temporary tactical alliances; the Bolsheviks were the only revolutionary Marxist party in Russia.

(4) Lenin and Stalin were correct in insisting on unremitting struggle against anti-Leninist opposition groups because, although not enemy agents, the Mensheviks and Socialist Revolutionaries (Essars) in fact objectively aided the bourgeoisie by their practices.

(5) Until the July Days, Lenin's line was peaceful development

40. *Ibid.,* p. 743.
41. *Ibid.,* p. 24.

of the revolution, which was at that point undermined by the Mensheviks and Essars.

(6) Industrialization, full collectivization, and thus the foundations of socialism were achieved only with difficulty; but the party led the people to these successes, which are dated as accomplished by 1932.

The heavy publication schedule of official historiography which continued throughout the year reflected the stabilization of policies and interpretations.[42] But the pressure to fulfill production plans and bring to publication a wide variety of volumes on Soviet history forced a reorganization of the Institute of History under the Academy of Sciences.[43]

We can round out the picture of historiography in 1959 by taking note of a proliferation of historians' meetings and readers' conferences throughout the spring and summer. From all the available indications in the published accounts, these conferences were the scene of some genuine discussions, largely revolving around the problem of defining the extent of scholarly interpretation and permissible debate on party and Soviet history.[44] Even the brief published accounts of the conferences reveal con-

42. On July 31, *Pravda* stated that a new six-volume *History of the Great Patriotic War* was in preparation, to be issued during 1960 and 1961. On August 12, it announced publication of the first five volumes of a ten-volume *World History*. The new *History of the Civil War in the USSR* continued to appear; volume 4 was put out in September. During September and October the press discussed the draft history program for secondary schools presented by the Academy of Pedagogy. Moreover, during the autumn of 1959 the program for teaching party history was completely rewritten on the basis of the new *History of the Communist Party* text and the decisions of the Twentieth and Twenty-First Congresses. The new program was prepared by the Department of Teaching of Marxism-Leninism of the USSR Ministry of Higher and Secondary Education. A. A. Zemskov and I. G. Mitrofanov, "O nekotorykh voprosakh izucheniia istorii KPSS v vyshei shkole," *Voprosy istorii*, no. 10 (1959), pp. 137–151.

43. *Voprosy istorii* reported that, pursuant to the decision of the academy's general meeting on March 27, 1959, the institute had been partially reorganized — the most important changes having taken place in the department of history of Soviet society. The topical sectors of this department had been dissolved and replaced by "creative scholarly groups devoted to basic planned works." "Nekotorye itogi raboty Instituta istorii Akademii nauk SSSR za 1959," *Voprosy istorii*, no. 5 (1960), pp. 195–206.

44. See I. I. Semenov, "Konferentsii chitatelei zhurnala 'Voprosy istorii,'" *Voprosy istorii*, no. 7 (1959), pp. 201–207; N. K. Sidorov, "Konferentsiia chitatelei zhurnala 'Voprosy istorii' v Leningrade," *ibid.*, no. 8 (1959), p. 184; and V. T. Berezin, "Chitatelskaia konferentsiia v Moskovskoi vyshei partiinoi shkole," *ibid.*, no. 9 (1959), p. 191.

siderable variety of approach, methodology, and professionalism among historians. There was certainly no spokesman, whether official or not, for the entire discipline. The year closed with another attempt by the party's ideologists to end the confusion and set matters straight concerning Stalin's role in party history. An unsigned article in the December issue of *Kommunist* in honor of Stalin's eightieth anniversary points both to his services and to his mistakes.[45] It is noteworthy that these errors were not defined as exclusively post-1934: Stalin took the wrong stand on the Provisional Government until the April Theses were issued. On the basis of this "correct, full and objective characterization and evaluation" of Stalin by the CPSU, the formulation of Stalin as a tragic figure is introduced: "All that he did was done in the interests of communism; this was his tragedy."[46] Needless to say, this interpretation is essentially different from Khrushchev's depiction of Stalin in the secret speech as actively evil in his sickness, motivated by considerations of personal power even to the detriment of the interests of communism. We shall see, however, that this latter-day attempt of the regime to transform the image of Stalin from villainy into tragedy was also to prove transitory.

The year 1960. The chief preoccupation of the Soviet leadership during 1960 was foreign policy. On balance, though, it would appear impossible to detect a causal connection between the sudden tightening of foreign policy in the summer of 1960 and the writing of party history. The argument for direct political influence is in any case more impressive with regard to domestic politics. The domestic scene can best be described as one of consolidation of Khrushchev's reform policies and subdued conflict over their administration — in other words, a continuation of the general political temper of the preceding year. But within this ostensibly stable milieu, the differences among historians were once again becoming acute and more apparent, despite the fact that the revisionist historians had long since lost control of *Voprosy istorii.* If one examines closely the publications, official decrees, and other developments relating to the historical profession over the course of the year, one is struck by the growing

45. "I. V. Stalin (k 80-letiiu so dnia rozhdeniia)," *Kommunist,* no. 18 (1959), pp. 47–56.
46. *Ibid.,* p. 54.

bifurcation of Soviet historiography into coexisting scholarly and propagandistic dimensions. This in itself is not novel in the Soviet context, since the events of the early 1930s and of 1956 could be so categorized and were in fact more forthright debates. What is new is the growing separateness or professionalization of this divergence, its relative insularity from political winds, and the continuity of this more subtle altercation among historians despite the political atmosphere. Thus, whereas the political year was split midway into soft and hard periods with respect to international politics, the operative distinctions with regard to historiography do not appear on the calendar.

An important press campaign theme throughout most of 1960 was set out in the Central Committee resolution of January 9, "On the Tasks of Party Propaganda in Present-Day Conditions."[47] The rationale given for increased emphasis on ideological training is of interest here in support of my argument that the rejection of terror as the central instrument of control requires a much heavier reliance upon internalized or subjective norms. Explaining why the mastery of Marxism-Leninism is a vital necessity for every Soviet man, the resolution cites first the fulfillment of the goals of communist construction. Second, "as socialist democracy develops further and the socialist state system gradually evolves into communist public self-government, persuasion and education of the masses are becoming to an even greater extent the chief method of regulating the activity of Soviet society."[48] Specifically, the Central Committee demands that extensive study of party history be organized within the system of political education on a basis of differentiated methods and periods of study (calculated with respect to considerations of occupation, age, educational background, and so forth). Such a flexible program obviates the catechismic approach of the *Short Course* and requires more highly trained teachers, a rather large and varied literature on party history, and a certain independent responsibility at the instructor level.

Pravda on April 6 featured an editorial entitled "Make Ideological Work the Center of Attention," which for the first time publicly recognized the fact that there existed a perennial con-

47. "Postanovlenie Tsentralnogo komiteta partii," *Pravda,* January 10, 1960, pp. 1–2.
48. *Ibid.,* p. 1.

flict of loyalties and interests among even the most politically reliable historians. The editorial charged that certain central newspapers and journals were not setting an example for local publications: "The magazine *Voprosy istorii* stands aloof from the practice of propaganda work, even though the magazine's editors know that the Central Committee resolution poses the task of enhancing the role of the social sciences, including the historical sciences, in propaganda work."[49] This board, it should be noted, was the new group brought in in 1957 to rectify the damage done by Burdzhalov and the revisionists. The danger here for the regime would seem to be twofold. First, the senior and most important journal for historians was not fulfilling its traditional function of passing along official positions on various problems and topics to provincial scholars and ideological writers — partly, of course, because of the lack of official clarity on many issues. Second, there was developing a concept of the historian's role as a scholar standing somewhat apart from the contemporary scene.

In August leading workers of the party's history institutes (local branches of the Institute of Marxism-Leninism) met in Moscow to discuss the January Central Committee decree, with emphasis on the multivolume *History of the Communist Party of the Soviet Union* and possible improvements in the Institute of Marxism-Leninism.[50] And in July or early August the Section on Historical Sciences of the Academy of Sciences approved a reorganization of the structure and format of *Voprosy istorii*. Apparently a series of regional discussions with "historians in Moscow and several other of the country's scientific centers" had preceded the final decision. The journal would now consist of four sections or departments: "Articles," "Historical Science in the USSR," "Historical Science Abroad," and "Letters and Notes."[51]

49. "Ideologicheskuiu rabotu — v tsentr vnimaniia," *Pravda*, April 6, 1960, p. 2.
50. I. M. Filimonova, "K sozdaniiu mnogotomnoi istorii KPSS," *Voprosy istorii KPSS*, no. 5 (1960), pp. 229–330.
51. "O profile i strukture zhurnala 'voprosy istorii,'" *Voprosy istorii*, no. 8 (1960), pp. 19–21. Previously the journal's departments had been: "Articles," "Historiography," "Discussion," "Criticism and Bibliography," "Historical Science in the USSR," and "Historical Science Abroad." Since the second, third, and fourth departments in fact are easily subsumed under "Historical Science in the USSR," the reorganization was not of a radical nature.

All of this organizational tinkering and continued pressure on historians did, of course, register the party leadership's determination to keep historians within specified bounds and to utilize their talents. But this pressure was neither begun nor perceptibly intensified after the U-2 crisis in May. Orthodox or conservative trends were only part of the scene; persuasive arguments and some important signals pointed in the other direction. One example is the publication early in the year of part two of Sholokhov's frank novel of collectivization, *Virgin Soil Upturned*. Another is the fact that the Soviet Union was pleased to send delegates to the Eleventh International Congress of Historians, which met in Stockholm in August. The coverage of the congress in the press and historical journals was generally positive; although noises were made about the need to distinguish political from ideological coexistence, most journal articles were on a scholarly level and expressed eagerness for more contact with bourgeois as well as socialist historians abroad. It is important to note also that the Central Committee decree on party propaganda did not specify the 1959 *History of the Communist Party* as the required text for the intensified party history program. Similarly, the revised syllabus for courses on party history in higher schools failed to make this new book the official text, although the program expanded treatment of the post-October period at the expense of prerevolutionary years.[52]

It may be suggested too that the reorganization of *Voprosy istorii* announced in August was more complex than a straightforward attack on the journal by the Academy of Sciences' Historical Sciences Section. The journal's editorial in the June issue [53] is chiefly concerned with the January decree on propaganda, and one might expect the board to display contrition after the scolding it received from *Pravda* on this account. But the editorial merely gives a reportorial account of the Central Committee resolution and the section's complaints, neither ac-

52. B. F. Gaubikh, "Novoe izdanie vuzovskikh program po istorii KPSS," *Voprosy istorii KPSS*, no. 5 (1960), pp. 227–229. An interesting feature of the report on the revised syllabus was the lament that certain departments of party history and some instructors simply were ignoring the syllabus, which had been in effect for two years.
53. "Postanovlenie TsK KPSS 'O zadachakh partiinoi propagandy v sovremennykh usloviiakh i istoricheskaia nauka,'" *Voprosy istorii*, no. 6 (1960), pp. 3–9.

knowledging criticisms as correct nor undertaking to suggest improvements. The editors do admit that "some of the journal's executive personnel took an improper attitude to the criticisms of historians concerning the journal's content and were often overly sensitive,"[54] which of course does not answer the substantive charges. Even more surprising, the editors turned on the bureau of the academy's Historical Sciences Section and blamed its inaction for *Voprosy istorii*'s alleged shortcomings. Although the bureau made recommendations for the reorganization in August 1959, it had only recently taken measures to guarantee the revamping of the journal's work. It seems likely that not only the board of *Voprosy istorii* but also the members of the Historical Sciences Section were divided and quarreling among themselves. This editorial also gratuitously included a snide comment to the effect that the scientific councils of the Institute of History created in 1959 still were not working properly. Thus, although the format of *Voprosy istorii* was changed and its board and contributors scolded for neglect of propaganda in favor of specialized research, this episode was inconclusive. Certainly it little resembles earlier campaigns against erring journals.

The pressure from historians for higher standards of scholarship and better research facilities continued during 1960, and there is good evidence of at least partial success. The editorial in the August number of *Voprosy istorii*, which surveyed the state of the profession, referred in passing to a most interesting "recent decree" of the Central Committee and Council of Ministers.[55] This decree enacted a series of measures raising the degree requirements in Soviet universities and institutes. Buried among a number of routine recommendations was the grant to the Higher Certification Commission of Higher and Specialized Secondary Education of the power — upon the representation of an academic council of any institution of higher education or research institute — to divest a person of his academic degree if it has been mistakenly awarded or if the recipient is not active in creative work. The precise grounds are that the work of the "scientific-pedagogical workers" concerned lacks "value for sci-

54. *Ibid.*, p. 9.
55. "Sovetskaia istoricheskaia nauka na novom etape razvitiia," *Voprosy istorii*, no. 8 (1960), pp. 3–18.

ence and production, or when the scientific workers over the course of a long time produce no concrete results in the fields of their research and do not achieve a high quality of pedagogical work in the higher educational institutions."[56] Quite clearly, although the motivation for such a policy is the improvement of scholarship and the exposure of some of the fraudulent and badly trained scholars of the Stalin period, it could be an instrument of jealousy and unscrupulous ambition. As such, this mechanism requires careful supervision to avoid abuses. Nonetheless, the decree does represent a victory for the more serious, creative, and conscientious researchers and teachers.

But the official demand for higher standards extended not only to academic personnel but to the Central Committee's own Institute of Marxism-Leninism. In June the Central Committee sharply criticized the institute for "serious inadequacies," with specific reference to its neglect of party history and "factual errors and inaccuracies" in several published collections of party documents. Since one of the institute's most important tasks during the next several years would be the publication of the multivolume history of the CPSU, it must decisively raise the level of its work and the caliber of its workers. The Central Committee Department of Agitation and Propaganda for the Union Republics and the heads of the institute and its affiliates were directed to take whatever measures were necessary to bring to the institute highly qualified personnel — especially in the sectors for party history and the international communist movement.[57]

One more observation should be made. We have seen the development of distance between the political and the historiographical in the sense that events in the former sphere were now no longer automatically reflected in the latter. Historiography was beginning to maintain its own professionally oriented concerns, which involved the continuing coexistence of two strains of thought. This duality of the scholarly and political can be

56. "O merakh uluchsheniia kachestva dissertationnykh rabot i poriadka prisuzhdeniia uchenykh stepenei i zvanii," from a Resolution of the Central Committee and Council of Ministers, January 28, 1960, *Spravochnik partiinogo rabotnika,* 3rd ed. (Moscow: Political Literature Publishing House, 1961), pp. 511–516.
57. Resolution of the Central Committee, "O merakh po uluchsheniiu raboty Instituta marksizma-leninizma pri TsK KPSS," June 17, 1960, *ibid.,* pp. 542–545.

clearly seen in journal publications, scholarly books, and reported interchanges at historical meetings throughout the period. At times it became a confrontation or direct debate; but in most cases the term bifurcation is a more accurate description, since it often involved differentiated levels of discourse. An obvious example of this phenomenon is that of the diverse presentations of a historical topic in a scholarly monograph or *Voprosy istorii* as contrasted with those in *Kommunist* and *Partiinaia zhizn* — in descending order from scholarship to propaganda.

A less obvious kind of duality — which began to appear with some frequency in 1960 — is comprised within a single medium and can be illustrated by two articles in the same issue of *Voprosy istorii KPSS*.[58] One is a thoughtful exploration of a new periodization of 1917, which would designate the two and a half weeks immediately following the Kornilov episode as a second period of possible peaceful revolution. Sovokin makes a sophisticated analysis of documents as well as Lenin's works on the subject; he takes into account the opinions of other students. The Titarenko article is, in striking contrast, essentially a propaganda tract hammering away at the theme of party unity: historical experience appears as a device to show that only eradication of revisionism and opportunism could have achieved socialism in the USSR.

At first glance it would seem that the appearance of two such diverse pieces in the same journal could be explained quite simply as a temporal confusion — the Titarenko article representing the old-fashioned efforts of a party hack who is incapable of change, and Sovokin, the wave of the future. Under this interpretation, once the new and liberalized party line became completely evident, the Titarenko type would fade away. My argument here is rather that this duality points to real divergencies regarding substantive questions of party history among the political leadership, those party officials entrusted with guidance of history and related matters, and the historians themselves. Further, this multiplicity of voices claiming to speak for Soviet historiography is an aspect of the Soviet system that I see as a continuing one.

The Twenty-Second Congress. The months preceding the

58. A. M. Sovokin, "O vozmozhnosti mirnogo razvitiia revoliutsii posle razgroma kornilovshchiny," *Voprosy istorii KPSS*, No. 3, 1960, pp. 50–64; S. L. Titarenko, "V. I. Lenin o znachenii edinstva partii v borbe za pobedu sotsializma i kommuniszma," *ibid.*, pp. 159–169.

Twenty-Second Party Congress in October 1961 present a picture of low-key discussion of scholarly matters.[59] An unusual exchange took place during the year on the aesthetic properties of historiography. Interestingly, although both disputants were doctors of historical science — and were so described — their articles were printed in the newspaper addressed to writers and literary critics, *Literaturnaia gazeta*.[60] Turok's article, after presenting a collection of stylistic horrors, defined history as the "concentrated experience of many generations."[61] Historical books will pass along these experiences to succeeding generations only if they are well written. Thus Turok was making a functional argument for good style; but also implicit in his definition were the exclusion of doctrinal considerations from the evaluation of historical writing and the separation of historiography from politics. Despite the heretical overtones of his position, Turok was not taken to task until September, and then not in an abusive way. The other historian, Manfred, criticized Turok for reducing the historian's responsibility to matters of style; but he did not structure his argument from the vantage point of political authority. The debate over historical style was patently inconclusive, and Turok did not pursue it either before or after the congress.

The Twenty-Second Party Congress is another critical moment, since it represents — as do the two preceding party congresses — a temporal conjuncture of the political and the historiographical. Khrushchev expanded and further discretdited the antiparty group by adding Voroshilov, although after his confession was presented to the congress he was placed in an intermediate cate-

59. In April the scientific councils of the Academy of Sciences' Historical Sciences Section were given increased powers to coordinate research projects throughout the USSR within their respective fields. The May number of *Voprosy istorii* contained an announcement that *Vestnik Moskovskogo universiteta* had recently been reorganized from an all-university into a specialized journal, which would be exclusively devoted to history. The new *Vestnik* would now serve the university departments of history — including the Department of History of the CPSU (no. 5, pp. 157–159). The scholarly interest revealed in a wave of articles on local and republican soviets (with particular attention to the early years of the Soviet government), which had been notable since mid-1960, was furthered in September by the publication of the final four volumes of a seven-volume collection of documents on the soviets (" 'Sezdy Sovetov,' " *Izvestiia*, September 13, 1961, p. 4).
60. V. Turok, "Istorik i chitatel," *Literaturnaia gazeta*, February 4, 1961, pp. 2–3; A. Z. Manfred, "I uchenyi i pisatel," *ibid.*, September 12, 1961, p. 2.
61. Turok, p. 3.

gory and forgiven his mistakes. Still, the attack on Molotov, Kaganovich, and Malenkov — who had not confessed — was intensified. Khrushchev now revealed that these three, with Voroshilov "and others," had categorically opposed his proposal to lay Stalin's abuses of power before the Twentieth Congress and had continued their obstruction of the campaign against the personality cult even after the congress, "fearing that their role as accomplices in the repressions [of the purges] would come to light." Khrushchev was evidently trying to convey the impression that the threat from the antiparty group had been a real and continuing one, which was now ended. He described his past difficulties quite openly:

You can imagine how difficult it was to solve these questions when the Presidium of the Central Committee included people who had themselves been guilty of abuses of power, of mass repressions . . . [The factionalists] concentrated their fire primarily against me personally, as First Secretary of the Central Committee, inasmuch as it had fallen to me in the line of duty to raise these questions.[62]

In the speech by N. M. Shvernik, chairman of the Central Committee's Party Control Committee, details were supplied demonstrating the guilty participation of Malenkov, Kaganovich, and Molotov in the purges of party members during the period 1934–1937. Shvernik reported that since the Twentieth Congress there had been more than 70,000 appeals and over 15,000 reinstatements of purged party members.[63] The requisite process of reintegrating so many nonpersons into the historical narrative is, of course, in itself a staggering task for Soviet historians.

Finally, in the catalogue of substantive revisions of party history enumerated at the congress, there was the further detailing of Stalin's crimes, followed by the symbolic act of removing his body from the Lenin mausoleum.[64]

Thus was completed the intricate and multilayered history of Stalin's crimes, begun in February 1956, and the tangled series of revelations of the actions of the antiparty group — which were

62. "Zakliuchitelnoe slovo pervogo sekretaria TsK KPSS tovarishcha N. S. Khrushcheva," *Pravda*, October 29, 1961, pp. 1–3.
63. "Rech tovarishcha N. M. Shvernika," *Pravda*, October 26, 1961, pp. 3–4.
64. *Pravda*, November 1, 1961. For a more complete account of the historiographical aspects of the Twenty-Second Congress and an excellent interpretive analysis, see Adam B. Ulam, "Khrushchev and Boccaccio," *The New Face of Soviet Totalitarianism* (Cambridge: Harvard University Press, 1963), pp. 179–217.

progressively delineated in July 1957, December 1958, January 1959, and October 1961.

As observed in connection with the secret speech, Khrushchev's remarks to the Twenty-Second Congress wielded history as a bludgeon. Once again he raised the specter of the Kirov murder to frighten his political enemies. He provided a more complete account of the details of the assassination and observed, "The mass repressions began after the murder of Kirov. A great deal of effort is still necessary to determine fully who was guilty of his death."[65]

Historiography was also pressed into the service of Khrushchev's political reconciliation with the Soviet military — which was quite clearly aggrieved over his soft attitude toward the West and the resultant military budget cuts, his tendency to rely on nuclear weaponry at the expense of more traditional branches, and the ouster of Zhukov. In his speech to the Twenty-Second Congress Khrushchev now deplored Stalin's purges of military officers as well as party cadres in the 1930s, and on December 29 *Izvestiia* rehabilitated Marshal Tukhachevsky in a laudatory article.

Speculation upon the political motivations underlying these sensational revisions of party history has been dramatically facilitated since Khrushchev's ouster in October 1964. It seems quite clear now that those in opposition to Khrushchev within the Presidium continued to be disturbingly persistent and that he undertook to destroy their political power by discrediting their historical images. In crushing the antiparty group he created a patently fictitious unanimity of policy positions and ideological persuasion among men who stood both to the right and left of himself: it is difficult to imagine Malenkov and Molotov uniting on any domestic issue other than the deposition of Khrushchev. But such distortion of the historical views of defeated enemies is neither new nor puzzling on the Soviet political scene.

It is evident that Khrushchev in October 1961 still lacked sufficient support at the various levels of the party membership to expel his rivals from the CPSU. However, we cannot assume that at this point he was pressing for expulsion. As had happened at the Twenty-First Congress, a number of his close followers called for expulsion, but this cry was not taken up by others and no

65. "Zakliuchitelnoe slovo pervogo sekretaria TsK KPSS tovarishcha N. S. Khrushcheva," p. 3.

action was taken, although the initial Central Committee resolution on the antiparty group had in June 1957 explicitly demanded their exclusion from the party.

The official rationale for once again dragging these unsavory accusations of Stalin and the antiparty group before public gaze was, of course, on a more lofty plane than that of political advantage. *Pravda* explained the decision in this way:

Some ask: Why did the Party, at its Twenty-Second Congress, return to the question of the cult of the individual, condemned at the Twentieth Congress . . . ? . . . The Twenty-Second Congress vividly demonstrated that an end had been put in our Party once and for all to the faulty forms and methods of the period of the cult of the individual.[66]

It does not seem unreasonable to object that a more convincing demonstration of the end of the cult would have been just the opposite: the absence of lurid charges and recollections from the record of ensuing party congresses.

By contrast, Khrushchev's own explanation for returning to such a painful and dangerous topic was less instrumental and more convincing than the one later provided by *Pravda*. And, whatever the exigencies arising from his problems with the antiparty faction, it is difficult to pass off these remarks as mere oratory:

Comrades! It is our duty to make a thorough and comprehensive study of all such cases [as Kirov's murder] arising out of the abuse of power. Time will pass, we shall die, we are all mortal, but as long as we continue to work we can and must find out many things and tell the truth to the Party and the people. We are obliged to do everything possible to establish the truth now, for the greater the length of time that separates us from these events, the more difficult will it become to reestablish the truth. It is now too late to bring the dead back to life, as the saying goes. But it is necessary that all this be recorded truthfully in the history of the Party. This must be done so that phenomena of this sort can never be repeated in the future.[67]

One further aspect of historical revision at the Congress deserves mention here. Khrushchev not only tampered with matters of personalities in party history but he set out a new periodization

66. "XXII Sezd partii ob iskliuchenie posledstvii kulta lichnosti," *Pravda*, November 21, 1961, p. 2.
67. "Zakliuchitelnoe slovo pervogo sekretaria TsK KPSS tovarishcha N. S. Khrushcheva," p. 2.

scheme for the history of the CPSU. The occasion was adoption of the new party Program:

The adoption of the new Program marks the beginning of a new era in the history of the development of our Party and of all Soviet society. Each new Program of our Party corresponds to a specific stage in the country's development . . . [The first stage]: the overthrow of the rule of the exploiters and the establishment of the dictatorship of the proletariat [completed in October 1917]. [The second stage]: the building of socialism [not dated and not further amplified]. [The third stage]: the creation of a communist society [which begins with the Twenty-Second Congress and covers the ensuing twenty years].[68]

Developments in historiography during the several months following the Twenty-Second Congress are instructive on several levels of analysis. The congress itself did not lay down for historians any specific formulas or guidelines of a substantive nature — except for the reiteration and extension of the crimes of Stalin and the antiparty group, which did not drastically alter their official positions relative to those of February 1956 and July 1957. Nonetheless, there followed during the latter part of the year an elaborate series of conferences and publications designed to reinforce the implicit directives of the congress with regard to historiography.

On the most superficial level, Stalin was now unpersoned, as the geographical memorials to his name were removed. On November 10, 11, and 12, very brief notices in *Pravda* and *Izvestiia* stated that the presidiums of the appropriate supreme soviets had renamed Stalinsk, Stalino Province, Stalingrad, and Stalinabad. But the rest of the picture is considerably more complex.

Very soon after the congress, on November 15 and 16, the Academy of Sciences held a general meeting devoted to discussion of the Twenty-Second Congress and the tasks posed by it for the academy. This was immediately followed by two-day general meetings of the various academic sections — including the Historical Sciences Section — to discuss the congress as it related to the various disciplines.[69]

68. "O programme KPSS: Doklad tovarishcha N. S. Khrushcheva," *Pravda,* October 19, 1961, pp. 1–10.
69. For accounts of this meeting on November 15–16, 1961, see "Ha obshchikh sobraniiakh otdelenii. V otdelenii istoricheskikh nauk," *Vestnik akademii nauk SSSR,* no. 12 (1961), pp. 83–85; and "Sovetskie istoriki obsuzhdaiut zadachi nauki v svete reshenii XXII sezda KPSS," *Voprosy istorii,* no. 1 (1962), pp. 3–13.

From the rarefied circles of the Academy of Sciences, the party leadership moved the discussion into a broader and less scholarly arena. On December 25 an enormous four-day meeting, called by the Central Committee, opened in the Kremlin. The auditorium was packed with 1,300 ideological workers from local party organizations and 1,400 from the staffs of central institutions concerned with ideology. This was to be the living transmission belt to pass along party positions. On the presidium sat Koslov, Kosygin, Mikoyan, Suslov, Khrushchev, Shvernik, Grishin, Demichev, Ilichev, Ponomarenko, and Shelepin.[70]

This gathering was the first such broad and inclusive meeting of the professional ideologists and propagandists. It obviously points up the dramatic departure from the Stalinist system of dissemination of the party line, which was much tighter, more direct, and involved relatively few people at each administrative level. This huge conference could not be called a working discussion. Still it indicates that the leadership evidently saw a need to prepare these opinion formers in a rather complete and sophisticated manner for something more than a one-way presentation. Shortly after the conference of ideologists, a much less publicized meeting was held for heads of social science departments in higher educational institutions.[71]

It is not irrelevant to note that these conferences took place in the context of a wider spate of meetings, all dealing with the propagation of the results of the congress.[72] Despite all of these meetings, however, the final impression with regard to the leadership's program for historiography of the CPSU remains vague. Scattered throughout the discussion were such catch phrases as "no ideological coexistence," a "balanced" or "critical" appraisal of Stalin's work, "collective research," "better coordination of re-

70. "Vsesoiuznoe soveshchanie po voprosam ideologicheskoi raboty," *Pravda,* December 26, 1961, p. 1.
71. "XXII sezd KPSS i zadachi kafedr obshchestvennykh nauk. Doklad sekretaria TsK KPSS tovarishcha M. A. Suslova," *Pravda,* February 4, 1962, pp. 3–4.
72. On December 22 and 23 the third plenum of the board of the USSR Writers' Union met to discuss "the Twenty-Second Congress and tasks of Soviet literature." (*Literaturnaia gazeta,* December 23, 1961, p. 1.) On the same days the board of the All-Union Society for Dissemination of Political and Scientific Knowledge held its fourth plenary session, the agenda being the task of propagandizing the resolutions of the Twenty-Second Congress. (*Pravda,* December 25, 1961, p. 6.) And the plenum of the board of the USSR Journalists' Union, which met December 28, was also devoted to the journalists' duties with regard to the party's decisions at the congress. (*Pravda,* December 29, 1961, p. 3.)

search," "more use of documentary sources," "focus on contemporary issues," "rejection of both dogmatism and revisionism." But the precise balance of these often incompatible virtues and their application to real historical issues were necessarily left undetermined and therefore subject to individual interpretation.

What, then, were the effects on historiography of the revelations of the Twenty-Second Party Congress? In other words, were the speeches at the congress and the ensuing meetings and press campaign successful from the leadership's point of view? The answer must be qualified by our argument that the top political elite was not completely agreed on the purposes of the congress. As suggested above, there were differing opinions on what punishment should be meted out to the antiparty group as well as on other policies. If we confine ourselves to evaluating the effectiveness of the pronouncements on historiography by Khrushchev personally or his close supporters, the appraisal is again mixed: compliance with specific commands is coupled with continuing erosion of fundamental attitudes toward historiography and its functions. The new and more vicious denunciations of Stalin and the antiparty group were quickly incorporated into party history, as evidenced in journal articles, the popular press, and eventually in the second edition of the *History of the Communist Party of the Soviet Union* published in November 1962. This aspect of Khrushchev's new line is relatively clear and easy to follow. What is of more interest to us is the manner in which historians reacted to the signals from the congress and enusing meetings with regard to documentation, scholarly standards, and other professional concerns. Once again we must be impressed with the variety of responses to a rather vague general policy.

The implications for Soviet historiography within the general thrust of the Twenty-Second Party Congress are enormous. Khrushchev's remarks in defense of his exposure of Stalin, arguing that knowledge of the historical truth of the Stalin period was essential to social health and economic productivity, suggested that historical accuracy and documentation had functional value. This implication was generally perceived by both conservative and liberal historians and developed in varying ways and degrees by the more adventuresome. A kind of limited sanction was given to the liberals by the chief speaker at the meeting of the Historical Sciences Section of the Academy of Sciences held in mid-November. Academician Ie. M. Zhukov, secretary of the section, spoke at length on the topic of the Twenty-Second Congress as it related to the work of historians.[73] Most of the speech was a tedious rehearsal of clichés about party spirit, collective research, the need for further coordination among research institutes and higher educational institutions — but there were interspersed a number of remarks that amplified Khrushchev's position. Zhukov made clear that the regime was not entirely satisfied with the historians' performance since the Twentieth Congress and stressed that aspects of the record (specifically, the mistaken articles in *Voprosy istorii* in 1956 and 1957) were subject to continuing review. He went on to blast both dogmatists (Molotov was named as the inspirer of this kind of deviation) and revisionists (no Russians were included and only Yugoslavs were so specified). Finally, he attempted to square the circle, first pointing to Marx and Lenin as models of thorough factual and documentary research, and then charging Soviet historians to focus on contemporary issues whether or not documentary materials were available and to be guided in their work by party spirit. It is difficult to see how these confused directives could carve out an approved sphere for historical research. What did emerge clearly was the demand for more thorough research and better methodology.

Zhukov was also obviously concerned with the paucity of good historians and saw the central problem to be that of training more historians without lowering academic standards. He remarked quite defensively that indeed this must somehow be possible: after all, there were no fewer talented young scholars in history than in other fields of learning.[74]

Once again we have occasion to notice that the *Voprosy istorii* account of the discussion following Zhukov's speech is considerably more open than that in other journals. One example can be cited: V. M. Khvostov was quoted only in *Voprosy istorii* as explaining the "present acute shortage of highly qualified cadres" by the debilitating pressures of the Stalin years, when "many historians preferred to select themes far removed from questions of our times."[75] According to this same account, another prominent historian and corresponding member of the Academy of

73. Ie. M. Zhukov, "XXII sezd KPSS i zadachi sovetzkikh istorikov," *Voprosy istorii*, no. 12 (1961), pp. 3–13.
74. "Ha obshchikh sobraniiakh otdelenii. V otdelenii istoricheskikh nauk," *Vestnik Akademii nauk SSSR*, no. 12 (1961), p. 84.
75. "Sovetskie istoriki obsuzhdaiut zadachi nauki v svete reshenii XXII sezda KPSS," *Voprosy istorii*, no. 1 (1962), p. 10.

Sciences, M. P. Kim, hinted strongly that some documents in the archives had been tampered with and that Soviet historians thus faced special difficulties in their research: "Some materials and documents that were placed in the country's archives during the period from the 1930s to the early 1950s will require very careful study, since they bear traces of the influence of the cult of the individual."[76]

Thus, already at the initial meeting of the most prestigious group of historians at the academy, there were a variety of interpretations of what the party leadership — itself divided — had sanctioned.

The debate over historical sources set in motion by the Twenty-Second Party Congress reached a dramatic point with the publication in February 1962 of an authoritative article on documentation.[77] Because the author was I. Smirnov, who was then preparing the official short history of the USSR, *Kratkaia istoriia SSSR,* published by the Academy of Sciences Publishing House in 1963–64, and because his article appeared in the party's leading journal, *Kommunist,* it is of unusual significance. Despite evidence of progress in use of sources, the Smirnov article is full of now-familiar complaints: there was still no single system for classification of sources;[78] the minimum doctoral requirements in party and soviet history did not include any readings in source studies; no dissertations on source studies in the history of the party or the USSR had yet been defended in the universities or the History Institute; the History Institute's current seven-year plan showed neither works on source studies for the Soviet period nor a catalogue of the central archives; the historical journals did not give enough attention to the problems of courses for the Soviet period; memoirs were generally neglected as historical sources. Moreover, many authors and editors still did not understand the importance of citing fully their sources:

The actual course of historical development in the sources is not

76. *Ibid.,* p. 9.
77. I. Smirnov, "Dostovernye fakty — osnova istoricheskogo issledovaniia," *Kommunist,* no. 3 (1962), pp. 75–83.
78. It should be noted in this connection that Soviet bibliographical sources show publication in 1962 of a *Scheme of Unified Classification of Documentary Materials of the State Archive Fund of the USSR in Catalogues of State Archives (Soviet Period),* edited by G. A. Belov. The completeness of this system and its authority and implementation remain problematical, however.

always followed. In the final analysis this methodological short-coming becomes a historiographical shortcoming, and the scholarly level of the study is lowered. As a rule such authors do not give a list of their sources, but at best enumerate the collections . . . remarking only that all these sources are "of great importance." Some publishing houses consider it "a matter of honor" to simplify the scholarly apparatus of a monograph despite categorical complaints from writers.[79]

Smirnov's review of Soviet source studies provides evidence of the continued opposition to de-Stalinization within certain circles and institutional sectors of the historical profession. Of special interest is a series of lectures in the Party History Department of Moscow University, published in 1961, which Smirnov brands an "unsuccessful experiment" and "a departure from the principles of Party orientation."[80]

The authors and editors of this work, which was sent to press in March 1961 — five years after the historic decision of the Party Central Committee "On Overcoming the Cult of the Individual and its Consequences" — took an uncritical attitude toward the evaluation of Stalin's works and gave them an even higher estimate than they had received during the reign of the cult of the individual. Many of the errors in these works were ignored.[81]

More than this, the lectures provided only inadequate and incorrect treatment of Lenin's works, maintained that newspaper accounts of Lenin's speeches were authentic historical sources, largely ignored and completely bypassed the point of Lenin's Testament. Several victims of the purges, later rehabilitated, were still called in this volume enemies of the party.

Smirnov's attack on this publication makes clear that these serious breaches of the party's policy on historiography were neither accidental nor isolated, but rather were part of a continuing and conscious interpretation within at least one important academic faculty:

It is quite obvious that a book containing such serious ideological errors could have appeared only if the Party history department of Moscow University's history faculty and Professor N. V. Savinchenko, the department head, had taken an irresponsible attitude toward the publication of literature for students. The guilt of the

79. Smirnov, "Dostovernye fakty," pp. 78–79.
80. The book referred to is *Obzor istochnikov istorii KPSS (kurs lektsii)*, P. B. Zhibarev and M. D. Stuchebnikova, eds. (Moscow: State University Publishing House, 1961).
81. Smirnov, "Dostovernye fakty," p. 81.

leaders of the department and the officials of the faculty . . . is the greater in that the "Review" is based on a course of lectures that has been given in the history faculty for a number of years.[82]

Here is more reason for caution in setting up easy categories of academic affiliation as equal to revisionist or liberal orientation, and official party position as sure indication of ideological conservatism: the writer in the party's ideological journal in this instance exposed Stalin's apologizers in the university. This incident also illustrates the observation that special caution must be exercised when identifying and analyzing the views of historians of the CPSU, since there is evident interchange of personnel between academic departments of party history and those party organs responsible for party history and ideology. In this connection, it is interesting to observe that editor Stuchebnikova — who was alleged to have ignored Lenin's Testament and last articles published after the Twentieth Party Congress in her own article — had maintained in 1961 the uncompromising position that distinguished her remarks to the *Voprosy istorii* conference in January 1956. She was in 1956 identified as a member of the Marx-Engels-Lenin-Stalin Institute and now as on the history faculty of the University of Moscow.

Smirnov pointed to another critical problem for historians attempting to comply with the request for more factual material and better research of original documents: the need to integrate large and sudden infusions of factual material into the existing body of historical knowledge and published works. He put it this way:

Strange as it may seem, certain textbooks and other study aids also introduce confusion into factual materials on the history of Soviet society. This happens when authors of textbooks introduce important but completely unknown facts, or else introduce new data that are not in accordance with the facts current in scholarship. It is impossible to be indifferent to them and yet it is not the custom for textbooks to include references to archives. Of course a textbook should not be overloaded with references. But it is the duty of authors . . . to give the basis for any new factual material.[83]

Obviously his concern was not confined to the need for giving references but extended to the more sensitive question of who will undertake to unravel and resolve the inconsistencies caused by

82. *Ibid.*, p. 82.
83. *Ibid.*, p. 79.

the new and contradictory facts, and how this could be done with the least disturbance. Such a public reference to this aspect of historical rewriting is rare, possibly unique.

It is a measure of the duality mentioned earlier that Smirnov personally had internalized the conflicts and contradictions of the competing strains within Soviet historiography. One senses that whatever he might have been ten years ago, this man was in 1961 no longer a hack; nor was he a rebel. He was beginning to experience a sincere commitment to good methodology and honest scholarship, but at the same time fearful of losing his philosophic grounding. Like Zhukov, he was uneasy over some of the possible complications that might arise from the new emphasis on scholarship. Caught in this crossfire, he evolved a formula that would, he hoped, allow him to remain both scholar and believer: he would reconcile party spirit and scholarly objectivity.

Party spirit demands political acuity and qualifications in the approach to sources from which is drawn the factual basis of historical research. Just because the Marxist-historian conceives historical developments from the vantage point of the most decisive and consistent force of social progress — from the position of the working class — he can conduct fundamental objective scientific research, faithfully depict the historical process, present correct and well-founded views.

Works written by historians of the Party and of Soviet society must be based on strictly documented historical facts and on the correct interpretation of these facts from the point of view of Marxism-Leninism.[84]

This was a perilous acrobatic exercise. But in ensuing years such a balancing act was to become less exciting. This was not because the man on the high wire was any less brave or skilled — if anything, his perch became more precarious — but because in some strange way the whole circus was beginning to be passé.

84. *Ibid.*, pp. 75, 83.

If we pause for a moment midway in the rush of events that crowd the years 1956–1966, we will see that 1962 was a landmark in the maturation process of Soviet historiography: history was becoming less a political weapon and more a self-contained and existential pursuit. Forces were developing within the councils of responsible political decision making as well as among historians themselves, which would over the following years professionalize historiography to a remarkable degree. And yet to posit a growing sense of group identity among historians and an increasing focus on scholarly concerns is not to argue that historiography moved suddenly beyond the purview of the larger political context. The suggestion here is one of relative rather than complete depolitization, occurring within the general context of a highly politicized system.

We must first consider those political trends and events that are of relevance to Soviet historiography during the entire period under review, 1962–1966. Although developments in Soviet historiography in substance suggest a natural break at the end of 1962 and in number require that a separate chapter be devoted to that year, an analysis of the political and intellectual milieu would suffer considerably from being artificially divided. Therefore the more general and political aspects of the discussion will be treated in terms of the larger period. There is, of course, no intended implication that the developments selected for treatment here are of more importance in Soviet politics than those not considered: the criterion is quite explicitly that of direct relationship to Soviet historiography, specifically of the CPSU.

On the international scene, the heightening tension with the Chinese was probably of most significance to Soviet historiography. By lending support and providing a forum for the arguments of those elements of the Soviet bureaucracy and intelligentsia opposed to de-Stalinization, the Chinese polemic intensified domestic disputes over Stalin's historical role and related issues. In the last analysis, the Chinese attacks on Soviet "revisionism" probably helped the liberal or revisionist Soviet historians, by ranging their hard-line opponents on the side of the foreign antagonist.

But despite the ferocity of this interchange — which reached crisis proportions with the Chinese-Indian border conflict at the end of 1962 and again in the summer and autumn of 1963 and the spring of 1964 — the explicit connection between disputed doctrinal issues and related historical questions has been only rarely and incompletely made in the Soviet Union.[1] Thus, it must be concluded that the impact of the Sino-Soviet dispute on Soviet historiography has been of a derivative rather than direct character. Although the dispute clearly did have the effect of articulating the arguments of domestic dogmatists, the association of these views with the Chinese was not helpful to the Soviet conservatives; and in any case it is impossible to infer a direct, causal response among historians.

If we turn to the sphere of internal Soviet politics, we are on safer ground — having at least eliminated the complicating factors of national rivalry and mistrust and the problem of international communication. Several domestic events and policies immediately suggest themselves as of certain relevance to Soviet historiography of the CPSU. One such is the dramatic shift in cultural policy at the end of 1962, when Khrushchev — off balance from the Cuban crisis and facing opposition to his plan to bifurcate the party — violently attacked the "formalists" in literature and the arts. As we shall see, the cultural crackdown had relevance for historians because of the recent appearance of a number of stories, novels, and memoirs of historical quality and sensationally revisionist thrust. But the severe attacks on liberal writers did not spill over into a campaign against troublesome historians; the impact of the whole affair upon the debates among historians seems to have been negligible.

The second relevant moment of political crisis was the accession to power of Brezhnev and Kosygin in October 1964 and the denigration of Khrushchev. In this case there was double cause to expect explicit reflection of political developments in party historiography: not only had the central figure in recent history been exposed as a hare-brained schemer, but said leader had himself significantly rewritten the history of the CPSU to his own political requirements. What would happen now? The amazing fact is that very little happened in historiography.

The new leadership did not immediately, or indeed later, press

1. See R. V. Viatkin and S. L. Tikhvinsky, "O nekatorykh voprosakh istoricheskoi nauki v KNR," *Voprosy istorii*, no. 10 (1963), pp. 3–20; and K. Kuznetsov (candidate of history) and R. Terekhov (party member since 1912), "Vazhnaia vekha v zhizni leninskoi partii," *Pravda*, May 26, 1964, p. 2.

for substantive revisions to portray themselves in more favorable or more prominent positions. While Khrushchev's solitary glory faded, Brezhnev and Kosygin were not promoted to fill the vacancy. The reasons for the absence of massive official intervention in historical interpretation are both political and historiographical. An examination of post-Khrushchev historiography yields few indications or hints of direct political interference or pressure on historians beyond the superficial expunging of Khrushchev's preeminence; there is nothing comparable to the secret speech, the 1956 attack on the revisionist historians, or the denigration of the antiparty group.

The most obvious explanation is that devolving from the purposes and style of the new leadership. Its desire was initially — and this has continued — to protect an image of stability; careful and moderate shifts of policy and reform; a calm, businesslike approach to the problems of rule, including those problems relating to intellectual matters. An editorial in *Pravda* very soon after Khrushchev's ouster reiterated the correctness of the Twentieth, Twenty-First, and Twenty-Second Congresses.[2] Specifically, the new leaders pledged not to interfere arbitrarily and precipitously with social scientists working in good faith but rather to rely on regular liaison between scholars and their institutional party committees. This line has since been neither rescinded nor seriously questioned, although many of Khrushchev's specific economic and administrative reforms have been nullified.

This is all quite well in answer to the what and how of post-Khrushchev politics as they impinge on historiography. But why these policies, methods, and style? Clearly, any new regime in a situation of irregular succession must distinguish itself as dramatically as possible from its predecessor, which must be depicted as bumbling and inefficient at best and traitorous, tyrannous, stupid, and brutal at worst. Another obvious factor is that of the length and eventfulness of the preceding leader's tenure: to erase a Khrushchev is easier and much less traumatic than to demote a Stalin, simply in terms of the quantity of history involved. Further probing brings us to considerations of personal character, temperament, and experience: certainly there were sharp cleavages between Khrushchev, the self-made man of the 1930s, and his

2. "Revoliutsionnaia teoriia osveshchaet nash put," *Pravda*, November 5, 1964, p. 2.

well-educated successors, who knew the early struggles of the party only at second hand. While allowing for human variety that is purely individual in origin, it must be seen that the formative influence of two quite different historical and psychological environments is at work here.

It is impossible at this point to reject the argument that Brezhnev and Kosygin are concerned with reform and moderation only until one of them feels secure enough to seize unilateral, and ultimately despotic, control. However that may be, it seems clear that there were real risks in ousting the man who destroyed the Stalin cult and who therefore — whatever his faults — symbolized a new liberalization to the Soviet population. Further, the coalition behind Brezhnev and Kosygin was created by virtue of its members' mutual dissatisfaction with Khrushchev rather than any new collective policies — another fact that has induced caution. But this topic lends itself not to prediction but to speculation. It would be fallacious to conclude on the basis of their sober, faceless caution to date that Brezhnev and Kosygin and their successors have finally eschewed personal charisma and cultism as a foundation for political control, even though the weight of the evidence certainly points that way at present. Although these two do not appear to have the talent or taste for it, and although the memory of Stalin is now an effective political deterrent, there is no genuine institutional or ideological bar to personal rule under altered future circumstances.

The third and final political event of significance for Soviet historiography of the party is the Twenty-Third Congress, which took place at the end of March 1966. Once again, as in 1962 and late 1964, our interest is attracted by what was not said and what did not happen.

In brief, the Twenty-Third Congress was remarkable for its studious avoidance of problems of historiography — and specifically, Stalin's place in Soviet history — since the months preceding it were rife with debate, innuendo, and rumor. And it may be perceived that this official silence, the party leadership's refusal overtly to endorse the demands of either the neo-Stalinists or the liberals, was in itself a conscious decision and a signal understood by the party hierarchy as well as the intelligentsia. Thus, in an oblique way, the political and intellectual developments leading to the congress brought about a political decision; but that decision was to maintain the status quo. The Siniavsky-Daniel trial, the Chinese dispute, growing dissatisfaction among party functionaries over Khrushchev's reforms, and the very fact of the impending congress created political pressures for a general tightening of ideological policy and a revision of party history to reinstate Stalin. But these pressures were outweighed by other factors.

I would suggest that the leadership's reasons for holding to the established historical treatment of Stalin were not entirely political. Significantly, the gradual development of a sophisticated and self-conscious sense of scholarly identity among many of the best historians coincided in 1966 with the emergence of a primitive political pressure group dedicated to maintaining a moderately liberal official policy toward historiography. Thus the growth of rudimentary apolitical professionalism apparently contributed to the creation of a nascent group activsm. But this is anticipating what needs to be shown in more detail. The point to be made here is that the political events and the debate swirling around the Twenty-Third Party Congress had a clear and enormous impact upon party historiography. But it was no longer the traditional relationship between Soviet politics and historians.

Nineteen hundred and sixty-two opened with an event, unheralded and largely unnoticed at the time, which was to prove symbolic of historiography during the entire year. The first number of *Voprosy istorii* was published under a new superscription: at the top of the title page immediately below the familiar "USSR Academy of Sciences, Section of Historical Sciences" appeared "USSR Ministry of Higher and Secondary Specialized Education." This additional sponsorship of the journal, although it must have entailed certain organizational shifts, was nowhere announced in this or any other issue. The editorial policies did not undergo perceptible changes as a result, although the board took on four new members and removed one.

Of more moment is the very fact of the decision to incorporate the educational bureaucracy, with its special purview and prerogatives, into the supervision and control of *Voprosy istorii*. This would seem to reflect both a growing awareness of the need for close contact by the editors with university faculty members and a commitment to the training of more and better young historians. It is because of these considerations and their implications for the historical profession that this action was described as symbolic: much of the action by the political leadership with regard to historiography and by the historians themselves during 1962, and in ensuing years, can be seen as directed to improvement of academic standards and historical education.

The concern for more competent historiography was reflected in continuing discussions of source work and methodology in the historical journals. A significant step toward the improvement of historiography was taken by the Central Committee and Council of Ministers during the spring of 1962. *Pravda* on May 18 featured a summary of an undated resolution "On Measures for the Further Improvement of the Selection and Training of Scientific Cadres," which laid out several specific measures to raise academic standards.[3]

Literature and Art as Modes of Historical Revision

A striking development during 1962 was the rather sudden and extensive utilization of fictional writing and other art forms as vehicles for historical revision — especially with reference to history of the party and the USSR — which started with the publication of Kazakevich's story, "Enemies," in *Izvestiia* on April 21.[4] It is hard to believe that such an inflammatory topic as Lenin's relations with the Menshevik Martov could be treated in the official government newspaper without sanction at a very high level. There is substantiation of this view in the fact that the revised 1962 edition of the *History of the Communist Party of the Soviet Union* included a new paragraph that stressed Lenin's forbearance toward Bukharin and his allies in 1918: "Despite the extreme bitterness of the struggle against the 'Left Communists,' Lenin strictly adhered to the standards which had formed in the Party. He was forbearing and used the method of persuasion."[5] Although it would be a mistake to assume that this softened attitude could now be extended to all political enemies, this passage does imply something more than a specific exception for

3. It is interesting that the official compilation of decrees, *Spravochnik partiinogo rabotnika*, 4th ed., 1963, reproduces not the decree itself but this same *Pravda* summary (pp. 418–423).
4. Em. Kazakevich, "Vragy," *Izvestiia*, April 21, 1962, p. 6.
5. *History of the Communist Party of the Soviet Union*, 2nd rev. ed., p. 278.

the Left Communists by referring to "the standard which had formed in the Party." An additional factor suggesting official sponsorship is the obvious rarity of a fictionalized account in *Izvestiia*. Kazakevich is, however, careful to point out that his story is not pure fiction and recounts a true occurrence.

As the title suggests, "Enemies" deals with an antagonistic human relationship; upon perusal of the story, however, the reader is soon aware that the author is subtly calling in question the applicability of the term "enemy" with regard to the political rivalry of Lenin and Martov. The plot develops Lenin's decision to conspire with Madame Martova to get her former husband secretly on the last train to the West before the outbreak of war with Poland. Of course, the title would in the Soviet context instantly bring to mind Stalin's unique concept of enemies of the party and state and the historical treatment of the Mensheviks. Thus it may be argued that there were for the Soviet reader clear symbolic overtones, whereby Lenin's treatment of Martov had reference to the more general question of the proper policy of a communist regime toward socialist dissenters.

The problems raised by "Enemies" turned out to be complex and a source of argument among critics. Only in July was there an attack on Kazakevich's portrayal. It is interesting to observe that the format was not that of the usual literary critique but was cast in the form of one letter in a correspondence column in *Oktiabr*.[6] Dymshits castigated Kazakevich for not clearly setting out Lenin's motivation: Lenin helped other oppositionists as well as Martov, "believing they would be less dangerous for the republic outside than inside." He characterized Lenin as a "great revolutionary humanist" whose primary concern was for the revolution and only incidentally for troublesome individuals.

An important genre in the literary historiography which now began to appear in quantity was the memoir. And probably the most significant for public opinion and the whole intellectual milieu was Ilia Ehrenburg's "People, Years, Life," which *Novyi mir* serialized beginning in 1962 until well into 1965. Ehrenburg's unique position as a bellweather of Soviet cultural policy has been frequently described, and it should be borne in mind when assessing the significance of his frank descriptions of what he and his fellows in the artistic community endured during Stalin's later

6. A. Dymshits, "Chelovek i obshchestvo," *Oktiabr*, no. 7 (1962), pp. 182–192.

years. His chapters dealing with the purges appeared in May and June.

The very same issues of *Novyi mir*, numbers 3, 4, and 5, carried a novella by Iury Bondarev, "Silence," set in the postwar years. A bitter picture of that period emerges, which does not flinch at frank discussions of midnight arrests, false denunciations, and the miasma of fear hovering over loyal Soviet citizens. The critical reaction was mixed (as it was toward Ehrenburg's memoirs) but revealing. In September reviewers in *Oktiabr* and *Zvezda* were harshly disparaging of this "melodrama" for the unfair treatment of party workers who failed to protest against the purges: after all, "people could not then draw the generalizations" that later became evident.[7] But then the appraisals suddenly mellowed, and the later reviews were profuse in praise of this "honest" and "powerful" work.[8] Certainly if one were to select journals reflecting Khrushchev's cultural policy of controlled innovation during this period, the choice would run to *Pravda*, *Izvestiia*, *Literaturnaia gazeta*, and *Novyi mir*. *Oktiabr* and *Zvezda* would be recognized as the organs of the literary conservatives. Thus it may be surmised that after the hostile comments in *Oktiabr* and *Zvezda*, word was passed from the party Secretariat to trusted personnel of other papers that such impressions needed prompt correction.

During the autumn the debate over prose style in historiography was reopened in *Izvestiia*. The final word went to Academician Tikhomorov, who crushed "the strange theory [in a recent article] that artistic expressiveness is of secondary importance in works of history" and charged that much contemporary historical writing was "careless and incredibly dull."[9]

As the year proceeded, the literary allusions to the wisdom of de-Stalinization took on the proportions of a campaign and acquired a more intensely partisan identification with Khrushchev. On October 24 *Pravda* gave prominent place to Yevtushenko's poem "Stalin's Heirs," despite some recent jibes in the press at his poetry readings in Maiakovsky Square. The poem became an

7. Iury Idashkin, "No esli zadumatsia," *Oktiabr*, no. 9 (1962), pp. 212–213; also V. Gusarov, "Uspekh ili neudacha?" *Zvezda*, no. 9 (1962), pp. 209–211.
8. See Z. Boguslavskaia, "Chelovek razmyshliaet," *Literaturnaia gazeta*, October 23, 1962, pp. 2–3; K. Paustovsky, "Srazhenie v tishine," *Pravda*, April 18, 1962, p. 6.
9. M. Tikhomirov, "Letopis nashei epokhi," *Izvestiia*, October 31, 1962, p. 5.

instant sensation for its evocation of a strangely superstitious fear that Stalin had perhaps somehow prevailed:

Let some repeat over and over:
"Relax!" — I cannot be
       calm.
As long as Stalin's heirs exist on earth
It will seem to me
       that Stalin is still in the mausoleum.

The reference to political disputation and the claim to authority for his position were clear in the phrase, "The Party ordered me not to be quiet."

This attempt to demonstrate the final end of Stalinism with no turning back was reiterated in a set of poems written by Boris Slutsky for *Literaturnaia gazeta*. After the horrors of the Stalin period were recalled, there followed the insistent refrain that the people had survived the hardships and were eagerly responsive to the new:

But people — for good or for ill —
Keep well in cold storage.
People who have fatigued, like rails
Over which the whole world has driven locomotives,
Are receptive to any signal of good.
1961

Time for winding up the verses.

Time to dismantle and to clear away.
Time to bring the dreams to pass.[10]
1962

But the tidal wave came with the publication in *Novyi mir* of the novella *One Day in the Life of Ivan Denisovich*,[11] an unparalleled artistic document that in one stroke opened up the whole hideous history of the Siberian concentration camps to public discussion. As a turning point in Soviet historiography it can only be compared to Khrushchev's secret speech in 1956. And like the denigration of Stalin, the decision to publish Solzhenitsyn's novella could only have been taken at the apex of the political leadership. Not even the outspoken and courageous chief editor Tvardovsky would have presumed to take such a step on his own authority.

10. Boris Slutsky, "Stikhi raznykh let," *Literaturnaia gazeta*, November 24, 1962, p. 2.
11. A. Solzhenitsyn, "Odin den Ivana Denisovicha," *Novyi mir*, no. 11 (1962), pp. 8–74.

The piece received immediate and very favorable reviews and was nominated for a Lenin Prize. Simonov wrote in *Izvestiia* that this was an important step in a process of exposing Stalin's errors: "Sooner or later both history and literature will throw light on every single aspect of Stalin's activity."[12] The *Literaturnaia gazeta* review, in praising *One Day* as a "purifying pain," tackled directly the argument against recalling past oppression: "Old, healed wounds do not pain. But a wound that still bleeds must be healed and not cravenly hidden from sight. And there is only one cure — truth. The Party summons us along this path of truth."[13]

Khrushchev perhaps overplayed his hand when he told the Central Committee on November 23 that he had personally authorized publication of both "Stalin's Heirs" and *One Day* (which had appeared only the previous day). He specifically stated that top officials had tried to stop Solzhenitsyn's novel, but did not name his opponents.[14] At this point Khrushchev was under considerable pressure on several fronts. The Cuban fiasco had erupted just a month earlier, exposing him to conservative attack as an international adventurer; on September 9 Ie. Liberman's *Pravda* article on profits as a tool of economic rationalization and planning had touched off a debate; only a few days earlier, on November 19, Khrushchev had shocked the Central Committee with his radical proposal to split the party into agricultural and industrial wings. Thus the wave of "formalist art" and questionable literature — crowned by the politically explosive publications just mentioned — was placed in jeopardy by concurrent international tensions and political disputes among Khrushchev and his peers.

After Khrushchev's famous visit to the Exhibition of Works by Moscow Artists at the Manezh took place on December 1, it was all over for the formalists. A barrage from the press ensued, which culminated in a large formal meeting of party and government leaders with representatives of literature and the arts on Decem-

12. Konstantin Simonov, "O proshlom vo imia budushchego," *Izvestiia*, November 18, 1962, p. 5.
13. Grigory Baklanov, "Chtob eto nikogda ne povtorilos," *Literaturnaia gazeta*, November 22, 1962, p. 3.
14. For a detailed chronological outline of Soviet cultural policies from 1962 to early 1966, see Peter Viereck, "The Mob Within the Heart," *Soviet Policy-Making*, Peter H. Juviler and Henry W. Morton, eds. (New York: Frederick A. Praeger, 1967), pp. 83–120.

ber 17. A new and harsh line was laid down in no uncertain terms by Khrushchev and Ilichev, providing "complete freedom to struggle for communism."[15] But there had evidently been opposition within cultural circles, including letters to Khrushchev asking him to prevent a repetition of cultural repressions such as occurred under Stalin and — according to his remarks on March 8, 1963 — "even a plea for 'peaceful coexistence' of *all* trends in art." This suggestion was harshly rejected.

Such spirited discussion in the face of an official blast can only indicate great personal courage and the perception by many artists that the political leadership was fundamentally split on the problem of defining the desirable limits of artistic freedom. The soundness of their analysis was confirmed by the appearance of a series of very unfriendly critiques of One Day in Literaturnaia rossiia, Oktiabr, and Moskovskaia pravda,[16] as editors sniffed the conservative winds. These criticisms were ultimately answered at length early in 1964, and the debate continued.[17]

All of this is singularly related to historiography both by reason of what it suggests about the political split over de-Stalinization during this period and because the most controversial literary works that sparked the general crackdown had historical themes and opened new aspects of party history to public discourse. To understand this dimension of the matter, it must be emphasized that Khrushchev had very early in the controversy identified himself as Solzhenitsyn's and Yevtushenko's sponsor, thereby committing his own prestige to literary de-Stalinization and historical revision. Tvardovsky remarked to Henry Shapiro of UPI, "At the first meeting [of political leaders with cultural figures on December 17] Nikita Sergeevich mentioned Solzhenitsyn in the course of his speech and introduced him to all of those present."[18]

Thus, amid all the confusion and pressure toward tightening of cultural controls at the end of 1962 and into the spring of 1963,

15. "Tvorit dlia naroda vo imia kommunizma," *Pravda*, December 18, 1962, p. 1.
16. Lidiia Fomenko, "Bolshie ozhdaniia," *Literaturnaia rossiia*, January 11, 1963, pp. 6–7; Georgiy Lomidze, "Nekotorye mysli," *Literaturnaia rossiia*, January 18, 1963, p. 6; N. Sergovantsev, "Tragediia odinochestva i 'sploshnoi byt,'" *Oktiabr*, no. 4 (1963), pp. 198–207; and I. Chicherov, "Vo imia budushchogo," *Moskovskaia pravda*, December 8, 1962, p. 3.
17. V. Lakshin, "Ivan Denisovich, ego druzia i nedrugi," *Novyi mir*, no. 1 (1964), pp. 223–245.
18. "Literatura sotsialisticheskogo realizma vsegda shla ruka ob ruku s revoliutsiei," *Pravda*, May 12, 1963, pp. 4–5.

Khrushchev succeeded in promoting and protecting certain literary works of historical significance while blasting formalism, in pursuance of his own policies of controlled political reform. These favored publications were deliberately and carefully distinguished from other innovative artistic efforts, which were ruthlessly suppressed. The striking aspect of this whole episode is the harsh treatment accorded by the political elite to purely literary works vis-à-vis literature of a historiographical nature. And further, the sudden tightening of cultural controls had no equivalent or repercussion in the realm of scholarly historical research.

In his second major incursion into revelatory historiographical revision, then, Khrushchev's instrument became fictional literature rather than history as such. We can only speculate on his reasons: perhaps he felt that the camps and other aspects of the Stalin purges were too painful and explosive to be dealt with on a factual level but must be approached obliquely; perhaps he realized that proper documentation would be a problem. But both of these objections could be made with regard to the more tragic episodes of the history of World War II, and yet Soviet historians have themselves undertaken its revision. It seems plausible that one of the reasons for Khrushchev's use of literature at this juncture was the relatively greater integrity and lesser malleability of Soviet history, in comparison with the more exposed and defenseless position of belles lettres. There may have been the feeling that history written to order was less convincing and more difficult to manage than it had been even as recently as 1956.

Such a suggestion requires further investigation into developments in historiography during late 1962. Some important events took place at this time under official or semiofficial auspices, so that if the crushing of artistic deviation did indeed have an echo among historians, it would have been instantly apparent.

In November the party journal *Partiinaia zhizn* published a summary of an undated Central Committee resolution "On the Journal 'Voprosy istorii KPSS.' "[19] Reviewing the journal's work during the five years since its creation, the resolution noted that

19. "V tsentralnom komitete KPSS. O zhurnale 'Voprosy istorii KPSS,' " *Partiinaia zhizn*, no. 22 (1962), pp. 44–46.

much had been accomplished. However, *Voprosy istorii KPSS* was accused of not having succeeded in

achieving the level of work required by the XXII Party Congress and not [having] taken the leading place in scholarly study of the history of the CPSU. The journal has included insufficient work directed toward overcoming subjectivism and dogmatism in historical science and toward a thorough investigation of the facts and events which took place in the period of the cult of Stalin's personality.[20]

Here is more evidence of a continuing split among historians with regard to the official denigration of Stalin, with malperformance extending as far up the editorial hierarchy as *Voprosy istorii KPSS*. It was charged that discussions of little-researched questions of party history rarely appeared in its pages; many works were reviewed only after a long delay; there was not enough attention to research done by provincial historians concerning their localities; the state of historiographical work and source work was poor. The editorial board was specifically directed to publish

scholarly articles, collections and documents relating to the pre-October period of the Party's activities, with the aim of liquidating the mistakes and distortions of historical truth promulgated by the cult of the personality of Stalin . . . to publish systematically articles and materials on questions of historiography and sources in the field of history of the CPSU; in reviews to give objective evaluation of the scientific significance of the most important works on Party history, to inform readers concerning the state of scholarly research work in the Institutes of Party History under the central committees of the communist parties of the union republics.[21]

In order to accomplish these tasks, *Voprosy istorii KPSS* would from January 1, 1963, be a monthly instead of a bimonthly journal.

Thus we are presented with the unusual spectacle of the Central Committee urging its journal toward higher standards of scholarship on party history and making specific provisions to that end. Imputation of motivation must remain on a speculative level, but the most plausible explanation would appear to be the Central Committee's concern that the party maintain at least a competitive, if not controlling, position in party historiography. *Voprosy*

20. *Spravochnik partiinogo rabotnika*, 4th ed. (1963), p. 454.
21. *Ibid.*, p. 456.

istorii — which had sheltered the troublemakers in 1956 — was shunted toward more general problems when *Voprosy istorii KPSS* was created; and in order for the latter to compete and establish itself as dominant in historiography of the CPSU, it would have to achieve the scholastic level of the older journal. Obviously, if the party archives were to be opened, the party functionaries in the Central Committee would prefer to have publication remain as much as possible in the hands of its own journal, rather than pass by default to others.

The Second Edition of the Official Party History
During the year the *History of the Communist Party of the Soviet Union* was revised to bring it into line with the Twenty-Second Party Congress. On November 10 *Pravda* announced the appearance of the second edition, in which it was asserted that the question of the personality cult was "more extensively covered."[22] In a number of ways the 1962 version makes significant revisions of even so recent an official account as the 1959 text. Several passages further modify the treatment of the Mensheviks, the Left and Right Oppositionists, and even Trotsky, so that although their policies continue to be mercilessly castigated, they personally are portrayed more as political or ideological foes rather than traitors and enemies of the Soviet state and people.

Although the second edition thus works toward a less vitriolic and more objective treatment of oppositionists, the image of Stalin has been dramatically defaced. No longer are the authors content to eliminate the laudatory passages and neutralize his influence: now virtually all positive references to Stalin have been deleted, and attributions of his speeches or decisions are usually made to the Central Committee or to the party leadership in general. And in place of a rather passive downgrading, Stalin is directly and severely criticized. It was he personally who — by calling for a higher rate of collectivization in December 1929,[23] by underestimating the peasant's attachment to his household and plot,[24] and by falsely accusing and confusing the party rank and file with his "Dizzy with Success" article[25] —

22. "Novoe izdanie 'Istorii Kommunisticheskoi partii Sovetskogo Soiuza,'" *Pravda*, November 10, 1962, p. 2.
23. *History of the Communist Party of the Soviet Union*, 2nd rev. ed., p. 413.
24. *Ibid.*, p. 444.
25. *Ibid.*, pp. 445–446.

caused the excesses of collectivization. Most dramatically, Stalin is directly charged with using the Kirov murder to bring on the "wholesale repressive measures and the most flagrant violations of socialist legality" of the purges.[26] And Stalin's long-range responsibility for the Soviet lack of preparedness in 1941 is further amplified by naming of the purged generals;[27] explaining in detail the harm done to industrialization by purges, irrational personnel shifts, and repressive treatment of factory managers and experts;[28] and pointing to the "gross violations of the Leninist standards of Party life and socialist legality" which hampered defense preparations and the whole of society.[29] In the new edition specific treatment of the situation in the USSR on the eve of the war involves Stalin directly: in place of a rather mild comment on "Stalin's misappreciation of the strategic situation,"[30] the reader is given a lengthy discussion of "Stalin's impermissible misappraisal of the strategic situation," his naive reliance on the Soviet-German nonaggression treaty, his "lack of vigilance toward fascism [which] deprived the Party and government bodies of the possibility of taking precautions."[31] Needless to say, however, the new edition reiterates the proposition that despite the damage caused by the personality cult, it could not alter the nature of the socialist system or stop its progress.[32]

In the 1959 edition Khrushchev stands quite alone as the post-Stalin leader, the architect of reform. But three years later, although there is certainly no cult surrounding his person, he completely dominates the scene and appears in new historical perspective with respect to the Revolution, Civil War, and Second World War. The local soviet in the Donets, of which he was elected chairman in May 1917, is singled out as an example of early centralization of authority in the soviets.[33] It is Khrushchev's report to Stalin from the Kiev Special Military District in April 1941 which is chosen to illustrate the "serious concern" of party bodies and military commands;[34] the account of the

26. *Ibid.*, p. 487.
27. *Ibid.*, p. 537.
28. *Ibid.*, p. 520.
29. *Ibid.*, p. 534.
30. *Ibid.*, 1960, p. 548.
31. *Ibid.*, 2nd ed., p. 538.
32. *Ibid.*, p. 506.
33. *Ibid.*, pp. 223–224.
34. *Ibid.*, p. 538.

battle of Stalingrad becomes much more detailed, and Khrushchev is named with General Yeremenko as responsible for the Stalingrad front.[35] But the text carefully quotes Khrushchev's remark to the Twenty-Second Congress that all credit should go to the Central Committee and Presidium rather than to him personally.[36]

As the figure of Stalin was blackened in the 1962 edition of the basic text on party history, that of Khrushchev took on greater luster, though for somewhat different reasons. The denigration of Stalin clearly followed from political decisions taken at the Twentieth and Twenty-Second Party Congresses. But the inflated treatment of Khrushchev would seem to be less directed than inferred or self-imposed by the historians responsible for the textbook — whether at the contributing author level or the editorial level or both, we cannot say. Certainly a man like Academician Mints, who was one of the authors, perceived such flattery as necessary or justified in view of his praise of a new history of the Ukrainian Communist Party as "perhaps the first scholarly work containing extensive information about the glorious life of N. S. Khrushchev."[37]

The All-union Conference of Historians, December 1962

During late December 1962 — while the recalcitrant writers and artists were enjoying the company of party leaders at a reception and a large group of young Muscovites was receiving special attention from the Central Committee's Commission on Ideology[38] — two very unusual and exciting conferences of historians

35. *Ibid.,* pp. 551–552.
36. *Ibid.,* p. 715.
37. I. Mints, "Stranitsy geroicheskoi borby Ukrainskogo naroda za kommunizm," *Pravda,* July 25, 1962, pp. 2–3. This same review incidentally lends substance to the proposition that there is no longer a centralized and known line to guide even so sensitive and semiofficial an effort as the revision of Ukrainian party history. Mints criticized the omission from the discussion of the UCP during World War II of the "people's partisan war without precedent," which was waged under the leadership of the Ukrainian Central Committee, "headed by N. S. Khrushchev." Both the 1959 and 1962 editions of the CPSU history paid extensive attention to the partisan movement, a fact which somehow the author of the Ukrainian study failed to notice, or did not want to notice.
38. There was a reception for the "intelligentsia of the arts" given by party and government leaders in Moscow on December 17, at which Ilichev spoke. The speech was carried in full by *Pravda* (December 22, pp. 2–3) and *Izvestiia* (December 23, pp. 3–4). On December 24 and 26 the commission

took place. One was devoted to problems of reminiscences as historical source material. *Voprosy istorii KPSS* reported in brief a conference held on December 28 at the Central Party Archives of the Institute of Marxism-Leninism, which brought together its editorial board and a number of Old Bolsheviks for the purpose of developing systematic publication of their memoirs.[39] Such an attempt to encourage the writing of memoirs and to help organize their publication represented a new departure from the traditional official posture toward the Old Bolsheviks, which had been inherited from Stalin and was one of simple manipulation. This followed from the new interest in original sources and the obvious fact that the makers of the October Revolution were now a tiny and vanishing remnant. On the other hand, the decision to harness the Old Bolsheviks to the party's own journal of history certainly was a bid to exert direct editorial supervision over their writings.

The second meeting to which reference has been made deserves considerable attention. This was the conference required by the May 18 decree of the Central Committee and Council of Ministers, now designated the All-Union Conference on Measures To Improve the Training of Scientific-Pedagogical Cadres in the Historical Sciences and held in Moscow on December 18–21, 1962. The meeting was organized jointly by the Academy of Sciences, the Ministry of Higher and Specialized Secondary Education, and the Academy of Social Sciences and Institute of Marxism-Leninism, both under the Central Committee. About two thousand historians attended. Such massive participation and authoritative sponsorship is significant: this was the first all-union professional conference of Soviet historians which could be said to resemble a national mass gathering. All-union conferences of ideologists have been quite frequent, and sometimes concerned with matters of historiography; pedagogical meetings or conferences of social scientists have touched on historical problems; there were after 1956 several small specialized

held a special session with about 140 young writers and artists working in Moscow, which also featured an address by the indefatigable Ilichev, secretary of the Central Committee and chairman of the Commission on Ideology. For a full transcript of his speech, see *Sovetskaia kultura,* January 10, 1963, pp. 1–3.
39. "Ob uchastii starykh bolshevikov v rabote zhurnale," *Voprosy istorii KPSS,* no. 2 (1963), pp. 155–156.

conferences of historians dealing with specific issues, such as the October Revolution or the party's role in collectivization. But there was not in 1962, and there still has not been, an institutionalized periodic convocation of Soviet historians; nor is there any organization of historians, like the unions of artists, writers, journalists, or teachers, which would generate a feeling of professional identity.

The All-Union Conference of Historians in December 1962 thus provides an unparalleled occasion for observation of Soviet historians as a group. But the record presents a special problem in analysis: there is projected at the same time both an overwhelming impression of dualism, of people speaking past one another and on different frequencies, and a rudimentary sense of group solidarity. Following a two-day plenum featuring a report by B. N. Ponomarev and remarks by participants, the conference was divided into three working sessions on the following topics, each consisting of a report and discussion: the history of the CPSU, world history, and the history of the USSR. The report to the session on party history was delivered by P. N. Pospelov. A final plenary session followed on December 21, when a resolution was passed, after concluding remarks by Ponomarev. However, the dualism referred to did not relate to disciplinary subdivisions or conference organization, but was rather an intensification of a phenomenon seen earlier: a growing split among historians based upon their varying concepts of the craft, their self-identification as historians within the Soviet system, and their approaches to methodology.

The most obvious evidence of this dualism can be read in the shape of the published materials themselves. Initially the meeting received a broad but selective and in some ways superficial treatment from the press.[40] Two years later, however, the "Science"

40. *Pravda* reported the convocation and carried an abstract of Ponomarev's address. ("Vsesoiuznoe soveshchanie istorikov," *Pravda*, December 19, 1962, p. 4.) There were accounts of varying length in historical journals and in *Izvestiia* and *Kommunist*, summarizing the remarks of some of the speakers and presenting the full text of Ponomarev's speech and the resolution passed by the conference. See B. Ponomarev, "Istoricheskuiu nauku i obrazovanie — na uroven zadach kommunisticheskogo stroitelstva," *Kommunist*, no. 1 (1963), pp. 10–35; "Vsesoiuznoe soveshchanie istorikov," *Voprosy istorii*, no. 2 (1963), pp. 3–75; B. N. Ponomarev, "Zadachi istoricheskoi nauki i podgotovka nauchno-pedagogicheskikh kadrov v oblasti istorii," *Voprosy istorii*, no. 1 (1963), pp. 3–35; "Vsesoiuznoe soveshchanie istorikov," *Istoriia SSSR*, no. 1

Publishing House brought out the "abbreviated stenogram" of the meetings.[41] The following analysis of the historians' conference is based on this volume, which runs to 511 pages. There are significant differences between the more complete record and that designed for public and party functionaries' consumption in the press. The stenographic record, even as edited, brings the discussion to life; and issues become visible that were hidden in bland reportage. The carefully fostered impression of unanimity now vanishes. And the two treatments relate to the audiences to which they were directed. The stenographic record was put out in an edition of 5,000 copies — which compares favorably with that of most scholarly monographs in history and which could be expected to reach all the serious and advanced historians (and only them). It must be remembered that such a readership is markedly more selective than that of even the smallest and most erudite of the historical journals, *Voprosy istorii*, which was in 1964 being published in an edition of approximately 13,800. Thus, for purposes of my argument, the journal reports of the conference can be taken to have a mass audience and the stenogram to have a select one.

Within the context of the proceedings themselves, there was another striking polarization of approach to the perceived problems of Soviet historiography, which can be roughly characterized as liberal-conservative. But there was also a surprising amount of fragmentation of attitude. After 1955, concomitant with a general commitment to better scholarship, greater diversification had developed among historians as to the purposes, methodology, focus, and scope of such research. This whole situation was displayed in microcosm at the 1962 conference of historians. A summation of the discussions here would be neither possible nor useful; but an attempt will be made to examine the condition of party history as seen by the participants, to point to the main lines of argument represented by different groups of Soviet historians, and finally to determine whether there was any professional group consciousness among the participating historians.

(1963), pp. I–VII; "Vsesoiuznoe soveshchanie istorikov," *Istoriia SSSR*, no. 2 (1963), pp. 214–219; Ie. Popova and Iu. Sharapov, "Posle bolshogo soveta," *Izvestiia*, March 3, 1964, p. 5.
41. *Vsesoiuznoe soveshchanie o merakh uluchsheniia podgotovki nauchno-pedagogicheskikh kadrov po istoricheskim naukam* (Moscow: "Science" Publishing House, 1964).

If we proceed to the question of the state of party history, Pospelov's speech (published only in the 1964 volume) is a remarkable document. The first half of the report — subtitled "Liquidation of the Consequences of the Personality Cult and Raising the Level of Research on Party History" — was essentially an amplification with respect to party history of Ponomarev's more general remarks. Briefly, the common themes were the need for vigilance to eradicate continuing distortions of Stalin's role and for further research into Stalin's mistaken ideas and practices,[42] for collective research and writing, for better coordination — led by the Institute of Marxism-Leninism — among historians working on related subjects to avoid duplication of effort, for greater concern by writers and journals to demolish Western falsifications of party history, for better planning — by the Ministry of Higher and Specialized Secondary Education, Gosplan, the Central Statistical Administration, in particular — to discover the number of historians needed in the near future, and, overarching all of these preoccupations, the shortage of qualified historians.

Part two of Pospelov's remarks is of more interest to us. In the process of arguing for improvements in the training of historians of the party, Pospelov lays bare the abysmal academic level of this subdiscipline. He begins on a brave note, asserting that the proportion of teachers of Party history possessing academic degrees has risen from 48.6 percent in 1956 to 52 percent in 1962. After these opening remarks the tone of the report immediately darkens, as he begins to decry these cadres as hopelessly inadequate to the tasks, and the remainder of his speech is devoted to exposing the shortage and shoddy preparation of historians specializing in the CPSU. In the course of his remarks he provides much information otherwise unattainable by the external observer but presumably well known to his audience.

Pospelov sees a fundamental handicap in the failure of state planning organs to subdivide their general category "history" into "history of the USSR," "history of the CPSU," "world history," and so forth. However, he calculates on the basis of figures of the Ministry of Higher and Secondary Specialized Education

42. Pospelov specified the periods 1908–1909, the spring of 1917, at the time of the Sixth Party Congress, and October 1917 — with respect to Stalin's relationship to Kamenev and Zinoviev. *Ibid.*, p. 201.

that during the five years from 1957 to 1962 only 422 aspirants in history of the CPSU were produced. Not only does party history lag in total number of specialists being trained, it is at a competitive disadvantage vis-à-vis other historical disciplines in attracting and keeping students; this debility is more pronounced in the provincial universities, and of course it is self-perpetuating. Other problems common to Soviet academic history as a whole become more pronounced, or acute, in the case of party history, Pospelov says. If in history generally not more than 10 percent to 12 percent of the dissertations are successfully completed and defended, the number is still lower in party history; dissertation topics are more difficult to select and more frequently changed; many advisers cannot and do not help their charges because they themselves do not carry on any research and are unfamiliar with the problems their students face.

This brings Pospelov to his major recommendations, which are slipped in almost casually. He traces the small numbers, enormous dropout rate, and academic inadequacies of the aspirants in party history to the fact that they have not had the specialized preparation that students in other disciplines have received on the undergraduate level.

History of the CPSU is now the only science the cadres of which are composed as a rule of people who have not specialized in their field of knowledge at the university level . . . Only two of all the universities— Moscow and Kiev — provide specialization in history of the CPSU, with a total number of not more than 100 students.[43]

Even more surprising is his remark that until as recently as seven or eight years ago the training of these two universities was duplicated at a number of others, including Leningrad University. A discussant at this session, P. R. Sheverdalkin of Leningrad University, recounted that until 1953 the university had such a department but that "then it, for reasons unknown to us, was closed. For three years we tried to reopen it and only in the past year have we received permission for students in the

43. *Ibid.*, p. 215. This dismal picture should not, however, blind us to the enormous improvement after Stalin's death. Another speaker noted that data of the Higher Attestation Commission show that during the fifteen years following publication of the *Short Course* in 1938, by contrast, only one doctoral dissertation was completed in the Soviet Union on party history (p. 242).

history faculty to specialize in history of the CPSU."[44] This seems strange at first glance, because the Twentieth Party Congress — which took place six years before — was designed in large part to open up and rejuvenate the study of party history. What caused the opposite effect? Probably the increased scope for interpretation and pressures for better scholarship, given the generally low level of academic training of party historians, proved frightening to most of them. Only a few historians with this specialty could respond to the new challenges, and university administrations perhaps found the best solution to be curtailment of courses in this field. Sheverdalkin's remarks hint at another factor in this development: the scorn and resentment felt by academically trained and oriented historians toward departments of party history whose members were usually not scholars, and the sudden opportunity for those traditional historians to get rid of the parvenues during the confusion after Stalin's death.

Pospelov's solutions go to the issues of insufficient numbers and poor training.[45] The recorded remarks of the discussants of his speech reveal general agreement. Ponomarev had quoted Khrushchev at the March 1962 Central Committee plenum:

In the interests of science it is necessary to strengthen control over the subjects of scientific research for candidates' and doctoral dissertations. We have opened wide the doors of science for able people. Along with this we must close the door to hack work, to dull, useless research. Such control we do not now have. This requires raising the level of scientific research.[46]

44. *Ibid.*, p. 235.
45. First, the Ministry of Higher and Secondary Specialized Education together with the planning agencies must raise the quota of young specialists being prepared in party history in universities, allocate the necessary resources to this end, and create separate departments where needed. The ministry's recent decision to make one of the four required fields of preparation for candidate status in history of the CPSU — history of the USSR (nineteenth and twentieth centuries) — a related rather than mandatory discipline does not satisfy Pospelov. He argues that even with this reduction in the number of examinations, an insufficient period of only about a year and a half remains for the completion of a dissertation. The solution is to formalize the practice in use at a number of universities of accepting into aspirant status students who have already partially completed the candidate's minimum requirements. With the time gained, the standards of knowledge of the classics of Marxism-Leninism, of foreign languages, and of international workers' and communist movements can and should be raised.
46. B. Ponomarev, "Istoricheskuiu nauku i obrazovanie — na uroven zadach kommunisticheskogo stroitelstva," *Kommunist*, no. 1 (1963), p. 31.

The division of opinion among the participants at this conference thus revolved around possible means toward an agreed end. But, although set in this more modest context, some of the discussions were so penetrating as to involve basic goals and to blur the somewhat artificial distinction between ends and means.

The statements of Pospelov and the other participants in the Section on History of the CPSU can be seen as forming two conceptual clusters or poles, which may be referred to as scholarly vis-à-vis administrative solutions. The latter cluster compromises suggestions granting priority to efficiency and control: the concern with lagging production of both researchers and studies, insistence upon collective authorship as the best mode of scholarship, an attempt to eliminate duplication of research effort among historians and institutes, emphasis on the crying need for regularization of standards so that all teachers at specified levels should have appropriate academic degrees and institutions involved in similar kinds of research should fall within the same administrative category with regard to salary scales and the like. Those proposals or preoccupations described as the scholarly cluster include such topics as: an overwhelming concern with the quality of academic training being given advanced students of party history; a special determination that aspirants be granted more time for independent study and for the completion of a dissertation that actually constitutes a contribution to the body of general scholarship; insistence upon more complete, sophisticated, and honest use of archival materials and upon required university courses in the use of sources; pressure for more opportunity for Soviet historians to keep up with Western work in their fields. These polar positions can be given shorthand definitions according to their respective goals: for some the historian's craft seemed to be the discovery and portrayal of historical *truth* (albeit truth in a Marxist frame, this concern is new and exotic on the Soviet scene), and for others the aim or focus remained on *control*.

The schizophrenic atmosphere of the conference can perhaps be best portrayed by pointing to historians at both poles. At the one extreme, we find a man like B. S. Telpukhovsky, of the Institute of Marxism-Leninism, whose concept of the historian's duty was "to propagandize deeply and continually [the CPSU's] glorious history" and who blandly stated that in the near future coordination councils would be created in the Institute of Marx-ism-Leninism.[47] The argument of A. K. Pankseev, of the Institute of Party History under the Estonian Central Committee, is also interesting. He advocated a uniform official line on troublesome historical questions in order to combat bourgeois falsifiers (spe-cifically of Baltic history) and to attract the emigrés in Switzer-land and elsewhere.[48] Finally, there was V. S. Zaitsev's speech, which is an outstanding example of faithful conformity to the superficial and political aspects of Khrushchev's reformist policy in tandem with a very unreformed concept of what party history is all about. In general he tried to support the official demand for more archival research. But the rationale Zaitsev offered for improved scholarship was the historians' duty to further expose Stalin. He then defended Khrushchev's opening of the archives by railing against Molotov and Kaganovich, who allegedly defended the *Short Course* at a 1956 Presidium meeting, op-posed the new party history text, and protested the authors' access to party documents. Zaitsev also provided an unintended illustration of historical revision in the service of the political leadership by contending that there was opposition to Stalin in the early 1930s from within party ranks: three Old Bolsheviks who formed a group to withstand the Stalin cult in 1933, two of whom were later shot.[49] In addition to these remarks, there were numerous references throughout the session to unidentified historians who pined for the period of the cult, who continued to write in those terms despite numerous criticisms.

At the other pole were participants who, though their requests were not included directly in the transcript, according to Pos-pelov "raised the question of whether it would be possible to give to researchers in the party archives broad access to all un-published party documents and materials." It is truly remarkable that such a proposal was openly entertained, since it in effect demanded the end of party control over the writing of party his-tory. Pospelov's reply was direct and to the point:

Such a proposal cannot be supported. The Party archive is not the property of one or another researcher or even of the Insti-tute of Marxism-Leninism under the Central Committee, CPSU, or of comrades who work in the archive. The Party archive is

47. *Vsesoiuznoe soveshchanie*, p. 277.
48. *Ibid.*, p. 254.
49. *Ibid.*, pp. 289–291.

the property of our Party and only the Central Committee can be in charge of it.[50]

One of the most devastating comments on the condition of Soviet historiography from a scholarly perspective was presented in the Session on History of the USSR.[51] Because it was unusually sharp in tone and because the speaker was E. N. Burdzhalov, it deserves mention here. Obviously, Burdzhalov's being a recognized discussant after his long public silence and the inclusion of his remarks in the edited record are significant in themselves. Moreover, the stenogram indicates that no rebuttal or reproof was offered Burdzhalov at any point in the conference. This bespeaks a more sophisticated, secure, and mature atmosphere among historians as well as the unwillingness of the party leadership to continue the vendetta against him. The reappearance of Burdzhalov also indicates that he was never completely disgraced or even removed to the provinces: he was now listed as attached to the V. I. Lenin Pedagogical Institute in Moscow. It is clear that Burdzhalov had not changed his analysis of Stalin and other leaders of the party in 1917 for which he was fired from *Voprosy istorii*. His remarks provide a number of examples of distortions (including some committed by his old enemies Bugaev and Sidorov) and suppression of documents unfavorable to Stalin after 1956 and even since the Twenty-Second Congress. Unlike other speakers, he refused to utter the usual formula that much progress had been made in overcoming the cult, although some errors persist. Burdzhalov still perceived the situation to be very grave.

Assuming this duality of thrust, can these ideas be meaningfully associated with individuals of any certain categories, groups, or institutions? Obviously the very limited number of historians represented in this discussion requires that any identifications of this type be inferential examples rather than definitive samples capable of generalization. Still, the model of polarization and fragmentation of opinion is congruent with most of the other adduced evidence. Let us, then, see what it shows.

Of the thirty recorded discussants at the Section on History of the CPSU, twelve were identified as having academic — university or Academy of Sciences — affiliation; six were historians

50. *Ibid.*, p. 296.
51. *Ibid.*, pp. 367–370.

associated with institutions of the party, such as the Institute of Marxism-Leninism, various institutes of party history, and *Voprosy istorii KPSS*; four were historians attached to technical institutes or schools; five were Old Bolsheviks. The picture is complicated somewhat by the fact that P. E. Yemelianov, who was listed as at the Moscow Institute of Chemical Machine Construction, was chiefly preoccupied with the Moscow city party organization and its experiences in planning and coordinating the research of teachers of party history at higher educational institutions in Moscow. For purposes of analysis, I shall treat his party affiliation as primary. This case of dual professional and political identity is, of course, only a more extreme form of a ubiquitous condition among Soviet historians of the party, virtually all of whom are closely linked with party activities. This instance has been treated specially simply because the historian himself overtly chose to speak from the platform of party association rather than that of academician. The attempt is made in all cases to work within the discussant's own frame of reference for purposes of classification.[52]

The scheme is further complicated by the presence of three historians who were not identified. One, however, A. Nosov, was referred to by another speaker as being associated with Moscow University. The second, V. S. Zaitsev, is known to be a candidate of historical sciences and one of the editors of *History of the Communist Party of the Soviet Union*; he might well be a member of the staff of the Institute of Marxism-Leninism.

If the initial classification is modified to accommodate Yemelianov, Nosov, and Zaitsev, the pattern of associations as shown in Table 3 emerges. The question then becomes one of discovering whether there are any patterns of personal-ideational relationships here. It might be expected that the academics and possibly the technicals would comprise the scholarly pole, whereas the party and the Old Bolsheviks (because of their less than scholarly background and long experience as party functionaries) would compromise the administrative pole. In fact,

52. It is interesting that Yemelianov was identified in his capacity of party functionary in the lengthy report on the conference in *Voprosy istorii* ("Vsesoiuznoe soveshchanie istorikov," *Voprosy istorii*, no. 2 [1963], p. 37). There he was described as president of the Section on History of the CPSU of the Commission for Coordination of Scientific-Research Work under the Moscow City Committee of the party.

Table 3

Academic	13
Technical	3
Party	8
Old Bolshevik	5
Unknown	1

seven academics represent a firm and positive scholarly approach, as defined. The other six academics fall on several points along a spectrum stretching from halfhearted or apparently superficial support for the scholarly position to lack of concern for the problem to strong support for administrative measures. Two professors manage to speak in favor of both points of view; and the most clever of them all — Academician Mints — by insisting on more archival research on a specific and much vexed problem, in effect rejects a very scholarly and carefully documented argument of Lenin's secretary which he finds embarrassing.

Only four of the eight party people come out strongly for coordination and supervision of research by the Institute of Marxism-Leninism, a centrally imposed line for CPSU historiography, and similar proposals. The others make very bland and noncommittal remarks, or — like the chief editor of *Voprosy istorii KPSS* — bury the whole issue in publication plans, or — like Zaitsev — demonstrate in their own comments the reality of centralized authority over sensitive topics without directly advocating it.

Of the three historians with technical affiliation, one is quite clearly in favor of administrative control over historians and their greater "participation in life"; one is concerned only with making historiography more oriented to the details of technology; and the third demands simultaneously more truth and better propaganda in history.

The Old Bolsheviks prove the most interesting both in terms of the substance of their remarks and in the underlying spirit or goals. They were the revisionists of the conference, and the total impact of their speeches is electrifying. Unlike the other groups, the Old Bolsheviks are not split between the two poles of my model but are unanimous in support of the scholarly position. The differences among them are of form rather than substance — that is, although two address themselves to a certain historical development or figure (Kokovikhin is concerned with the nature of local party organizations and their membership in 1905, Kravchenko is outraged at the historical obliteration of Krupskaia), the other three elevate their demand for particular truths into a general and more theoretical argument for historical veracity and honest methods of scholarship.

Iu. K. Milonov opens this more general attack by advancing M. S. Olminsky-Alexandrov rather than Lenin as the father of party history. Snegov's speech is even more forceful: "An honorable relationship to documents, honest Party sources are the chief safeguard . . . against distortion and falsification." "Each of us" historians, he insists, bears the burden of the Stalin cult, but the party has forgiven historians for writing lies during that dark period. As far as Snegov is concerned, greater guilt is borne by those historians who still persist in the cult; but he is willing to rely on argumentation to correct them — "don't take bayonets to them!"[53]

Although M. V. Fofanova's remarks are much more particularistic, revolving around the question of the exact date on which Lenin returned to Petersburg in the fall of 1917, they deserve to be defined as primarily of a methodological and hence general nature. The basic point at issue between her and Mints is the authentication of documentary sources: Mints stands on the decision of a special meeting of historians supported by the Central Committee, which agreed that October 3 was the earliest possible date; Fofanova contends that other documents prove an earlier date, even if they were not "official Party documents." In other words, she maintains that a historical problem cannot be settled by administrative fiat, even if arrived at by vote of the leading specialists.[54]

Thus we are faced with a complex pattern of attitudes at the all-union conference: only half of the academic and party people can be found at their expected poles, with their brethren badly split; the technicals are completely split; only the Old Bolsheviks are consistent. The chief point of this exercise is to offer further substantiation for one of the arguments of this book, that attitudes among Soviet historians are no longer easily explainable

53. *Vsesoiuznoe soveshchanie*, pp. 272, 275.
54. This controversy will be discussed further in Chapter Seven.

or predictable from such simplistic classification devices as party job, or institutional affiliation, or career background, or even age. Some observers have felt youth to be a general mark of liberalism or revisionism; but the Old Bolsheviks' performance here disputes that. Other and more subtle categories are needed if we are to account for the widely disparate attitudes toward the Soviet historiographical enterprise, categories that in their complexity and elusiveness closely resemble those one might construct for a similar study of American or other Western historians. This is not at all to say that Soviet and Western historians live in identical political environments. The periphery of the Soviet historian's professional sphere is still restricted, although not with the rigidity of the Stalin period, and this creates unique problems of method and interpretation for him. Nonetheless, insofar as he now has some uncertainty and choices within that circumference, his experience becomes analogous to that of historians in less controlled systems.

On the basis of expressed principles and opinions at this conference, then, it is possible to construct some more meaningful categories with regard to Soviet historians, which might point toward a model of behavior and approach. The total known life and professional experience of the historian would have to be sifted for attitudinal clues; some attempt at psychological observation would have to be made. As an example of what might be attempted, one thinks of the insightful comparative study by Leopold Haimson, which portrayed the unique concepts, styles, and psychological orientations of Old Bolsheviks, the Stalinist middle-aged, and the post-Stalin young intellectuals.[55] Haimson characterized the Old Bolsheviks as "remarkably unchanged" by the Stalinist experience, possessed of an inner resilience and hopefulness and true to older Russian and European intellectual traditions. I might add that the special burden of horror and sacrifice suffered by this earliest generation and the torment of their ideals have given them a hatred of Stalin which goes beyond that of younger members of the society.

Relative dependence upon institutional support and association should be determined: perhaps older age and retirement can act as a liberating factor to permit greater independence and eccentricity, as does a large private income in capitalist countries. The

55. Leopold H. Haimson, "Three Generations of the Soviet Intelligentsia," *Foreign Affairs*, January 1959, pp. 235–246.

type and quality, as well as quantity, of education (whether technical, scientical, or humanistic) would certainly be relevant. The factor of talent is extremely important: is this historian really good, is he respected in his special field by his peers, does he have popular acclaim as well as quiet self-confidence; or is he a bit belligerent and unsure because he fears himself inadequate as a scholar? A look at the discussants from this angle is interesting because it does tend to confirm the hypothesis that those who can be seen to have higher professional status as historians — in terms of appointment at more prestigious institutions, more pub- lications, and the like — were in general those who spoke out more courageously for the scholarly viewpoint. On the larger scene, we have seen evidence that association with a leading insti- tution such as Moscow University provides a significant degree of insulation from the official pressure on historians to denigrate Stalin; several discussants pointed to the persistence of the Stalin cult among professors at Moscow University. Unfortunately, the matter of personal rivalry — whether originating in a tempera- mental disagreement or arising out of a scholarly difference — cannot be ignored as a purposeful force in ostensibly theoretical or academic arguments. For example, when I. S. Smirnov of the Institute of History, who takes a strongly scholarly position, cites two works as illustrations of the tenacity of the Stalin cult and specifically identifies them as produced by historians at Moscow University, is his motivation one of personal enmity against the individuals involved or of rivalry between the institute and the university's history faculty, or is Smirnov simply outraged at the books and attempting to warn others?

Finally, the capital-provincial distinction is useful in this con- text, since it seems often to work in tandem with the factor of professional talent to create a syndrome. At the conference, for example, some of the most vociferous arguments for administra- tive control over erring or adventuresome historians came from provincial figures who were patently afraid of new scholarly methods and standards they had not the ability or training to apply. The provincials represented were also noticeably slower to absorb de-Stalinization and more resistant to the new official en- couragement of historical scholarship. This is a matter requiring caution, since it is obviously impossible to impute the original causes of the recalcitrance observed among many historians from outlying areas: it may spring from the retarding effect of distance upon communication of ideas as distinct from directives, or from a generally less talented and thus more insecure and rigid body of people, or it may simply reflect the cautious self-protective reaction of those who feel themselves far removed from the centers where policy and style are set and who are trying to hedge against future reversals.

Before leaving the topic of the dualistic and yet fragmented nature of the all-union conference, I should emphasize that dualism existed on the internal or psychological level as well. Again it is apparent that the remarks of various historians at this meeting substantiate suggestions in other published materials. Many of the discussants quite obviously were somewhat confused; some apparently did not sense the full implication of their own liberal recommendations and made arguments on other matters that were in fact contradictory; a few attempted quite knowingly to maintain both the administrative and the scholarly position.

Pospelov emerges as such a dualistic, transitional figure par excellence. Here is an Old Bolshevik, who received his first academic degree from Moscow Agricultural Academy in 1916 and joined the party in the same year, who climbed the Agitprop ladder and was elected a member of the Central Committee in 1939, who became an historian only in 1944 by virtue of appointment as Professor of Party History at the Higher Party School. Under Khrushchev he became increasingly prominent and in 1961 was made director of the Institute of Marxism-Leninism. Simultaneously with the subject conference he went on the editorial board of *Voprosy istorii KPSS*,[56] and in 1963 he became a member of the bureau of the Section on Historical Sciences of the Academy of Sciences. Ostensibly he is only enunciating the official encouragement of better scholarship, and yet at many points in his speech one senses that he is going beyond an instrumental demand to a primary concern and identification with the historical profession: he insists on earlier and better specialized training and the kind of academic standards and profesional pride which he not only never received but was taught to disparage. Still he is quite certain that the CPSU must retain control of the archives. In short, Pospelov exemplifies many historians who had been caught between sincerely held but conflicting loyalties. And the leadership's policy was both cause and effect of this personal dualism.

56. His name first appears in the opening issue of 1963.

My third task is to attempt some appraisal of the strength, basis, and content of group feeling or professional identification among the two thousand Soviet historians present at the all-union conference. I have pointed to other indications of such a development, and the resolution adopted at the conference provides some further evidence; but the conclusions offered here must remain tentative. First of all, the resolution again displays the same uneasy coexistence of goals which permeated the discussions. Passages that could adorn propaganda tracts are jumbled together with recommendations to raise standards of academic training and the like. But it is easily seen that the propagandistic remarks form only a small proportion of the entire resolution and that they most certainly do not represent the main objective. Moreover, the thrust of the language is toward group goals rather than individual purposes: there hangs in the air throughout the whole conference the historians' sense of shame at their own distortion of history and betrayal of truth under Stalin and a determination to regain self-respect and public esteem. This goes well beyond the leadership's quite instrumental policy of encouraging more convincing historiography, to the point of becoming a genuine group dynamic.

The resolution demands from various state and party agencies all manner of resources — personnel, funds, access to archives, publications, planning and coordinating facilities — which are needed to do a better job of historical research and teaching. Specifically, the historians of the CPSU ask for more contact between specialists on the party and those working on the USSR; they request a unified scholarly council in the Institute of Marxism-Leninism on problems of party-Soviet history to encompass these and other related fields. In this way the historians of the party are attempting finally to break out of the isolation that the *Short Course* imposed upon them, to take on the higher standards and thereby acquire the greater academic respectability of other historians of the modern period.

In all of this there is the implicit recognition that historians do have a group identity, common needs and goals distinct from those of propagandists, teachers, or other social scientists. The 1962 conference was an important step in the gradual development of a rudimentary group feeling out of a common sense of shame and guilt.

In contrast to the wealth of historical debate and publication that characterized the previous year, 1963 was one of relative quiet. During the course of the year following the Central Committee resolution "On the Journal 'Voprosy istorii KPSS' " published in late 1962, thousands of teachers, researchers, and propagandists attended over forty readers' conferences held by the editorial board in various cities.[1] Historical journal articles for the most part reflected and responded to problems and arguments developed earlier. Clearly, a good deal of effort was being expended to fulfill the demands of the 1962 Central Committee decree on measures to improve the training of specialists, which had been amplified at the All-Union Conference of Historians in December: much of the published discussion concerned methods of raising scholarly standards. Also, there is evidence that the departments of history at Moscow University were subject to considerable attention because of the charges of crypto-Stalinism leveled at a number of university historians at the conference.[2] A flurry of reorganization surrounded the Academy of Sciences and its Institute of History.[3]

The debate over *One Day* and other works continued to be pressed in literary journals during 1963. Until early in the year it had remained exclusively within the format of literary criticism, but now an interesting variation appeared: new fiction designed to rewrite the historical record presented by Solzhenitsyn. As might be expected, the revisionary concentration-camp literature appeared principally in *Zvezda* and *Oktiabr*. The initial story rejected Solzhenitsyn's interpretation of Siberian camp life as brutalizing its victims and extolled the bravery and humanity of many imprisoned communists, who were pictured as unbroken.[4] It was favorably reviewed in *Oktiabr*;[5] and at about the

1. "Bolshoi razgovor s chitateliami," *Voprosy istorii KPSS*, no. 2 (1964), p. 153.
2. For example, a conference on problems of historiography was held in the history faculty of Moscow University in late January. The accounts stressed that the meeting dealt largely with sources, methodology, and analysis. Ie. E. Belina, "Istoriographicheskaia konferentsiia v MGU," *Istoriia SSSR*, no. 4 (1963), pp. 217–220; and V. S. Shulgin, "Istoriograficheskaia konferentsiia v Moskovskom Universitete," *Voprosy istorii*, no. 7 (1963), pp. 117–119.
3. *Spravochnik partiinogo rabotnika*, 5th ed. (1964), pp. 230–235; "Vse sily nauki — stroitelstvu kommunizma," *Pravda*, May 17, 1963, p. 2; "Osnovnye sily nauki — na glavnye napravleniia," *Pravda*, July 5, 1963, p. 4; "Institut istorii AN SSSR v 1963 godu," *Istoriia SSSR*, no. 1 (1964), p. 216.
4. Boris Diakov, "Perezhitoe," *Zvezda*, no. 3 (1963), pp. 177–196.
5. N. Sergovantsev, "Nesgibaemye dukhom," *Oktiabr*, no. 10 (1963), pp. 212–215.

6 DEPERSONALIZING THE DEPERSONALIZER, 1963–1966

same time another account — this time presenting a true case of camp heroism by an unjustly imprisoned plant selectionist — was published in *Kazakhstanskaia pravda.*[6] This latter story about the biologist, who was identified as a disciple of Michurin, was obviously part of the controversy swirling around Lysenko; but it also should be seen as in the same vein as the Diakov story, providing an argument for the ability of a proud and strong human being to turn injustice and tragedy into a positive social contribution. Thus we have not only historiography by fiction but the fictionalized revision of historical truth, both versions representing and presumably encouraged by political factions within the party leadership.

The End of the Khrushchev Decade

An unusual item in the February 7, 1963, *Izvestiia* deserves notice: the piece entitled "Colonel Starinov's Secret," which was actually an inflated anecdote recounting Khrushchev's modest bravery in 1941. According to this story, despite Colonel Starinov's request that he evacuate his Kharkov headquarters, Khrushchev continued his work for several days while a system of booby-traps was laid in advance of the expected German occupation.[7] This flattery is striking for its blatancy: in all probability the story was greatly exaggerated or completely fictional. However, the *Izvestiia* story did not generate more such historico-mythical literature.

Khrushchev's seventieth birthday was celebrated on April 17, 1964, with great fanfare; and he was awarded the Order of Lenin and the Gold Star. Another incursion into Khrushchev's historical image within the fictional context occurred at about this time. A novel published by *Oktiabr* and favorably reviewed by the conservative critic Dymshits in *Izvestiia* portrayed Khrushchev in the guise of an enlightened but downtrodden party leader during the latter years of Stalin's rule.[8]

This kind of spasmodic and minor tampering with history to create niches for Khrushchev has the flavor more of separate perceptions by various historians of what was now appropriate than

6. "My ostavalis liudmi," *Kazakhstanskaia pravda,* October 6, 1963, p. 4.
7. O. Gorchakov, "Taina polkovinka Starinova," *Izvestiia,* February 7, 1963, p. 4.
8. Nikolai Sizov, "Trudnye gody," *Oktiabr,* no. 3 (1964), pp. 3–79, and no. 4, pp. 33–118; and A. Dymshits, "Roman o trudnykh godakh," *Izvestiia,* May 10, 1964, p. 6.

of a centralized campaign to build up the leader's image. Laudatory references were not uncommon, but they were almost invariably isolated statements obviously inserted into the flow of
the historical narrative. Thus, when the time came, it was relatively easy to erase Khrushchev as a historical figure, by omitting
the few passages that featured his exploits and giving credit to
others in the one-volume *History of the Communist Party of the
Soviet Union.*

A more difficult problem apparently arose with respect to a
motion picture that seems to have been designed to eulogize
Khrushchev but that, owing to the lengthy production process
of films, was ready for distribution only in late 1964. We are left
to puzzle over its appearance at all: Was it deemed too great a
financial loss to suppress it, or did "The Chairman" simply wend
its way through the bureaucratic maze and into the public view
without discussion? Or was it a parting gift, a last argument for
Khrushchev's leadership, by some of his supporters? At any rate,
the critics — and, we may assume, the public — saw the hero as
a likeness of Khrushchev.

The most forthright criticism of the movie appeared in December in *Komsomolskaia pravda.*[9]

Outwardly not very attractive, thickset, stocky, brusque, he leaves
one with the impression of vast inner strength . . . All concern, all
command, a fanatic for work, a man possessed! . . . [He is] scrupu-
lously upright, selflessly working for a better life for farmers, but
crude . . . Before us is a chairman, a leader, who sees himself as
a commander . . . in the sense that he knows only one way of
addressing subordinates — by command.

Most interesting to us is the critic's attempt to place Khrushchev
in historical perspective, to examine this model of leadership
in the context of the conditions of his day. In doing so, he rejects
what was apparently a familiar argument from historical inevitability in defense of Khrushchev's style:

It will be said that the circumstances of the times demanded just
this sort of iron-willed, ruthless, masterful leadership. [But it is
more accurate to say] that the difficult circumstances gave rise to
this type of leader. Whether he was best even then is open to
question. Is he today? Of course not. After all, this is the leader
who decides for all, he alone . . . He gives orders and interferes
in literally everything.

9. M. Kuznetsov, "Pobedy i porazheniia Egora Trubnikova," *Komsomolskaia
pravda,* December 12, 1964, p. 3.

We may note in passing that this repudiation of the Khrushchev type was answered the following month by a favorable review in *Izvestiia,* which pointed out that the hero's shortcomings were merely an extension of his virtues: it was his love for the people, rather than heartlessness, which prompted his severe demands on them.[10] Moreover, the film's leading actor received a Lenin Prize for that role.[11]

The essence of this whole discussion is the fact that in party history — as in related spheres of Soviet policymaking — the most fundamental of Khrushchev's innovations were allowed to stand after his ouster,[12] even though the style and form of their appearance or their organizational trappings were denounced and discarded. Khrushchev's rewriting with respect to Stalin and the antiparty group, his encouragement of more frank historiography on collectivization, the purges, and the concentration camps, were not reversed. But Khrushchev's inimitable bombast and some of his hobbyhorses vanished overnight from historiography in October 1964.

Probably the most convenient approach to an analysis of the extent and nature of historical revision following upon Khrushchev's retirement consists of a comparison of two versions of the introduction to the new six-volume *History of the Communist Party of the Soviet Union. Pravda* serialized this introduction to volume one (which covers the years 1883 to 1903) on September 21–23, 1964, in what was ostensibly final form. The introduction as printed in *Pravda* was featured in the earliest printing of volume one, which was sent to press on August 27, 1964, in an edition of 220,000 copies. At that point it was noted that copies 1 through 100,000 were being put out. This first printing was recalled from circulation within the Soviet Union (although at least one copy has been preserved in the United States) and replaced by a second printing of copies 100,001 through 235,000, which was sent to press on October 20, 1964.

10. Ie. Surkov, "Yegor Trubnikov i ego vremia," *Izvestiia,* January 23, 1965, p. 3.
11. *Pravda,* April 22, 1966, p. 1.
12. "Revoliutsionnaia teoriia osveshchaet nash put," *Pravda,* November 5, 1964, p. 2, reiterated the correctness of the Twentieth, Twenty-First, and Twenty-Second Party Congresses; the article "Edinstvo, aktivnost, delovitost," *Partiinaia zhizn,* no. 2 (1965), pp. 8–16, upheld the general line of the Twentieth and Twenty-Second Congresses.

This second printing is interesting on several counts: it enlarged the edition by 15,000 copies; the title page, ostensibly identical with that of the first printing, dropped P. A. Satiukov from the editorial board of the multivolume series; and the introduction was revised.[13] At no point was this revision indicated, and considerable editorial effort was evidently expended to obscure the fact that the new printing was anything more than a release of more copies. Thus the format is identical, and in both printings the flyleaf reads simply "Moscow: 1964." The post-Khrushchev changes, though not fundamental, were certainly noticeable: there is no other plausible explanation for the revisions than the removal of Khrushchev.

The most obvious difference is the absence of the personal references to Khrushchev in the later version. Beyond the reappraisal of Khrushchev as a historical figure, the revised introduction no longer betrayed his uniquely individual interpretive stamp. The bombastic and vicious sections dealing with the Left Essars and Mensheviks were omitted or replaced by less violent comments.[14] The concluding pages of the introduction no longer contained a number of very truculent passages that denounced the Chinese schismatics. Khrushchev's dramatic characterization and detailed description of the latter Stalin years were also missing from the final introduction, replaced by abbreviated general phrases. And at a still more general and analytical level, the final version deleted Khrushchev's bid for recognition as a theortical historian: the scheme of "three world-historic stages" of the working class and its party, which he had put forward in his concluding remarks to the Twenty-Second Party Congress.[15]

Thus the historiographical aspects of Khrushchev's denigration were pale renditions of a political event that had been purposely drained of as much drama and sensation as possible. Aside from the removal of the figure of Khrushchev from the historical narrative of the party, which was indeed not a difficult task, the post-Khrushchev revisions were of style and emphasis rather than of substance.

13. *Istoriia Kommunisticheskoi partii sovetskogo soiuza*, I, "Formation of the Bolshevik Party, 1883–1903," ed. P. N. Pospelov (Moscow: Institute of Marxism-Leninism under the Central Committee, Political Literature Publishing House, 1964), pp. v–liv.
14. *Ibid.*, pp. xxi, xxii, xxiv, xxv, xxvii.
15. See Chapter Four above.

Methods and Memoirs

The chief preoccupation during 1964 among Soviet historians was the problem of methodology, which was officially formulated in 1963 in terms of ideology and which came gradually during 1965 and 1966 to involve a debate over the nature and significance of facts, the definition and merits of historical truth as against myth. Various questions of a methodological cast had been raised after 1956 by virtue of the wealth of documents newly available to historians and the modern techniques of research being imported from the West. But it was only in 1964 that a fully self-conscious and explicit discussion began. Significantly, it took place not within the confines of the discipline but in the larger context of the social sciences — and historians of the CPSU, except for Mints and Pospelov, were conspicuous by their nonparticipation.

The discussion opened on an interdisciplinary and semiofficial level in early January 1964, with a meeting of the Section on Social Sciences of the Presidium of the Academy of Sciences, which discussed the report of Academician P. N. Fedoseev (philosopher) and Member-Correspondent Iu. P. Frantsev (social scientist).[16] The Fedoseev-Frantsev report raised a storm during the meeting because, in seeking to establish better methods and categories of research, it actually erected a new philosophical framework for historiography in relation to other social sciences. Fedoseev and Frantsev defined the functions of history as, first, to create "an understanding of historical experience [that] provides a real possibility of developing sound policies of the party" and "second [to supply] the means of a communist education of the masses."[17]

At this point something new enters as the authors develop a revised hierarchy and relationship for the social sciences. It is precisely this aspect that becomes the focus of discussion among the participants (who divide almost evenly for and against) and sparks a train of scholarly articles. Briefly, the revisionists are concerned with the problem of the relationship of history to sociology, which has been emerging from the Stalinist outer darkness of neglect and opprobrium. The renewed official sponsorship of sociological studies directly coincides with the debate among his-

16. For the text of the Fedoseev-Frantsev report and the resolution, as well as a condensed record of the discussion, see "O metodologicheskikh voprosakh istoricheskoi nauki," *Voprosy istorii*, no. 3 (1964), pp. 3–68.
17. *Ibid.*, pp. 17, 18.

torians over introduction of sociological techniques of research.[18] It is perhaps not irrelevant that a year later an article in *Pravda* recommended establishment of a separate discipline of political science to evaluate reorganizations, analyze programs such as the virgin-lands project, and so forth.[19] This proposal has not been seriously followed up, however. What Fedoseev and Frantsev suggest is that sociology take on the task of discovering universal laws and release historians to study their particularistic manifestations — which, of course, would require very different methods of study.[20] "Analysis of the laws operative in all or almost all social formations is for the most part a matter for the sociologists. History studies these laws not only within the framework of a given formation, but within the framework of specific historical epochs."[21] The historian should not merely state historical laws and use historical evidence as illustration. He is obliged "to use not only historical documents, but also to adopt the method of concrete social research. This is the study of statistical data, the carrying on of investigations, use of questionnaires, organization of surveys, etc."[22]

Proceeding from this base, the revisionists among the historians developed arguments in several directions over the next few years. These methodological formulations took the form of definitions of history and may briefly be characterized as follows:

(1) History is a science.
(2) History is empirical social science research.
(3) History is a composite form of logic and aesthetics.[23]

18. See F. Konstantinov and V. Kelle, "Istoricheskii materializm — marksistskaia sotsiologiia," *Kommunist*, no. 1 (1965), pp. 9–23; V. Shubkin, "O konkretnykh issledovaniiakh sotsialnykh protsessov," *Kommunist*, no. 3 (1965), pp. 48–57.
19. F. Burlatsky, "Politika i nauka," *Pravda*, January 10, 1965, p. 4.
20. How this division of labor was received by the nascent sociologists does not directly concern us, but they have shown remarkable ability to ignore it in favor of very pragmatic research into what Western social scientists would term industrial sociology and management techniques.
21. "O metodologicheskikh voprosakh," pp. 15–16.
22. *Ibid.*, p. 20.
23. These positions may be traced out by aid of the following: S. D. Skazkin, M. A. Barg, and V. M. Lavrovsky, "Istoriia i sovremennost," *Izvestiia*, September 18, 1962, p. 3; V. M. Lavrovsky, "K voprosu o predmete i metode istorii kak nauki," *Voprosy istorii*, no. 4 (1966), pp. 72–77; E. N. Gorodetsky, "Voprosy metodologii istoricheskogo issledovaniia v posleoktiabrskikh trudakh V. I. Lenina," *ibid.*, no. 6 (1963), pp. 16–34; I. Maisky, M. Nechkina, A. Manfred, and L. Shkarenkov, "Istoricheskii zhurnal i sovremennost," *Kommunist*, no. 4 (1964), pp. 87–93; N. E. Zastenker, "Problemy istoricheskoi nauki v trudakh K.

These versions of the nature of history certainly portray significant trends among Soviet historians. But these concepts have not won the day and are countered by more traditional arguments. It is difficult to support the conclusion of one scholar that the discussion of methodology initiated at the January 1964 meeting of social scientists and continuing over the next two years represents the complete separation of politics from scholarship, the conscious recognition by Soviet society that "scientific socialism" has passed its usefulness and must be discarded as a cumbersome myth.[24] Although many historians and philosophers clearly have rejected the pseudo-science of deterministic historical laws in favor of much more complex and fact-oriented analysis, they are not advocating value-free historiography such as they perceive in the West. A good example of this commitment to Marxism-Leninism as a basic ordering principle — on the part of an historian who has shown himself to be a good scholar rather than a polemicist — is the rebuttal of Academician Druzhinin to his fellow student of the nineteenth century, Franco Venturi:

I regard as unjustified your contrasting of facts to theories, and the individual to schema. Facts cannot be gathered, critically verified and combined by an internal connection if the historian does not have an overall point of view with respect to the criteria of selection, criticism, and causal explanation of historical phenomena . . . It is precisely such a methodological support that is provided to us by the theory of historical materialism.[25]

A more accurate assessment of the impact of this debate would show how the more venturesome Soviet scholars carved out a considerably more spacious area within which to conduct historical research unencumbered by the need constantly to illustrate vari-

Marksa i F. Engelsa," *Voprosy istorii*, no. 6 (1964), pp. 3–26; O. I. Shkaratan, "Methodologicheskie aspekty izucheniia istorii sovetskogo rabochego klassa," *ibid.*, no. 4, 1966, pp. 3–15; A. Ia. Gurevich, "Obshchii zakon i konkretnaia zakonomernost v istorii," *ibid.*, no. 8 (1965), pp. 14–30; E. M. Staerman, "O povtoriaemosti v istorii," *ibid.*, no. 7 (1965), pp. 3–20; "Nekotorye aspekty izucheniia sotsialnoi istorii," *ibid.*, no. 10 (1964), pp. 51–68; A. V. Gulyga, "O predmete istoricheskoi nauki," *ibid.*, no. 4 (1964), pp. 20–31, and "Poniatie i obraz v istoricheskoi nauke," *ibid.*, no. 9 (1965), pp. 3–14; G. V. Dubov, "Seminar po filosofskim problemam istoricheskoi nauki," *ibid.*, no. 7 (1964), p. 161; L. V. Cherepnin, "Istoricheskie vzgliady Gogolia," *ibid.*, no. 1 (1964), pp. 75–97.
24. Arthur P. Mendel, "The Rise and Fall of 'Scientific Socialism,' " *Foreign Affairs*, October 1966, pp. 98–111.
25. "Akademik N. M. Druzhinin. Otvet Franko Venturi," *Istoriia SSSR*, no. 5 (1964), p. 200.

ous dogmatic stances. They have done this not by denying Marxism-Leninism as their overarching philosophic foundation or by discarding the basic tenets of historical materialism as their guiding methodology: many historians have transferred those doctrinal concerns to a larger and more general sphere, transforming them into universal laws or sociological trends, while maintaining history as within the realm of the particular, regional, and temporal.

The whole argument of the avant-garde in this debate would seem to be a secularizing one, in a certain sense recapitulating the development in Western Europe of the idea of scholarship as distinct from the Church but loyal to its cultural and moral norms. Any such analogy is necessarily complicated, however, by the problem of perspective. One can clearly see movement in a secular direction, but we cannot judge how far along the continuum Soviet historiography has moved; nor can we assume that the end of the process will be the separation of history from politics (a problematic concept in any case) on the model of Western pluralistic systems.

During 1965 there developed a variant of the continuing debate over methodology, which turned on the evaluation of memoirs as historical sources. As on so many occasions, the journal *Novyi mir* was foremost in the innovation itself and the first to articulate the issues raised by such literature. The discussion was opened by Alexander Tvardovsky, in his editorial in honor of the fortieth anniversary of *Novyi mir*.[26] Explaining why his journal had opened its general prose section as well as the specialized "Diaries and Memoirs" department to the flood of memoirs following the Twentieth Congress, Tvardovsky stated his belief that the suppression and falsification of personal testimony during the Stalin era would permanently hamper Soviet historiography. For this reason, it was vital to recoup as many of these losses as possible through contemporary memoirs written under better conditions, even though the manuscripts were often very uneven in value.

He further defended this genre — despite criticism of a number of the memoirs he had published — by pointing to the inadequacy of Soviet historiography: "Undoubtedly, the reader's special attention to the memoir form indirectly expressed a dissatisfaction with professional literature, a desire to supplement it with

26. Alexander Tvardovsky, "Po sluchaiu iubileia," *Novyi mir*, no. 1 (1965), pp. 3–18.

facts it either did not touch upon at all or touched upon super-ficially."[27] From this argument he also justified the utilization of fiction as a kind of historiography and, indeed, a better vehicle for historical truth than historical writing itself.[28]

The historians did not pick up this challenge, and Tvardovsky's opinions were eventually answered on a philosophical and politi-cal rather than literary level. An article in *Izvestiia*, which ex-plicitly replied to Tvardovsky, stressed that there were two forms of truth: the truth of events and the truth of life, which are not necessarily coterminous: "Of course it is true that in the early period of the war there were instances of disorganization, confu-sion and at times even panic . . . This is the truth, but only the truth of events, of fact, and not *the truth of life and of the people's struggle*."[29] The relationship of such a concept of truth to Khrushchev's slighting reference to the mere "arithmetical majority" that tried to unseat him in June 1957 is a close one.

Since the Twentieth Congress the use of memoirs has presented problems for Soviet historians on several levels: evaluation and verification as sources, methodology or techniques of utilization, and ideology.[30] And on a very pragmatic level, memoirs can cause embarrassment. But with the ouster of Khrushchev and the accession of a leadership not personally linked to the Stalin regime, the peril of memoir literature lessens. Not only can Ehren-burg now with impunity depict the deification of Stalin as a systematic process requiring confederates,[31] but it can be said out loud that not all of the influential figures during the dark days of the mid-1930s were silent and cowed.

It is noteworthy, however, that such revisions did not appear in the historical journals. There are two outstanding examples. The first is a piece in the most important legal journal, which after delineating Vyshinsky's illegal prosecutions during the purges, points to an oppositionist circular of the former chairman of the Supreme Court. The authors conclude: "It is essential to empha-size that even in these years there were prosecutors and court

27. *Ibid.*, p. 9.
28. *Ibid.*, pp. 11–12.
29. Yevgeny Vuchetich, "Vnesem iasnost," *Izvestiia*, April 15, 1965, p. 3.
30. For a discussion of the kinds of issues raised by reminiscences, see M. Nechkina, "Monografiia: Ee mesto v nauke i v izdatelskikh planakh," *Kom-munist*, no. 9 (1965), pp. 77–83; and L. I. Kliuchnik, "O memuarnoi literature," *Voprosy istorii KPSS*, no. 2 (1966), pp. 150–153.
31. "Liudi, gody, zhizn," *Novyi mir*, no. 1 (1965), pp. 103–125.

officials who undertook attempts to halt or mitigate repressions and arbitrariness."[32] The inexorable pressure for further revision that this kind of revelation generates can be seen in the second example, drawn from a book review in *Kommunist*.[33] The writer quotes from page 270 of the 1964 *Short History of the USSR*: "Many delegates to the Seventeenth Party Congress, particularly those of them who knew Lenin's testament, felt the time had come to transfer Stalin . . . to other duties." He then indignantly observes that "The reader, naturally, would like to know the names of at least some of these delegates, to learn what concrete steps they took in this direction, and finally to be told the source that served as the basis for this statement. But this is not given."[34] The source probably is an article by a delegate to the Seventeenth Congress, published in February 1964, which used almost identical phraseology and was equally vague.[35]

There are some indications of official support for more careful verification and accurate publication of memoirs. Most impressive in this respect is the fact that a *Pravda* article reiterated many of the complaints and criticisms earlier published in historical journals and *Novyi mir*. The item in question was written by a docent of the Moscow Historical Archives Institute, who — after carefully rationalizing his concern for honest memoirs in terms of the education of youth — launched into a frank description of tampering with such documents.

textual alterations have been made frequently in the posthumously reprinted memoirs of Old Bolsheviks. It seems to us that the only thing permissible in such reprinting is the clarification or emendation of texts according to extant manuscripts, with mandatory references in footnotes . . . The publication of certain memoirs was attended by unwarranted cuts violating historical truth. [36]

32. N. V. Zhogin, USSR Deputy Prosecutor General, "Ob izvrashcheniiakh vyshinskogo v teorii sovetskogo prava i praktike," *Sovetskoe gosudarstvo i pravo*, no. 3 (March 1965), p. 25.
33. M. Naidenov, "Sereznye nedostatki nuzhnoi knigi," *Kommunist*, no. 17 (1965), pp. 126–128.
34. *Ibid.*, p. 127.
35. "As later became known, the thought sprang up among some congress delegates, particularly those who well remembered Lenin's Testament, that the time had come to shift Stalin from the post of General Secretary to other work." L. Shaumian, delegate to the Seventeenth Party Congress, "Na rubezhe pervykh piatiletok," *Pravda*, February 7, 1964, p. 2.
36. M. Chernomorsky, "Memuary–sredstvo revoliutsionnogo vospitaniia," *Pravda*, August 22, 1966, p. 3.

Not only are new memoirs needed, but there should be a reprinting "without distortion [of] such books, long since vanished from the bookshops, as the reminiscences of N. K. Krupskaia, Ie. D. Stasova . . ."

The Twenty-Third Congress

During 1966, the debate among historians — over questions of methodology, the Stalin cult, appraisal of Stalin's role, and the definition of history — burst out of the confines of the scholarly press and professional meetings and into the more general political arena. This widening of scope coincided in time with the buildup toward the February trial of the writers Siniavsky and Daniel which began with a vilification in *Izvestiia* on January 13, the press campaign that preceded the congress, and a number of official statements or actions pointing in a conservative direction. However, the developments of 1966 do not warrant the simple analysis of organized official repression of those revisionist historians and others who had misinterpreted the nature of de-Stalinization. Nor was it a matter of a sudden political battle of the hards against the softs which spilled over onto the historians. Instead we see the continuation of a lengthy discussion, now conducted on an expanded stage and before a larger audience.

The year opened on an ominous note, with the attack on the writers. There followed shortly an article in *Pravda* by three historians, which has been widely interpreted in the West as a severe criticism of de-Stalinization and the signal for a general tightening.[37] On careful reading, however, the article proves to be quite ambiguous. The authors in no way repudiate the Twentieth Congress, and they are vehement in decrying the deadening of creativity and the passivity of what passed for historical research under Stalin. Specifically they insist that the widely used formula "the period of the personality cult" is "an erroneous, non-Marxist term," which ignores the many positive achievements of the Soviet Union under Stalin. Once again, we must observe that these instructions are familiar but very difficult to follow: the only tangible item is the repudiation of a specific phrase.

A more disturbing signal appeared in *Izvestiia* and *Pravda* for February 25 and 26, respectively, in connection with the seven-

37. Ie. Zhukov, V. Trukhanovsky, and V. Shunkov, "Vysokaia otvetstvennost istorikov," *Pravda*, January 30, 1966, p. 2.

tieth anniversary of Andrei Zhdanov's birthday. *Izvestiia* praised Stalin's ideological hatchetman as "a true son of the people," and *Pravda* hailed him as an "outstanding Party figure."

Further evidence that the overthrow of Khrushchev had revived discussion of the historical treatment of Stalin was afforded by a speech of the Georgian party secretary. D. G. Sturua's verbiage was considerably more vehement than that of *Pravda* and certainly not ambiguous, but it never reached the central press. He says:

Some overly zealous critics attempted, under the banner of struggle against the consequences of the personality cult of Stalin, to rehabilitate Trotskyism, right-wing deviationism, bourgeois nationalism and other anti-Leninist ideological currents in our Party . . . Some historians switched over painlessly from unrestrained eulogy to scathing criticism.[38]

Even with allowance for the factor of Georgian nationalism and its unique pride in Stalin, it is clear that Sturua's fulminations do not stem from individual idiosyncracy. His solution for the disorder of the Soviet ideological front is basically that of the conservatives at the all-union conference of December 1962 and ever since — namely, centralized coordination and control.

A student, for instance, hears at a lecture and reads in a textbook that collectivization was the greatest revolutionary transformation in the countryside . . . But the same student may read in the writings of some of our men of letters from the camp of the "criticals" and "negators" that collectivization was a long chain of mistakes, violations, crimes, etc. But who must coordinate all our manysided ideological work? The Party, of course, its leading organs . . . as there is a lack of coordination in the work of our ideological institutes.[39]

It is evident from the phraseology, and from the seven-day delay in publishing his speech, that Sturua was arguing with opponents within the CPSU hierarchy as well as some of the scholarly and literary community in urging the party to reoccupy positions of command it had defaulted. The thought that this reversal to centralized control might be difficult, self-defeating, or indeed impossible had either not occurred to him or — more likely — was not admitted for tactical reasons.

38. "XXIII sezd Kommunisticheskoi Partii Gruzii, rech tov. D. G. Sturui," *Zaria vostoka*, March 10, 1966, p. 2.
39. *Ibid.*

If this exhausted the developments in the early part of 1966, it would be easy to infer that at some point in late 1965 or early 1966 the political leadership had arrived at a firm decision to retreat from de-Stalinization to a more "balanced" view of Stalin and to accede to the demands of hardliners in the party that history be re-revised accordingly. The point would then be made that shortly before the Twenty-Third Congress the regime reversed itself, owing chiefly to pressures from foreign communist parties. Such a scheme would seem unduly mechanistic in view of the complexity of events and discussion in Soviet historiography. It ignores the crosscurrents and indecisiveness in both the political and intellectual spheres, and tends to assume that the whole controversy over cultural and intellectual policy arose *de novo* on the eve of the congress.

It will be remembered that the open discussions concerning methodology, the use of memoirs, and the concept of truth in history were continuing during the early months of 1966 and were resumed in the late summer.[40] The historical profession displayed an unflagging interest in problems of sourcing and documentary materials. In January a new archival journal appeared: *Sovetskii arkhiv*, published six times a year by the Chief Archives Administration under the Council of Ministers with the help of the Institute of Marxism-Leninism and the Academy of Sciences' Institute of History. And if some conservative historians had been allowed to publish their arguments in *Pravda*, the same paper also featured the rather scholarly account of an archivist's attempt to verify an incident in Lenin's life, which was in itself a demonstration of the historian's craft as a search for truth.[41] The spring of 1966 also saw the rehabilitation of the Old Bolshevik historian of the party, V. I. Nevsky, who was purged in 1935 "on a false charge" for his unpopular historical writings.[42]

The argument among historians over Stalin's position showed no signs of having been settled by political fiat in early 1966. Of interest in this regard is an emigré press account — described as an abridged stenogram of a session held on February 16 of the

40. See V. Lakshin, "Pisatel, chitatel, kritik," *Novyi mir,* no. 8 (1966), pp. 216–256; L. Kryachko, "Pravda ne razediniatsia," *Literaturnaia rossiia,* October 28, 1966, p. 17; V. Ivanov, "Realizm segodnia," *Literaturnaia gazeta,* October 29, 1966, p. 1, and November 10, 1966, p. 3.
41. Grigory Khait, "Poiski leninskikh strok," *Pravda,* January 20, 1966, p. 4.
42. "Propagandist, narkom, istorik," *Izvestiia,* May 14, 1966, p. 4.

Department of History of the Great Fatherland War of the Institute of Marxism-Leninism.[43] The discussion was of N. M. Nekrich's book *22 June 1941* and became very heated. There were cries of "Who was guilty?" followed by "noise in the hall," and "not only Stalin . . . ," drowned out by "Stalin was chiefly guilty!" and "Stalin was a criminal!"

A more detailed account — apparently of this same discussion — has been published in the English journal *Survey*.[44] According to this record, the meeting often became a shouting interchange featuring defenders of Stalin — notably Professor G. A. Deborin of the Institute of Marxism-Leninism, G. F. Zostavenko of the Institute of Marxism-Leninism, and an unidentified Telegyn — who in general maintained that Stalin was not solely guilty for the military unpreparedness of the Soviet Union in World War II. He received poor information from advisers, they argued; moreover, Nekrich's condemnation of Stalin was simply a reflection of Khrushchev's exaggerated criticisms. From the record presented, however, it is clear that the neo-Stalinists were in the small minority at the meeting and that they received heavy abuse.

The talk against Stalin, Voroshilov, and Budenny by most discussants was violent. Petrovsky of the Institute of Historical Archives insisted that official sanction for his calling Stalin a criminal rested in the fact that the Twenty-Third Congress removed him from the mausoleum. Historian Yakir (of the Institute of History of the Academy of Sciences, son of army commander I. Yakir who perished in the purges) furiously as-

43 "Voennie istoriki osu zhdaiut Stalina," *Posev*, January 13, 1967, pp. 3–5. The reader must be cautioned at this point with respect to this document — a version of which was also published in *Survey* (see note 44 below) — and with respect to the protocol concerning an alleged meeting on the third volume of the multivolume party history. The authenticity of these protocols cannot be verified: the editorial note preceding the *Posev* item simply says that the document was received from Moscow, and the *Survey* article gives no indication of source. Furthermore, these protocols have been challenged as forgeries by at least one competent and careful scholar (Christian Duevel, "First-Rate Documents or Forgeries?", Radio Liberty Research CRD 529/67, Munich, September 29, 1967). Despite these problems of verification, however, I find the protocols extremely interesting and plausible accounts, which ring true in context of all the surrounding evidence. They are therefore presented to provide admittedly controversial and circumstantial, yet nonetheless enriching, background material. A more detailed analysis of the Nekrich affair is presented later in connection with the problem of the Soviet leader in historiography.
44. "The Personality Cult," *Survey*, April 1967, pp. 170–180.

serted that "Comrade Stalin" was an improper expression. "Stalin was nobody's comrade and, above all, not ours."[45]

Other remarks were even more significant in terms of historiography and scholarship. Dachichev — who is identified as "of the Staff," presumably of the Institute of Marxism-Leninism — is quoted as follows:

What is most serious is that Soviet sources for everything relating to that period are not always accessible. For example, in order to discuss the report of the Soviet attaché in Berlin that war would break out on 22 June one has to consult the books of the English historian Erickson. When shall we finally be given access to all the sources?[46]

Once again it remained for the Old Bolshevik Snegov to add the final touch. After having noted that "Stalin ought to have been shot" instead of "whitewashed," he asked why Deborin tries to justify Stalin. "How can one be a communist and speak smoothly about Stalin?" Deborin's retort was chilling: "As for Snegov's contribution, we have heard more than once what he told us about Poland; but we heard it from the opposite [capitalist] camp . . . It is strange that Snegov should here hold the same point of view. Comrade Snegov, you ought to tell us which camp you belong to!"[47] There was an uproar and Deborin was shouted down. Snegov's reply was classic:

The Kolyma [concentration] camp . . . I thought this was to be a scientific discussion; but instead of a scientific demonstration, Deborin has produced 1937-type arguments. But it's not easy to frighten us with concentration camps. We won't let ourselves be intimidated. Times have changed, and the past won't come back.[48]

The record notes applause at this point.

The meeting on *22 June 1941* further illustrates the complexity of alignments among historians on such controversial issues as World War II defense. For example, several staff members of the Institute of Marxism-Leninism spoke strongly against Stalin and were clearly at odds with the conservatives or neo-Stalinists. Among them, Anfilov insisted, "Stalin remains the chief culprit,"[49] and Dachichev felt that Nekrich should have gone even

45. *Ibid.*, p. 178.
46. *Ibid.*, p. 175.
47. *Ibid.*, p. 179.
48. *Ibid.*, pp. 179, 180.
49. *Ibid.*, p. 175.

deeper into Stalin's crimes: "Stalin had assumed the responsibility of sole driver. His guilt is immense."[50]

But one of the most dramatic actions with regard to historiography during this precongress period was not taken by historians. Although there was no inkling of this in the Soviet press, the *New York Times* reported that in February twenty-five famous Soviet "scientists, writers and artists" had sent a petition to Brezhnev warning against any movement away from de-Stalinization.[51] The report does not clarify the precise issues protested, but most probably the signers were concerned with the general problem of freedom of expression, the petition having been triggered by the Siniavsky-Daniel trial.

It is significant that although the "reliable sources" reported that all twenty-five were party members, they chose to bypass the usual channels of the CPSU hierarchy — the primary organizations in their institutes or unions. It is also notable that not a single revisionist historian felt sufficiently confident of his position to politicize his scholarly attitude — and with good reason. No Soviet historian in any field, and certainly not a specialist on the CPSU, could acquire the kind of social distance from politics possible for a physicist or an artist. We have no way of knowing what impact the petition had upon party leaders, but they undoubtedly realized that these twenty-five signers were the top of an iceberg and that the resources of the intellectual community cannot be readily calculated in numerical terms. Conversely, it is logical to assume that no such approach would have been broached to a political leadership that was completely united on the issue.

After this prelude, the congress itself was anticlimactic. As several observers have noted, there was little turnover in membership of the Central Committee, no startling changes in the personnel of top party organs, and "all the vital issues were swept under the carpet."[52] Khrushchev was never mentioned, although his policies and methods were castigated. The conflict with China was not openly discussed, economic reforms in progress were treated with great reticence, and the sensational trial of the writers just concluded was dismissed with a few sentences of abuse by Sholokhov.

50. *Ibid.*, p. 176.
51. Peter Grose, "25 Soviet Intellectuals Oppose Any Elevation of Stalin's Status," *New York Times*, March 21, 1966, p. 2.
52. Leonard Schapiro, "The Twenty-Third Congress of the CPSU," *Survey*, July 1966, pp. 72–84.

The first secretary of the Moldavian party solved the problem of literary pessimism by offering the formula of the right of every Soviet artist to create — coupled with the right of party and government agencies to select what will be printed.[53]

Interestingly enough, there was a reference by Georgian First Secretary Mzhavanadze to historiography at the congress, which took the form of disparaging authors who were too free, even "disrespectful, in their treatment of history. This applies first of all to the authors of memoirs."[54] Mzhavanadze accuses some memoir writers of being motivated by conceit to perpetuate their own names and gives as an example Ivan M. Maisky, former ambassador to Britain, now retired, whose "Recollections of a Soviet Ambassador" was published in *Novyi mir*. Maisky, it should be noted, was one of the writers who reportedly signed the petition to Brezhnev; certainly he was the nearest approximation to a political figure or historian among the known petitioners.

It is perhaps possible at this point to assess the intent of the congress. Apparently in the spring of 1966, despite the harsh sentencing of Siniavsky and Daniel, the leadership was internally divided over how to contain, without choking off, the scholarship and creativity of the intellectuals. Thus the congress remained nearly silent on the matter, except for a few ill-tempered remarks, in an attempt to preserve the uneasy balance that had evolved after 1956. Khrushchev's denunciation of Stalin was neither reiterated nor retracted. The regime refused to satisfy either of those elements pressing from both sides and indicated that it would muddle along. The Siniavsky-Daniel trial, it seems, would stand as a border marker to warn the most adventuresome, but intellectuals could continue to move in a broad area short of this bound.

Certainly, the liberals were not crushed. Tvardovsky was not present at the congress nor was he reelected a candidate member of the Central Committee; but he was not dismissed as editor of *Novyi mir* and that journal did not alter its controversial publication policies. The publication of Kuznetsov's novel *Babi Yar* lifted the taboo from another hidden tragedy in Soviet history.[55]

53. "Rech tovarishcha I. I. Bodiula," *Pravda*, April 3, 1966, pp. 3–4.
54. "Rech tovarishcha V. P. Mzhavanadze," *Pravda*, April 1, 1966, p. 2.
55. Anatoly Kuznetsov, "Babi Yar," *Iunost*, no. 8 (1966), pp. 7–42; no. 9, pp. 15–46; and no. 10, pp. 23–49.

There was, of course, no lack of expression by the more conservative historians and critics. Ehrenburg and other memoirists were still being attacked for attributing contemporary knowledge and attitudes to historical actors during the Stalin period, for "imagining" doubts not present in the 1930s.[56] Much energy was being devoted to preparations for the jubilee year for party historians: the fiftieth anniversary of the October Revolution. The amount of work in progress was revealed by the draft publication plan published in *Voprosy istorii KPSS*.[57] *Pravda* announced on August 24 that volume two of the six-volume *History of the Communist Party of the Soviet Union* had appeared, bringing the account up to the eve of October; and work on the third volume continued apace.

One of the most persuasive — and dramatic — proofs that the Twenty-Third Congress neither upgraded Stalin nor crushed the liberal historians is provided by an account of a closed meeting held at the Institute of Marxism-Leninism some time after the congress to discuss the draft third volume of the new multivolume *History*, which covers the October Revolution.[58] Present were two hundred and fifty historians of the CPSU and Old Bolsheviks, under the chairmanship of P. N. Pospelov.

The discussion revived some old quarrels. Fofanova again presented documentation for her assertion that Lenin returned to Petersburg early in September; she had been quoted in the circulated draft as saying that he arrived at the end of the month. Other Old Bolsheviks railed against the continued presentation of Stalin's opponents as traitors to the party. Feelings were high and the language passionate. Most participants, according to the report, seemed jubilant that — in Snegov's words — although "some people expected the Twenty-Third Congress to rehabilitate Stalin, nothing has come of it and nothing will!" The single Old Bolshevik who defended Stalin was shouted down. Bugaev's attempt to shunt the participants away from their fixation on Stalin and his crimes — "We are not writing a multivolume biography of Stalin" — was unsuccessful.[59]

56. For example, K. Bukovsky, "Otvet na lestnitse," *Oktiabr*, no. 9 (1966), pp. 199–201.
57. "Vo vsesoiuznom sovete po koordinatsii nauchnoi razrabotki istorii KPSS," *Voprosy istorii KPSS*, no. 6 (1966), pp. 153–157.
58. "The Personality Cult," *Survey*, April 1967, pp. 159–169. See note 43 concerning the authenticity of this document.
59. *Ibid.*, pp. 165, 168.

Perhaps the most fascinating aspect of this meeting in terms of the future of the profession is its confirmation of an informal alliance between the bolder young historians of the CPSU and the outspoken Old Bolsheviks. This is a phenomenon reminiscent of the attachment of liberal young writers to Boris Pasternak. Evidently the young historians who tried to gain admission to the first session were rather rudely turned back. The Old Bolshevik Zorin furiously attacked this decision, suggestively linking their exclusion to the Institute of Marxism-Leninism's monopoly on Leninist documents:

It is shameful that yesterday young historians were not allowed in. If you sit by yourselves on top of enormous material, so much the worse for the material. Who will write history after you? To sit on top of historical material like a cur on a stack of hay, to keep Lenin's documents under lock and key — these are crimes indeed.[60]

The Old Bolsheviks were especially indignant that the historian Yakir was refused admission. On the second day one young historian, Petrovsky, did gain entry and his remarks are worth quoting:

I have spoken to old Bolsheviks several times and said, your ranks are getting thin, you are leaving us while all you say remains within four walls, and the protocols of your conferences will not become the property of historians for a long time. You say that the history of the party will be written by young communists when you are gone. I would like to say that they already write it and write it well.[61]

This is an alliance in a race against time.

In the last analysis, although many brave words were spoken, the effect of the meeting on the forthcoming final version of the third *History* volume was negligible. Pospelov rejected the suggestion that a commission (presumably of Old Bolsheviks) be formed to "assist in the writing." He reported that over one thousand comrades had submitted comments on the draft. But the fears of Old Bolshevik Oslikovskaia were not unfounded:

Comrade Pospelov names organizations and people from whom he received comments on the third volume of the *History*, but he did not say to what extent these comments were used. What will happen about our statements here? Are our observations and suggestions made merely for later editions and not for this one? Why is our criticism not heeded?[62]

60. *Ibid.*, p. 164.
61. *Ibid.*, p. 167.
62. *Ibid.*, p. 161.

It seems clear that the multivolume official *History* did not significantly alter positions taken in the one-volume text with respect to Stalin and other leaders in the early years of the USSR. But it is also apparent that some historians — significantly led by the very old and the very young — left these formulations far behind.

The Brezhnev-Kosygin regime has remained committed, after the Twenty-Third Congress as before, to upgrading the teaching and research being done in historiography as in the other social and physical sciences. Conclusive evidence was provided by an undated decree of the Central Committee and Council of Ministers published early in September 1966,[63] which evidently was promulgated in fulfillment of the 1962 decree on improving the training of scientific cadres. The text betrayed a strange blend of centralization of controls in some respects with decentralization and "further democratization" of authority in others. This uneasy tension of goals was reinforced by the decree's dual empowering clauses running to both the CPSU and the Ministry of Higher and Specialized Education. Taken in the context of the discussions among historians pressing for better scholarship, the decree was indeed quite promising for an improvement in the quality of Soviet historiography.

63. "V Tsentralnom Komitete KPSS i Sovete Ministrov SSSR. O merakh po uluchsheniiu podgotovki spetsialistov i sovershenstvovaniiu rukovodstva vysshim i srednim spetsialnym obrazovaniem v strane," *Pravda,* September 9, 1966, pp. 1–2.

He who wants to hide
from the reflected substance of events,
Beware the mirrors,
                        do not look at them:
They are able to reveal everything.

You cannot withdraw from the evidence.
Mirrors
        remember everything.
They may fall
        from the walls,
But from the splinters —
        No one escapes
                No one —
No matter who he may be.

Simyon Kirsanov, "Mirrors,"
Znamiia, no. 3, 1967

HISTORY AS
THE MIRROR OF CONSCIENCE:
SOME CASE STUDIES 3

Soviet history is now a much more complex, scholarly, and sophisticated matter than under Stalin: although still sensitized to politics to a degree unknown in less centralized states, it can no longer be passed off as the mirror reflection of political occurrences. But in a more general sense, historiography remains consistent with the more complex political milieu of the USSR after 1956. With the disappearance of Stalinist totalitarianism, the one-way and directive relationship of political elite to historian has been replaced by a subtle pattern of interaction between the world of political and social reality and the historian's artifice: the picture of that world as it existed in the past.

This new relationship is, by its very nature, elusive: it does not lend itself to easy categorization, any more than does the political system of which it is a part. The ultimate questions for the political analyst have become: In what respects and to what degree has the USSR departed from a total system of controls enforced by terror? And under what conditions could these modifications be rescinded, or is the evolution of the political system since Stalin's death irreversible? But behind the political question of the current status of administrative controls is the concomitant theoretical — and historical — problem of the disposition of political opposition. The most sensitive and politically significant aspect of party history now becomes the treatment accorded to political dissidents and opponents. As the CPSU today shows no signs of softening its ban on "bourgeois" or "fascist" political movements, so Soviet historians remain adamantly scornful of the whole spectrum of parties and nationalist groups in Russian history to the right of the socialists. Still, as the monolithic communist camp has divided into a variety of socialist regimes and the USSR itself has espoused revisionist economic and social programs, so the historical treatment of non-Bolshevik socialists has been modified. Historiographical as well as political factors have been at work in this process, however. Once Soviet historians were instructed to take a fresh look at 1917, the stereotypes of the Mensheviks and Essars in the *Short Course* were no longer plausible.

It was, of course, the Twentieth Party Congress that initially inspired historical interest in Bolshevism's domestic opponents of the left. For long years they had been caricatured and disposed of by imprecation: now in 1956 three developments at the congress sparked a more genuine appraisal. First, the implication of Khrushchev's denunciation of Stalin was to discount Stalin's personal discrediting of his political rivals; second, there was Khrushchev's direct command to historians to study party history and replace the *Short Course*; third, the dramatic repudiation by Khrushchev of violence as an absolutely necessary condition of revolutionary change had a pacifying effect upon the historiography of the October Revolution.

From these authoritative bases, the historiography of the CPSU has generated a considerable, and perhaps by now autonomous, momentum of revisionary scholarship on the non-Bolshevik left. This revision has taken place inside the theoretical framework specifying Bolshevism as the only true Marxism and Lenin as the sole Russian leader capable of perceiving the Russian historical situation and acting upon such knowledge. The rival parties and persuasions are still portrayed in Soviet literature as irredeemably boggled in their social and historical analysis and inept in tactics. Within this general purview, however, quite significant changes have come about.

The matters at issue here, though, are not only the content of the new historiography with regard to political dissenters and opposition parties but the political implications: What political — and historiographical — factors are helpful in explaining the official concern with these problems; and, conversely, what relevance do such scholarly reappraisals have to Soviet political reality? If the infallibility of the CPSU is the essential criterion of the USSR as a unique form of dynamic, ideologically oriented, mass-society autocracy, then the historical treatment of that party's rivals and detractors is a critical test of its control.

Rather than pursue a chronological approach, it will perhaps be more productive to articulate the key issues as they are perceived and discussed by Soviet historians. It must be emphasized that these problems overlap and that they represent my own analytical device rather than any such articulation by the historians themselves. The central clusters of issues with regard to opposition, then, may be briefly outlined as follows:

1. The Bolsheviks and the revolutions of 1917: their leadership role, efficiency, and internal unity.
2. The Bolsheviks and the Mensheviks and Essars: the related problems of their roles in 1917, coalition and collaboration, rivalry in the countryside, and the concept of violence.

3. The special problem of the Left Essars: the case of the purloined agrarian program.

4. The CPSU and internal oppositionists in the twenties and thirties: can opposition to the CPSU leadership be qualified as relatively progressive or pernicious, or is it always anathema?

The Bolsheviks and the Revolutions of 1917

It would not be far from the truth to say that the whole discussion of 1917 during all the years since is in reference to Burdzhalov's 1956 articles in *Voprosy istorii*. Although the issues raised by Burdzhalov had lain dormant since 1957, early in 1962 the historical journals began once more to feature some articles on the subject of Bolshevik tactics in the spring of 1917. The matter was reopened in *Voprosy istorii KPSS* on quite a high scholarly level, which has generally been maintained.[1] Without referring either to Burdzhalov's demand for an objective appraisal of the Mensheviks and other oppositionists or to his controversial findings, Yevgrafov in effect substantiated and amplified Burdzhalov's work. He described in full detail the quarrels over tactics during early 1917 among the staff of *Pravda*, the bureau of the Petersburg Party Committee, and the bureau of the Central Committee. He also admitted the existence of unified Bolshevik-Menshevik committees during the spring and pointed out that "even in proletarian Kharkhov" several Bolsheviks observed at a unified meeting on March 23 that conditions did not warrant the existence of two separate wings of the RSDLP. Nor did Stalin appreciate the gravity of the differences between the factions within the party.[2] Yevgrafov was careful, however, to show that the majority of party organizations in March and early April were in fact Bolshevik organizations by virtue of Bolshevik leadership of most unified committees.[3]

The same issue of *Voprosy istorii KPSS* included a set of documents[4] described in the foreword by the Institute of Marxism-Leninism as being from its archives and "showing the activity of the Bolshevik party and its leading center — the bureau of the CC RSDLP(b) — during the period from the February bourgeois-democratic revolution to the return of V. I. Lenin from

1. V. E. Yevgrafov, "Nekotorye voprosy taktiki partii v marte–nachale aprelia 1917 goda," *Voprosy istorii KPSS*, no. 3 (1962), pp. 35–61.
2. *Ibid.*, p. 57.
3. *Ibid.*
4. "Protokoly i rezoliutzii biuro TsK RSDRP(B) (mart 1917g.)," *ibid.*, pp. 134–157.

abroad in April 1917."[5] The foreword did not discuss the issue of the unified committees, nor was this suggested by any of the documents presented. Stalin's errors were briefly described under the rubric of "mistaken positions" on many questions.

This publication of the protocols in *Voprosy istorii KPSS* — on the high authority of the Institute of Marxism-Leninism and coincident with a number of articles elsewhere dealing with Bolshevik tactics in the spring of 1917 — is a good example of what I have referred to as official or semiofficial initiative in historical revision. But in this instance, as in many others, the official revision proved unsatisfactory to more liberal historians. Although no one disputed the protocols in print, the Old Bolshevik Snegov was outspokenly critical in his remarks at the all-union conference of historians in December 1962. Snegov used strong language, ridiculing the institute's editors for their half-truths and deceptive phrases which disguised Stalin's Menshevik position and active support of Kamenev. He accused them of writing the foreword simply to muffle the devastating exposure of Stalin contained in the documents themselves and, further, of implying that this was a complete collection of bureau protocols while consciously omitting the record of the session on April 1, which shows that Stalin proposed unification with the Mensheviks.[6] Burdzhalov himself, at this same conference, castigated the omission of the April protocol.[7] It is indicative of the confusion of the debate among historians on this point that the April protocol had already been included in another collection published by *Voprosy istorii KPSS*.[8]

For Snegov, this misuse of documents was a greater sin than the efforts of those several other historians who glossed over Stalin's errors in a number of articles on 1917 tactics appearing at about the same time.[9] Only I. I. Mints's article in *Pravda*

5. *Ibid.*, p. 134.
6. *Vsesoiuznoe soveshchanie a merakh uluchsheniia podgotovki nauchno-pedagogicheskikh kadrov po istoricheskim naukam*, pp. 272–274.
7. *Ibid.*, p. 368.
8. "Protokoly Vserossiiskogo (martovskogo) soveshchaniia partiinikh rabotnikov (27 marta–2 aprelia 1917 g.)," *Voprosy istorii KPSS,* no. 6 (1962), p. 139.
9. Snegov does not specify the pieces he has in mind, but it is likely that they include I. F. Petrov, "Osveshchenie nekotorykh problem Oktiabrskoi revoliutsii v istoriko-partiinoi literature," *ibid.,* no. 5 (1962), pp. 5–26; and G. N. Golikov, "K izucheniiu istorii Velikogo Oktiabria," *ibid.,* no. 11, 1962, pp. 33–53.

met with Snegov's approval, for stating that there was absolutely no difference between Kamenev's and Stalin's positions in March and April 1917.[10] Once again we catch a glimpse of the variety of opinion and forthrightness among historians, with Mints — whom no one could accuse of liberalism — and the Old Bolshevik Snegov joining this one time to lead a crusade for objective research and honest use of documents.

There are obvious reasons why those historians who were driving toward a more honest portrayal of 1917 initiated their revisions by way of Stalin's tactical errors in 1917: denigration of Stalin was an officially sponsored project. Since 1956, historians have progressively, but not without arguments, extended back to April 1917 the period during which Stalin remained in a "semi-Menshevik position" with Kamenev.[11] But the problem of the Bolshevik relationship to the February and October revolutions also has a number of more controversial aspects.

Closely linked with the problem of mistaken Bolsheviks is the post-Stalin treatment of the April Theses. Again, it has been a process of gradual and spasmodic elaboration stemming from revelations about the *Pravda* editorial board. Soviet historians can now give some details of the opposition that greeted Lenin's program, using Lenin's own complaints and the treatment of his speech in *Pravda* as source materials. Probably the most frank presentation to date is that of Snegov, which shows how *Pravda* on April 5 tampered with Lenin's text and points to the overt public opposition of the board to Lenin's Theses and the fact that it was not until April 14 that Stalin came out in support of Lenin.[12]

Even though Snegov emphasizes that the party rallied to the Lenin program "after a short time," this picture of March and April remains sharply distinct from more official accounts designed for a mass audience. For example, the second edition of the one-volume *History of the Communist Party of the Soviet Union,* which appeared in November 1962, is content to present a much more abbreviated version, which drains the narrative of any impression of real conflict:

10. "Vtoraia revoliutsiia v Rossi," *Pravda,* March 12, 1962, p. 4.
11. See A. V. Snegov, "Neskolko stranits iz istorii partii (Mart–nachalo aprelia 1917 g.)," *Voprosy istorii KPSS,* no. 2 (1963), pp. 15–30, for a discussion of this problem and summary of other literature on the subject.
12. *Ibid.,* pp. 29–30.

In the new situation some of the Bolshevik committees and several leading Party members adopted an incorrect attitude towards the Provisional Government . . . Stalin adopted a similar attitude . . . In mid-April 1917 he abandoned his erroneous position . . . Within the Party, the April Theses were opposed by Kamenev, Rykov, Pyatakov and a handful of their followers . . . In the course of two to three weeks the whole Party rallied round Lenin's theses.[13]

The third volume (book one) of the six-volume *History of the Communist Party of the Soviet Union,* which was sent to press in June 1967, presents considerable detail on the process of intraparty debate on the April Theses.[14] However, with regard to the Bolshevik elite, the account is much less frank than Snegov's: Lenin's rift with the *Pravda* board is not recognized, and virtually the entire burden of opposition to Lenin at the Seventh (April) Conference is thrust upon Kamenev, Rykov, and Pyatakov. Stalin's position during this month is ignored completely. In fact, the only mention of him is a brief notation that the report on the nationality question was presented to the April Conference by Stalin, followed by a gratuitous remark to the effect that the relevant resolution was written by Lenin.[15]

If the history of 1917 can be viewed as a morality play, the appearance and reappearance of Lenin center stage in April and October are certainly dramatic high points, almost a *deus ex machina.* Certainly Soviet historiography, however revisionist, has consistently cast the drama of 1917 in precisely those terms: the air of almost hopeless ineptitude and confusion which hangs over most accounts of party activities in the early days of 1917 dissolves into purpose and hope on April 3. And Lenin's reappearance in October signals the denouement. But even more important for party infallibility, Lenin's return has traditionally in Soviet treatments marked the beginning of purposeful preparations for the armed uprising. Lenin in Petrograd embodies the party's claim that the Bolsheviks alone organized the October Revolution. So the seemingly trivial dispute among

13. *History of the Communist Party of the Soviet Union,* 2nd rev. ed., pp. 213, 214, 220. For another typically rosy assessment geared to popular education, see P. Volobuiev, "Genialnaia programma sotsialisticheskoi revoliutsii," *Pravda,* April 17, 1967, pp. 2–3.
14. *Istoriia Kommunisticheskoi Partii Sovetskogo Soiuza,* III, book 1 (Moscow: Political Literature Publishing House, 1967), pp. 58–63.
15. *Ibid.,* p. 76.

Soviet historians of the CPSU over the precise date of Lenin's arrival takes on an almost desperate urgency.

The quarrel among historians over the date of Lenin's return has apparently been smoldering for a number of years, and has only occasionally flashed into flames. One such occasion was the December 1962 conference of historians, when the Old Bolshevik who had been Lenin's secretary, M. V. Fofanova, passionately tried once more to restore Lenin as the single architect of the October Revolution by contending that he reentered the city on September 22.[16] She made her argument on the basis of both personal recollection and documentary evidence and showed that the facts were already being distorted by Stalin in 1922.

One of the many fascinating aspects of Fofanova's speech is the direct challenge to Academician Mints to prove his contention that Lenin could have returned only after the Central Committee resolution authorized it on October 3. Her appeal to him is a study in complex motivation: fear, hatred, pride in her own direct relationship with Lenin, and scorn for Mints's secondary connection, mixed with the need to appeal to his power. She evidently assumed that if she could convince Mints to change his stand, others would follow. Mints's recorded remarks were a brief and cold rejoinder to Fofanova. He did not deal with her argument except to contend that the matter had been settled by a special conference in 1961, which had resolved in favor of an October date.[17] Unfortunately, other published evidence does not permit final resolution of this discrepancy in dates.

Yet there are sufficient incidental references in the scholarly literature to indicate that many historians do not share Mints' satisfaction that the matter has been finally established. Most striking is the delicate and inconclusive treatment of Lenin's return presented in the first book of volume three of *History of the Communist Party of the Soviet Union*. It seems clear that the editorial board itself, of which Mints is a member, is divided. The account states that Lenin took part in the Central Committee meeting held in Petrograd on October 10, noting that "Several days had already passed since he returned illegally to Petrograd from Finland." The text proceeds, but at this point a footnote gives the number of the locomotive and the name

16. See M. V. Fofanova's remarks, *Vsesoiuznoe soveshchanie*, pp. 280–285.
17. *Ibid.*, p. 292.

of the engineer who had the honor of bringing Lenin from Vyborg. This piece of information is followed in the footnote by the fact that, upon his return, Lenin was hidden in the apartment of M. V. Fofanova and it gives the address. Only then is there a discussion of the problem of dating Lenin's arrival:

There is conflicting information concerning the date of Lenin's arrival in the sources and literature. They do not permit the citation of the exact date with certainty. In the protocol of the Central Committee meeting of October 3 the decision is recorded: ". . . To suggest to Ilich that he return to Peter . . ." (Protocols of Central Committee RSDLP(b), August 1917–February 1918, page 74.) In the memoirs of contemporaries, including persons who had a direct relationship to the organization of the journey (Rakhia, Shotman, Fofanova), it is shown that Lenin came from Vyborg to Petrograd at the end of September, but in the interests of conspiracy wrote his letters to the Central Committee ostensibly from Finland. In the XIV volume of the first edition of Lenin's collected works, published before his death in 1921, this very date [sic] was given. In several sources, including the memoirs of N. K. Krupskaia, a different date of return is given — October 7. This date entered the literature beginning with the thirties.[18]

It is difficult to fathom the reluctance of Mints and his supporters except on personal grounds, since it would appear that Lenin's presence from late September could only enhance Bolshevik claims to having engineered the revolution. But these men do not share with such emotion the determination of the Old Bolshevik to eradicate Stalin's image. The whole issue has undoubtedly become a matter of personal and professional pride for those historians who are being asked to retract long-standing pronouncements. And perhaps it is not outlandish to suggest that Mints may have especially resented being taken to task by two women — Fofanova and Ye. D. Stasova — Old Bolsheviks or no.

But there may also be a political aspect to the dispute. Such an account as presented in the new third volume of the official history obviously raises more questions than it settles, and the discussion does skate perilously close to the whole issue of Lenin's style of leadership. Any reader of this passage must wonder just how narrow was this "conspiracy" to conceal Lenin's

18. *Istoriia Kommunisticheskoi Partii Sovetskogo Soiuza,* III, book 1, pp. 300, 301.

true whereabouts and might suspect that most, if not all, of the central committee had been kept in the dark until some time after Lenin's appearance, in disguise and under an assumed name, at the October 10 meeting.[19] If in 1917 there were conspiracies within conspiracies, as the confusion in the sources readily suggests, Lenin's concept of decision making was very elitist indeed and his style of leadership not a collective one.

Again we have occasion to note that the entire debate remained beyond the purview of popular texts: the first and second editions of the one-volume party history simply state that Lenin moved into the Vyborg district of Petersburg on October 7.[20]

The specific events of October provide a focal point for consideration of an important aspect of Bolshevik leadership. A review in *Voprosy istorii KPSS* points to some journal articles that call in question the CPSU claim of direct organization of the Petrograd armed uprising.[21] These proposed revisions would destroy the impression of party prescience in favor of a much more opportunistic development of tactics. The third volume of the new history approaches the matter very cautiously; the final account seems to be the result of compromise and does not settle the real arguments. There is no claim that the central committee had decided in advance to conduct the uprising on the night of Otcober 24–25, although the party's general preparations are presented as well organized. Not until the evening of October 24 did Lenin order a specific plan of action.[22]

The historical problem of Bolshevik leadership of the 1917 Revolutions is not, however, limited to October. Post-1956 Soviet historiography also opened up a whole new aspect of the question of Bolshevik historical uniqueness and necessity. As historians have for the first time since the 1920s probed local

19. *Ibid.*, p. 301.
20. *History of the Communist Party of the Soviet Union*, 1st ed., p. 251; 2nd rev. ed., p. 246. Also A. A. Panfilova, V. Ia. Zevin, M. Ia. Pankratova, A. Ia. Velikanova, and S. P. Kiriukhin, "K voprosu o date vozvrashcheniia V. I. Lenina iz Finliandii v Petrograd oseniu 1917 g.," *Voprosy istorii KPSS*, no. 12 (1963), pp. 70–75. This article contains a review of the arguments in historical literature on behalf of a September date.
21. E. F. Yerikalov, "Osveshchenie Oktiabrskogo vooruzhennogo vosstaniia v Petrograde v istoriko-partiinoi literature 1956–1966 gg.," *Voprosy istorii KPSS*, no. 5 (1966), pp. 121–127.
22. *Istoriia Kommunisticheskoi Partii Sovetskogo Soiuza*, III, book 1, pp. 322–323.

and provincial situations and utilized party archives in those areas, it has become increasingly evident that the revolution was much more complex and difficult than earlier portrayals of provincial situations as merely later and less disruptive copies of the city uprisings. John Keep cites a number of Soviet books and articles which have, in the attempt to show a smoothly functioning Bolshevik organization with far-flung local representatives, inadvertently also betrayed evidence that the Bolsheviks were in fact very poorly organized in many instances, badly staffed, plagued by a lack of communications. Further, they were — demonstrably from these Soviet sources — encountering armed resistance in some areas until March 1918, and were in the minority in many local soviets even after October.[23] This kind of factual material, no matter how carefully rationalized, has an obviously corrosive effect upon the myths of party infallibility and popular appeal. It also weakens the historical argument for current centralized control by revealing the extent of local autonomy within the Bolshevik ranks in 1917 and 1918.

The eradication of spontaneity from the February Revolution, of course, is even more of a problem for the Soviet historian. Interestingly enough, the Khrushchev history texts of 1959 and 1962 attribute more leadership to the Bolsheviks than did Stalin's *Short Course,* which gave a terse and highly impersonal account: "On February 18, 1917, a strike broke out at the Putilov Works . . . On February 24 . . . the demonstration was resumed with even greater vigor . . . On the morning of February 26 . . . the political strike and demonstration began to assume the character of an uprising." The Bolsheviks entered the scene only on February 26 by issuing a manifesto for continued armed struggle.[24]

We can only speculate whether it happened by dint of ambition to provide a model for bourgeois revolutions in developing areas, or by virtue of Khrushchev's penchant for placing the party at the center of every development — but the official post-Stalin versions have moved the Bolsheviks to the center of the stage at an earlier point in the action:

On February 23 there were demonstrations . . . The St. Peters-

23. John Keep, "October in the Provinces," in *Revolutionary Russia,* Richard Pipes, ed. (Cambridge: Harvard University Press, 1968).
24. *History of the Communist Party of the Soviet Union, Short Course,* pp. 175–176.

burg Committee of the Bolsheviks called for a political strike
. . . The next day . . . the Bolsheviks decided to continue the
strike and turn it into a general strike and then into an insurrection . . . On the following morning, February 26, in response
to the Bolshevik appeal, the workers passed from political strike
to armed revolt.[25]

This is one of the few instances after 1956 when official or political pressure has evidently been exerted to revise party history
in flagrant violation of the facts and sources. As such, this situation has posed difficulties for most historians, and the increment
in scholarship on the February Revolution has not been as great
as otherwise would have been expected.[26] And, perhaps just
because the research has been running against documentary evidence, the old warrior Burdzhalov has chosen the early days of
the February Revolution as a research project. In 1964 the Moscow State Pedagogical Institute, with which Burdzhalov is affil-
iated, published an article dealing with the origins and initiation
of the February Revolution in a monograph collection of research
papers.[27] With the exception of his published remarks at the historians' conference in December 1962, this appears to have been
his first printed work since the *Voprosy istorii* articles of 1956,
and just as sensational.

Whereas he agrees that Bolshevik involvement occurred as early
as February 23, Burdzhalov interprets the February Revolution
as having begun on the 18th with spontaneous street distur-
bances and strikes: he makes no attempt to show Bolshevik
organization of these events, but rather gives the impression that
the spark was hunger and the women's demand for bread. Adding insult to injury, he quotes the memoirs of the Old Bolshevik
V. Kairov with respect to a factory meeting of Bolsheviks on
February 23: "It is clear that the idea of an armed uprising had
long ago already arisen among the workers, but at that moment
. . . no one thought of such a near possibility of revolution."[28]

25. *History of the Communist Party of the Soviet Union*, 2nd rev. ed., pp. 202–
203.
26. For a list of the relevant works in Soviet historiography after the Twentieth Congress, see I. A. Aluf, "O nekotorykh voprosakh Fevralskoi revoliutsii,"
Voprosy istorii KPSS, no. 1 (1967), p. 17.
27. E. N. Burdzhalov, "Nachalo vtoroi russkoi revoliutsii," *Materialy i issledovanie po istorii SSSR* (Moscow: State Pedagogical Institute named for V. I.
Lenin, 1964), pp. 131–159.
28. *Ibid.*, p. 141. Quoted from "Shest dnia Fevralskoi revoliutsii," *Proletarskaia
revolutsiia*, no. 1 (1923), p. 158.

Early in February 1967 Burdzhalov's book on the February Revolution appeared,[29] and it did indeed fulfill the promise of the paper published three years earlier. Once again his research is meticulous and his analysis well reasoned. There had been nothing in Soviet historiography on the early months of 1917 approaching this level of scholarship and integrity of argument since the 1920s. It must be observed that, although this is a small edition (5700 copies), it can be expected to reach the scholarly community quite adequately.

Burdzhalov may be faulted by non-Soviet historians for neglecting the ultimate riddle of the February Revolution and failing to unravel the tangled threads of underlying causes and the triggering events. Nonetheless, in the context of the Soviet Union, his treatment is breathtaking. From the perspective of the work at hand, we may identify several intriguing problems or themes with which Burdzhalov is principally concerned: the divisions within the Bolshevik leadership over tactics, the loose and often ineffective coordination among Bolshevik organizations, even in Petrograd, and the critical role of the worker masses — not just in executing but in initiating the uprising.

The final paragraphs of the book have a quasi-populist ring, and the Bolsheviks are mentioned almost casually as an afterthought.

The chief role in the victory of the second Russian revolution was played by the proletariat of Petrograd. The workers of Peter were the initiators and inspirers of the uprising against tsarism. They were the first to enter the struggle and, attracting the mass of soldiers to themselves, they succeeded in achieving victory . . .
Gaining the victory in the capitol, the Petrograd proletariat undermined the foundations of tsarist power in the whole country . . .
Having overthrown tsarism, the workers and peasants of Russia under the leadership of the Bolsheviks carried the revolution further, into the socialist epoch.[30]

Burdzhalov was answered indirectly early in 1967.[31] Although no specific mention occurs in the text of Aluf's article on the February Revolution, reference is made to the Burdzhalov arti-

29. E. N. Burdzhalov, *Vtoraia russkaia revoliutsiia* (Moscow: "Thought" Publishing House, 1967). See also the book review by William G. Rosenberg in *Kritika*, Spring 1968, pp. 1–12.
30. Burdzhalov, *Vtoraia*, p. 406.
31. Aluf, "O nekotorykh voprosakh."

cle in a footnote. Aluf's argument is interesting on several counts. For one thing, he follows Burdzhalov's lead in quoting from a significant number of sources on the February Revolution — both historical interpretations and memoirs — originating in the 1920s, which had not been referred to by Soviet historians in decades. Secondly, Aluf presents a more subtle claim for Bolshevik leadership than is customary: no attempt is made to place Bolsheviks literally at the head of street demonstrations and strikes, but the argument is cast in terms of secondary causation: "The events of February 23 were not planned in advance, and in this regard they appeared spontaneous . . . But this is only one side of the matter. The other consists of the many tactics of the Bolshevik party prior to February 23 in preparation for revolution, all its work with the masses."[32] Clearly, if such a formulation is designed to demolish Burdzhalov's evidence of spontaneity, it does not succeed. But the need to answer Burdzhalov has moved the dialogue onto another and more sophisticated level.

It seems apparent that the troublesome issues presented and carefully documented by Burdzhalov's latest volume will continue to agitate historians in the scholarly press for some time to come. However, the extent and pace of any spillover of these more subtle interpretations into popular historiography can only be conjectured. Perhaps most significant is the tenacity of Burdzhalov's interpretations and his personal integrity. He has not trimmed; and indeed the wind may be shifting toward his sail.

The Bolsheviks and the Mensheviks and Essars

There has been since 1956 a real change in Soviet appraisal of the behavior of the rival socialist parties in 1917. The Mensheviks and Essars no longer are portrayed as enemy agents and saboteurs of the Revolution, but as bad Marxists who could not or would not comprehend the unique condition of Russia and the significance of the historical situation. Thus — subjectively loyal to the goal of socialism — they objectively acted to defeat its coming. That this modification has moved from scholarly precincts into the popular domain is evident from the less vindictive treatment accorded the Mensheviks and Essars in the 1959 and 1962 texts on party history as compared to the *Short*

32. *Ibid.*, p. 24.

Course. Although all three of these mass-edition texts proclaim that the Mensheviks and Essars deserted to the counterrevolutionary bourgeoisie,[33] the tone of the account of their activities has become less abusive, and the summary statement in the *Short Course* that the "non-Communist parties . . . all became bourgeois parties even before the October Revolution and fought for the preservation and integrity of the capitalist system"[34] is missing from the post-Stalin versions.

The dramatic increase in available archival materials and memoirs, with the enormous research effort in conjunction with the fiftieth anniversary of the October Revolution, have combined with this more sophisticated approach to produce what one rather unhappy Soviet reviewer calls "a series of arguments and undecided questions." It is impossible to trace out here all of these quarrels; but I shall attempt to schematize those historical issues that illuminate the problem of opposition in the Soviet system.

Scholarly debate still centers on 1917, and indeed the roots of the problem lie there. Soviet publications have revealed some really astonishing arguments over the past several years. The basic issue is that of the historical necessity of violence in October, upon which the CPSU has erected both its domestic legitimacy and its claim to world socialist primacy. A number of journal articles have presented evidence to show that the accepted line — that only for three or four days in September was a peaceful development of the revolution possible — needs revision to lengthen this period in September and also to include various numbers of days immediately following Kornilov's defeat.[35]

Other historians approach this position by stressing the period between February and October as one of primarily legal political activity by the Bolsheviks in winning over a majority of the soviets.[36] Such a treatment, of course, dangerously blurs the dis-

33. *History of the Communist Party of the Soviet Union, Short Course,* p. 188; *History of the Communist Party of the Soviet Union,* p. 262, and 2nd rev. ed., p. 257.
34. *Ibid.,* p. 224.
35. For a summary and rebuttal, see Yerikalov, "Osveshchenie Oktiabrskogo vooruzhennogo vosstaniia," p. 124.
36. For examples of this argument at the mass level as well as the scholarly, see G. N. Golikov, "Partiia-vdokhnovitel i organizator Velikoi Oktiabrskoi

tinction between Bolsheviks and Mensheviks, and its proponents must be careful to interpret Lenin's tactics of "All Power to the Soviets" as having "nothing in common with the reformist-conciliator calls for social peace, for cooperation of antagonistic classes, for rejection of revolutionary means of struggle."[37] This is obviously a difficult position to maintain and to defend, but the attempt is made.[38] Tangential to this discussion, there has proceeded a debate over the precise meaning of Lenin's policy toward the soviets, carried on within innumerable journal articles on the history of the soviets. The frame of the dilemma is: Did Lenin advocate transfer of power to the soviets before or only conditional upon their complete control by the Bolsheviks? Clearly if he approved the former, it was tantamount to a temporary sharing of power with other parties.

A more theoretical version is developed by Frantsev, who posits that the revolutionary process consisted of various coexisting historical tendencies. The mode of armed struggle came to the fore in October. "But there was another tendency, which, however, in those conditions did not prevail — the peaceful tendency of development of the revolution. The study of the world-historic significance of the experience of the October Revolution includes as well a study of such opportunities as were unrealized."[39] This theoretical explication, which gains considerable prestige from its publication in *Izvestiia*, dovetails with the markedly less bloody accounts of 1917 that have appeared since 1956. It also is congenial with current official stress on the significance of the July Days as ending the stage of peaceful development of the revolution. By their repression of the popular July demonstrations, the Mensheviks and Essars joined the counterrevolution and forced the Bolsheviks to take power by force. Thus in popular as well as specialized works it is the rival socialist parties who bear the onus of violent revolution, which was thrust upon

sotsialisticheskoi revoliutsii," *Voprosy istorii KPSS*, no. 12 (1963), pp. 63–69; and P. Volobuiev, "Genialnaia programma sotsialisticheskoi revoliutsii," *Pravda*, April 17, 1967, pp. 2–3.
37. Golikov, "Partiia-vdokhnovitel i organizator," p. 65.
38. For a revealing critique of such a balancing act, see A. Kuchkin, K. Gusev, and A. Konstantinov, "Kuiga po istorii Velikogo Oktiabria," *Kommunist*, no. 12 (1963), pp. 123–125. This is a review of *Istoriia Velikoi Oktiabrskoi sotsialisticheskoi revoliutsii*, P. N. Sobolev, ed. (Moscow: Academy of Sciences Publishing House, 1962).
39. Iu Frantsev, "Vosprianyl rod lindskoi," *Izvestiia*, November 6, 1965, p. 2.

the reluctant Bolsheviks. This is, of course, a dramatic revision of earlier Soviet historiography; but it also creates new peripheral inconsistencies with regard to the claim that some of the more violent rebels of the tsarist period were precursors of Bolshevism.

There is, moreover, a strain of opinion among some historians which argues for more careful analysis of the class composition and attitude toward revolutionary action with respect to bourgeois parties, groups, and leaders. A pair of articles appearing in *Istoriia SSSR* on the topic of periodization of the October Revolution provide a good example of this kind of debate. The earlier piece[40] declaims against all the non-Bolshevik leaders as unchanging counterrevolutionary ideologues. The second article calls this analysis too simplistic.[41] The author, Burganov, argues that Lenin characterized classes pragmatically by their relationship to revolution, first having determined "what revolution we are talking about." Further, Lenin realized that party label and class were in themselves inadequate indicators of political position: he even talked of some leaders of the soviets as counterrevolutionary. Burganov concludes that "it seems to us incorrect to talk of all petty-bourgeois democrats as counterrevolutionary."[42]

Rosenberg's review calls attention to Burdzhalov's highly unusual consideration of Essar and Menshevik participation in the February Revolution.

Among the workers were not only Bolsheviks, but Essars and Mensheviks as well. During the decisive days of struggle against tsarism a mighty revolutionary force seized the whole mass of workers and welded it together . . .

In the streets of Petrograd together with the worker-Bolsheviks there struggled other workers — Mensheviks, Essars, nonparty workers. In the course of their struggle the unity of their aims was revealed and the unity of their actions took shape.[43]

There is one more aspect of this cluster of issues which is of interest to us: the treatment accorded the unified Bolshevik-Menshevik committees in 1917 and 1918. Burdzhalov raised the lid in 1956 by demanding that historians stop ignoring the awk-

40. N. E. Naidenov, "Leninskaia periodizatsiia istorii velikoi oktiabrskoi sotsialisticheskoi revoliutsii," *Istoriia SSSR,* no. 6 (1963), pp. 3–18.
41. A. Kh. Burganov, "K voprosu o periodizatsii istorii Velikoi Oktiabrskoi sotsialisticheskoi revoliutsii," *Istoriia SSSR,* no. 3 (1964), pp. 3–16.
42. *Ibid.,* p. 3.
43. Burdzhalov, *Vtoraia russkaia revoliutsiia,* pp. 123, 156.

ward fact that unified committees had existed. Since then, Soviet historians have grappled with the problem in varying ways.[44] Some studies of October point to confusion with regard to unified committees among the Bolshevik ranks, especially in the provincial areas.

Much of the research with respect to these committees has been to show Stalin's erroneous "semi-Menshevik" position in support of unification despite Lenin's strictures in the spring of 1917.[45] One specialist on the Revolution has used this aspect of Stalin's denigration to raise a very sensitive theoretical issue: essentially he is calling into doubt the historical necessity of the eradication of rival socialist parties during the building of socialism. Gorodetsky attacks Stalin for insisting that the basic task of the Soviet government before the victory of socialism was the overthrow of the exploiting classes, with economic and cultural construction not receiving serious attention. He then says: "Stalin considered the necessary and general characteristic of the dictatorship of the proletariat to be the one-party system, ignoring the experience of the real, albeit brief, existence after October of a bloc of two parties — the Bolsheviks and Left Essars."[46] And the Bolshevik tactic of the "left bloc" alliance during the interrevolutionary months is now openly discussed. As the treatment of the socialists has become more objective since Khrushchev's eclipse, so have the accounts of Bolshevik tactical cooperation with them grown somewhat less strident. The best illustration of this trend is the contrast between the *Pravda* version in September 1964 and the final introduction to the *History of the Communist Party of the Soviet Union,* which appeared a few months later.[47] The *Pravda* introduction, published while Khrushchev was in power, is laced with derogatory and insulting references to the Mensheviks and Essars, as "petty-bourgeois traitors to socialism," who pursued a "treacherous, antirevolu-

44. V. V. Anikeev, "Svedeniia o bolshevistskikh organizatsiakh s marta po dekabr 1917 goda," *Voprosy istorii KPSS,* no. 2 (1958), pp. 126–193, and no. 3 (1958), pp. 96–168.
45. A good example is A. V. Snegov, "Neskolko stranits iz istorii partii (mart-nachalo aprelia 1917 g.)," which reproduces the essence of his remarks at the December 1962 all-union conference.
46. E. N. Gorodetsky, *Rozhdenie sovetskogo gosudarstva: 1917–18,* Institute of History, Academy of Sciences (Moscow: "Science" Publishing House, 1965), p. 18.
47. See Chapter Six above.

tionary position [and] stood for preservation of the capitalist wage slavery system." These passages were deleted from volume one as it appeared in final form after Khrushchev's fall. In place there was inserted a new paragraph:

The chief strategic task of the party throughout this stage of struggle for the dictatorship of the proletariat consisted of guaranteeing the *hegemony of the proletariat* as the decisive condition for the defeat of tsarism and capitalism, attracting to the side of the proletariat the broadest span of workers and oppressed peoples of the national regions of Russia. This task was achieved in the sharp and continuous struggle against the bourgeois and petty-bourgeois parties, first of all against the Kadets, Mensheviks and Essars. Along with this, during the democratic stage of the revolution the Bolsheviks in their struggle for the masses, in the interests of achieving unity of the working class, entered into partnership and blocs with other parties and social groups active in workers' movements, with representatives of the petty-bourgeois revolutionary democrats (the tactic of the "left bloc").[48]

The Left Essars

A measure of the magnitude of the doctrinal and political problems raised for the Soviet leadership by the historical Left Essars is the fact that no serious work was produced on the subject after Stalin's death until 1963. At that point there appeared a slim volume by K. V. Gusev, a well-known and conservative authority on early party history.[49] This monograph was published for the specialized scholarly community — in an edition of 6000 copies — but it touched off a furor that quickly spread the discussion into wider circles. The book has been the subject of a number of articles in historical journals; in March 1964 it was the topic of a special session of the *Voprosy istorii* editorial board with the Department of History of Soviet Society at Moscow University; and the tone of a number of party publications indicates that the debate reached middle- and lower-level functionaries.

Gusev had, it appears, raised the two most sensitive issues relevant to this most threatening of all parties to the Bolsheviks: its class composition and the extent and time span of its partnership with the Bolsheviks. From an analysis of these questions,

48. *Istoriia Kommunisticheskoi Partii Sovetskogo Soiuza*, I, xxi–xxii.
49. *Krakh partii levykh eserov* (Moscow: Social-Economic Literature Publishing House, 1963).

the ultimate problem inevitably came under review: Do the traditional historical arguments provide a convincing rationale for the one-party state? Since the 1920s such questions have not been asked in Soviet historiography; and one can argue that they were not thoroughly investigated even in the twenties, because historians were too close to events and lacked the special perspective they would acquire under Stalin's regime.

Gusev's study appears on the surface to be quite orthodox. The footnotes include references to some research done in the 1920s, but far more common are quotations from Lenin's works and citations of official protocols or other documents. Gusev's avowed purpose is to clarify mistaken impressions and outright falsifications perpetrated by Western and emigré historians of the Essars, to correct the near complete neglect of the subject in the USSR "from the beginning of the thirties until 1956" and even later. Why, then, are his findings so radical? The clue probably lies in his attack on O. H. Radkey's work,[50] as "trying to show that the Bolsheviks had no support among the peasantry, which in the main was linked to the Essars, and that the crushing of the latter was the result of Bolshevik intrigues and some tactical mistakes of the Essars' leadership, which were made use of by their enemies."[51] It is this effort to prove that the Bolsheviks did have peasant support, and that the Essars were doomed by large historical developments, which forces Gusev to take the party seriously and to press beyond superficial cliches. But when he does this, he is in trouble.

I have said that the crucial issues pertinent to the Left Essars are the class composition of the party and its joint activity with the Bolsheviks. Gusev's research effectively renders useless previous Soviet analysis on the first point. Emphasizing that at the time of the 1917 revolutions this was a party "the social basis of which was the laboring peasantry,"[52] he summarizes his findings as follows:

From what has been said the conclusion follows, that the social base of the Left Essars during the period of formation of this party was the laboring peasantry . . . The definition of the party

50. O. H. Radkey, *The Agrarian Foes of Bolshevism* (New York: Columbia University Press, 1958).
51. Gusev, *Krakh partii*, p. 16.
52. *Ibid.*, p. 90.

of Left Essars in this period as the party of the peasantry or working peasantry is given in several works of V. I. Lenin.[53]

According to Gusev, their fall from grace began in the spring of 1918, when the Left Essars became increasingly infected by kulak elements opposed to the social revolution in the countryside.[54] It is generally assumed by Marxist historians, whether or not they would support Gusev's argument, that the factor of class composition is a critical one. Thus much of the debate has consisted of allegations that the party was indeed a kulak party in 1917 as well as in 1918, or that the proportion of kulak membership began to increase only in 1918.[55]

For Gusev, then, there is no difficulty in justifying Lenin's alliance in 1917 with this peasant party as undertaken in good faith to gain the support of the rural poor. This bloc does remain, however, a major hurdle for those historians who refuse to consider the Left Essars as an honorable party — as of proper class composition. Such historians rely upon much more instrumental or tactical rationalizations. An example of this approach is a 1965 article by V. V. Garmiza,[56] which explains that Lenin utilized the Essar slogans without accepting their program because the poor peasants believed in that program.

The alternative interpretation, which Gusev's account fosters, has been developed quite extensively and apparently has had an impact in some unexpected places. Perhaps the outstanding example of revisionary historiography on the Left Essars has been presented by A. S. Smirnov in *Voprosy istorii KPSS*.[57] If anything, Smirnov is more revisionary than Gusev. Displaying thorough knowledge of a wide variety of source materials, he builds a complex network of interaction, political support, and joint activities of the Left Essars and Bolsheviks even before the formal alliance at the Seventh Conference of the Bolsheviks in April

53. *Ibid.*, p. 89.
54. *Ibid.*, p. 90.
55. See V. V. Garmiza, "K. V. Gusev. *Krakh partii levykh eserov*, M., Sotzekgiz, 1963," *Istoriia SSSR*, no. 3 (1964), pp. 170–174; K. I. Sedov, "Obsuzhdenie knigi K. V. Guseva 'Krakh partii levykh eserov,' " *Voprosy istorii*, no. 10 (1964), pp. 176–181; D. Iu. Bakhshiev, "Iz istorii borby leninskoi partii protiv opportunizma," *Voprosy istorii KPSS*, no. 3 (1967), pp. 121–125.
56. "Kak esery izmenili svoei agrarnoi programme," *Voprosy istorii*, no. 7 (1965), pp. 31–41.
57. "Ob otnoshenii bolshevikov k levym eseram v period podgotovki Oktiabrskoi revoliutsii," *Voprosy istorii KPSS*, no. 2 (1966), pp. 14–28.

1917. Smirnov elaborates a whole series of instances in which the Left Essars supported the Bolsheviks in further preparations for October: the two parties are depicted as cooperating in the countryside, in the soviets, in military garrisons, and in mass organizations such as factory committees and workers' and soldiers' clubs.[58] He points out that Left Essars as well as Bolsheviks were arrested in the aftermath of the July Days and their press shut down.[59] In short, the reader perceives that this was a genuine partnership between political parties which shared at least some goals. As Gusev does, Smirnov blames the Left Essars for destruction of the bloc, when in the summer of 1918 the party leadership abandoned its agrarian program and opted for adventurism and counterrevolution, leaving the rank and file to go over to the Bolsheviks.[60]

It is interesting to see how much of this interpretation and data have found their way into more conservative or semiofficial historiography. The works of E. Bugaev are usually a good touchstone for these purposes, and one of his articles says:

On the eve of October the Left Essars with their demand for equalization of landholding (in contrast to the Center and Right Essars) actually reflected the views of the major part of the peasantry. Therefore the Bolsheviks called for a bloc with the Left Essars, as carrying out the idea of unifying the workers and peasants. Formally this bloc was created after the II Congress of Soviets. In actuality it was already formed . . . in the course of preparing for the October armed uprising.[61]

If, then, a significant number of Soviet historians now see the Left Essars as having made a real contribution to the revolution as genuine partners of the Bolsheviks, degenerating only in mid-1918, they are faced with a serious dilemma: When and how is the one-party state legitimated? On this point, not surprisingly, there is considerable variety of opinion. Not even Bugaev will accept for the Bolsheviks the responsibility of eradicating the Left Essars, or indeed any other party. It was the sharp class struggle abetted by international imperialism and intervention which in the end forced those parties that had initially supported the Bolsheviks

58. *Ibid.*, p. 23.
59. *Ibid.*, p. 26.
60. *Ibid.*, p. 28.
61. E. Bugaev, "Klassy i partii Rossi v kanun Oktiabria," *Kommunist,* no. 16 (1966), p. 18.

(including the Left Essars) to become counterrevolutionary, while their better elements joined the Bolsheviks.[62] This process of repudiation and self-liquidation inevitably brought about hegemony of the Bolsheviks.

Gusev himself clearly understood the political implications of his historiography: the legitimation of a multiparty system. His phraseology is significant:

The Bolsheviks did not aim for the creation of a single-party system, and V. I. Lenin more than once spoke of the desirability of creating a coalition Soviet government. And it was not the Bolsheviks who created the one-party system and as a result thereof the one-party government, but the historical conditions of the revolution in Russia and the policy of the party of the Left Essars, which, turning away from the people and showing up on the other side of the barricades, led to this system.[63]

And one of Gusev's supporters was willing to take this a step further to argue:

The coalition of the Bolsheviks with the Left Essars shows that V. I. Lenin and the communist party allowed the possibility of partnership of the soviet government with other parties which had a soviet platform, that the dictatorship of the proletariat does not exclude, as is now seen in the example of the countries of people's democracies, the existence of a multiparty system under conditions of preservation of leadership for the communists.[64]

Along these lines it is instructive to explore Gusev's treatment of the Left Essars for its illustration of the multilayered structure of Soviet historiography. I have argued for the development since 1956 of a spectrum of professional opinion, which varies with the historical issue, within a more general condition of conservative-revisionist polarity. But this model does not tell the whole story and must be reinforced by the perspective of the medium or audience. Thus one may observe a number of simultaneous versions of any particular historical episode or person, which differ in substance or style; and the criterion of these differences is that of the consumer. The case in hand is of particular interest since it displays this stratification as performed by a single historian.

In addition to his scholarly monograph on the Left Essars pub-

62. *Ibid.*, p. 20.
63. Gusev, *Krakh partii*, p. 239.
64. Garmiza, "K. V. Gusev. *Krakh partii levykh eserov*," p. 170. For a similar interpretation, see E. G. Gimpelson, "Iz istorii obrazovaniia odnopartiinoi sistemy v SSSR," *Voprosy istorii*, no. 11 (1965), pp. 16–30.

lished in 1963, Gusev also wrote two different articles on the subject which appeared in 1966. One was a contribution to a volume put out by the Department of History of the CPSU of the Central Committee's Academy of Social Sciences, on the topic of the party's struggle against opportunism.[65] It may have been the product of a symposium held by the department. Gusev's article is a veritable *tour de force* in which are assembled all of the angry Lenin quotations against the Essars that were omitted from his monograph. The source work is comparatively superficial, the language is declamatory, and the Essars are portrayed as socialists in name only. Gusev finds it advisable to glide quite quickly over the Left Essars, and almost all of the references to them deal with their position on the war. He sums them up in a few words: "As to the Left Essars, while they joined the Bolsheviks and supported, although inconsistently, the basic directives of soviet policy, they received support from only limited sections of the workers."[66]

At about the same time, Gusev was commissioned to write a pamphlet on the non-Bolshevik parties for the propaganda effort, and in April 1966 there appeared number 9-10 in the history series put out under the auspices of the All-Union Society for the Dissemination of Political and Scientific Knowledge.[67] This was to be a sixty-page essay dealing with a very broad subject; in fact, though, Gusev treats only Essars and Mensheviks. The brush strokes are necessarily broad, and the point is clearly — in terms of vocabulary, simplicity of style, and paucity of source work even in comparison with the Academy of Social Sciences article — to present an argument for party workers to pass along. The Left Essars are treated only briefly, and their main function appears to be to demonstrate the disarray and disunity within the Essar party. This time there is "nothing of socialism in the program of the Essars."[68] The reader first meets the party's left wing at the Third Congress of the Essars in May 1917;[69] their contribution

65. "V. I. Lenin o melkoburzhuaznoi suchshnosti i politicheskom avantiurizme programmy i taktike eserov," *Iz istorii borby leninskoi partii protiv opportunizma* (Moscow: "Thought" Publishing House, 1966), pp. 82–132.
66. *Ibid.*, p. 132.
67. K. V. Gusev, *Krakh melkoburzhuaznykh partii v SSSR* (Moscow: "Knowledge" Publishing House, 1966).
68. *Ibid.*, p. 9.
69. *Ibid.*, p. 29.

to the October Revolution is ignored and the reader is reminded that at the first congress of the Left Essars one of their leaders spoke out against an armed uprising;[70] and the possibility of a positive social role for the Left Essars is shown as destroyed in January 1918, when they refused to accept the Bolsheviks' offer of coalition because they "could not desert their petty-bourgeois tendencies."[71]

It requires some effort to recall that the same man wrote all three pieces. But this disparity poses difficulty only for the outsider: quite clearly historians and their various readers within the Soviet Union understand the multiplicity of voices with which historiography speaks and automatically adjust their perception according to the nature and scope of the publication.

It may be objected that Gusev's several renditions are not exactly coincident in time and that the differences observed may simply be the effect of a change in "the line." But the available data simply do not warrant presumption of a definitive single official line on most historical problems. Further, there are many similar stratifications of historiography on other topics — some of which do coincide in time — which mitigate against such an assumption. And if there had been such a general and effective suppression of the conclusions of Gusev's monograph between 1963 and 1966, Smirnov's or indeed Bugaev's articles (to cite only two) could not have appeared in 1966.

The CPSU and Intraparty Opposition
The treatment in party history of dissidents within the CPSU has undergone some sea changes since 1956. The oppositionists can be categorized as belonging to four groups, as seen from the perspective of Soviet publications:

1. Opposition within the CPSU to Stalin after 1934.
2. The Right and Left Oppositions of the 1920s.
3. The antiparty group of 1957.
4. The figure of Trotsky.

There are obvious differences in substance and tone among the treatment meted out to these various categories in revisionist or small-edition monographs as well as in the mass media and official texts. For instance, one may roughly posit that the four groups

70. *Ibid.*, p. 36.
71. *Ibid.*, p. 40.

show an ascending scale of resistance to amelioration of the harsh judgment imposed by the *Short Course*. It should be noted, however, that although the antiparty group is still outside the pale, Khrushchev's ouster has certainly put its members in a better position for future rehabilitation.

The general trend since 1956 has been, despite the variations among opposition categories, consciously in the direction of a more rational and documented repudiation of intraparty oppositionists and away from vicious abuse. This has required more detailed explication of the policies of these groups, and the whole process has of course moved in tandem with the program of rehabilitation of those party members wrongly purged by Stalin. One more generalization should be made before introducing a few examples of this trend: the initiative for public or published revisions of historiography with regard to opposition groups in the CPSU has come almost exclusively from the regime or quasi-official sources such as the editorial boards of textbooks on party history. In such delicate matters the Soviet historian is extremely cautious, and with reason.

A brief synopsis of some of the textual changes will amplify these remarks. First, with regard to the opposition groups of the 1920's, a comparison of the analysis of the Fifteenth Party Congress in the first and second editions of *History of the Communist Party of the Soviet Union* reveals the following changed evaluation of the Right Opposition:

Shortly after the Congress, many of the expelled participants in the Trotsky-Zinoviev opposition began to submit applications, breaking with Trotskyism and asking to be reinstated in the Party . . . The majority of the expelled fulfilled their undertakings and were reinstated in the Party. *But, as subsequent events showed, the behavior of the leaders of the Trotsky-Zinoviev opposition was doublefaced. They returned to the Party with the same provocative aim — to disrupt it from within, to overthrow the Leninist Central Committee, to usurp the leadership of the Party and to frustrate the building of Socialism in the USSR.*[72]

This version is already quite mild in comparison with the castigation in the *Short Course* of the opposition at the Fifteenth Congress as "enemies of the people, spies recruited by foreign espionage services," whose recantations were "false and hypocritical from beginning to end," designed by these "political

72. *History of the Communist Party of the Soviet Union*, p. 423 (italics added).

swindlers" to insinuate themselves once again into public confidence.[73] But the passage is further modified in the 1962 edition. so that the italicized sentences are replaced with the following:

Many Communists — mostly from among the rank and file — who had adhered to the Trotsky-Zinoviev opposition but had seen that the Party's Leninist line was correct and that Trotskyism was an anti-Leninist trend, were working honestly in the Party, taking part in the struggle to build socialism.

Trotsky, a rabid enemy of Leninism, did not lay down arms.[74] Thus the great majority of the oppositionists are exonerated, the whole affair takes on the coloration of political interaction, and Trotsky is stripped of his following to become a lone eccentric.

The treatment accorded Bukharin and his allies is especially interesting. The official Khrushchev texts show little mercy toward Bukharin and the other Left Communists of 1918, who opposed the conclusion of a peace treaty with Germany. Finding themselves a minority in the Central Committee,

Bukharin and his followers adopted a policy of disorganizing the entire work of the Party and the Government . . . [But] Lenin unmasked the 'Left Communist' group as accomplices of the German imperialists and the Russian bourgeoisie . . . explained that their theory of "speeding up" the international revolution had nothing in common with Marxism . . . [Their] policy of wrecking the Brest-Litovsk peace treaty suffered a fiasco.[75]

Despite the continued harsh judgment of the early Left Communists, in the second edition of the new text a paragraph has been inserted which puts the whole episode on a different footing, that of a sincere opposition to policy rather than sabotage:

Despite the extreme bitterness of the struggle . . . Lenin . . . was forbearing and used the method of persuasion . . . In the same year — 1918 — the "Left Communists" publicly admitted their mistake and joined vigorously in the activities of the Party and the state.[76]

The real changes in appraisal of the Right Opposition, however, are observed later in the account. In the context of domestic policy — whether with regard to Bukharin's and Preobrazhensky's

73. *History of the Communist Party of the Soviet Union, Short Course*, pp. 290, 291.
74. *History of the Communist Party of the Soviet Union*, 2nd rev. ed., p. 419.
75. *History of the Communist Party of the Soviet Union*, pp. 280, 281; 2nd ed., pp. 275, 276.
76. Page 278.

proposals to the Sixth Party Congress (which become "opportunist" rather than "Trotskyist" in the second edition)[77] or with regard to Bukharin's position against collectivization — the modifications in both substance and tone from the *Short Course* are dramatic. Bukharin, Rykov, and Tomsky are now called simply "Right-wingers" or "Right-wing defeatists," rather than an anti-party group, "defenders and intercessors" for the kulaks, who were inevitably "bound to join hands with the remnants of the bloc of Trotskyites and Zinovievites for common action against the Party." Further, the later versions present a much clearer picture of just what Bukharin's theoretical arguments and policies were, and what political activities the Right Opposition actually engaged in.[78]

The implication of traitorous deception is eased in the second edition: the Right leaders' acknowledgment of error in November 1929, from "a maneuver of double-dealers . . . [who] in secret . . . continued their undermining activity,"[79] becomes a "waiting game."[80] Absent entirely from the post-Stalin accounts is the vicious *Short Course* fiction of the "Bukharin-Trotsky gang of spies, wreckers and traitors to the country" and its deserved "annihilation" in 1937.[81] Instead, the official texts condemn Stalin's "erroneous thesis that the class struggle in the country would intensify as the Soviet State grew stronger," which only "served as a justification for mass repressions against the Party's ideological enemies who had already been routed politically."[82] The second edition further omits the caveat that under victorious socialism it was still "necessary to be on guard against certain elements from among the routed opposition groups of the Trotskyists, Zinovievites, Right-wingers and nationalists."[83]

In short, then, both Right and Left Oppositionists of the 1920s have become ideological and political opponents rather than

77. *History of the Communist Party of the Soviet Union*, p. 239; 2nd rev. ed., p. 234.
78. *History of the Communist Party of the Soviet Union, Short Course*, pp. 291, 293, 294; *History of the Communist Party of the Soviet Union*, pp. 427–430, 349; 2nd rev. ed., pp. 422–425, 343.
79. *History of the Communist Party of the Soviet Union*, p. 431.
80. Second rev. ed., p. 426.
81. *History of the Communist Party of the Soviet Union, Short Course*, pp. 346–348.
82. *History of the Communist Party of the Soviet Union*, pp. 512, 513.
83. *Ibid.*, p. 512; 2nd rev. ed., pp. 504–505.

archfiends and enemies of the Soviet people. All of these revisions have been faithfully adhered to in journal articles as well as in the Soviet press.

This general trend toward a more reasoned, if not objective, treatment of Lenin's opponents within Bolshevism is apparently continuing. As noted earlier, volume three — and especially book one thereof, which deals with March 1917 to March 1918 — presented an unusually sensitive set of problems and personalities for the editorial board of the six-volume *History*. That this was early recognized is apparent from the official concern and volatile professional reaction at the discussion of the draft text.[84] Further evidence of confusion and debate is afforded by the unusually long period that elapsed between the dates on which the text was given to the typesetters (September 3, 1966) and signed to the press (June 9, 1967). It is perhaps significant that book two of volume three (covering March 1918 through 1920) also was held up almost a year, from October 12, 1966, to September 13, 1967; the first two volumes of the series were processed in a matter of one to three months.

This is not the occasion for a general review of the six-volume party history, which is still in process of publication. But some leading themes with regard to political opposition should be recognized. In an informative and perceptive evaluation of the volume for 1917–1918,[85] Robert V. Daniels observes that in basic interpretation the new account presents neither novel information nor ideas but is rather an expanded version of the 1962 edition of the official one-volume history. He is disappointed to encounter *partiinost* "as firmly in force as ever."[86] But what really strikes Daniels is the radically altered commentary on Lenin's intraparty opposition.

The entire tone has changed in the treatment of the fallen angels of Communism. Trotsky, Zinoviev, Kamenev are frequently mentioned, singly or in lists, in an altogether neutral fashion. The worst they are charged with, at points of actual or alleged disagreement with Lenin, is "errors," "opportunism," and "disorienting influence." Gone is the familiar denunciation for counter-revolu-

84. See "The Personality Cult," *Survey*, April 1967, pp. 159–180.
85. "E. I. Bugaev *et al.*, editors, *Istoriia Kommunisticheskoi Partii Sovetskogo Soiuza. Tom tretii: Kniga pervaia (mart 1917–mart 1918 g.)*," *Kritika*, Spring 1968, pp. 58–66.
86. *Ibid.*, pp. 59, 60.

tionary designs and betrayal, even with reference to Zinoviev's and Kamenev's opposition to the insurrection . . . in Volume III of the Party History, the strongest language employed against them is a paraphrase of Lenin on their "strikebreaking." Zinoviev is even mentioned in a footnote (p. 159) as Lenin's companion in hiding in the haystack after the "July days," a fact up to now suppressed in all the revolutionary museums and guidebooks.[87]

From the perspective of comparison with earlier official histories of the CPSU — the *Short Course* and the one-volume texts put out only a few years ago — the shift would indeed appear astounding. In view of all the discussions and interpretive revisions exposed in professional journals and monographs since 1956, this development is not completely unexpected. Nonetheless, the fact that the oppositionists have been promoted from traitors and unpersons to very lively albeit mistaken political opponents is very significant. The gradual migration of such a stance from Burdzhalov's heretical suggestions in 1956 to a canonized text in 1967 provides official sanction for historians to discuss not only these individuals but their policies in a more detailed and rational manner.

Having said this, a note not so much of caution as of discrimination must be entered. There remain real and fascinating distinctions among official evaluations of the several "fallen angels." Bukharin and Trotsky are still in special categories. Bukharin's position is now dealt with more seriously than in the earlier party histories and his arguments are explicated in some detail: in this respect he is clearly recognized as a theorist of talent whose ideas require countering. His "mistakes of principle" and "erroneous positions,"[88] while not those of a class enemy, do seem to put him in a category apart from Kamenev, Zinoviev, and similar figures, whose errors were more political and tactical. Further, the new volume three gives rather detailed evidence that Bukharin and the Left Communists had, at least in late 1917 and early 1918, "quite significant support in the leading organs of a series of party organizations."[89] Thus the reader gains the impression that Bukharin was always a more serious threat to Leninism than most

---

87. *Ibid.*, pp. 62–63.
88. *Istoriia Kommunisticheskoi Partii Sovetskogo Soiuza*, III, book 1, pp. 184, 185.
89. *Ibid.*, p. 528.

other oppositionists because his challenge was at a more basic level. It would seem reasonable to expect that Bukharin will remain fixed in his present limbo even if Zinoviev and Kamenev are allowed to inch their way back to a state of grace — unless the political leadership should some day adopt a significant part of his policies. In such an event, of course, his historical rise might be spectacular.

One further observation should be made: despite the rather remarkably improved scholarship and increased sophistication of the new official historiography, pictorial representations continue to maintain an iconographic function. The reader looks in vain through the latest volumes of the *History* for pictures of Zinoviev, Kamenev, Trotsky, or Bukharin; small ones of Stalin[90] and Kossior[91] are included. There is evidently retained in the Soviet political culture some version of the primitive belief that the graphic image has a reifying impact. And although the verbal acknowledgment of political opposition figures is now tolerable, dignifying them visually is somehow not only threatening but blasphemous.

There has also emerged, and still only within the circles of historians and Old Bolsheviks, a new historical category: the Bolshevik opposition to Stalin during the 1930s, which was loyal to the party while attempting to curb or bring down its leader. One case was referred to by Zaitsev at the conference of historians in December 1962, when he recounted the expulsion from the CPSU in 1933 and ultimate death of three distinguished Old Bolsheviks, who were discovered by Stalin to have held "conversations concerning the replacement of Stalin." One died accidentally (at least ostensibly), and two were shot. Zaitsev concludes:

In this way, the facts show that forces existed in the party fighting against Stalin's evil methods of leadership, against the creation of the cult of his personality. But these people belonged neither to the right nor to the Trotskyites, although they were accused of both the one and the other.[92]

Zaitsev reported that these three were being rehabilitated. And there have been allusions to other such instances of real opposi-

90. *Ibid.*, p. 307; *ibid.*, book 2, p. 321.
91. *Ibid.*, book 1, p. 327; *ibid.*, book 2, p. 350.
92. Remarks of V. S. Zaitsev, *Vsesoiuznoe soveschanie*, p. 291.

tion, as distinct from party members who were wrongly accused of disloyalty.

The figure of Trotsky remains that of the archvillain, seemingly one of the few fixed points in Soviet historiography. In both editions of the party history text, he and his supporters are represented as "agents inside the Party of the class enemies, mouthpieces of the hostile capitalist encirclement,"[93] "ready to stab the Soviet country in the back, the moment the imperialists attacked it."[94] Nonetheless, the post-Stalin picture of Trotsky shows some definite revisions of the devilish figure encountered in the *Short Course*. They relate, for the most part, to Trotsky's motivations.

In the *Short Course* Trotsky is shown as deciding in 1923 to take advantage of Lenin's illness "to smash the Party and overthrow its leadership."[95] In the Khrushchev text, which has not been discredited on this score, Trotsky is presumed to be proposing alternative leadership and policies, which of course would have been disastrous but all the same represent something beyond simple wrecking of the party and state. The comparable passage reads:

Taking advantage of the fact that Lenin, the Party leader, was incapacitated by grave illness, Trotsky resumed his fight against the Leninist Central Committee, against the Party. He decided that the country's difficulties gave him a favorable opportunity to realize his designs — to take the leadership of the Party into his own hands and pursue his own line, one that, in the end, would have led to the restoration of capitalism.[96]

This is a subtle shift, but it fosters the impression that Trotsky did not directly aim for the restoration of capitalism and that he was more a political foe than a traitorous plotter.

There have been some occasional rumors picked up by Western journalists and tourists in the USSR that Trotsky would be reconsidered in one or another forthcoming historical work; but this has not materialized. Trotsky has appeared briefly in a film;[97] and a few years ago *Pravda* found it necessary to slash A. Shtein for his play "Between the Cloudbursts" on the Kronstadt upris-

93. *History of the Communist Party of the Soviet Union*, p. 408; 2nd rev. ed., p. 405.
94. *Ibid.*, 1st ed., p. 409; 2nd rev. ed., p. 406.
95. *History of the Communist Party of the Soviet Union, Short Course*, p. 265.
96. *History of the Communist Party of the Soviet Union*, p. 381; 2nd rev. ed., p. 379.
97. The film, entitled "The Salvo of the Aurora," was criticized in *Krasnaia zvezda* for underrating Trotsky's talents; see Chapter One.

ing: "The author refers to Trotsky . . . so unclearly — if not ambiguously! — that if the reader had no distinct idea of his role . . . he could get an absolutely false impression that this figure was on the whole positive!"[98]

Evidence exists of considerable discussion with regard to the proper treatment of Trotsky occasioned by preparation of the third volume of the *History of the Communist Party*. The pressure to produce a believable account in time for the fiftieth anniversary was apparently considerable, and the practical concern and emotional involvement of many Old Bolsheviks have been enormous. According to the unofficial account of a closed meeting on the third volume, attended by some Old Bolsheviks and historians of the party, the matter of Trotsky was in dispute. Clearly a truthful record of 1917 cannot be produced until substantial revisions are made to acknowledge Trotsky's leadership. Two Old Bolsheviks, Dinitas and Milonov, allegedly made direct suggestions to this effect:

The distribution of forces on the eve of October is wrongly presented in the third volume. It should be shown who were the *mezhraiontsy* — Manuilsky, Uritsky, Lozovsky. Trotsky was at the head of them. They left their mark on the revolution. This must be mentioned.[99]

On November 6 1918 Stalin published an article in *Pravda* maintaining that Trotsky, Chairman of the Petrograd Soviet, participated directly in all the work connected with the leadership of the rising. Stalin maintained that the party owed its victory in October first and foremost to Trotsky. Strange as it is, this article was reprinted in the collection *October Revolution*, published in 1932.[100]

The latter remark is especially interesting in its attempt to utilize Stalin's own authority to destroy the Stalinist version. Perhaps Milonov was attempting to gain the support of the pro-Stalinist historians, or perhaps he was merely enjoying the irony.

Certainly no such restoration of Trotsky has occurred. There are, however, in volume three significant changes in the historical figure of Trotsky — who would be unrecognizable to the devout reader of the *Short Course*. The new text, even in comparison with the 1962 *History*, portrays a more complex personality, a

98. "Otvetstvennost khudozhnika," *Pravda*, July 12, 1964, p. 4.
99. "The Personality Cult," p. 161.
100. *Ibid.*, pp. 161–162.

man who is no longer the agent of class enemies but whose failure to comprehend social events and driving personal ambition lead him to disastrous tactical mistakes.

Trotsky is never seen as a genuine Bolshevik, but as always attempting to substitute his own programs for Leninism.[101] He is a "falsifier of history,"[102] who not only misunderstood the historical situation but distorted it both at the time of action and in retrospect. This phenomenon is not perceived as anything beyond willful misperception, stubbornness, and deceit: the assumption is of course that any true Marxist-Leninist could and did understand history. Much is made of Trotsky's "haughty manner and dictatorial ways," his continual flouting of central committee instructions during the Civil War, his lack of faith in the creative abilities of the workers and peasants, his "excessively centralizing and bureaucratic aspirations."[103] In short, Trotsky was neither a spy nor a class traitor; he was a personal and political disaster to the cause he served.

Such a portrayal necessarily requires historiographical skill and some subtlety. The references to Trotsky's specific activities or ideas are selective and reveal only the negative aspects of the man — his egotism, mistakes, overweening ambition, and desire to dominate. With some effort the reader can piece together from the text a record of Trotsky's official career, but he will not gain any concept of his enormous and positive role in events. Trotsky has thus become not a nonperson but a partial person or semiperson. Almost by definition, such a status is inherently dynamic. Clearly to maintain this partial picture in a state of suspense (literally and figuratively) will be a difficult task.

How can an infallible CPSU have been led by so many Bolsheviks who — if no longer traitors and tools of the imperialists — were so muddle-headed and blind to events? And why must the Mensheviks and Left Essars be so thoroughly discredited if they were indeed sincere socialists, with some programs now revealed as remarkably similar and relevant to subsequent Soviet policies? Why could and should the Bolsheviks have worked together with the Mensheviks in 1917–1918? Where is the fine distinction be-

101. *Istoriia Kommunisticheskoi Partii Sovetskogo Soiuza*, III, book 1, p. 194.
102. *Ibid.*, p. 541.
103. *Ibid.*, book 2, pp. 70, 276, 376, 378.

tween Lenin's mercy toward errant old comrades, his idealized commitment to internal party democracy, and his doctrine against factions within the party?

It is difficult to overstate the enormity of the political as well as historical implications which these matters raise in the Soviet context. The existing revisions and refinements call in question the legitimacy of one-party government during the building of socialism — that is, prior to 1936. And if Stalin's rule after 1934 was that of a criminal and madman, as the Soviet public has been encouraged to believe, perhaps later one-party rule was also unjustified. Even more explosive is the problem of the legitimacy of political opposition within the CPSU, suggested by some recent scholarship. The question becomes: If the opposition to Stalin during the 1930s by some party members was in the best interests of the CPSU and justified by events at the time as well as in later historical perspective, how can the party regulation condemning any and all opposition to the leadership stand? If the historian attempts to distinguish between party oppositionist heroes during the purges and, say, Trotskyite wreckers during the 1920s, what criteria will he establish as marking justified opposition to the power structure? And how can the Khrushchev assertion that socialism may come to power in many areas by way of a parliamentary majority be held up out of the reviled Menshevik doctrine of a peaceful growing into socialism?

In an oblique manner the problem of political opposition in Soviet historiography resolves itself into the temporal dimension. The observer is struck by the strong backward impetus of denigrations in Soviet party history: the tendency to push the evil deeds and motives of any recently discredited leader back into his earlier career is well documented in the progressive unmasking of Stalin, Trotsky, or the antiparty group. This is probably a function of the Marxist claim to be a lawful and scientific theory with universal applicability. But these presumptions of generality can conceivably create a serious reverse momentum if intraparty opposition is proclaimed virtuous at any specified point in time.

It may also be seen that the issue of political opposition has an important spatial dimension in that it intensifies the theoretical and political dispute over whether the Soviet Union is the model for all socialist states. It is no longer possible for even the most nimble Soviet historian to sustain both the one-party system as an essential category of the dictatorship of the proletariat and the Soviet Union's role as prototype. The considerable political motivation to maintain leadership among the socialist community of states and over foreign communist parties might work toward the repudiation of Stalin's repressive tactics toward his socialist rivals.

The question of defining tolerable limits of political diversity, dissent, and opposition is clearly the central dilemma for the Soviet political leadership as well as for the Soviet historian. The discussion must be historical because of its political sensitivity, yet it cannot successfully be confined to the past. Of all historical topics, this one presents the primary threat to maintenance of the Soviet system as we have come to know it.

The Twentieth Congress opened the floodgates for historical research on topics that had for many years been out of bounds. Certainly the collectivization of agriculture was high on the list of proscribed subjects, and the response of historians to the permissive signal issued in 1956 has been dramatic. The developments were well summarized in one of a series of journal articles on the historiography of collectivization:

After the Twentieth Congress of the CPSU, favorable conditions were created for the study of the history of the collectivization of agriculture in the U.S.S.R., as also for the development of other areas of historical science. Many documents became available. Researchers received permission to study unpublished materials of the plenums of the Central Committee (November 1929, December 1930, January 1933, June 1934, and others). The materials of various commissions of the Central Committee, VKP(B), on questions of collectivization are valuable sources on the history of the development of concrete acts, methods, and forms of collectivization. Interesting letters of workers, kolkhozniks, party and soviet workers to the Central Committee, VKP(B), the People's Commissariat on Agriculture, U.S.S.R., directly to J. V. Stalin, declaring warm wishes to help in the socialist transformation of the countryside. Materials of the funds of central agricultural institutions have been researched . . . Remarkable changes have occurred in the study of statistical data. Documents of local party and soviet organizations have been broadly introduced into the scientific purview.
All this produced positive results. Monographs and scientific articles of wide circulation have appeared dealing with the history of kolkhoz construction. Qualitative changes in the treatment of this theme have taken place — reflecting the profound and many-sided researches on cardinal problems . . . Our representations of collectivization have become more complete and have changed in many ways.[1]

When one examines the research and critical literature on this topic since 1956, it becomes evident that at any moment several works were being prepared while others were appearing in print, that communication was imperfect among scholars working on the topic, that the dialogue cannot be neatly dissected and each rejoinder ordered in time. Nevertheless, it may be useful to trace the main outlines of the developing interpretations and analyses of collectivization as they have appeared in Soviet historical literature.

1. M. A. Viltsan, N. A. Ivnitsky, Iu. A. Poliakov, "Nekotorye problemy istorii kollektivizatsii v SSSR," *Voprosy istorii*, no. 3 (1965), p. 3.

The initial studies were concerned to utilize some of the wealth of new research materials and data, at first to make the point that collectivization was indeed historically necessary and rational. A leading and prolific scholar in this field argued in 1956 that both rural mechanization and collectivization were essential to create the material-technical base for a productive and advanced agricultural system. Only complete collectivization could provide social relationships in the countryside appropriate to the use of the new machines and techniques. Collectivization had to pace industrialization if a serious socal contradiction were to be avoided.[2]

A second theme also appeared very early in this period and became of central focus: the organizing and guiding role of the party in developing the policy and carrying through the collectivization. In an important, trendsetting critique of the literature published late in 1958, V. I. Pogudin stresses the political aspects of collectivization, explicitly rejecting explanations that would dispose of it as simply a reflection of "a law of necessary relationship between two wings of production," or as the inevitable result of the development of an adequate material-technical base, whereby "collectivization would develop of itself, following mechanization."[3] Pogudin insists that the policy of collectivization be recognized by the historian as a deliberate, political choice made by the CPSU. This policy decision was, moreover, rational and worked to the quickest and most efficient ordering of agricultural production. The spread of collectivization stimulated agricultural machinebuilding and related industrial production. In turn, the growth of machine construction directed attention to the party's policy of strengthening the kolkhoz. "In this manner, the social and technical revolutions in agriculture developed simultaneously."[4]

In his criticism of a series of works Pogudin consistently employs the categories of amount of factual material introduced and the extent to which specific activities of the CPSU and especially its local organizations are displayed. He finds almost all studies to be inadequate in their treatment of the internal functioning

2. V. P. Danilov, "Materialno-tekhnicheskaia baza selskogo khoziaistva SSSR nakanune sploshnoi kollektivizatsii," *Voprosy istorii*, no. 7 (1956), pp. 3–17.
3. "Nekotorye voprosy istoriografii kollektivizatsii v SSSR," *Voprosy istorii*, no. 9 (1958), pp. 121, 122.
4. *Ibid.*, p. 123.

of party organizations, the work of local party organizations in training rural communists and attracting the best elements in the rural population to the party.

This article also sets out the need for Soviet historians of the collectivization period to devote more attention to the work of mass economic organizations in implementing the policy. He mentions the trade unions, the machine tractor stations, the state farms.

Pogudin comes to grips with the "mistakes" and "excesses" in the kolkhoz program. Soviet historans had for the past year or more been acknowledging these problems, but in a superficial and gingerly fashion. Pogudin is forthright: "It is well known that along with broad successes in the building of kolkhozi at the begining of 1930 serious mistakes were made and distortions of the party line. The fundamental mistake was distortion of the Leninist principle of voluntarism in kolkhoz construction."[5] While not evolving his own systematic explanation for these mistakes, Pogudin discerns inadequacies in all of the reasons offered hitherto by other scholars:

1. Leftist deviations of elements within the CPSU.
2. The phenomenon of numbers of local leaders being carried away by success and losing touch with actual conditions.
3. The intrigues of enemies of the party and the kulaks' machinations and propaganda.
4. Mistakes in collectivization methods, such as sovkhoz-kolkhoz combinations.

Such explanations must be rejected as inadequate, he says.

Finally we may note that Pogudin takes the first step toward a new interpretation of Stalin's role, by refusing to give him any credit for holding back the more foolish and vicious elements within the party at the beginning of 1930. He says: "the correction of mistakes and inadequacies in the kolkhoz movement is linked by several historians only with the name of J. V. Stalin, while the great work of the party and the Central Committee remain in the shadow."[6]

The course of scholarly opinion on collectivization in the years after this article has been essentially a process of elaboration, substantiation, and — in the case of Stalin's role — intensification of Pogudin's outline. Important conferences of historians were

5. *Ibid.*, p. 132.
6. *Ibid.*, p. 133.

held to deal specifically with problems of the peasantry and kolkhoz construction in 1958 and 1961.[7] In the reports of these meetings and in other sources, collectivization is repeatedly identified as the fulfillment of Lenin's plan for cooperative agriculture, although the idea of collectivization had been attributed to Stalin during the years 1936 to 1953, and Lenin's significance in agricultural organization is wrongly limited to the early New Economic Policy period.[8]

The conclusion of the period of struggle for kolkhoz building was dated in the one-volume text *History of the Communist Party of the Soviet Union* as 1932, rather than 1934, as was stated in the *Short Course*. The explanation given is rather unsatisfactory:

As is known, in January–February 1932 the XVII Party Conference established that the decisions of party congresses regarding the building of the foundations of a socialist economy had been fulfilled in this period in the countryside as well as the city.[9]

This statement does not accord well with the text itself, which states that it was decided "the foundations of socialism" had been laid at the time of the Central Committee and Central Control Commission joint plenum held in January 1933, in connection with the completion of the First Five-Year Plan.[10] These inconsistencies indicate a certain amount of confusion in moving toward a new periodization; but at any rate it is established that the collective farm system was set up at least

7. E. N. Oskolkov and L. A. Etenke, "Nauchnaia konferentsiia o voprosakh kollektivizatsii," *Voprosy istorii KPSS*, no. 4 (1958), pp. 212–214; V. P. Danilov, "K itogam izucheniia istorii sovetskogo krestianstva i kolkhoznogo stroitelstva v SSSR," *ibid.*, no. 8 (1960), pp. 34–64; and V. P. Danilov, "Nekotorye itogi nauchnoi sessii po istorii sovetskoi derevni," *ibid.*, no. 2 (1962), pp. 20–43.
8. See book review, by V. V. Mavrodin, N. G. Sladkevich, and A. L. Fraiman, of *Istoricheskie zapiski*, A. L. Sidorov, ed. (Moscow, 1954–1955), in *Voprosy istorii*, no. 10 (1956), pp. 141–155; V. M. Selunskaia, "O kandidatskikh dissertatsiiakh po istorii kollektivizatsii selskogo khoziaistva v SSSR," *ibid.*, no. 11 (1956), pp. 195–201; V. P. Danilov, "K itogam izucheniia istorii sovetskogo krestianstva i kolkhoznogo stroitelstva v SSSR," *ibid.*, no. 8 (1960), pp. 34–64; V. M. Selunskaia, "Kooperativnyi plan V. I. Lenina v trudakh sovetskikh istorikov," *Voprosy istorii KPSS*, no. 9 (1964), pp. 107–116.
9. E. I. Bugaev and N. V. Ruban, "Put borby i pobed leninskoi partii," *Voprosy istorii KPSS*, no. 4 (1959), p. 20.
10. *History of the Communist Party of the Soviet Union* (Moscow: Foreign Languages Publishing House, 1960), pp. 474–475; 2nd rev. ed., pp. 468–469. 468–469.

a year prior to the convening of the Seventeenth Party Congress on January 26, 1934. It seems likely that the underlying reason for the reperiodization of the building of the collective farm system is to separate it further in time — and thus in influence — from the beginnings of the Stalinist excesses, which are shown in the new text as developing soon after the Seventeenth Congress.

The interpretation of Stalin's role in the decision to speed the pace of collectivization and in the practice of forced collectivization and other excesses has been one of gradual blackening. The first steps in the reevaluation process were, with regard to the specific topic of collectivization as well as to Stalin's image in general, concerned to chip away the richly layered baroque encrustations of false praise for nonexistent achievements and contributions. Thus, an article in *Voprosy istorii,* which surveyed candidate dissertation topics dealing with the collectivization of agriculture between 1947 and April 1956, complains that scholarship in this field is still marred by the Stalin cult of personality.[11] It is evident that the chief criticism made by the author of this article concerns the inadequate research and shabby treatment accorded the party by historians of collectivization. The formulation of Stalin's role is quite cautious: "The role of J. V. Stalin in collectivization and in further development of the Leninist theory of the socialist organization of agriculture is indisputable. However . . . the actions of the entire Russian Communist Party (B) were of decisive significance."[12] Selunskaia calls for more detailed study of the work of the rural raikoms during the campaign for full collectivization, which would show their methods and contributions to the program. She feels that most mistakes in the dissertations arise from lack of critical analysis of the sources and literature, not from lack of material. An interesting — and not a typical — aspect of her argument is to the effect that more careful research into raikom activities would correct the mistaken assertion in most dissertations that Stalin singlehandedly struggled against the Trotskyites and Right Opportunists during this period.

Several dissertations incorrectly identify provocative enemy actions with mistakes of members of the party and soviet workers.

11. V. M. Selunskaia, "O kandidatskikh dissertatsiiakh po istorii kollektivizatsii selskogo khoziaistva v SSSR," *Voprosy istorii,* no. 11 (1956), pp. 195–201.
12. *Ibid.,* p. 197.

These authors cite the proposition in the *Short Biography of J. V. Stalin* that "leftist" distortions were the result of deliberate acts of enemies of the party. But such an evaluation of "leftist" deviations contradicts the resolution of the Central Committee of 15 March 1930 and opinions of J. V. Stalin where "leftist" deviations were described for the most part as mistaken actions and unconscious revivals of the Trotskyite relationship to the middle peasant, which appeared as a result of giddiness from success.[13]

The approach to the problem of Stalin was thus in this early period (late 1956) a careful one, moving always in the cause of the good name of the party, with heavy reliance on Lenin and the central committee, and even making use of Stalin's words to scale down his own image.

The first edition of the 1959 *History of the Communist Party* represents a significant change in the official treatment of Stalin, specifically with regard to the period of full collectivization. There is no fulminating against "pigheaded attempts" to skip the artel form, or against "heedless" and artificial forcing of the pace of collectivization "on the part of Party workers," which marked the *Short Course*.[14] Also absent are such trenchant pieces of analysis as:

Comrade Stalin's article ["Dizzy with Success"] was of the utmost political moment . . . The broad mass of the peasants now saw that the line of the Bolshevik Party had nothing in common with the pigheaded "Left" distortions of local authorities. The article set the minds of the peasants at rest.[15]

Rather, we read that

Carried away by the initial success of collectivization, some Party organizations infringed the decision of the Central Committee of the Party of January 5, 1930, concerning the rate of collectivization.[16]

Stalin's famous article is disposed of in two sentences, which emphasize that it was published by decision of the central committee, that it simply "clarified the Party line . . . and directed the members of the Party toward rectifying the mistakes committed."[17] There follows a description of organizational mea-

13. *Ibid.*, pp. 197–198.
14. *History of the Communist Party of the Soviet Union (Bolsheviks), Short Course*, p. 307.
15. *Ibid.*, p. 308.
16. *History of the Communist Party of the Soviet Union*, p. 449.
17. *Ibid.*, p. 450.

sures taken by the central committee to end forcible collectivization and "Left" distortions. But we now see that it takes more
than a journalistic piece to reassure the peasantry: *"These
energetic measures of the Party* to put right the mistakes made
set the minds of the peasants at rest" (emphasis added).[18]

The portrait of Stalin has darkened perceptibly in the second,
revised edition of the *History* put out after the Twenty-Second
Party Congress. Whole new sections have been added to the
chronicle of collectivization which stress Lenin's warnings of the
difficulties involved in restructuring agriculture for the first time
in history, and which quote his strictures against "undue haste"
at the Eighth Congress.[19] Now the blame for artificial speed and
excessive pressure on local party and government organs is
placed directly upon Stalin:

Stalin's underestimation of the power of the peasants' attachment
to their small, privately owned households, and his refusal to
lend ear to the reasonable proposals made by local Party
officials were the greatest miscalculation and a source of
numerous mistakes at the beginning of the mass collective-farm
movement.[20]

He is described as ignoring earnest requests from local and
regional party committees for clarification of policy. But the
CPSU did not stand passively before Stalin. Now we can see in
more detail the action taken not only by the central committee
but also by local, regional, and territorial party leaders. Alarmed
by "dangerous signs of resentment on the part of the peasant
masses . . . the Central Committee of the Party immediately took
steps."

At the end of February 1930 the leaders of a number of territory
and regional Party organizations met to discuss problems of
collectivization . . . At the instance of the leaders of local Party
organizations and a number of members of the Political Bureau
of the CC, the Central Committee late in February specified and
amended the Model Rules for the Agricultural Artel.[21]

The appearance of this passage immediately following a diatribe
against Stalin is sufficiently interesting to warrant a digression
here to point to the parallel development of concern for more

18. *Ibid.*, p. 451.
19. *Ibid.*, 2nd rev. ed., p. 442.
20. *Ibid.*, p. 444.
21. *Ibid.*, p. 445.

accurate party history and the progressive denigration of Stalin, which pace each other, in this period. We see here a graphic example of the fascination that the lower- and middle-level party organizations hold for historians during the Khrushchev period, especially notable in connection with collectivization. A large body of research grew up after 1956 documenting the role of the lower party organizations in carying out collectivization. A number of these studies have been of particular national areas.[22] For our purposes, an illustration from the literature on the Ukraine is most relevant because of Khrushchev's personal involvement there. A review praising a book on the early kolkhoz movement in the Ukraine (1921–1925) stresses the great contribution of the party and — even more interesting — details the popular support for the party in this program as well as its successful utilization of other institutions and organizations in kolkhoz construction. The author is credited with the presentation of a wealth of new facts and documents,

testifying to the enormous work of propagandizing the collective form of agriculture which was carried out by the CP(B) Ukraine through its goubernia, uezd and volost organizations, the soviet, cultural educational institutions and the party press . . . [Named as leaders in the formation of kolkhozi are] not a few demobilized Red Army men, Komsomol leaders, women and so forth . . . Much factual material collected by the author indisputably shows that the popular masses actively supported the policy of the Communist Party.[23]

Other articles elaborate on the work done by the village correspondents' movement, the cooperatives, and the sovkhozes in preparing for full collectivization and — after 1933 — the political departments of the machine tractor stations.

But we must return to the question of the progressive identification of Stalin with the unfortunate "excesses" of collectivization, which parallels the increasing interpretation of collectivization as a mass movement. It remains to be noted that in the second edition of the 1959 party history, Stalin's initiative is finally denied with respect to halting the forced collectivization. Stalin

22. See M. E. Naidenov, "Sovetskaia istoricheskaia nauka nakanune XXII sezda KPSS," *Voprosy istorii*, no. 10 (1961), pp. 3–24, for a survey of this literature.
23. M. E. Naidenov, reviewing A. F. Tchmiga, *Ocherki po istorii kolkhoznogo dvizheniia na Ukraine (1921–1925)* (Moscow, 1959), in *Voprosy istorii*, no. 2 (1960), pp. 182, 184.

is now said to have written "Dizzy with Success" on instructions from the political bureau of the central committee, but he failed to clear it with other Politburo members. Therefore, although favorably received by the middle peasants because it rejected compulsory collectivization, it caused confusion among the party cadres which resulted in "large numbers" of peasants bolting like kolkhozes.

Although collectivization had been urged from above, by Stalin, he used his article to put the blame for the mistakes in collective-farm development *entirely* on local officials, whom he groundlessly accused of bungling . . . The kulaks and various other elements opposed to collective farming profited by these developments to discredit the collective farms, rural Party and government organizations, and officials who had been carrying out collectivization.[24]

The criticism of Stalin stops here, but it is clear that such a commentary in official Soviet historiography is devastating to the Stalin image. The significant aspect of the quoted phraseology is the implication that Stalin's viciousness in blaming lower party cadres for his own errors aided the kulaks and other class enemies. This in the Soviet lexicon is defined as objectively aiding the enemy.

There is, however, evidence that the official appraisal of Stalin's activities with regard to collectivization has fluctuated once more. A 1966 journal article demonstrated a marked lessening of the passion with which Stalin's excesses were described during Khrushchev's regime.

When the excesses had reached mass proportions, the articles "Dizzy with Success" and "An Answer to Comrade Kolkhozniks" were published, which played an important role in the establishment of Lenin's principles of kolkhoz construction. It is true that . . . Stalin onesidedly accused the local workers of bungling.[25]

24. *History of the Communist Party of the Soviet Union*, 2nd rev. ed., p. 446.
25. N. A. Ivnitsky, "Opyt KPSS po pretvoreniiu v zhizn leninskogo kooperativnogo plana," *Voprosy istorii KPSS*, no. 2 (1966), p. 102. This trend has been confirmed by the third edition of the official text, *History of the Communist Party*, 3rd rev. ed. (Moscow: Political Literature Publishing House, 1969), which deletes even more of the colorful and personal details regarding Stalin's role in collectivization. "Dizzy with Success" is now described as playing a "large positive role" in correcting the excesses that had occurred in kolkhoz construction; however, it is specified that Stalin did not in his article fully clarify the reasons for these mistakes but laid the basic responsibility on local party workers (p. 405).

A further complicating factor is the possibility that Stalin may have been joined by Molotov as an accomplice in the distortion of Lenin's cooperative plan. A journal article published in 1963 clearly cast Molotov in the supporting role:

At the November [1929] Plenum of the Central Committee Molotov, with the agreement and support of Stalin, launched a critique of the idea of completing collectivization during the course of five years . . . The proposition of Stalin and Molotov for a maximal forced tempo of collectivization, without consideration of objective conditions, was the basic reason for the gross distortions in kolkhoz construction.[26]

However, this opening wedge for a new perspective in the denigration of Molotov (and possibly other members of the 1957 antiparty group) has not been followed up since Khrushchev's fall from power.

A principal preoccupation of Soviet historians in recent years has been to show that collectivization was a fulfillment of Lenin's cooperative plan, historically necessary and essential to the building of socialism. Lenin's plan is continually buttressed with more and more doctrinal references, made a central part of his thinking, and pushed further and further back in time. One scholar spells it out:

It is especially important to emphasize that the plan for the building of socialism was worked out not from above, but by degrees, as a measure of fulfillment and development of experience and practice. Thus it would be incorrect to consider, as is done nowadays in literature, that the cooperative plan of V. I. Lenin was stated only in his last articles.[27]

After listing a series of works — many of which are not dealing with agriculture per se but with other aspects of the economy — he concludes: "In this way, the Leninist cooperative plan is an organic part of his general plan for the building of socialism in our country."[28]

Closely related to the effort to dissociate collectivization from the repressions and terror of the 1930s by stressing Lenin's creative part in it is an insistence on the part of official writings that the artels were well under way as a popular movement before the

26. M. L. Bogdenko, "K istorii nachalnogo etapa sploshnoi kollektivizatsii selskogo khoziaistva SSSR," *ibid.*, no. 5 (1963), p. 24.
27. Ivnitsky, "Opyt KPSS," p. 98.
28. *Ibid.*

Stalin era. An article in *Selskaia zhizn* written by a group of veterans of the collectivization campaigns shows this argument very well. Here the regime has called on the authority of Old Bolsheviks to buttress both the historical and doctrinal legitimacy of the kolkhozes. The authors criticize a number of recent studies (which are not specifically cited) for linking the realization of Lenin's cooperative plan "only with the beginning of the period of full collectivization. [But] the collective form of agriculture became widespread immediately after the victory of Great October, and by 1929 there were quite a few good agricultural artels in the countryside."[29]

Within a few months this theme had made the rounds of specialized journals and appeared in the mass media. A *Pravda* article, summarizing a number of recent entries in the column "Against Bourgeois Falsifiers of the History of the CPSU" of *Voprosy istorii KPSS,* emphasized that not only "the working class and its party but also . . . the peasant masses themselves" realized the necessity of a socialst transformation of agriculture. This is attested "by the movement for forming the collective farms, which had attained broad scope by the end of the 1920s."[30]

The excesses and distortions brought on by Stalin most emphatically do not alter that fundamentally positive evaluation of collectivization. The Soviet experience is also explicitly seen by most historians as of international significance, to be used creatively by other communist and workers' parties. "Despite the great national idiosyncrasies of conditions and traditions in each country, general laws are at work."[31]

During the period under review collectivization is increasingly described as a mass movement led by the CPSU: the formulation of the *Short Course,* that full collectivization was a second revolution equal to October but carried out from above, is explicitly rejected.[32] Much of the literature dealing with the transformation of agriculture not only stresses the role of the party cadres (who admittedly were mostly concentrated in the cites) but insists that

29. "K Voprosu ob osveshchenni istorii kollektivizatsii — Vernoi dorogoi otsov," *Selskaia zhizn,* February 25, 1966, p. 3.
30. "Otpor falsifikatoram," *Pravda,* August 17, 1966, p. 2.
31. Ivnitsky, "Opyt KPSS," p. 106.
32. For a clear presentation of this argument, probably the most useful single source is S. P. Trapeznikov, "Sotsialisticheskaia kooperatsiia — leninskii put krestian k kommunizmu," *Voprosy istorii KPSS,* no. 1 (1962), pp. 44–62.

Lenin's plan called for the union of the urban and rural workers, the latter now defined as including the middle as well as the poor peasants. For example, we may note crticisms made in *Voprosy istorii KPSS* of a book on collectivization published in 1964. The author has alleged with regard to Lenin's plan that "only the proletariat can destroy exploitation and classes. Therefore, the socialist reorganization of the countryside can be accomplished by the working class under the leadership of the Communist Party." "But," says the reviewer, "this raises the question: what does the role of the laboring peasantry as the partner of the working class consist of . . . ?" The author answers that the leading role of the proletariat and party in the socialist transformation of agriculture consists of nothing less than accomplishing the party's agrarian program. "All remaining questions relate to tactics and methods of leadership by the proletariat in leading the peasantry into socialism." The reviewer, rejecting this attitude as patronizing, retorts that Lenin saw the association of peasants and workers as not merely tactical, but a permanent and strategic relationship.[33]

The 1959 *History of the Communist Party* formulates it in the following manner, when summing up the period 1929 to 1932:

The social basis of the dictatorship of the proletariat had been extended and consolidated. The collective-farm peasantry had become the firm mainstay of Soviet power. This was already a *new* class . . . Lenin's wise policy of an alliance between the working class and the poor peasants, on the one hand, and the middle peasants, on the other, had helped to draw the bulk of the peasantry into socialist construction . . . The alliance of the working class and the collective-farm peasantry was being established on *a new basis — the community* of their interests.[34]

So far, so good. The mass basis of collectivization has been broadened dramatically. But it is impossible and undesirable for Soviet historians to ignore the existence of "the kulaks and other elements" who did most firmly oppose collectivization. The class enemy is of course necessary to a Marxist appraisal of collectivization as a historical phenomenon. The party history of 1959 does not significantly alter the bland account given in the *Short*

33. G. A. Chigrinov, reviewing V. N. Yakovtsevsky, *Agrarnye otnosheniia v SSSR v period stroitelstva sotsializma* (Moscow, 1964), in *Voprosy istorii KPSS*, no. 8 (1966), p. 127.
34. *History of the Communist Party of the Soviet Union*, p. 469.

Course. At the end of 1929 the party was able to undertake a policy of elimination of the kulaks as a class, we are told.

The essence of this policy was to *deprive the kulak class of the means of production essential for its existence and development* . . . Local organs of Soviet power in the districts of solid collectivization were granted the right to evict the kulaks to districts far removed from their places of residence and to confiscate all their means of production . . . The kulaks were completely expropriated. This was the only way to deal with kulaks.[35]

This bloodless account takes on somewhat more human overtones and becomes more explicit in some of the articles addressed to professional historians. For the first time in 1958 a change in scholarly treatment can be detected with the appearance of two articles that rely heavily on archival materials.[36] Several scholarly volumes pursued this treatment further.[37]

Moreover, a number of journal writers are for the first time publicly incensed at the slanderous statements of bourgeois critics that "liquidation of the kulaks meant the physical annihilation of that class."[38] Such charges have not been referred to in previous Soviet historiography and, in an effort to refute them, new information is being introduced into Soviet accounts.

P. V. Semernin fills in some details of the work of the special Politburo subcommission on the kulak problem created under the commission on kolkhozes in late 1929. The subcommission divided kulaks into three categories: depending on their economic status they were stripped of their capacity to exploit. The first category consisted of those with an active counterrevolutionary role (the richest), to whom repressive measures were to be applied: "arrest, arraignment before a court and confiscation of

35. *History of the Communist Party of the Soviet Union,* 2nd rev. ed., pp. 440–441.
36. P. V. Semernin, "O likvidatsii kulachestva kak klassa," *Voprosy istorii KPSS,* no. 7 (1958), pp. 72–85; V. K. Medvedev, "Likvidatsiia kulachestva v nizhnevolzhskom krae," *Istoriia SSSR,* no. 6 (1958), pp. 9–28.
37. For a detailed survey of the literature since 1952, see M. L. Bogdenko, I. E. Zelenin, "Istoriia kollektivizatsii selskogo khoziaistva v sovremennoi sovetskoi istoriko-ekonomicheskoi literature," *Istoriia SSSR,* no. 4 (1962), pp. 133–151.
38. A. V. Kornilov and N. S. Shevtsov, reviewing S. P. Trapeznikov, *Istoricheskii opyt KPSS v sotsialisticheskom preobrazovanii selskogo khoziaistva* (Moscow, 1959), in *Voprosy istorii KPSS,* no. 6 (1959), p. 199. Also, V. I. Tetiushev, "Protiv izvrashcheniia istorii kollektivizatsii selskogo khoziaistva SSSR v burzhuaznoi istoriografii," *ibid.,* no. 11 (1964), pp. 128–138.

all means of production"; they and their families would be exiled. The second group was defined as economically powerful and exploiting and received somewhat less repressive treatment: "expropriation of all means of production and the kulaks themselves to be exiled to remote northern areas." Those less powerful and not active against the Soviet power were to be taken into kolkhozes on trial for two to three years, their capital resources transferred to the kolkhoz fund, with a decision to be made by the kolkhoz as to their permanent status after the trial period. There is an obvious problem here, which Semernin notices, namely, that the 1930 Statute on Agricultural Artels specifically excluded from kolkhoz membership all people deprived of voting rights — which would extend to the third category of kulaks.[39] He feels this contradiction is solved by a resolution of the Central Executive Committee of the Sovnarkom of July 3, 1931, which provided for restoration of political rights to a kulak if five years' probation shows him to be an honest and willing worker.[40] This article seems to be usually detailed. Many scholarly as well as popular accounts are still written in more general terms, merely stating that elimination of the kulaks meant not physical annihilation but expropriation of the means of production and exile, with the opportunity to work in their new areas of residence.[41]

On the subject of the use of force against the kulaks, we may again look to V. I. Pogudin, whose 1958 article had opened the discussion of collectivization, in light of his demonstrated ability as synthesizer and harbinger.[42] In his 1965 article he reviews the literature on collectivization: he sees that much has been accomplished since the Twentieth Congress but that the problem of the kulak remains the least studied aspect of agrarian history. After this brief introduction, he quite calmly and with an air of innocent surprise hurls a bombshell. He cannot understand why since World War II there has not been a general reconsideration

39. Semernin, "O likvidatsii kulachestva," pp. 81–83.
40. *Ibid.*, p. 83. The source of this resolution is given as *Kollektivizatsiia selskogo khoziaistva. Vazhneishie postanovleniia kommunisticheski: partii i sovetskogo pravitelstva, 1927–1935* (Moscow: Academy of Sciences, 1957), p. 391.
41. For an example see Bogdenko, "K istorii nachalnogo etapa," p. 34.
42. "Problema likvidatsii kulachestva kak klassa v sovetskoi istoriografii," *Voprosy istorii*, no. 4 (1965), pp. 142–149.

of the question of the method of liquidation of the kulaks utilized in the USSR. In brief, he contends that, although elimination of the rural bourgeoisie is a general law for all countries building socialism, it is impossible in the face of the varied paths to socialized agriculture in the people's democracies to explain the continuing viewpoint in Soviet literature that "the deprivation of the kulaks of their means of production by means of direct force is in general, always and everywhere, the only possible way to liquidate the kulak class."[43] He provides copious citations from Lenin (in terms of volume and page only) to the effect that Lenin felt expropriation to be necessary for landowners but not obligatory in reforming the kulaks. Lenin recognized two possible methods of liquidating the kulak class — by economic measures or by forcible expropriation — and the choice of method would depend upon the specific historical situation.

Pogudin argues that the scholarly fixation on forcible expropriation was engendered by Stalin's emphasis on this method, perpetuated in the *Short Course*. But he also notes that this choice of policy was arrived at by the party after sharp discussion and for good and sufficient reasons that had to do with the unique internal and international conditions of the USSR in 1929 and 1930. It is thus impossible for anyone to maintain that the Soviet means of eliminating the kulak class is universal. Moreover, even in the Soviet Union the course of expropriation varied in different parts of the country, as several recent regional studies have shown.

Such an argument — for all its obeisance to the party's decision to use force as appropriate to the conditions of Russia in late 1929 and to the historical lawfulness of the liquidation of this class — is ultimately a dangerous one precisely in that it subtly suggests the possibility of another choice, within the USSR as well as in the people's democracies. The admission that Lenin was of two minds on the issue, and the linking of Stalin with forcible measures, is damaging to the concept of party infallibility. The terminology itself is bound to be disturbing: force now enters into the discussion of collectivization, albeit in unspecified form.

It is not clear whether the appearance of this article portended

43. *Ibid.*, p. 143.

another extension of the area of discussion. An indirect and partial response appeared in *Voprosy istorii KPSS* early in 1966. There Ivnitsky argues for the lawfulness of the Soviet experience, its usefulness for creative emulation in other socialist countries. He proceeds to build a three-stage model of producer cooperatives in socialist countries, which culminates in the kolkhozes and sovkhozes of the USSR as the most advanced types.[44]

There are some powerful political reasons for the rewriting of official accounts of collectivization. The most obvious and plausible was Khrushchev's determination to discredit Stalin as cruel, excessive, and given to bad judgments. The era of collectivization provides an obvious opportunity for such a portrayal. There exists a further possibility of expected personal political gain for Khrushchev — who was during the years of collectivization far from the seat of central power — by the implication of Molotov. It is certainly possible that had Khrushchev continued in power, Malenkov and Kaganovich — who were in the 1930s presumably in a position to influence Stalin's policies and to modify his excesses — might have been added to the list of Stalin's accomplices in the horrors of collectivization.

More recently we may perceive that the history of collectivization is being adjusted to remove traces of Khrushchev's agricultural policies and predilections. Thus, for example, the remarks of a prominent agricultural historian should be read in the context of Khrushchev's frequently articulated preference for state farms over collectives as more socially advanced. Professor V. Logunov, head of the department of party history at Voronezh Agricultural Institute and candidate of historical science, in writing a critical review of recent historical literature on collectivization, comes down hard on some "mistaken interpretations." And high on his list are

attempts to oppose sovkhozes to the kolkhozes as the highest and even the only real form of socalist relations in the countryside . . . The history of Soviet agriculture must reveal the close dialectic unity of kolkhoz and sovkhoz construction. Both one and the other are essential.[45]

Such factors are useful in appraising the treatment of individual

44. Ivnitsky "Opyt KPSS," pp. 106, 107.
45. V. Logunov, "Kolkhoznii stroi — Narodnoe zavoevanie," *Selskaia zhizn,* February 25, 1966, p. 3.

leaders, but, as we have seen, the interest of historians in collectivization as a historical episode extended far beyond a mere pinning of blame. The general trend has been to rework the policy and attendant events so as to make collectivization a consistent, historically lawful, palatable, and legitimate use of policy-making power by the CPSU. The official rewriting evinces a concern to interpret the policy as rational and carried out by administrative measures and persuasion rather than by force. The portrait of the CPSU that emerges is of responsible and sober cadres, who know the difference between Lenin's cooperative plan and excessive pressure and forced pace. This is a party that deservedly won broad popular support for its agricultural policy. Collectivization is revealed as sanctified by Lenin. Not imposed from the top, it was carried out by a responsible party apparat — despite the temporary excesses of its leader — as part of a long-range plan for socialism.

But the more the story of collectivization is discussed, the less the issues and differences are settled. The question of the use of force against reluctant peasants refuses to go away. And historians are troubled by analogous problems, such as the role of the party in organizing and channeling this "revolution from below" and the necessity for direct state as well as party intervention in 1929 and the early 1930s. Quite clearly, confusion and quarreling over the interpretation of collectivization has continued among historians as it has among their readers.

This ferment may be expected to persist, reinforced by the publication of thirty volumes of documents on collectivization.[46] The projected series is sponsored by the Institute of Marxism-Leninism and its affiliates, the various institutes of history and economics of the Academy of Sciences of the USSR and the union republics, and the state archives of Moscow "and many other cities." It will include three summary volumes, the rest to be concerned with special problems and specific union republics or regions.

Despite the reservations of one prominent authority — M. L. Bogdenko — principally with regard to techniques of verification and sourcing, these documents obviously provide the basis for a more complete and frank treatment. Bogdenko notes that the

46. M. L. Bogdenko, "Pervye toma obshchesoiuznoi serii dokumentov i materialov po istorii kollektivizatsii selskogo khoziaistva SSSR," *Voprosy istorii*, no. 8 (1966), pp. 147–154.

papers go against common interpretation on several counts: by showing that in at least some areas the party began to combat excesses in February rather than only in March 1930 (before Stalin's "Dizzy with Success"), that the liquidation of the kulaks at the beginning of 1930 was carried out not generally but at very divergent rates and with varying success in different regions, and that the excesses in kolkhoz construction in the winter of 1929–30 were the result "not only of mistakes by low-level [party] workers, but also of incorrect directives by representatives of the center."[47] The fact that Stalin is not mentioned in the review cannot be taken as a valid barometric reading of his role in collectivization, because in the nature of these localized materials top-level policy documents would not appear. It is more difficult to evade such issues, or course, in the general volumes, and perhaps that explains the earlier appearance of the regional collections.

Perhaps the historian's dilemma can best be demonstrated by reference to a very hard-line and conformist account appearing in *Voprosy istorii* late in 1967.[48] The author is G. V. Sharapov, candidate of historical science, who two years earlier had called publicly for more positive historical treatment of collectivization.[49] In the earlier article — published in the central newspaper for agricultural workers — he was furious at the ammunition being fed to "bourgeois falsifiers of Soviet history" in the West by "certain historians and writers" who "have asserted that in our country the necessary conditions for carrying out mass collectivization were absent, [and] have placed in doubt the lawfulness of liquidation of the kulaks as a class." Although giving no specific citations, Sharapov and his coauthor accused "some historians, writers, creators of movies and theatrical works [of having] portrayed the process of kolkhoz construction as only a stream of mistakes and inadequacies." They drew the lesson that "The duty of Soviet historians, writers, and artists is to describe the heroic struggle of the people of our country for fulfillment of Leninist ideas, the socialist transformation of agriculture." No one, then, can accuse Sharapov of revisionism or fail to appreciate that his intent is to present the policy of collectivization in the most favorable light. But with the best possible will, his

47. *Ibid.*, pp. 151–152.
48. G. V. Sharapov, "Reshenie agrarnogo voprosa v SSSR," *Voprosy istorii*, no. 10 (1967), pp. 95–112.
49. P. Aleksandrov and G. Sharapov, "Za marksistko-leninskoe osveshchenie istorii kolkhoznogo stroitelstva," *Selskaia zhizn*, December 29, 1965, p. 3.

attempt — as manifested in the 1967 article for a historical journal — fails. The tone and purpose are evidently those of rationalization and apology. Collectivization was a success in the main, we are told; some mistakes were made but quickly corrected by the party and Council of Ministers. He says, on the one hand, that liquidation of the kulaks was the work of peasant masses and, on the other, that working-class participation in collectivization was of critical importance, especially in 1929–30, when many workers moved to the countryside and joined collectives. Sharapov also attempts to associate the policy of eliminating the kulaks with Lenin, omitting any reference to Stalin, by stressing that the party's struggle against the wealthy peasantry dates from the very beginning of Soviet power in 1917.

Most interesting is Sharapov's rather novel treatment of the questions of voluntarism and force. The policy of relying on voluntary entrance of peasants into the collectives, he tells us, could and did lead only to an intensification of capitalism in the countryside. For explanation the reader is given only the cryptic observation that in the 1920s the presence and leadership of urban workers (note that he does not say the party per se) in rural areas was weak. It seems clear that Sharapov is trying to refer tactfully to the peasantry's legendary drive to individual proprietorship in the land and its rejection of land socialization no matter who the sponsoring party was. He concludes that the success of cooperative agriculture could not have come about without the strong "support of the proletarian state."[50] Thus Sharapov is pushed back to reliance upon the state as the decisive agent in collectivization, having found himself unable or unwilling to argue convincingly that the mass of the peasantry, or the CPSU (which presumably had successfully united the workers with poor and middle peasants), or the rusticated urban workers were sufficiently motivated or competent to do the job.

One is left with the unhappy and untidy picture of the genie who can be neither cajoled nor forced back into the jar. The Soviet historian of collectivization — whatever his personal or professional commitments, whether to the regime, to career advancement, to some kind of objective history, or to the Marxist laws of history — is faced with insoluble contradictions and dilemmas. He must choose among several interpretations and, whatever the decision, he lays bare a national tragedy.

50. Sharapov, "Reshenie agrarnogo voprosa," p. 100.

As soon as one begins to examine closely party historiography with regard to political leadership, it becomes quite clear that the relationship is a complex one. One strand flows from the political reality to its mirrored reflection in historical records: this has been described above as part of the barometric function of Soviet historiography.[1] In that context it was argued that any Soviet leader over time generates symbolic overtones and that the most important political figures come to represent whole clusters of ideas and policies which are associated in the popular mind with their personalities. Thus the historical figures of Stalin, Trotsky, and others are very specific characters in the morality play that is party history. Although the official purpose may well be didactic, the average reader is also instructed on a more subtle level in the intricacies of Soviet power politics. Thus, by following the twists and turns of the reappraisals of Stalin in the press, he can decipher to some extent the covert debate within the leadership over the syndrome of policies and style of rule associated with Stalin's name. Moreover, as Khrushchev so dramatically showed, the manipulation of a leader's image can be an effective — if dangerous — weapon in the hands of an ambitious politician.

But this is only one side of the relationship, albeit the most visible. If we stop at this point we are left with a very neat and mechanistic model, in which there is a programmed response for each political stimulus, a simple pattern whereby a shift within the political leadership is causative and the scholarly or journalistic activity is reflexive. Although it is clear that much historical discussion of Stalin and other leaders can be satisfactorily explained by direct reference to the designs of the current regime, to consider such an analysis complete would, I feel, seriously impoverish our understanding. In general, evidence of more shadowy and complex aspects of the political-historical relationship concerning leadership is found in the historical journals, monographs, records of professional meetings, and the like, whereas perusal of the mass-circulation media, texts, and official speeches yields a series of examples of the more direct and obvious pattern.

A brief synopsis of the haunted wanderings of Stalin's ghost after 1956 is perhaps an effective initial approach to the problem.[2]

1. See the discussion in Chapter One.
2. For a detailed explication of the process of de-Stalinization, see Thomas B. Larson, "What Happened to Stalin?" *Problems of Communism,* March–April 1967, pp. 82–90.

Larson has summarized the period 1953–1956 as focusing on the deflation of Stalin as a symbol [which] involved, first, the removal of Stalin's name from national political "institutions" such as the party, the Constitution, and the ideology, and ultimately from even the most insignificant organization and localities of the USSR, followed by the discrediting, minimization, or "forgetting" of Stalin's writings and doctrines.[3]

The crucial moment for the historical Stalin remains, of course, the Twentieth Party Congress in February 1956, when Anastas Mikoyan made the first public negative reference — followed by Khrushchev's sensational secret speech.

If we were to pursue the record of de-Stalinization as a seismographic phenomenon, we would initially confront a jagged graph marked by several spectacular peaks and valleys. Stalin-watching as a daily spectator sport is, however, palpably more exciting than taking a long backward look at the past decade and a half. As so often happens, a more distant perspective reveals some mountain ranges and undulating plateaus, where the immediate view produced only precipitous cliffs.

The seismograph of de-Stalinization shows three peaks of activity — the Twentieth Congress in February 1956, the Twenty-Second Congress in late 1961, and the final months of 1962 — each officially engendered by the political leadership. As pointed out, the political explosiveness of the Stalin image is so tremendous as to make initiative for change impossible from any other quarter than the elite. Other chapters have reviewed the events of those periods.[4] The first two, of course, represent overt and stinging denigrations by Khrushchev personally; whereas the third campaign was carried out chiefly in literary works and journals, although Khrushchev made it clear that it was begun and pursued under his auspices, despite the objections of other leading members of the regime.

All of this is obvious. Confusion enters with regard to the periods occurring between the peaks; daily viewing shows apparently broad oscillations. Some observers have pointed to moments of strong and hard reaction against the de-Stalinization program; others have predicted its complete reversal. The example of this kind of sudden official "hardening of the line" most frequently

3. *Ibid.*, p. 84.
4. See pp. 62–76, 117–129, and 137–145.

cited is that of the spring of 1963 and centers on Khrushchev's March 8 speech to a group of intellectuals.[5] This speech should be read in the context of the crackdown on writers and artists which the regime instituted in December 1962. But to perceive Khrushchev's remarks on Stalin as a simple extension of a general and uniform hard line and a reversal of the 1956 posture is not warranted. Khrushchev's remarks were rather, I would suggest, an attempt to create a workable formula that could be used by artists and scholars to avoid the obvious perils of the early months after the secret speech and the uproar surrounding the recent revisionist fiction.

Some specific remarks of Khrushchev on March 8 could be easily misinterpreted, if not read against the larger tenor of the speech. For example,

the Party renders Stalin's services to the Party and the Communist movement their due. We believe even today that Stalin was devoted to communism; he was a Marxist, and this cannot and must not be denied . . . At Stalin's funeral many people, myself among them, had tears in their eyes. They were sincere tears.[6]

But Khrushchev was counteracting a pendulum swing he found extreme. Thus he applied strong pressure in the other direction, to return to a desirable midpoint — and it is precisely this attempt to find a moderating counterweight which has appeared to some observers as a push to the opposite extreme. Khrushchev placed these positive references in the midst of new revelations of Stalin's intended but narrowly averted purges of Moscovite and Ukrainian intellectuals and a very forthright reaffirmation of the party's repudiation of Stalin's crimes:

Our viewpoint on this question has been fully and quite clearly explained more than once in Party documents . . . The Party has implacably condemned and condemns the gross violations of Leninist norms of Party life, the arbitrariness and abuse of power, committed by Stalin . . . His fault was that he committed gross mistakes of a theoretical and political nature, violated Leninist principles of state and party leadership, and abused the power entrusted to him by the Party and the people.[7]

Another period of turmoil is identified with the months pre-

5. "Vysokaia ideinost i khudozhestvennoe masterstvo-velikaia sila sovetskoi literatury i iskusstva," *Pravda*, March 10, 1963, p. 1–4.
6. As quoted in Larson, "What Happened to Stalin?" p. 89.
7. *Ibid*.

ceding the Twenty-Third Congress in March 1966. As discussed above,[8] there are sound indications in the central and regional press of a dispute within the political leadership, some Politburo members probably pressing to take the occasion of the congress to reformulate the assessment of Stalin. Especially important is the famous January 30, 1966, article in *Pravda,* in which three historians undertook to chastise some of their brethren for subjectivism (attempts at "abstract, non-class, historical 'truth' ") and to repudiate the concept of "the period of the personality cult" as ignoring the positive accomplishments of Stalin's USSR.[9] The most dramatic evidence of a political debate over de-Stalinization — and of the fact that the upheaval extended deep into the intellectual and artistic communities, possibly with severe repercussions in the broader population — was, of course, the petition of the twenty-five intellectuals to Brezhnev warning against any restitution of Stalin.[10]

But, although a detailed graph of the early months of 1966 shows real pressures at high political levels to upgrade the image of Stalin — which were of course especially frightening to more liberal elements in conjunction with the trial of Siniavsky and Daniel — I cannot agree that this should be represented as a sudden plunge from the 1962 crest. It can more accurately be perceived as a period of indecision and nearly submerged conflict over policy and style, which surfaced in the debate and tensions surrounding the symbolic Stalin.

An official position was apparent only in March 1966 with the Twenty-Third Congress, a decision best characterized as a non-decision. Stalin's name went ostentatiously unspoken, and the personality cult was only infrequently referred to. The regime's policy on Stalin was a refusal to move either right or left, a continuation of the attempt at stabilizing the denigration. Since the congress the new leadership has not basically altered its balancing posture. The Central Committee's theses for the fiftieth anniversary of the October Revolution made very brief reference to Stalin and specifically approved the destruction of the personality cult;[11] this pattern has been generally followed since.

8. See Chapter Six.
9. Ie. Zhukov, V. Trukhanovsky, and V. Shunkov, "Vysokaia otvetstvennost istorikov," *Pravda,* January 30, 1966, p. 2.
10. See p. 178.
11. "50 let velikoi oktiabrskoi sotsialisticheskoi revoliutsii," *Pravda,* June 25, 1967, pp. 1–5.

It would thus appear that — as is true with respect to political historiography in general — Khrushchev's successors have determined to secure the political and social benefits of de-Stalinization while avoiding the political backlash he experienced. The official statements are therefore altered from those of Khrushchev more in style than in content, to remove the personal invective and the colorful and inflammatory language. In the process, the figure of Stalin has been eased offstage.

Briefly, then, this seismographic record of official policy on Stalin shows three earthquakes caused by Khrushchev's dramatic attacks on the cult; each was followed by a lengthy and jagged shock wave during which official pressure was in a repressive direction in order to stabilize, rather than reverse, the general movement.[12]

Stalin as a Political Symbol

We must now move to more subterranean levels, from official policy to the increasingly murky regions of politics and scholarship.

Distinguishing between the "official" and phenomena termed for purposes of this discussion "political" necessarily implies a conscious interpretive stance toward the Soviet system which is not that of the classical theory of totalitarianism, with its push-button responses to a single central authority. The focus here is on usages or attempted usages of the Stalin figure in historiography for political ends, to press the regime toward quite specific policies and styles of leadership. It would be presumptuous on the basis of this study to essay a definitive reworking of this theory; however, a perusal of some political interpretations of the Stalin image by various individuals and groups will perhaps suggest interesting directions and aspects for a more general reinterpretation.

The best-known example of pressure on the top political leadership from a group committed to a generalized style or method of rule has been cited: the petition of the twenty-five intellectuals

12. It is worth a footnote to record an incident at Stalin's graveside near the Kremlin Wall in the summer of 1968. Responding to a visitor's reference to Stalin's removal from the mausoleum, the Intourist guide said that, yes, indeed, he used to be in the mausoleum but he — or rather, his family — had requested transference of the body to the family cemetery plot. For convenience of the Soviet public, however, the grave was now in this more central location. Such an explanation, which could only have originated in an official briefing and not in the individual creativity of one guide, might foreshadow increasing obscurity for Stalin.

against any reversal of Khrushchev's denigration of Stalin. Although there may be some uncertainties as to how representative the *ad hoc* twenty-five are of the larger intelligentsia segment of the population, the fact of their self-conscious utilization of a historical leader to deter the regime from the methods he symbolizes cannot be blinked.

The central press and specialized journals also contain some interesting references to Stalin which support specific policies under debate. For example, writing in one of the professional journals for lawyers, F. M. Burlatsky graphically cited Stalin's misuse of constitutional theory in order to frame his own argument for some legal hedges against the use of force.[13] He stressed the need for a new constitution to correspond to the present stage of development, stipulating that "many of the democratic forms of life provided by the USSR Constitution of 1936 did not at the time find proper development and were distorted."[14] But Stalin's worst error was exaggeration of the importance of coercion and the use of constitutional theory to justify mass repressions. It would, says Burlatsky, scarcely be worth referring to Stalin's mistakes in this sphere, "were it not that there are even now people abroad who in every way laud to the skies precisely those mistaken propositions of his and exaggerate the role of coercion in building socialism and communism."[15] Similarly, another legal writer argued for more specific constitutional provisions by noting that Stalin was mistaken in refusing to include the ultimate goals of communism in his 1936 constitution.[16]

The Stalin image has also proved to be useful to the progressives in the debate over economic rationalization. One stratagem is the linking of an opponent's line of argument to Stalin: thus one author in *Kommunist* observed that a typical error of the period of the personality cult was that of subjectivism, which he defined as ignoring the significance of profit and cost-value categories.[17] And on the occasion of Voznesensky's sixtieth anniversary, a

13. F. M. Burlatsky, "O nekotorykh voprosakh teorii obshchenarodnogo sotsialisticheskogo gosudarstva," *Gosudarstvo i pravo*, no. 10 (1962), pp. 3–14.
14. *Ibid.*, p. 9.
15. *Ibid.*, p. 11.
16. A. Denisov, "Nekotorye teoreticheskie problemy konstitutsionnogo ustroistva sovetskogo gosudarstva," *Sovetskaia iustitsiia*, no. 23 (1966), pp. 3–5.
17. A. Gatovsky, "Rol pribyli v sotsialisticheskoi ekonomike," *Kommunist*, no. 18 (1962), pp. 64–65.

writer for *Pravda* attacked Stalin for so destroying those concerned with a balanced structure of the economy in 1929 as to remove any incentive for the compilation of grain and other balances necessary to scientific planning.[18]

Also, observations about Stalin in a pair of articles appearing in *Voprosy istorii KPSS* late in 1964 can be read as cryptic arguments on behalf of proponents of heavy industry in their perennial quarrel with the advocates of consumer goods. Ekshtein recalls with horror that Soviet industry was until 1940 incapable of meeting the plan, that it produced less and less each year. He blames this largely on Stalin's wishful brand of planning and his large-scale repression of industrial cadres. And Kasianenko attributes the party's difficulties in the technological reequipping of industry to Stalin's frequent and faulty independent decisions.[19]

Stalin's name has since the 1920s been intimately associated with Soviet policy toward the minority nationalities. Part of the denigration process has been to point out that the major (and correct) lines of nationality policy were of course laid down by Lenin in the early 1920s and only elaborated by Stalin. Even before this theme appeared, though, Soviet historians began to reappraise the standard derogatory treatment meted out to national movements and leaders during Stalin's ascendancy. The official repudiation of Stalin's repressive policies and Great Russian chauvinistic historiography can quite easily be turned to nationalistic purposes, however. The reader need not be a Stalinist to detect a thrust toward greater national pride and cultural autonomy in such arguments as the following. The writer, an Uzbek, details the pernicious effects on the history of national movements caused by the personality cult — such as the removal of museum exhibits, which have not yet been restored, and the attribution of national uprisings in Central Asia to foreign intrigues. But his remedy would go considerably beyond mere correctives:

This situation must be corrected with the help of historians. A thorough study of the history of national movements can be suc-

18. G. Sorokin, "Vydaiushchiisia deiatel leninskoi partii," *Pravda,* December 1, 1963, p. 4.
19. A. Ekshtein, "O partiinom rukovodstve razvitiem chernoi metallurgii v predvoennyi period (1937–1941)," *Voprosy istorii KPSS,* no. 11 (1964), pp. 68–80; V. I. Kasanenko, "Deiatelnost partii po tekhnicheskomu perevooruzheniiu promyshlennosti," *ibid.,* pp. 28–41, esp. p. 40.

cessfully carried out with coordination on a republic scale in the Academy of Sciences of the Uzbek SSR and establishment of close creative contacts with scholars of other sister republics.[20]

Stalin and the Military. One of the most dramatic and explosive dimensions of the reappraisal of Stalin's role in Soviet history revolves around his leadership during the early years of World War II, his treatment of military cadres during the thirties, and his general defense policies. The exquisite sensitivity of this area of discourse is not difficult to appreciate, in light of the purges of officers in the prewar years, the tremendous war losses, and the unwholesome aura of the Nazi-Soviet Pact and unpreparedness that hang over the tragic year 1941.

The reader must be warned against hoping for (or dreading) an exhaustive study of the Soviet diplomatic or military historiography of World War II, which is obviously a book-length project in itself.[21] My focus is more narrowly upon reappraisals of Stalin's military policies during the decade 1956–1967, in light of political ramifications. Unfortunately for any aspirations toward a tidy analytical format, this aspect of de-Stalinization is marked by an intricate interweaving of what I have categorized as the political and scholarly realms of discourse. But, perhaps for this very reason, the quarrel over those events and policies of Stalin's career touching the military and the war is especially illuminating.

It is not difficult to perceive an active determination on the part of military leaders to work their revenge upon Stalin's memory and in the process to clear the record of those officers purged and then defamed in the *Short Course*. And there has persisted throughout the post-1956 period a complex interrelationship of political pressures and historical revisions to link the fate of Stalin with that of the miltary heroes who were his victims. Once more the observer is struck by a strong sense that time has been compressed into a confusion of decades because the temporal dimension has been dissolved: Stalin, Zhukov, Brusilov, Konev,

20. Kh. T. Tursunov, "K voprosu izucheniia istorii natsionalno-osvoboditel-nogo dvizheniia narodov Srednei Azii," *Obshchestvennye nauki v uzbekistane,* no. 11 (1965), p. 30.
21. For a thorough analysis of Soviet histories of World War II to the early sixties, see Matthew P. Gallagher, *The Soviet History of World War II,* (New York: Frederick A. Praeger, 1963). Another excellent source is Seweryn Bialer, ed., *Stalin and His Generals: Soviet Military Memoirs of World War II* (New York: Pegasus, 1969).

Tukhachevsky, all are contemporary and rivalrous historical actors.

The most immediate observation is that there seems to be a dependent and inverse relationship between the status of the historical Stalin and that of his purged generals. But this did not extend to Khrushchev's own rival, Zhukov. Khrushchev's secret speech did not expose Stalin's purges of the armed forces and only glancingly mentioned the need for new texts on the history of the Civil War and World War II. It remained for Zhukov to use his brief political ascendancy to press for the rehabilitation of purged military heroes.[22] But the campaign was only partially successful; Khrushchev clearly resented and feared his personal popularity and ambitions to restore military prestige and elan. Considerably after Zhukov's removal from the Ministry of Defense, the second edition of the one-volume party history followed its attack on Stalin's "unwarranted repressive measures before the war," "lack of vigilance toward fascism," and "impermissible misappraisal of the strategic situation on the eve of the war,"[23] with the stipulation:

A considerable share of the blame for the Red Army being unprepared to repulse the enemy attack falls also on S. K. Timoshenko and G. K. Zhukov, who were in charge of the People's Commissariat of Defense and the General Staff respectively, and yet did not take immediate measures to deploy the Red Army in battle order.[24]

But with the intensified and more explicit enumeration in the second edition of Stalin's responsibility for the early defeats, comes also the first specific mention of the executed generals:

The Red Army was short of experienced leaders. Many prominent army chiefs, including V. K. Blucher, A. I. Yegorov, M. N. Tukhachevsky, I. P. Uborevich and I. E. Yakir, had been subjected to unwarranted repressive measures before the war and had lost their lives.[25]

Certainly the decisive moment was the Twenty-Second Party Congress in October 1961, at which Stalin was punished for newly revealed and grisly crimes by ejection from the Lenin

22. Roger Pethybridge, *A Key to Soviet Politics* (New York: Frederick A. Praeger, 1962), p. 153.
23. *History of the Communist Party of the Soviet Union*, 2nd rev. ed., pp. 537, 538.
24. *Ibid.*, p. 538.
25. *Ibid.*, p. 537. The third edition of November 1969 omits this passage.

Mausoleum. It was only now — with Zhukov safely excluded from the political scene — that Khrushchev felt a need to effect better rapport with the military bureaucracy and publicly deplored Stalin's purges of military officers during the 1930s. The complete and triumphant rehabilitation of Marshal Tukhachevsky soon appeared.[26]

Now the tempo of military rehabilitation began to quicken. Pacing it was the publication of memoirs of high officers, which grew from a trickle in 1962 and 1963 into a flood by 1964. These appeared in the central press — *Pravda, Izvestiia, Literaturnaia gazeta, Sovetskaia rossiia;* literary monthlies — *Ogonyok, Oktiabr,* and *Novyi mir;* in party journals — *Kommunist* and *Partiinaia zhizn;* military publications — *Krasnaia zvezda* and *Voenno-istoricheskii zhurnal;* and historical journals — *Voprosy istorii KPSS* and *Voprosy istorii.* Bialer counts over 150 book-length memoirs and several hundred articles between 1956 and 1967.[27]

These records are intrinsically interesting on several counts, but their most significant dimension here is the pursuit of two main themes: professional military competence and Stalin's brutality and ignorance of strategic matters. One by one the great generals and admirals present their own perspectives on campaigns they led and their individual experiences with Stalin. Their views may differ in detail, but their common concern is to rescue the honor of themselves and their men. The few occasions when Stalin is defended can usually be traced to professional rivalry, such as that between Marshal Konev and Marshal Zhukov.[28] Or, if Stalin is portrayed as a wise and rational wartime leader, this wisdom is illustrated by the fact that although he did have his own military strategy in this or that situation, he was prevailed upon to shelve it in favor of the plan of whatever officer is writing the memoir.[29]

The common concern with military honor must not be overemphasized so as to blur the distinctions that do exist among

26. Ia. Gorelov, "Zolotoe oruzhie," *Izvestiia,* December 29, 1961, p. 6.
27. *Stalin and His Generals,* p. 16.
28. P. I. Troianovsky, "Doroga na berlin," *Sovetskaia rossiia,* April 16, 1965, pp. 2–3; I. Konev, "Na berlin!" *Pravda,* April 21, 1965, p. 4; I. Konev, "Sorok piatyi god," *Novyi mir,* no. 5 (1965), pp. 3–60.
29. I. Konev, "Na berlin!" *Pravda,* April 21, 1965, p. 4; P. Derevianko and O. Rzheshevsky, "Muzhestvo i iskusstvo polkovodsta," *Krasnaia zvezda,* September 30, 1965, p. 4.

these memoirists with regard to Stalin. Several of them follow their critical remarks with formulations to the effect that all wartime setbacks cannot be simply disposed of as Stalin's personal fault.[30] Other divergencies can perhaps be traced to individual or interservice rivalries. For example, some historical treatments indicate that the military intelligence services have been particularly outraged and embittered by certain historical accounts of the weeks preceding June 1941 and Hitler's "surprise attack," which imply that Stalin was not adequately informed by Soviet intelligence of Hitler's plans.[31] One author indicts Stalin for underrating his military intelligence advisers.[32] But Konev recalls Stalin showing intelligence reports to Zhukov and himself — implying that he had taken account of their advice.[33]

These elements of partiality and prejudice among nonhistorian memoirists are recognized by the regime as counterproductive to its own purposes: *Pravda* called for more objectivity toward Stalin in military memoirs on January 4, 1967. And they have been deplored by more professionally minded military historians.[34] At any rate, for whatever reasons — perhaps nothing more sinister than the exhaustion of the supply — the great wave of wartime memoirs has receded since 1965.

In light of this fragmentation of viewpoint among military memoirs, it is important to take note of the quite uniformly positive presentation of Stalin's leadership during the battle for Moscow. On the occasion of the twenty-fifth anniversary, the Soviet press developed a large-scale campaign in November and December 1966. In these reminiscences of the Moscow crisis — whether written by political or military figures — any mention of Stalin is laudatory. The writers usually refer to his magnificent psychological calm, organizational skills, and especially his

30. Marshal I. Bagramian, "Trudnoi leto," *Literaturnaia gazeta*, April 17, 1965, pp. 1–2; Admiral N. G. Kuznetsov, "Pered voinoi," *Oktiabr*, no. 11 (1965), pp. 134–171.
31. For one such treatment, see "Chitateli obsuzhdaiut knigu," *Voprosy istorii*, no. 2 (1966), pp. 154–156.
32. I. P. Prusonov, "Povyshenie organizuiushchego i napravlia-iushchego vliianiia partii v vooruzhennykh silakh (1956–1964)," *Voprosy istorii KPSS*, no. 2 (1965), pp. 4–6.
33. I. Konev, "Sorok piatyi god," *Novyi mir*, no. 5 (1965), p. 38.
34. I. Grudinin, "O dialektike obektivnogo i subektivnogo v voine," *Voenno-istoricheskii zhurnal*, no. 1 (1967), pp. 3–13.

brilliant determination to hold a triumphal parade on November 7, 1941, in celebration of the October Revolution, with the Germans just a few miles outside the city.

Stalin the hero of Moscow proved, however, to be a transitory figure, circumscribed both in time and events; the praise did not stretch into other periods or aspects of his leadership, and the press campaign was turned off in December as suddenly as it had been inaugurated. This episode should not be interpreted as a shift to a period of mellowing toward Stalin, but as yet another controlled balancing maneuver. I would agree with Bialer's formulation, that we are witnessing an end to the anti-Stalin campaign rather than a new campaign to rehabilitate Stalin.[35]

The Historians' Debate

We have been tracing out some of the more visible patterns of relationship between the aspirations of the military elite and the portrayals of Stalin as wartime leader. But, important as these political pressures and accommodations have been in revamping Stalin's wartime record, they do not tell the whole story. For within the framework of official oscillations, academic historians have also been conducting their own skirmishes on a battleground distinct but not separate from politics.

The debate among historians over the treatment due Stalin is less clearly manifest in their substantive works — although differences in tone and choice of historical material are perceptible — than in their professional critiques and discussions. Again, this is a function of their reluctance to deviate in print on such an inflammatory topic. But there have occurred several face-to-face debates within the profession which have crystallized opinion. Here I will broaden the focus to include discussions of Stalin's career as a whole.

The first of these discussions — which occurred at the conference of historians in December 1962 — has been discussed in detail in Chapter Five. Although the meeting was in no way formally directed to the problem of Stalin, his baleful presence was felt by most of the participants. Pospelov's report to the session on party history contained an important section on "Liquidation of the Consequences of the Personality Cult and Raising

35. *Stalin and His Generals*, p. 31.

the Level of Party History," in which he made specific suggestions for scholarly investigation into Stalin's mistaken ideas. Ponomarev's plenary address also included this theme. So it is not surprising that the conference proceedings revealed clearly only one side of the debate with respect to Stalin: that of the revisionists, who were pressing for further exposure and denigration. That they continued to be opposed by pro-Stalin historians is clear from many remarks, which — unfortunately for the outside observer — were usually vague. The plainest references were to the effect that the history faculties at Moscow University were a center of resistance to de-Stalinization.

Brief mention should be made of the annual meeting of the departments of history of the Academy of Sciences held on December 28–29, 1963.[36] Although the account in *Voprosy istorii* gives no record of remarks by members, it is evident that Professor V. G. Trukhanovsky's report reflected one side of a continuing debate among members of the academy. Referring to the work of *Voprosy istorii* in overcoming the legacies of the personality cult, he argued that "some authors go into this complicated work in an oversimplified manner. In particular, investigating one or another aspect of the building of socialism in a certain period, they explain all the difficulties and failures exclusively by the cult of personality."[37]

There were similar overtones at the June 1965 all-union conference of historians in Kiev, devoted to the topic "V. I. Lenin and Historical Science." A journal account of the meeting noted that many participants brought up the question of the cult, and that one speaker had called for a more objective appraisal of the *Short Course* than "in recent times." However, the participants managed to agree on a compromise formulation: that historians must be guided by the Central Committee resolution of June 30, 1956, "in which the great damage of the cult of personality is noted, together with Stalin's services as an outstanding actor in our party and government."[38]

Also pertinent is the account of two conferences of military historians held at the end of 1965 to discuss the newly published

36. Iu. V. Bromlei and V. I. Neupokoev, "V otdelenii istorii AN SSSR i nauchnykh sovetakh," *Voprosy istorii*, no. 6 (1965), pp. 140–151.
37. *Ibid.*, p. 151.
38. V. G. Sarbei, "Vsesoiuznaia nauchnaia sessiia po probleme 'V. I. Lenin i istoricheskaia nauka,'" *Istoriia SSSR*, no. 6 (1965), pp. 213–214.

Great Patriotic War of the Soviet Union, 1941–1945, a Short History.[39] One historian is recorded as challenging the book's interpretation of the German attack as a surprise to Stalin as well as to the armed forces and the Soviet people. Stalin and several other (unnamed) leaders, he asserts, "over the course of several prewar months received sufficient data on the preparation of the attack." During the question period, such malcontents were treated to one of the finest pieces of dialectical convolutions one can find. The head of the authors' collective, Professor M. M. Minasian, first accepted the picture of Stalin as not paying attention to and "incorrectly evaluating" warnings of the impending attack, and thus making wrong decisions, which were described in the text as "serious political errors." But then:

The serious political error on the question of the threat of war is an objective fact. The incorrect evaluation of disregarded signals lies at the root of the practical measures carried out by the government apparatus.
It follows that for the government and military apparatus everything that happened on 22 June 1941 was a surprise. Thus the events of 22 June were like thunder out of a clear sky for Stalin also.[40]

It is difficult to imagine that this circular reasoning could satisfy or silence critics in any but the most superficial manner.

The most spectacular evidence available of the bitter quarrel among historians over Stalin is to be found in two underground accounts of meetings held in 1966. In neither instance has the Soviet press presented its own version, nor can the protocols be verified as authentic. One was the meeting of 250 historians, members of the ideological section of the central committee, and Old Bolsheviks to discuss the draft third volume of the new six-volume party history.[41] The storm center was within the Old Bolshevik group. It is, however, very clear from the *Survey* account that at least two historians were openly vociferous against the editorial board for its failure to give a realistic portrayal of Stalin in 1917-1918 and its persistence in defaming or obliterating Bukharin, Piatakov, Trotsky, Zinoviev, and Kame-

39. "Chitateli obsuzhdaiut knigu," *Voprosy istorii KPSS*, no. 2 (1966), pp. 154–157.
40. *Ibid.*, pp. 155, 156.
41. See Chapter Six; and "The Personality Cult," *Survey*, April 1967, pp. 159–160.

nev. These two were Piotr Yakir, son of a prominent purged general, veteran of fourteen years in a concentration camp, who has since become famous for "antisocial" activities to protest the secret trials of writers in 1967 and 1968 and his sensational petition to Soviet scientists and artists to act against "ominous symptoms of a restoration of Stalinism." The second is identified in the protocol only as "Petrovsky (a young historian)."

Pospelov, president of the editorial board, maintained a generally defensive attitude. But it is interesting that he was perceived by one of the outspoken critics as excessively trusting of the contributing authors rather than a neo-Stalinist himself, and he seemed to be shocked and dismayed at Petrovsky's complaint that he had been unjustly excluded from an earlier session.[42] Pospelov's ambivalent stance is reminiscent of his behavior at the 1962 conference and is important for an understanding of his subsequent demotion.

Finally, we must consider what has come to be called the Nekrich affair, for what it reveals of political-military and scholarly debate over Stalin's wartime performance. The focal point is a meeting of the Department of History of the Great Fatherland War of the Institute of Marxism-Leninism on February 16, 1966, as described in the second of the two underground reports.

At the time of publication of his *22 June 1941* in the spring of 1965,[43] Doctor of Historical Sciences Nekrich had earned the reputation of a respected and politically reliable military historian. He was a member of the Academy of Sciences' Institute of History and the author or editor of a number of important books and pamphlets on Soviet foreign affairs. But with his book on the early months of World War II he lost all of this: despite a favorable early review in *Novyi mir*, by the autumn of 1967 he had been expelled from the party and subjected to a vicious attack in *Voprosy istorii KPSS*.[44] Presumably, he also was dis-

---

42. "The Personality Cult," pp. 169, 167.
43. A. M. Nekrich, *1941, 22 iiunia* (Moscow: "Nauka" Publishing House, 1965). See also the review by Sanford Lieberman in *Kritika*, Winter 1968, pp. 47–54.
44. G. Fedorov, "Mera otvetstvennosti," *Novyi mir*, no. 1 (1966), pp. 260–263. (It is interesting that it was *Novyi mir* which rescued Nekrich from ensuing oblivion by publishing a book review under his name in its first issue for 1968. G. A. Deborin and B. V. Telpukhovsky, "Videinom plenu i falsifikatorov istorii," *Voprosy istorii KPSS*, no. 9 (1967), pp. 127–140.

missed from the Institute of History. It is a safe assumption that others were dragged down in Nekrich's sudden fall: men who could be expected to recognize the dangerous errors and implications of his book and either insist on revision or prevent its clearance by the censors — but who failed to do so. In June 1967 Pospelov was replaced as director of the Institute of Marxism-Leninism by the party philosopher P. N. Fedoseev, and two months later the director of the Institute of History — Nekrich's immediate superior, V. M. Khvostov — was dismissed and given a less important position. There may well have been other casualties.

It is quite clear from the nature of the charges made against Nekrich in the *Voprosy istorii KPSS* article that the heart of the matter lies not in any new facts adduced but with the author's unorthodox analysis. The language of the critique is extremely harsh and the accusations are cast in political terms: Nekrich has fallen into "ideological captivity to the bourgeois falsifiers of history, betrayed the scientific principles of Marxist historiography." Thus his crime was one of conscious ideological deviation, not that of mere scholarly inaccuracies.

The alleged discussion at the Institute of Marxism-Leninism and the text itself bear this out. His descriptions of historical events cannot be faulted; but the devastating fact is that Nekrich is simply not working within Marxist-Leninist historical categories. As his critics point out, Nekrich's portrayal of Britain and the United States "utterly ignores the class forces involved" and suggests more of a realpolitik explanation of their warnings to Stalin on the eve of the Nazi attack. Equally fundamental is Nekrich's refusal to cast the tragic early months of the war as a prelude to inevitable victory in the framework of Marxist historical law. Failing "to show that the setbacks were of a temporary nature, that there were factors of decisive importance objectively dictating the victory of the USSR," he necessarily "presents the victory of the Soviet Union and the defeat of Germany as fortuitous events, not determined by historical laws."[45] Moreover, for Nekrich the heroic role during the war was played not by the party or the government, but by the people. The final section of the book, "Great Feat of the People," credits

45. *Ibid.*, pp. 136, 128.

the "high moral spirit of the people" with more than compensating for the economic and military inferiority of the USSR. The party is portrayed essentially in a supporting role, as having unified and channeled this popular strength.[46]

But it is his treatment of the oppressive figure of Stalin which ultimately dooms Nekrich. In this respect, most of the public Soviet discussion of the book avoids the real point. The important implications of Nekrich's portrayal run along a deeper and more unsettling course than that of amplifying Stalin's failings. In one account he is quoted as decrying popular submissiveness to the leader, saying that it was "Because of us, the little people, Stalinism began."[47] Moreover, his indictment of Stalin's schematic "understanding of the outside world" as causing his mistakes in foreign policy is a specific rendering of one of the underlying themes of the book: the need for pragmatic, realistic political leadership that is not imprisoned by rigid theoretical (Marxist-Leninist) preconceptions.[48]

It is not surprising, then, that it was a discussant of Nekrich's book who articulated the ultimate dilemma of Stalinism. Historian Kulish tried to shift the debate away from personality to the political system itself. One can only imagine the consternation and fright his statement must have caused:

To ask whether Stalin's guilt was total or limited is still a typical attitude of the personality cult. One is still concentrating on Stalin. We should look into the problem more deeply. We should ask how such a situation was able to come about. How did the government, under Stalin's direction, govern the country? How did it defend our people against the danger? Was it equal to its responsibilities? The answer is: No. We must analyze the process which allowed Stalin, who was not equal to his task, to become head of the Party and the state, with unlimited powers.[49]

It was precisely because Nekrich's historical probing had produced this kind of public heresy that he had to be punished. For the first time a Soviet scholar had clearly linked the individual despot with the nature of the system and its philosophical underpinnings. Thus the scholarly and political worlds have

46. Nekrich, *22 June 1941*, pp. 163, 164.
47. "The Personality Cult," p. 179.
48. *22 June 1941*, p. 132.
49. "The Personality Cult," p. 177.

been joined most dramatically in the historical question of Stalin.

The confrontation of historians over the Nekrich affair was on two levels — the scholarly quarrel over an accurate portrait of Stalin and the basic causes of the early military defeats of the war, and a more politically oriented scramble for preferred position among the historical actors. These aspects of the discussion were completely entangled with each other in reality, although it may be useful to view them as distinct phenomena for analytical purposes. Let us examine some of the political motivations and pressures involved.

For example, consider the denunciations by Anfilov — evidently a military historian attached to the general staff — of Voroshilov, Budenny, Golikov, and Kuznetsov. Voroshilov, he says, completely supported Stalin during the purges; Golikov and Kuznetsov — who present themselves as heroes in their own memoirs — knew of Hitler's Barbarossa Plan and even reported it to Stalin, but with the injunction that this was nothing more than a provocation. Anfilov further quotes Marshal Zhukov as accusing General Golikov (during the war, head of intelligence for the Red Army staff) of withholding necessary information from Zhukov (the chief of staff) and Marshal Timoshenko (commissar for defense), reporting only to Stalin.[50] But Gnedich undertakes to defend Golikov — to be sure, in a backhanded way — by stating that he himself had seen all the reports on Hitler's plans which were sent to Stalin and Molotov over the course of two years. Golikov was mistaken in interpreting these reports, but blame for failing to act on them falls on Stalin alone. "Golikov bears responsibility for the repression of GRU cadres, but for the neglect of defense measures Golikov is not guilty."[51] All of this suggests a many-faceted squabble among officers of different commands, using the controversy over Stalin to protect the reputation of their own outfit and denigrate others.

There is also some evidence that Piotr Yakir, of the Institute of History, was able to rally considerable high-level support among the military to press for his father's rehabilitation, despite his own well-known liberal tendencies. *Pravda* on August 15, 1966, carried a eulogy of Commander I. E. Yakir, who was

50. *Ibid.*, p. 175.
51. "Voennie istoriki osuzhdaiut Stalina," *Posev,* January 13, 1967, p. 4.

disgraced and executed in 1937, on the anniversary of his birth, written by Marshal Bagramian. Quite possibly it is this continuing loyalty toward the son of an old comrade which generated influential protection for young Yakir, from men who disagree with his politics. In any case, Piotr Yakir's dual identity — as an active liberal and courageous historian as well as a member of the military elite by family ties — provides a fascinating case study of a special kind of scholar-activist.

From observation of the historiographical perambulations of Stalin, it is apparent that academic discussion of a personal leader cannot be understood as merely the function of official policy. The debate over Stalin provides the most likely occasion and format for a perusal within the USSR of the more general and sensitive problem of political leadership and the system. Such public discussions are still furtive and truncated: nonetheless, they seem to represent a trend.

The Theory of Collective Leadership

It is perhaps fair to say that the central task the party leadership has set for itself and its historians since 1956 is a kind of contained revisionism. With regard to the problem of the political hero — most dramatically, Stalin — the official effort, only partially successful, has been to seal off the disease in time and space. Thus we have the formula that Stalin's excesses did not seriously damage the march toward socialism and the rejection of the initial concept of a negative "period of the cult of personality" in favor of the picture of an epoch of achievement despite certain problems.

There are now serious efforts toward a more positive solution of the problem of the hero in politics, namely, the development of a theory of collective leadership. As the theory has matured, it has begun to generate supportive historical evidence: what was initially in the late 1950s presented by the regime as the ideal for Soviet leadership is ten years later increasingly shown as the actual historical pattern.

The prime example of this aspect of official party history is P. A. Rodionov's book *Kollektivnost*[52] — proclaimed on the fly-

52. P. A. Rodionov, *Kollektivnost — Vysshii printsip partiinogo rukovodstva* (Moscow: Political Literature Publishing House, 1967).

leaf to be "designed for leading party workers, teachers in departments of history of the CPSU and party structure of higher educational institutions, and also for propagandists and party activists." The authority of the book is attested to by the career and status of its author, who has spent most of his adult life in the agitprop apparat, earning a degree of Candidate of Historical Sciences in the Academy of Social Sciences in 1958. Since 1964 he has been second secretary of the Georgian Central Committee and since 1966 a candidate member of the CPSU Central Committee. At the same time, it must be noted that Rodionov's book appeared in the context of a series of journal articles debating the precise nature of collective leadership, particularly its relationship to individual administrative responsibility and party infallibility.[53] Thus, though collective leadership has become a shibboleth, basic political questions are still raised within discussions of the exact definition and implications of collectivity.

Rodionov's treatise is an interesting example of historiography in its function of legitimation of policy. In its own way it is a tour de force. He undertakes first to show the special place of collectivity in Marxism-Leninism (a comparatively easy process of culling out appropriate quotations from the classics) and second (much more creative) to demonstrate how the operation of this principle guided party action under Lenin and afterward, "in particular, in the years when the appearance of the cult of personality was especially pronounced."[54]

In order to impress the contemporary theme of collective leadership upon historical materials, Rodionov relies heavily on a unique periodization of Soviet history. The foreword concerns theory and the period up to the beginning of NEP and is called "The Principle of Collectivity and Its Place in Marxist-Leninist Teachings on the Party." Chapter one is labeled "The Leninist Style" and treats the period 1921–1957. The second chapter picks up the story at 1959 and carries it to 1967 under the heading "The Development of the Leading Role of the CPSU in Communist Construction and the Strengthening of Collective

53. See F. Petrenko, "Kollektivnost i otvetstvennost," *Pravda*, July 20, 1966, pp. 2–3; D. Kunaiev, "Kollektivnost — Vysshii printsip partiinogo rukovodstva," *Partiinaia zhizn*, no. 19 (1966), pp. 8–15; and A. K. Kolesnikov, "Sobliudenie leninskikh printsipov rukovodstva — Osnova uspekhov v borbe za generalnuiu liniiu partii," *Voprosy istorii KPSS*, no. 4 (1967), pp. 102–114.
54. *Kollektivnost*, p. 5.

Leadership." Obviously such a time sequence enables him to treat the phenomenon of Stalinism as a relatively minor aberration, and in fact Stalin enters only after two thirds of the narrative has elapsed without him (including the discussions of collectivization, the First Five-Year Plan, and the New Opposition).

Rodionov follows well-worn formulas about Stalin's relationship to the system. The book is otherwise remarkable only for an unusual attempt to explain the onset of the personality cult by citing important objective conditions — the machinations of surrounding enemy states, internal enemies, the fact that the USSR had no model to follow and thus had a strong need for concentration of power as well as some temporary limitations on democracy. Also, alas, there were the unfortunate personal factors that Lenin had noted in his Testament.[55]

Finally, Rodionov places Khrushchev's dismissal in context by stating that the central committee plenum "recognized the inexpediency of combining in one person the duties of first secretary of the Central Committee and president of the USSR Council of Ministers in the future."[56] And at this juncture, his historiography becomes explicitly prescriptive, an attempt to influence rather than merely reflect political reality.

The attempt to portray the post-Stalin style of collective leadership as the general and historical pattern for the USSR is of course part of the "return to Leninism" initiated soon after Stalin's death. But quite evidently the Brezhnev-Kosygin partnership is a very different type of collectivity than what can be attributed to Lenin by even the most imaginative historian. The problem here for historians goes to the heart of the central dilemma of the political regime: How can a profoundly personal rule be safely transformed or institutionalized by its successors in the midst of radically changing domestic and international circumstances?

As Robert Tucker has pointed out, depersonalization of a hero such as Lenin is impossible, and the cult of the dead leader militates against transmission of his charisma to any successor.

. . . insofar as the charisma of a successful charismatic leader survives in the form of a cult of the dead leader, it does not cease

55. *Ibid.*, pp. 190–195.
56. *Ibid.*, p. 219.

to be personal in quality; it remains his even in death. The cult, in other words, may be a special form of "routinization" of his charisma, but is not a "depersonalization" of it.[57]

Thus, whatever the bases for political succession in the Soviet Union, the transference of Lenin's personal authority will not be at issue as long as his body is worshipped in the Lenin Mausoleum.

Stalin's crashing failure to attire himself in Lenin's mantle will stand as the only attempt at apostolic succession by one of his generation. It remains to be seen whether a political partnership lacking in charisma can depersonalize Stalin and simultaneously exploit the cult of Lenin, all under the rubric of historical and contemporary collective leadership. Historians of the CPSU are a talented group, they have survived much and most of them have earned a respite. But with such problems before them, one cannot predict any quick improvement of their situation.

57. Robert C. Tucker, "The Theory of Charismatic Leadership," *Daedalus*, Summer 1968, pp. 731–756.

Almost ten years ago, I wrote a work on Kievan Rus. Due to circumstances beyond my control, however, I was forced to interrupt my researches on the origin of the Imperial Russian State; now, as a historian, I hope to be compensated for that loss by being a witness to the end of that state . . . On the question of how long the regime can survive, several interesting historical parallels may be cited. At present, at least some of the conditions that led to the first and second Russian revolutions probably exist again . . . If I have determined the time of the outbreak of war with China correctly, the collapse of the regime will occur sometime between 1980 and 1985.

Andrei Amalrik, *Will the Soviet Union Survive until 1984?*

HISTORY AS PORTENT 4

This has been a difficult task: the unraveling of the tangled skein of relationships between historiography and politics within a political system that strives for total control and that reserves for history a central role at once scientific and mystical. I must now attempt some evaluations and conclusions.

It is, of course, true that the historical record of any state has an impact upon the practice of politics as well as upon the political norms, myths, and beliefs of that system. Historiography is everywhere not only informally influenced by the social fashions, political taboos, and current concerns that agitate the public arena, but in some cases it has been and is the object of quasi-official or official attempts at censorship and manipulation. Moreover, it seems clear that history — especially as it deals with the recent past — frequently has a powerful impact upon the contemporaneous politics of the host system, whatever its structure or coloration. To the extent that this is true, then, my findings have some general relevance for the broader field of comparative politics. A number of the phenomena discussed have present-day counterparts elsewhere or can be seen to resemble past institutions or practices outside the USSR.

However this may be, it seems equally clear that the political system of the USSR and its use of historiography — specifically and especially that which records the exploits of the CPSU — present these universal political-historical relationships in unique combinations and intensity. Marx and, to a greater degree, his revisionist disciple Lenin held a curiously ambivalent view of history as both scientific and mystical, deterministic and voluntaristic, fundamental and instrumental, sacred and degenerate. In fact, the Marxist-Leninist fixation upon history as the driving force of politics has proved pervasive in rendering the Soviet disposition of political historiography qualitatively as well as quantitatively distinct from that of authoritarian or traditionally repressive states. We find that historians within the USSR are very highly rewarded and charged with sociopolitical functions beyond those observable in other political systems, but they are as a group simultaneously distrusted, divided, and curbed by the political regime to a degree unusual even in the Soviet context.

A major portion of this book has been devoted to a close

examination of events during the decade following the Twentieth Party Congress in February 1956, in an effort to trace out the links and relationships between the daily operation of politics and scholarly and popularized historical accounts of earlier political events. The focus in essentially on the history of the CPSU, on the assumption that the extremely sensitive nature of the subject generates an intensive official concern for supervision and also exposes more of the mechanics of that surveillance to scrutiny.

Because of the enormous bulk of source material, the chronological survey of events is selective or analytical rather than comprehensive in scope; but several key developments have been treated extensively. The period opens with the dramatic revelations of the secret speech, Khrushchev's demand that both the party organization and party historiography be redefined: his bid for political primacy in the future on the basis of supervision of the past. On such an occasion, historiography and politics merge. But beyond the denigration of Stalin and the reaffirmation of faith in the strength, initiative, and dignity of the CPSU, the congress opened long-forbidden archives and topics of historical research and placed party historians under higher professional standards than they had known since the twenties. Essentially the historical record of the ensuing years has been one of continuing elaboration of the generalized and vague instructions given Soviet historians by Khrushchev, Pankratova, and Malenkov at the Twentieth Congress.

As historians moved out from the oppressive but secure categories of Stalin's *Short Course,* they began to respond to the regime's often confusing demands in a variety of ways and to initiate modifications for themselves. The difficulties of the regime in silencing the revisionist historians in late 1956 and 1957 suggest a self-propelling momentum within historiography engendered by substantive historical revisions and liberalization of controls over scholarship. A review of the literature shows that the revisionist interpretations and methodology which touched off the official repression of Burdzhalov and his group in 1956 and 1957 have in later years not only passed into general scholarly parlance but have filtered down to a surprising extent into mass-edition texts on party history. The most striking example of this vertical spillover from high-level, small-edition monographs and research articles into popularized historiography is indeed the whole issue of Bolshevik tactics in March and April of 1917, which was opened to discussion by Burdzhalov.

But the inherent momentum of historical change may be observed also in terms of horizontal spillover, a kind of contagious uncovering of forbidden topics and interpretations. The initial exposure of Stalin's brutal treatment of party members in the secret speech soon leaked into accounts of his earlier career and thus paved the way for franker accounts of his role in collectivization and some discussion of its human costs, and the first open admission of the existence of concentration camps. Thus items of historical revisionism — whether sponsored by Khrushchev and the party leadership or generated by confused or adventuresome historians — can be seen to develop an intrinsic viability, passing into the arena of scholarly and public knowledge and often shooting off sparks to inflame adjacent structures.

The chronological record shows an accumulating body of factual materials from newly opened archives, from memoirs, and from the renewed utilization by historians of long-forbidden historical research published in the twenties. Such resources, serving as documentation for the rapidly increasing numbers of texts and articles, and accompanied by a growing proficiency among historians of the CPSU in scholarly methodology, become important elements of this self-momentum. They force a more sophisticated level of discourse upon conservatives and liberals alike and make necessary an upgrading of personnel and methods in party institutions, such as the Institute of Marxism-Leninism, as well as in universities and the Academy of Sciences.

In short, an examination of the record of events reveals long-range liberalizing tendencies and more complex relationships, underlying another and more familiar pattern: the ebb and flow of short-range policy toward historiography of the CPSU. Moments of crisis and change alternate with periods of relative stability and consolidation. And, a further complication, we have observed the development of two quite separate domains within party historiography — one party-oriented and the other academic in outlook — both marked by attitudes of increasing professionalization or insulation from political winds. This traditional scholar-apparatchik divergence is now marked by a certain autonomy for the whole enterprise, in the sense that continuing debates within the profession are pressed by both factions with remarkably little concern for external political crises. This is not to contend that Soviet historians have suddenly moved beyond the larger political context. The phenomenon I am pointing to is that of an emergent professional group identity and pride, which has apparently infected to some degree even the conservative or apparatchik historians. The latter, for example, now seem to perceive certain issues of historiography — involving methodology, criteria of sources, style, even the matter of the historian's basic tasks — as perennial quarrels to be conducted on their merits with the liberals, despite a sudden freeze in the international atmosphere (in the summer of 1960) or a clampdown on writers (in December 1962) or the disclosure of an antiparty group in the political leadership (in June 1957). Any conclusions must be relative: history is becoming less of a political weapon and more a self-contained pursuit.

Having seen this bifurcation among Soviet historians, though, we must immediately go beyond it to stress another important conclusion from the analysis of developments since 1956. There is impressive evidence of a very broad division, within the liberal-conservative dichotomy, among historians as to the purposes, methodology, and scope of historical research.

This development is clearly related to the general commitment to better scholarship which grew up after the secret speech, and which was vividly displayed at the 1962 conference of historians on improving professional standards. In my treatment of that meeting historians were shown to be polarized into scholarly and administrative camps around cohesive clusters of attitudes, and simultaneously fragmented along a spectrum of opinion. The fact that only half of the participants expressed arguments that could be identified with their primary institutional affiliations and career backgrounds points up the complexity of this emerging professional group, the problems of individual identification within the group, and the need for a development of more subtle and personal categories of attitude and behavior beyond those of institutional associations, age, and career history. The functional alliance of outspoken Old Bolsheviks with some of the highly educated young historians to press for more truthful historical accounts of the early years of Soviet power, behavior such as Pospelov's at the 1962 conference, and the existence of such unexpected centers of Stalinism as the history faculty of the University of Moscow effectively destroy any easy assumptions that "old apparatchik" equals "Stalinist conservative" and "sophisticated academic" equals "liberal revisionist."

To obtain a functional analysis of historiography within the Soviet political system, I have delineated formal (explicitly acknowledged) and informal (unstated though often generally understood) functions. Within the first category is one function common to most systems: that of guardian of public tradition and legend. We also observe the overt utilization of history as a didactic tool: a function that remains at the unstated and sometimes even unconscious level in most other systems. In the informal category there are, again, both general and unique functions. Certainly the use of historiography to legitimate the political system is not peculiar to the Soviet Union; but other functions — as political barometer, vehicle of theoretical discussion, and political weapon — are systemically induced. The rationalizing function of history presents more of a problematic issue. Any political leadership will attract rationalizers in historiography, and pluralistic systems will tolerate detractors; authoritarian systems will reward the one and exterminate the other. Still there remains a special force and quality to the rationalizing function of Soviet historiography because of Marxist-Leninist theory, which accords history unchallenged authority and causative power. The particular role of party history within this system is thus far unique, although in time the Chinese may develop a similar conceptual framework by projecting their quite contemporaneous theory of the party back into the past.

Closely tied to the whole question of the functions of history are matters of evaluation of performance from the regime's point of view, the efficacy of controls, and the dysfunctional aspects of Soviet historiography. To develop these topics it was necessary to reconstruct the quite complicated network of state and party administrative controls — both formal and informal — which operate as a spur and a restraint upon historians. No significant institutional changes in this mechanism were discovered; consequently, the most creative and liberalizing developments in post-Stalin historiography have been and are of an interpretive or extrainstitutional nature. The revisionist challenge from liberal historians has come not only at the level of scholarly reinterpretation of specific events and figures but has appeared in the guise of literature and cinematography, and in the context of philosophic debate. Thus historiography has displayed clearly imperialistic tendencies, defined by some historians as incorporating fictional works and films and dealing with philosophical categories such as truth and aesthetic value. Still other scholars — acting apparently out of a like determination to free historiography from its political straitjacket — argue for a confinement of history to the realm of the particular and for the surrender of all concern with general laws and social theory (Marxism) to sociology.

Short of official renunciation or atrophy of the claim to infallibility by the CPSU, which cannot be expected in the near future, it remains within the capability of the regime — under conditions of international or domestic political crisis — to reinstitute severe controls. But the general outlook remains encouraging for a continued increment of knowledge of historical facts, higher standards of research and writing, increasing self-respect and group concerns, and a trend toward more objective historiography.

Any attempt at more subtle evaluation of the functioning of historiography within the Soviet system lays bare the deep and multiform dualities both among historians and within the regime. The political leadership is plagued by incompatible goals: it strives for an improved quality and increased quantity of historical works and attempts to retain the ultimate decision as to what constitutes heresy. With the rejection of terror, it must now rely on the development of internalized norms of behavior, a kind of automatic self-censorship, to augment official censorship. It sees the need for carefully circumscribed historical revision and that this can no longer be effectively induced by the old rough methods. Thus it must train better scholars and grant them access to archival materials. The inherent dangers are enormous. Moreover, the existence of the controlling bureaucracy itself can be seen to be dysfunctional in a number of ways: by generating family circles or mutual-protection groups among historians, by providing multiple points of access for dissidents within an unwieldy and redundant machine which enables them to exploit interagency inconsistencies and rivalries. Even the carefully structured system of elites fostered by the political leadership to combat the spillover of revisionist ideas has been converted by some of the more courageous historians into protected and self-contained elite groups that can shun their didactic role.

But the historian has also become increasingly ambivalent, as the burden of control over his production has fallen in greater measure upon his own shoulders. And this malaise, common among the more scholarly historians since the early 1930s, has come in recent years to affect the previously stolid and uncomplicated historians of the CPSU. The available evidence suggests not only a trend toward a larger number of highly trained historians choosing to specialize in party history but also an increase in the proportion of historians of the CPSU who are educated at universities rather than in party schools. Because the regime imposes more stringent standards of party loyalty and political participation upon historians of the CPSU than upon other historians, such developments are clearly productive of divided loyalties and a kind of schizophrenic orientation toward the goals and methodology of party history among the better qualified and more sensitive members of this group.

At this point the historian pauses and quietly draws the curtain, while the student of politics plunges rashly ahead into speculation. But there may be some comfort in the realization that — if the Western historian is skeptical, perhaps uninterested, and probably horrified — the Soviet historian would support the endeavor. For the historian of the CPSU is interpreting the present and predicting the future as he portrays the past; he is extrapolating from the party to the whole society; and he probably expects his critics to do the same. So I shall, in the last chapter.

Post-Stalin historiography of the CPSU should be viewed not as a mere reflection of politics but as a microcosm of the macrocosm that is the Soviet sociopolitical system. The fundamental duality of goals, tension in philosophy, and schizophrenia of identity produce in Soviet historiography an instability of policies which is analogous to that observed on the larger scene. But because of the exquisite sensitivity of the subject matter, party history often displays these dichotomies in exaggerated relief.

If we presume to cast the shadows observed in this specialized sphere upon the larger context, some intriguing questions arise. If there is a certain hard and accumulating residue of fact that accrues from each cyclical liberalization of policy and from the improved quality of historiography itself, is there also a self-momentum of social thought and habit that increasingly hinders a political retrenchment to the Stalinist type of control? Is the system of political elites more stable than that among historians? Can liberalism in economic management coexist over the long term with relatively tight ideological and cultural controls, or will there be repercussions? Can the historical figure of Stalin be excoriated by the top leadership (even if he were to be later exonerated in large part) without raising serious political questions about the system that for so many years harbored and adulated his policies as well as his person? Above all, is the new system of political control without terror — through incentives, legality, and the creation of internalized norms — adequate to the regime's goals?

It seems also apparent that historiography in any society is Janus-like: serious historiography foreshadows and helps to shape the future by first portraying past successes and failures and, second, by interpreting social costs and suggesting political priorities for the years ahead. But this general characteristic is acutely accentuated in the case of the USSR, because of the self-defined monopoly of the CPSU on power and political thought and the central but contradictory role reserved for history by its official doctrine. The element of utopianism in Marxism-Leninism — history perceived as a dialectical process that continually generates the new and progressive out of the old and decaying — requires the historian to understand the past as containing the future and to portray the past in terms of the future.

Thus, in the same manner that one would speculate upon the

larger Soviet system by moving outward spatially from the subsystem composed of Soviet writers of political history and their political mentors, one can extrapolate from that subsystem in terms of time. Let us then attempt to follow the future gaze of Soviet historiography.

If infallibility of the CPSU remains the essential legitimation of the attempt at total party control, then the historical treatment accorded that party's opposition is critical in an appraisal of its current social control as well as its future policies. This study has pointed to the quality of temporal compression, or the general tendency to merge historical periods, which is endemic in the historiography of the CPSU. It is, of course, closely linked to the special moral quality of this history and the resultant tendency toward one-dimensional and consistent character portrayal. Although the Mensheviks and Socialist Revolutionaries are no longer the fiends, traitors, and saboteurs of the *Short Course*, their new identity as stupid would-be Marxists (which became evident only in 1917) is nonetheless projected to their very early careers. Similarly, the denigration of Stalin and the antiparty group was a process of the gradual antedating of the onset of their crimes to earlier periods.

The exposure of such giant Bolshevik leaders as misled or criminal actors, and the ameliorated treatment of rival socialist parties, would appear to have severely corrosive effects on the theory of party infallibility and an intimate connection with such past political issues as the nature of Khrushchev's removal and such continuing problems as maintenance of the CPSU as model for other socialist parties. At some point in the near future the ingenuity of Soviet historians will be severely tested by the need to establish some theoretical categories — perhaps of legitimacy, historical necessity, or utility — with which to analyze political opposition to the Bolsheviks or to a specific Bolshevik leader. This would involve the development of criteria for the evaluation of political oposition per se, as a political phenomenon. Their solutions will bear both a derivative and a causal relationship to future Soviet politics, since any change in the definition of the acceptable limits of past political discourse and behavior would draw corresponding new boundaries for future discussion and action.

But there is another dimension to this phenomenon: the creation of new types of heroes, new models for political leadership, new modes of political behavior. It is possible to speculate upon such developments, if the treatment accorded the Mensheviks, Essars, and other opposition groups continues to mellow. Acceptance of the existence of these groups on the political scene of the past — even assuming that approbation would continue to be withheld — would in the Soviet context spell a kind of tacit approval. If revisionists continue to emphasize Lenin's alleged insistence on political rather than violent solutions to the problem of opposition, and if the official repudiation of Stalinist terror were maintained, liberal historians could over time develop a model of political competition among varieties of loyal socialist parties. Whether such a model could be acted out in any manner on the political stage would, of course, depend upon a multitude of imponderables both external and internal to the Soviet system.

Ultimately it would seem that the Soviet political elite has indeed committed the fatal error attributed by Marx and Lenin to every historical ruling class: it has created the insurgent group within the existing polity which will — at the proper revolutionary moment in time — bring it down. The catalyst in this case is the dissident intelligentsia. Small in number, it nonetheless represents the most fertile source of genuine political and moral challenge to the Soviet system as we know it. And Marxism-Leninism teaches the Soviet leadership that this elite (whether revisionist or revolutionary), were it to succeed somehow in forming a partnership with the working masses of the population, could take power. Just such an alliance, after all, nearly succeeded in Czechoslovakia in 1968.

Such a contingency in the USSR still remains remote. And yet the Soviet regime quite correctly claims that there exists a real danger of large-scale infection from certain recent activities of dissenting writers, students, and scholars, which it recognizes as essentially political acts. The event triggering the whole cycle was the trial of the writers Siniavsky and Daniel in early 1966. Upon that event have followed in fast-paced sequence a whole array of demonstrations, petitions to Soviet leaders, foreign communists, and world opinion, open letters to political and cultural figures, circulation of trial protocols, and other clandestine materials damaging to the regime's image. The protest movement received a new impetus and entered another cycle just two years after the Siniavsky-Daniel court case when four young students and writers were found guilty of antisocialist activity (some of which related to the earlier trial).

In defining the impact of these developments as political, I am focusing on the fact that in each case the protestors made a conscious appeal to a wider circle in the population than those few intellectuals personally involved, that they attempted to generate group support and action against established policy. This is a new departure in recent years — in Marxist terms, a dissent qualitatively different from the illicit reproduction and smuggling abroad of subversive fiction.

Without tracing out the protest movement in detail, I can point to a few episodes that bear special relation to political historiography. The first is the petition to Brezhnev signed by twenty-five intellectuals — party members all — warning against retreat to a Stalinist posture at the forthcoming Twenty-Third Party Congress.[1] Here a historical reference of great symbolic impact was consciously utilized to make a political point and create support for a viewpoint.

The second instance involves the circulation of a petition which is in some interesting ways different from its predecessors.[2] The document was drawn up and signed by three Moscow intellectuals: the historian Pyotr Yakir, Iuli Kim (self-described as a teacher), and Ilia Gabay (teacher and editor). They flay the trial procedures and the fabricated criminal charges against a whole series of defendants: they stress the lawlessness of these trials and insist on their moral right to protest. But their language is precise, and it is clear that they are leveling political as well as moral charges against the prosecutors in a new way. For one thing, their petition is directed overtly to a special elite group — "to USSR scientists, to those in culture and the arts" — who are urgently asked to act against "the impending dangers of new Stalins and Yezhovs." For another, the whole direction of the attack is against the perceived "ominous symptoms of a restora-

1. Peter Grose, "25 Soviet Intellectuals Oppose Any Elevation of Stalin's Status," *New York Times,* March 21, 1966, p. 2.
2. See "To Soviet Intellectuals," Radio Liberty Research Paper No. 21, 1968, for both Russian and English texts of this petition.

tion of Stalinism" as a system; the trials are introduced as one such symptom and are not the main concern.

Yakir's special professional concerns are readily apparent in the passionate spelling out of the "landmarks of Stalinism in recent years." Stalin's name is used positively — which, he says, might be excused as a "desire to portray history impartially" except that impartiality to a hangman is itself moral pathology and in any case this impartiality has not been extended to "telling the truth about the leading statesmen of the first decade of Soviet rule." He suggests that objectivity has yet to change the picture of Trotsky's "unmitigated sabotage." His bitterness is forceful: "In the social sciences the ruinous and irreversible dictate of politics continues to be mandatory. For a scientist, deviation from truth is death, but our historians who deal with most recent times, philosophers, and political economists are forced to do this every day." Most unusual is the point that it is lack of institutional guarantees within the political structure which make a reversion to Stalinism possible.

To be sure, repressions have not reached the proportions of those years. But we have sufficient basis for the fear that among state and party officials there are more than a few who would like to reverse our public evolution. We have no guarantees that the year 1937, little by little and without tacit connivance, will not come upon us again.

Yakir and his copetitioners insist that only action by "creative people . . . in whom our citizens have boundless faith" can turn back the remorseless process of restoration of Stalinism. The Stalinists are relying on the intelligentsia's "inertia, our short memory and our bitter habit of lacking freedom . . . Little by little with your tacit acquiescence, a new 1937 may come upon us."[3]

There is one last incident to be recited: the strangely quixotic demonstration that took place in Red Square on August 25, 1968. Seven Soviet citizens sat down at the historic spot of tsarist executions, unfurled small Czech flags and banners decrying the Soviet invasion of Czechoslovakia. They were instantly seized by political police, beaten, and arrested. The group was unusual in that it included a "worker" as well as two poets, a philologist, a linguist, a physicist, and an art critic. The other

3. *Ibid.*, pp. 8, 10–13.

notable aspect of the affair is that at least two participants were important organizers of the protest movement that had grown up around the series of trials of intellectuals: Larisa Bogoraz-Daniel and Pavel Litvinov. They were now extending the logic of their ideas and even their techniques of dissent to another discrete arena.

In larger perspective, some of the words spoken in the courtroom by the two leaders of the group will probably have more effect than the deed itself.[4] In their final pleas both Madame Daniel and Litvinov made frank and novel accusations of unconstitutional procedures on the part of the government. And even more striking are their references to Soviet history and its revisions. Litvinov puts this very nicely when he notes that the prosecutor recognizes that the defendants were opposed to a specific government policy and not to the society and system itself. He says he does not think even the prosecutor would say that all Soviet policies and political errors are the logical outcome of the system — "for then he would have to say that all the crimes of the Stalin times were the results of our social and state system."

To recognize this usage of political history is not to reduce the impact of post-Stalin historical revision to a manipulative level, although almost certainly this aspect has been to some degree present. More than an instrumental exploitation of history, one senses in the defendants' remarks first the deep shock and outrage of de-Stalinization and then the growing cynicism and intellectual independence toward official explanations which the intelligentsia developed out of the sweeping rewriting of history after 1956.

Madame Daniel says: "If I had not done this, I would have had to consider myself responsible for the error of our Government. Feeling as I do about those who kept silent in a former period [the rule of Stalin] I consider myself responsible." And Litvinov agrees: "As a Soviet citizen, I deemed it necessary to voice my disagreement with the action of my Government, which had made me very indignant." In other words, once Soviet historiography has confirmed that even one party ruler made policy mistakes which other leaders and the populace were too terrified

4. "Excerpts from the Proceedings of Trial in Moscow," *New York Times,* October 15, 1968, p. 14.

or apathetic to challenge, the historical lesson may be drawn that responsible citizenship requires political independence and occasionally overt opposition.

Litvinov raises the ultimately heretical question. If Stalin and the CPSU leadership could be wrong — if history itself could be so wrong for so many years — where is the infallible authority? "This is relevant," he insists. "Who is to judge what is in the interests of socialism and what is not?"

In an uncanny manner these events confirm the notion that in a system making such claims as the CPSU does on writers and social scientists, artistic or scholarly discontent has inevitable political overtones. Thus in the Soviet context, moral protest to be effective must become political action; issues are conjoined in a special way; and at least occasionally we witness a spillover from the world of the arts and academia to that of the policy maker and the would-be political participant.

It does seem, in the last analysis, that the history of the party and its appointed keepers are working against the general stability of the Soviet system. I would hazard the expectation that ultimately this cannot be rectified — all of the skeletons cannot be jammed back in the closet and the ghosts laid. Eventually, precisely out of the continued unraveling and evaluating of Soviet political history, will come some real and inescapable political alternatives. And out of the erosion of the myth of party infallibility will one day come the insight and courage to present these alternatives in the spirit of responsible citizenship.

Western Books

Amalrik, Andrei. *Will the Soviet Union Survive until 1984?* New York: Harper and Row, 1970.

Berlin, Isaiah. *Historical Inevitability*. London: Oxford University Press, 1954.

Bialer, Seweryn, ed. *Stalin and His Generals*. New York: Pegasus, 1969.

Black, Cyril E., ed. *Rewriting Russian History*, 2nd rev. ed. New York: Vintage Books, 1962.

Bober, M. M. *Karl Marx's Interpretation of History*. Cambridge: Harvard University Press, 1950.

Brumberg, A., ed. *Russia under Khrushchev*. New York: Frederick A. Praeger, 1962.

Cairns, Grace. *Philosophies of History*. London: Peter Owen, 1963.

Carr, Edward Hallett. *What Is History?* New York: Alfred A. Knopf, 1962.

Collingwood, R. G. *The Idea of History*. London: Oxford University Press, 1946.

Conquest, Robert. *Russia after Khrushchev*. New York: Frederick A. Praeger, 1965.

Counts, George. *The Country of the Blind: The Soviet System of Mind Control*. Boston: Houghton Mifflin Company, 1949.

Crankshaw, Edward. *Khrushchev, a Career*. New York: Viking Press, 1966.

Croce, Benedetto. *History, Its Theory and Practice*. New York: Russell and Russell, 1960.

Daniels, Robert Vincent. *The Conscience of the Revolution: Communist Opposition in Soviet Russia*. Cambridge: Harvard University Press, 1965.

D'Arcy, M. C., S.J. *The Meaning and Matter of History: A Christian View*. New York: Farrar, Straus and Cudahy, 1959.

Deutscher, Isaac. *Ironies of History: Essays on Contemporary Communism*. London: Oxford University Press, 1966.

Fainsod, Merle. *How Russia Is Ruled*, rev. ed. Cambridge: Harvard University Press, 1963.

Gallagher, Matthew P. *The Soviet History of World War II*. New York: Frederick A. Praeger, 1963.

Gorokhoff, Boris I. *Publishing in the U.S.S.R.* Washington, D.C.: Indiana University Publications, Council on Library Resources, 1959.

Gruliow, Leo, ed. *Current Soviet Policies — II. The Documentary Record of the 20th Communist Party Congress and Its Aftermath*. New York: Frederick A. Praeger, 1957.

Haimson, Leopold H. *The Russian Marxists and the Origins of Bolshevism*. Cambridge: Harvard University Press, 1955.

Hook, Sidney. *The Hero in History*. New York: John Day Company, 1943.

Hughes, Henry Stuart. *History as Art and as a Science*. New York: Harper and Row, 1964.

Katkov, George. *Russia 1917: The February Revolution*. New York: Harper and Row, 1967.

Keep, John, ed. *Contemporary History in the Soviet Mirror*. New York: Frederick A. Praeger, 1964.

Laqueur, Walter. *The Fate of the Revolution*. New York: Macmillan, 1967.

Leites, Nathan. *A Study of Bolshevism*. Glencoe: Free Press, 1953.

Leonhard, Wolfgang. *The Kremlin after Stalin*. New York: Frederick A. Praeger, 1962.

Lewin, Moshe. *La paysannerie et le pouvoir sovietique, 1928–1930*. Paris: Mouton and Co., 1966.

Lewis, H. D. *Freedom and History*. London: George Allen and Unwin, 1962.

Linden, Carl A. *Khrushchev and the Soviet Leadership, 1957–1964*. Baltimore: Johns Hopkins Press, 1966.

Mazour, Anatole G. *Modern Russian Historiography*, 2nd ed. Princeton: Van Nostrand, 1958.

Mehnert, Klaus. *Stalin versus Marx: The Stalinist Historical Doctrine*. London: George Allen and Unwin, 1952. German original published by Holzner Verlag, 1951.

Orlov, Alexander. *The Secret History of Stalin's Crimes*. New York: Random House, 1953.

Pethybridge, Roger. *A Key to Soviet Politics: The Crisis of the Anti-Party Group*. New York: Frederick A. Praeger, 1962.

Pipes, Richard, ed. *Revolutionary Russia*. Cambridge: Harvard University Press, 1968.

Popper, Karl R. *The Poverty of Historicism*. London: Routledge and Kegan Paul, 1957.

Problemi i realtà dell' URSS. Rome: Editori Riuniti, 1958.

Pundeff, Marin, ed. *History in the U.S.S.R., Selected Readings*. San Francisco: Hoover Institution on War, Revolution and Peace, Chandler Publishing Company, 1967.

Radkey, Oliver H. *The Agrarian Foes of Bolshevism*. New York: Columbia University Press, 1958.

———— *The Sickle under the Hammer: The Russian Socialist Revolutionaries in the Early Months of Soviet Rule*. New York, London: Columbia University Press, 1963.

Salmon, Lucy Maynard. *Why Is History Rewritten?* New York: Oxford University Press, 1929.

Schapiro, Leonard. *The Communist Party of the Soviet Union*. New York: Vintage Books, 1964.

———— *The Origin of the Communist Autocracy*. New York: Frederick A. Praeger, 1965.

Shteppa, Konstantin F. *Russian Historians and the Soviet State.* New Brunswick: Rutgers University Press, 1962.

Shukman, Harold. *Lenin and the Russian Revolution.* New York: J. P. Putnam's Sons, 1966.

Swearer, Howard R. *The Politics of Succession in the USSR.* Boston: Little, Brown and Company, 1964.

Ulam, Adam B. *The New Face of Soviet Totalitarianism.* Cambridge: Harvard University Press, 1963.

Urban, P. K. *Smena tendentsii v sovetskoi istoriografii.* Munich: Institute for the Study of the USSR, 1959.

Wetter, Gustav A. (trans. Peter Heath). *Soviet Ideology Today.* New York: Frederick A. Praeger, 1966.

Wolfe, Bertram D. *Khrushchev and Stalin's Ghost.* New York: Frederick A. Praeger, 1957.

Soviet Books

Burdzhalov, E. N. *Vtoraia russkaia revoliutssiia* [The Second Russian Revolution]. Moscow: "Science" Publishing House, 1967.

Chernomorskiy, M. N. *Istochnikovedenie istorii SSSR* [Source Work on History of the USSR]. Moscow: Higher School Press, 1966.

Dvadtsat piat let istoricheskoi nauki v SSSR [Twenty-Five Years of Historical Science in the USSR], ed. V. P. Volgin, E. V. Tarle, and A. M. Pankratova. Moscow, Leningrad: Academy of Sciences, 1942.

Gorodetsky, E. N. *Rozhdenie sovetskogo gosudarstva: 1917–18* [The Birth of the Soviet State: 1917–18]. Moscow: "Science" Publishing House, 1965.

Gusev, K. *Krakh partii levikh eserov* [The Collapse of the Party of the Left Essars]. Moscow: Socio-Economic Literature Publishing House, 1963.

Gusev, Kiril Vladimirovich. *Krakh melkoburzhauznykh partii v SSSR* [The Collapse of the Petty-Bourgeois Parties in the USSR]. Moscow: "Knowledge" Publishing House, 1966.

History of the Communist Party of the Soviet Union (Bolsheviks), Short Course. Toronto: Francis White Publishers, 1939.

History of the Communist Party of the Soviet Union, B. N. Ponomarev, ed. (trans. Andrew Rothstein). Moscow: Foreign Languages Publishing House, 1960.

History of the Communist Party of the Soviet Union, 2nd rev. ed., B. N. Ponomarev, ed. (trans. Andrew Rothstein and Clemens Dutt). Moscow: Foreign Languages Publishing House, n.d.

Istoriia i istoriki: Istoriografiia istorii SSSR [History and Historians: Historiography of History of the USSR]. M. V. Nechkina, ed. Moscow: Academy of Sciences, Institute of History, "Science" Publishing House, 1965.

Istoriia kommunisticheskoi partii sovetskogo soiuza, I: Sozdanie bolshevistskoi partii, 1883–1903 [History of the Communist Party of the Soviet Union, I: The Creation of the Bolshevik Party, 1883–1903]. Moscow: Political Literature Publishing House, 1964.

Istoriia kommunisticheskoi partii sovetskogo soiuza, II: *Partiia bolshevikov v borbe za sverzhenie tsarizma 1904–fev. 1917* [History of the Communist Party of the Soviet Union, II: The Bolshevik Party in the Struggle for the Overthrow of Tsarism, 1904–Feb. 1917]. Moscow: Political Literature Publishing House, 1966.

Istoriia kommunisticheskoi partii sovetskogo souiza, III: *Kommunisticheskaia partiia — Organizator pobedy velokoi oktiabrskoi revoliutsii i oborony sovetskoi respubliki, Mart 1917–1920* [History of the Communist Party of the Soviet Union, III: The Communist Party — Organizer of the Victory of the Great October Socialist Revolution and Defender of the Soviet Republics, March 1917–1920]. Moscow: Political Literature Publishing House, Book One 1967, Book Two 1968.

Istoriia SSSR: Epokha sotsializma (1917–1957) [History of the USSR: The Epoch of Socialism (1917–1957)]. M. P. Kim, ed. Moscow: Political Literature Publishing House, 1957.

Iz istorii borby leninskoi partii protiv opportunizma [From the History of the Struggle of the Leninist Party Against Opportunism]. Moscow: "Thought" Publishing House, 1966.

Kliucheva, E. I. *Kollektivnost — Vysshii printsip partiinogo rukovodstva* [Collectivism — the Highest Principle of Party Leadership]. Moscow: "Thought" Publishing House, 1966.

KPSS spravochnik [CPSU Handbook]. Moscow: Political Literature Publishing House, 1963.

Kommunisticheskaya partiia — Vdokhnovitel i organizator pobedi velikoi oktiabrskoi sotsialisticheskoi revoliutsii [The Communist Party — Inspirer and Organizer of the Victory of the Great October Socialist Revolution]. Moscow: Academy of Social Sciences under the Central Committee, Department of History of CPSU, 1957.

Kurs lektsii po istorii kommunisticheskoi partii sovetskogo soiuza [Lecture Course on History of the Communist Party of the Soviet Union], I. Leningrad: Leningrad University Publishing House, 1961.

Lekstii po kursu istorii kommunisticheskoi partii sovetskogo soiuza [Lectures for the Course on History of the Communist Party of the Soviet Union]. I. Moscow: Moscow University Publishing House, 1961.

Lenin i oktiabrskoe vooruzhenoe vosstanie v petrograde [Lenin and the October Armed Uprising in Petrograd], I. I. Mints, ed. Moscow: "Science" Publishing House, 1964.

Leninskaia partiia — Organizator oktiabrskoi revoliutsii [The Leninist Party — Organizer of the October Revolution]. Moscow: "Thought" Publishing House, 1965.

Maslov, Nikolai N. *Lenin kak istorik partii* [Lenin as Historian of the Party]. Leningrad: Leningrad Publishing House, 1964.

Nekotorie voprosy istorii KPSS [Some Questions of History of the CPSU], 3rd ed. S. M. Petrov, ed. Moscow: Higher Party School and Academy of Social Sciences under the Central Committee, CPSU, 1961.

O nekotorikh problemakh stroitelstva kommunizma v svete reshenii XXI sezda KPSS [Concerning Some Problems of the Construction of

Communism in Light of Decisions of the Twenty-First Congress of the CPSU], 2nd ed., S. M. Petrov, ed. Moscow: Higher Party School and Academy of Social Sciences under the Central Committee, CPSU, 1960.

Ocherki istorii istoricheskoi nauki v. SSSR [Sketches of History of Historical Science in the USSR], IV, M. V. Nechkina, ed. Moscow: "Science" Publishing House, 1966.

Outline History of the USSR. Moscow: Foreign Languages Publishing House, 1960.

Partiia-vdokhnovitel i organizator razvernutogo stroitelstva kommunisticheskogo obshchestva (1959–1961) [The Party — Inspirer and Organizer of Large-Scale Building of Communist Society (1959–1961)], V. N. Svetzov, ed. Moscow: Political Literature Publishing House, 1963.

Rodionov, P. A., *Kollektivnost — Vysshii printsip partiinogo rukovodstva.* [Collectivism — Highest Principle of Party Leadership]. Moscow: Political Literature Publishing House, 1967.

Shalagin, K. D. *Borba bolshevikov s trotskizmom (1907–1914)* [The Struggle of the Bolsheviks with Trotskyism (1907–1914)]. Moscow: Higher School Publishing House, 1965.

Soboleva, P. I. *Borba bolshevikov protiv menshevikov i eserov za Leninskuiu politiku mira (nov. 1917–1918)* [Struggle of the Bolsheviks against the Mensheviks and Essars for Lenin's Policy of Peace (Nov. 1917–1918)]. Moscow: Moscow University Publishing House, 1965.

Sovetskaia istoricheskaia nauka ot XX k XXII sezdu KPSS [Soviet Historical Science from Twentieth to Twenty-Second Congress of the CPSU], N. M. Durshinin, ed. Moscow: Academy of Sciences, 1962.

Spravochnik Partiinovo Rabotnika [Handbook of the Party Worker]. Moscow: Political Literature Publishing House. 1st ed., 1957; 2nd ed., 1959; 3rd ed., 1961; 4th ed., 1963; 5th ed., 1964; 6th ed., 1966; 7th ed., 1967.

Uchenie zapiski: Istoriia KPSS [Scholarly Notes: History of the CPSU], 1st ed., S. M. Petrov, ed. Moscow: Higher Party School and Academy of Social Sciences under the Central Committee, CPSU, 1959.

Uchenie zapiski: Istoriia KPSS [Scholarly Notes: History of the CPSU], 5th ed., F. D. Kretov, ed. Moscow: "Thought" Publishing House, 1966.

Voskresensky, Iury V. *Razgrom kommunisticheskoi partiei trotskistsko-menshevistskoi 'novoi oppozitzii' (1925–26)* [The Crushing of the Trotskyist-Menshevist "New Opposition" by the Communist Party (1925–26)]. Moscow: Moscow University Publishing House, 1962.

Vsesoiuznoe soveshchanie o merakh uluchsheniia podgotovki nauchno-pedagogicheskikh kadrov po istoricheskim naukam [All-Union Meeting Concerning Measures for Improvement of Training of Scientific-Pedagogical Cadres in Historical Sciences]. Moscow: "Science" Publishing House, 1964.

Articles in Western Journals

Achminov, Herman. "A Decade of De-Stalinization," *Studies on the Soviet Union,* 1965, pp. 11–19.

Billington, James H. "Six Views of the Russian Revolution," *World Politics,* April 1966, pp. 452–473.

Cocks, Paul M. "The Purge of Marshal Zhukov," *Slavic Review,* September 1963, pp. 483–490.

Daniels, Robert V. "Soviet Historians Prepare for the Fiftieth," *Slavic Review,* March 1967, pp. 113–118.

Dorotich, D. "Disgrace and Rehabilitation of M. N. Pokrovsky," *Canadian Slavonic Papers* (A. Bromke, ed.), VIII, University of Toronto Press, 1966, pp. 169–181.

Enteen, George. "Two Books on Soviet Historiography," *World Politics,* January 1958, pp. 327–353.

Fainsod, Merle. "Censorship in the USSR — A Documented Record," *Problems of Communism,* March–April 1956, pp. 12–19.

Fletcher, George. Review, "The New Party History," *Survey,* October 1965, pp. 162–172.

Frankel, Jonathan. "Party Genealogy and the Soviet Historians (1920–1938)," *Slavic Review,* December 1966, pp. 553–603.

Gilson, Jerome M. "New Factors of Stability in Soviet Collective Leadership," *World Politics,* July 1967, pp. 563–581.

Haimson, Leopold H. "Three Generations of the Soviet Intelligentsia," *Foreign Affairs,* January 1959, pp. 235–246.

Laird, Roy D. "The New Soviet Myth: Marx Is Dead, Long Live Communism!" *Soviet Studies,* April 1967, pp. 511–518.

Larson, Thomas B. "What Happened to Stalin?" *Problems of Communism,* March–April 1967, pp. 82–90.

McNeal, R. H. "Soviet Historiography on the October Revolution," *American Slavic and East European Review,* October 1958, pp. 269–292.

Mendel, Arthur P. "The Rise and Fall of 'Scientific Socialism,' " *Foreign Affairs,* October 1966, pp. 98–111.

"The Personality Cult," *Survey,* April 1967, pp. 159–180.

Rogger, Hans. "Politics, Ideology and History in the USSR: The Search for Coexistence," *Soviet Studies,* January 1965, pp. 253–275.

Schapiro, Leonard. "The Twenty-Third Congress of the CPSU," *Survey,* July 1966, pp. 72–84.

Schlesinger, Rudolf. "The October Revolution as the Background of the Institutional Setting," *Soviet Studies,* April 1967, pp. 519–526.

———. "Recent Soviet Historiography," *Soviet Studies,* April 1950, pp. 293–312; July 1950, pp. 3–21; October 1950, pp. 138–162; January 1951, pp. 265–288.

Skilling, H. Gordon. "Interest Groups and Communist Politics," *World Politics,* April 1966, pp. 435–451.

Slusser, Robert M. "The Forged Bolshevik Signature: A Problem in Soviet Historiography," *Slavic Review,* June 1964, pp. 294–308.

Sumner, B. H. "Soviet History," *Slavonic and East European Review,* April 1938, pp. 601–615.

"The Transient Hero in the USSR: Problems in Dismantling the Cults of Stalin and Khrushchev." Unsigned pamphlet, n.d.

Tucker, Robert C. "The Deradicalization of Marxist Movements," *American Political Science Review,* June 1967, pp. 343–358.

――― "The Theory of Charismatic Leadership," *Daedalus,* Summer 1968, pp. 731–756.

Ulam, Adam B. "The Moscow Congress: Prudence and Semantics," *The Reporter,* May 5, 1966, pp. 25–27.

――― "Reflections on the Revolution," *Survey,* July 1967, pp. 3–13.

"Voennie istoriki osuzhdaiut stalina," *Posev,* January 13, 1967, pp. 3–5.

Wolfe, Bertram D. "Leon Trotsky as Historian," *Slavic Review,* October 1961, pp. 495–502.

――― "Operation Rewrite: The Agony of Soviet Historians," *Foreign Affairs,* October 1952, pp. 39–57.

Yakobsen, Sergius. "Postwar Historical Research in the Soviet Union," *Annals of the American Academy of Political and Social Science,* CCLXIII (1949), pp. 123–133.

Articles in Soviet Journals

"Akademik N. M. Druzhinin. Otvet Franko Venturi" [Academician N. M. Druzhinin. Answer to Franco Venturi], *Istoriia SSSR,* no. 5 (1964), pp. 194–203.

"Aktualnye problemy marksistsko-leninskoi teorii" [Urgent Problems of Marxist-Leninist Theory], *Pravda,* June 5, 1966, p. 6.

Aluf, I. A. "O nekotorykh voprosakh fevralskoi revoliutsii" [Concerning Some Questions on the February Revolution], *Voprosy istorii KPSS,* no. 1 (1967), pp. 16–31.

Anderson, M. F., V. I. Kuzmin, M. D. Stuchebnikova, and N. I. Shatagin. "Uchebnoe posobie po istorii SSSR" [Textbooks on History of the USSR], *Voprosy istorii KPSS,* no. 1 (1959), pp. 180–190.

Anikeev, V. V. "Dokumenty tsentralnogo partiinogo arkhiva o deiatelnosti partii v period podgotovki oktiabria" [Documents from the Central Party Archives Concerning Party Activity in the Pre-October Period], *Voprosy istorii KPSS,* no. 11 (1966), pp. 122–127.

――― "Nekotorye novye svedeniia po istorii oktiabrskoi revoliutsii" [Some New Information on the History of the October Revolution], *Voprosy istorii KPSS,* no. 9 (1963) pp. 99–106.

――― "Svedeniia o bolshevistskikh organizatsiiakh s marta po dekabr 1917" [Information on Bolshevik Organizations from March to December 1917], *Voprosy istorii KPSS,* no. 2 (1958), pp. 126–193, and no. 3 (1958), pp. 96–168.

Arutiunov, G. A. Review, *Listovki kavkazskogo soiuza RSDRP, 1903–1905* [Leaflets of the RSDLP Union of the Caucasus, 1903–1905], in *Voprosy istorii,* no. 4 (1956), pp. 158–160.

Assaturova, M. I. "Obshchye sobranie otdelniia istoricheskikh nauk" [General Meetings of Departments of Historical Science], *Voprosy istorii,* no. 6 (1959), pp. 157–163.

Bakhshiev, D. Iu. "Iz istorii borby leninskoi partii protiv opportunizma"

[From the History of the Struggle of the Leninist Party Against Opportunism], *Voprosy istorii KPSS,* no. 3 (1967), pp. 121–125.

Baklanov, Grigory. "Chtob eto nikogda ne povtorilos" [So That This Will Never Happen Again], *Literaturnaia gazeta,* November 22, 1962, p. 3.

Balashov, V. N. "Sessiia otdelenii obshchestvennikh nauk AN SSSR po borbe s sovremennym revizionizmom" [Session of the Department of Social Sciences of the USSR Academy of Sciences on the Struggle with Contemporary Revisionism], *Voprosy istorii,* no. 7 (1958), pp. 171–190.

Beilina, E. E. "Istoriograficheskaia konferentsiia v MGU" [Historiographical Conference at Moscow State University], *Istoriia SSSR,* no. 4 (1963), pp. 217–220.

Berezin, V. T. "Chitatelskaia konferentsiia v moskovskoi vyshei partiinoi shkole" [Readers' Conference at Moscow Higher Party School], *Voprosy istorii,* no. 9 (1959), pp. 190–192.

Berezkin, A., and S. Mezentsev. "Geroicheskaia istoriia kommunistichesko partii sovetskogo soiuza" [Heroic History of the Communist Party of the Soviet Union], *Kommunist,* no. 10 (1959) pp. 53–65.

Bliakhin, P. "Film o podvig naroda" [A Film About the Exploit of the People], *Izvestiia,* January 3, 1957, p. 2.

Bogdenko, M. L. "K istorii nachalnogo etapa sploshnoi kollektivizatsii selskogo khoziaistva SSSR" [Toward a History of the Beginning Stage of Full Collectivization of Agriculture in the USSR], *Voprosy istorii,* no. 5 (1963), pp. 19–35.

Boguslavskaia, Z. "Chelovek razmyshliaet . . ." [A Man Reflects . . .], *Literaturnaia gazeta,* October 23, 1962, pp. 2–3.

"Bolshoi razgovor s chitateliami" [A Great Conversation with Readers], *Voprosy istorii KPSS,* no. 2 (1964), pp. 152–154.

Bondarevskaia, T. P., and A. Ia. Velikanova. "Peterburgskii sovet rabochikh deputatov v 1905 godu" [The Petersburg Council of Workers' Deputies in 1905], *Voprosy istorii KPSS,* no. 1 (1958), pp. 55–71.

"Broshiury o sezdakh i konferentsiiakh KPSS" [Brochures on Congresses and Conferences of the CPSU], *Voprosy istorii,* no. 2 (1956), pp. 124–129.

Bugaev, E. I. "K voprosu o taktike partii v marte-nachale aprelia 1917" [On the Question of Tactics of the Party in March–Early April 1917], *Voprosy istorii KPSS,* no. 1 (1957), pp. 13–36.

Bugaev, E. "Klassy i partii Rossii v kanun oktiabria" [Classes and Parties of Russia on the Eve of October], *Kommunist,* no. 16 (1966), pp. 9–21.

——— "Kogda utrachivaetsia nauchnyi podkhod" [When the Scientific Approach Is Lost], *Partiinaia Zhizn,* no. 14 (1956), pp. 62–72.

——— and N. V. Ruban. "Put borby i pobed leninskoi partii" [The Path of Struggle and Victory of the Leninist Party], *Voprosy istorii KPSS,* no. 4 (1959), pp. 17–34.

Bukovsky, K. "Otvet na lestnitse" [Reply on the Staircase], *Oktiabr,* no. 9 (1966), pp. 199–201.

Burche, E. F., and I. E. Mosolov. "Protiv iskazhenii istorii aviatsii" [Against the Distortion of the History of Aviation], *Voprosy istorii,* no. 6 (1956), pp. 124–128.

Burdzhalov, E. N. "Esche o taktike bolshevikov v marte–aprele 1917" [Again on the Tactics of the Bolsheviks in March–April 1917], *Voprosy istorii,* no. 8 (1956), 109–114.

—— "Nachalo vtoroi russkoi revoliutsii" [The Beginning of the Second Russian Revolution], in *Materialy i issledovanie po istorei SSSR* (Moscow, 1964), pp. 131–159.

—— "O taktike bolshevikov v marte–aprele 1917" [Concerning the Tactics of the Bolsheviks in March–April 1917], *Voprosy istorii,* no. 4 (1956), pp. 38–56.

Burganov, A. Kh. "K voprosu o periodizatsii istorii velikoi oktiabrskoi sotsialisticheskoi revoliutsii" [On the Question of Periodization of the History of the Great October Socialist Revolution]. *Istoriia SSSR,* no. 3 (1964), pp. 3–16.

Burlatsky, F. "Politika i nauka" [Politics and Science], *Pravda,* January 10, 1965, p. 4.

Chekhovich, O. D. "O nekotorykh voprosakh istorii Srednei Azii XVIII–XIX vekov" [Concerning Some Questions of the History of Central Asia in the XVIII–XIX Centuries], *Voprosy istorii,* no. 3 (1956), pp. 84–95.

Cherepnin, L. V. "Istoricheskie vzgliady Gogolia" [Historical Views of Gogol], *Voprosy istorii,* no. 1 (1964), pp. 75–97.

Chermensky, E. D. "Fevralskaia burzhuazno-demokraticheskaia revoliutsiia 1917 goda" [The February Bourgeois-Democratic Revolution of 1917], *Voprosy istorii,* no. 2 (1957), pp. 3–18.

Chernomorsky, M. "Memuary — sredstvo revoliutsionnogo vospitaniia" [Memoirs — a Means of Revolutionary Education], *Pravda,* August 22, 1966, p. 3.

Chicherov, I. "Vo imia budushchogo" [In the Name of the Future], *Moskovskaia pravda,* December 8, 1962, p. 3.

Chigrinov, G. A. "V. N. Yakovtsevsky, *Agrarnye otnosheniia v SSSR v period stroitelstva sotsializma,* Moscow: 1964" [V. N. Yakovtsevsky, *Agrarian Relationships in the USSR in the Period of the Building of Socialism*], *Voprosy istorii KPSS,* no. 8 (1966), pp. 126–130.

Danilov, V. P. "K itogam izucheniia istorii sovetskogo krestianstva i kolkhoznogo stroitelstva v SSSR" [Toward the Goal of Study of the History of the Soviet Peasantry and Kolkhoz Construction in the USSR], *Voprosy istorii,* no. 8, (1960), pp. 34–64.

—— "Materialno-tekhnicheskaia baza selskogo khoziaistva SSSR nakanune sploshnoi kollektivizatsii" [The Material-Technical Base of Agriculture in the USSR on the Eve of Full Collectivization], *Voprosy istorii,* no. 7 (1956), pp. 3–17.

—— "Nekotorye itogi nauchnoi sessii po istorii sovetskoi derevni" [Some Results of the Scientific Session on History of the Soviet Countryside], *Voprosy istorii,* no. 2 (1962), pp. 20–43.

Danilova, L. V., and V. P. Danilov. Review of "Rewriting Russian

History. Soviet Interpretations of Russia's Past" *Istoriia SSSR,* no. 6 (1959), pp. 188–200.

Denisov, G. M. "Ob osveshchenii v Bolshoi Sovetskoi Entsiklopedii deiatelnosti vydaiushchikhsia bolshevikov" [Concerning the Interpretation of the Activities of Leading Bolsheviks in the Great Soviet Encyclopedia], *Voprosy istorii,* no. 5 (1956), pp. 141–145.

Diakov, Boris. "Perezhitoe" [Days Lived Through], *Zvezda,* no. 3 (1963), pp. 177–196.

Drabkina, F. I. "Vserossiiskoe soveshchanie bolshevikov v Marte 1917" [The All-Russian Meeting of Bolsheviks in March 1917], *Voprosy istorii,* no. 9 (1956), pp. 3–16.

Dubov, G. V. "Seminar po filosofskim problemam istoricheskoi nauki" [Seminar on Philosophical Problems of Historical Science], *Voprosy istorii,* no. 7 (1964), pp. 159–162.

"XX sezd KPSS i zadachi issledovaniia istorii partii" [The Twentieth Congress of the CPSU and Tasks for Research on Party History], *Voprosy istorii,* no. 3 (1956), pp. 3–12.

"XXII sezd KPSS i zadachi ideologicheskoi raboty. Doklad sekretaria TsK KPSS tovarishcha L. F. Ilicheva" [The Twenty-Second Congress of the CPSU and Tasks of Ideological Work. Report of Secretary of the Central Committee of the CPSU Comrade L. F. Ilichev], *Pravda,* December 27, 1961, p. 2.

"XXII sezd KPSS i zadachi kafedr obshchestvennikh nauk. Doklad sekretaria TsK KPSS tovarishcha M. A. Suslova" [The Twenty-Second Congress of the CPSU and Tasks of the Faculty of Social Sciences. Report of Secretary of the Central Committee of the CPSU Comrade M. A. Suslov], *Pravda,* February 4, 1962, pp. 3–4.

"XXII sezd partii ob iskliuchenie posledstvii kulta lichnosti" [The Twenty-Second Congress of the Party Concerning Elimination of the Remnants of the Cult of Personality], *Pravda,* November 21, 1961, p. 2.

"XXIII sezd kommunisticheskoi partii Gruzii, rech tov. D. G. Sturui" [The Twenty-Third Congress of the Georgian Communist Party. Speech of Comrade D. G. Sturua], *Zaria vostoka,* March 10, 1966, p. 2.

Dykov, I. G., and F. V. Chebaevsky. "O nekotorykh monografiiakh ob ustanovlenii sovetskoi vlasti na mestakh" [Concerning Some Monographs on the Establishment of Soviet Power in the Provinces], *Istoriia SSSR,* no. 4 (1957), pp. 162–166.

———— "O nekotorykh voprosakh istorii ustanovleniia sovetskoi vlasti v Moldavii" [Concerning Some Questions on the History of the Establishment of Soviet Power in Moldavia], *Voprosy istorii,* no. 7 (1959), pp. 18–36.

Dymshits, A. "Chelovek i obshchestvo" [Man and Society], *Oktiabr,* no. 7 (1962), pp. 182–192.

———— "Roman o trudnykh godakh" [A Story of Difficult Years], *Izvestiia,* May 10, 1964, p. 6.

"Edinstvo, aktivnost, delovitost" [Unity, Activity, Efficiency], *Partiinaia zhizn,* no. 2 (1965), pp. 8–16.

"Edinstvo partii i razvitie kritiki" [Unity of the Party and the Development of Criticism], *Partiinaia zhizn,* no. 21 (1957), pp. 48–57.

Ehrenburg, I. "Liudi, gody, zhizn" [People, Years, Life], *Novyi mir*, no. 1 (1965), pp. 103–125; no. 4 (1965), pp. 29–83.

Fedoseev, P., and Iu. Frantsev. "Istoriia i sotsiologiia" [History and Sociology], *Kommunist*, no. 2 (1964), pp. 61–74.

————, I. Pomelov, and V. Cheprakov. "O proekte programmy soiuza kommunistov Iugoslavii" [Concerning the Draft Program of the Yugoslav League of Communists], *Kommunist*, no. 6 (1958), pp. 16–39.

Filimonova, I. M. "K sozdaniiu mnogotomnoi istorii KPSS" [Toward the Creation of a Multi-volume History of the CPSU], *Voprosy istorii KPSS*, no. 5 (1960), pp. 229–230.

"Film 'Oktiabr' nachinaet novuiu zhizn" [The Film "October" Begins a New Life], *Pravda*, October 28, 1962, p. 6.

Fomenko, Lidiia. "Bolshie ozhidaniia" [Great Expectations], *Literaturnaia rossiia*, January 11, 1963, pp. 6–7.

Frantsev, Iu. "Vosprianul rod liudskoi" [Mankind Has Awakened], *Izvestiia*, November 6, 1965, p. 2.

Garmiza, V. V. "K. V. Gusev. Krakh partii levykh eserov, M. Sotzeskgiz, 1963" [K. V. Gusev. The Collapse of the Left Essar Party, Moscow, Sotzekgiz, 1963], *Istoriia SSSR*, no. 3, (1964), pp. 170–174.

———— "Kak esery izmenili svoei agrarnoi programme" [How the Essars Changed Their Agrarian Program], *Voprosy istorii*, no. 7 (1965), pp. 31–41.

Gaubikh, B. V. "Novoe izdanie vuzovskikh programm po istorii KPSS" [New Edition of Higher Educational Institutions' Program for History of the the CPSU], *Voprosy istorii KPSS*, no. 5 (1960), pp. 227–229.

Gimpelson, E. G. "Iz istorii obrazovaniia odnopartiinoi sistemy v SSSR" [From the History of the Development of the One-Party System in the USSR], *Voprosy istorii*, no. 11 (1965), pp. 16–30.

———— "Nekotorye voprosy istorii velikoi oktiabrskoi sotsialisticheskoi revoliutsii na mestakh" [Some Questions on the History of the Great October Socialist Revolution in the Provinces], *Istoriia SSSR*, no. 3 (1958), pp. 221–227.

Golikov, G. N. "K izucheniiu istorii velikogo oktiabria" [Toward the Study of the History of Great October], *Voprosy istorii*, no. 11 (1962), pp. 33–53.

———— "K razrabotke istorii oktiabrskoi revoliutsii" [Toward Reconsideration of the History of the October Revolution], *Kommunist*, no. 15 (1956), pp. 44–57.

———— "Na perednem krae istoricheskoi nauki" [The Forefront of Historical Science], *Voprosy istorii*, no. 11 (1961), pp. 18–42.

———— "Ob izuchenii istorii oktiabrskoi revoliutsii" [Concerning the Study of the History of the October Revolution], *Kommunist*, no. 10 (1960), pp. 82–90.

———— "Partiia — vdokhnovitel i organizator velikoi oktiabrskoi sotsialisticheskoi revoliutsii" [The Party — Leader and Organizer of the Great October Socialist Revolution] *Voprosy istorii KPSS*, no. 12 (1963), pp. 63–69.

Gopner, S. I. "Martovskie i aprelskie dni 1917 goda" [The March and April Days of 1917], *Voprosy istorii,* no. 3 (1957), pp. 42–52.

Gorbatov, A. V. "Gody i voiny" [Years and Wars], *Novyi mir,* no. 3 (1964), pp. 133–156; no. 4 (1964), pp. 99–138; no. 5 (1964), pp. 106–153.

Gorchakov, O. "Taina polkovinka Starinova" [The Secret of Colonel Starinov], *Izvestiia,* February 7, 1963, p. 4.

Gorlovsky, M. A. "Pervaia mezhoblastnaia nauchnaia konferentsiia po istorii Urala" [The First Interoblast Scientific Conference on the History of the Urals], *Voprosy istorii,* no. 6 (1958), pp. 192–195.

Gorodetsky, E. N. "Voprosy metodologii istoricheskogo issledovaniia v posleoktiabrskikh trudakh V. I. Lenina" [Questions of Methodology of Historical Research in the Post-October Works of V. I. Lenin], *Voprosy istorii,* no. 6 (1963), pp. 16–34.

Guliga, A. V. "O predmete istoricheskoi nauki" [On the Topic of Historical Science], *Voprosy istorii,* no. 4 (1964), pp. 20–31.

——— "Poniatie i obraz v istoricheskoi nauke" [Idea and Image in Historical Science], *Voprosy istorii,* no. 9 (1965), pp. 3–14.

Gurevich, A. Ia. "Nekotorye aspekty izucheniia sotsialnoi istorii" [Some Aspects of the Study of Social History], *Voprosy istorii,* no. 10 (1964), pp. 51–68.

——— "Obshchii zakon i konkretnaia zakonomernost v istorii" [General Law and Concrete Lawfulness in History], *Voprosy istorii,* no. 8 (1965), pp. 14–30.

Gus, M. " 'Ostavatsia pri fakte' — i tolko?" ["Rest on the Facts" — and Only the Facts?], *Literaturnaia gazeta,* November 16, 1965, p. 1.

Gusarov, V. "Uspekh ili neudacha?" [Success or Failure?], *Zvezda,* no. 9 (1962), pp. 209–211.

Gusev, K. V. "Iz istorii soglasheniia bolshevikov s levymi eserami" [From the History of the Agreement of the Bolsheviks with the Left Essars], *Istoriia SSSR,* no. 2 (1959), pp. 73–94.

Gusev, S. I. "Iz istorii borby za stroitelstvo bolshevistskoi partii" [From the History of the Struggle for Construction of the Bolshevik Party], *Voprosy istorii,* no. 5 (1956), pp. 17–33.

Iakovlev, L. A., and V. A. Kondratev. "Novoe v rabote sovetskikh arkhivov" [News in the Work of Soviet Archives], *Voprosy istorii,* no. 1 (1957), pp. 192–194.

Iastrebov, L. B. "Obsuzhdenie problem istochnikovedeniia istorii SSSR sovetskogo perioda" [Discussion of the Problem of Sourcework in USSR History in the Soviet Period], *Istoriia SSSR,* no. 4 (1962), pp. 230–232.

Idashkin Iury. "No esli zadumatsia" [But If One Thinks], *Oktiabr,* no. 9 (1962), pp. 212–213.

"Ideologicheskuiu rabotu — v tsentr vnimaniia" [Ideological Work — in the Center of Attention], *Pravda,* April 6, 1960, p. 2.

Ignatev, G. S. "Oktiabrskoe vosstanie v Moskve" [The October Uprising in Moscow], *Istoriia SSSR* no. 4 (1957), pp. 126–140.

Ilin, A. F. "Problemy vtoroi piatiletki sovetskoi promyshlennosti v kandidatskikh dissertatsiiakh" [Problems of the Second Five-Year Plan of Soviet Industry in Candidates' Dissertations], *Voprosy istorii,* no. 1 (1957), pp. 185–192.

"Institut istorii AN SSSR v 1963 godu" [The Institute of History of the USSR Academy of Sciences in 1963], *Istoriia SSSR,* no. 1 (1964), pp. 214–217.

Ivanov, V. M. "Partiia v borbe protiv trotskistskoi revizii leninizma v 1924 godu" [The Party in Struggle Against Trotskyite Revisionism of Leninism in 1924], *Voprosy istorii KPSS,* no. 4 (1959), pp. 56–72.

—— "Realizm segodnia" [The Realism of Today], *Literaturnaia gazeta,* October 29, 1966, p. 1, and November 10, 1966, p. 3.

Ivnitsky, N. A. "Opyt KPSS po pretvoreniiu v zhizn leninskogo kooperativnogo plana" [The Experience of the CPSU in Bringing to Life the Leninist Cooperative Plan], *Voprosy istorii KPSS,* no. 2 (1966), pp. 97–107.

"Iz perepiski E. D. Stasovoi i K. T. Novgorodtsevoi (Sverdlovoi), mart–dekabr 1918" [From the Correspondence of E. D. Stasova and K. T. Novgorodtseva (Sverdlova), March–December 1918], *Voprosy istorii,* no. 10 (1956), pp. 85–101.

"K 50-letiiu pervoi russkoi revoliutsii" [On the Fiftieth Anniversary of the First Russian Revolution], *Voprosy istorii,* no. 2 (1956), pp. 197–199.

"K 70-letiiu so dnia rozhdeniia Akad. I. I. Mintsa" [On the Seventieth Anniversary of the Birth of Academician I. I. Mints], *Istoriia SSSR,* no. 1 (1966), p. 246.

Kanev, S. N. "Iz istorii borby V. I. Lennia protiv farktsionnykh gruppirovok (1920–1922)" [From the History of the Struggle of V. I. Lenin against Fractional Groups (1920–1922)], *Voprosy istorii KPSS,* no. 4 (1958), pp. 58–71.

"Kandidatskie dissertatsii po istorii KPSS, zashchishchennye s 15 maia po 31 dekabria 1958 goda" [Candidates' Dissertations on History of the CPSU, Submitted from 15 May to 31 December 1958], *Voprosy istorii KPSS,* no. 2 (1959), pp. 232–236.

Kardin, V. "Legendy i fakty" [Legends and Facts], *Novyi mir,* no. 2 (1966), pp. 237–250.

Kazakevich, E. "Vragy" [Enemies], *Izvestiia,* April 21, 1962, p. 6.

Khait, Grigory. "Poiski leninskikh strok" [A Search for the Leninist Line], *Pravda,* January 20, 1966, p. 4.

Khanazarov, K. Kh., and V. M. Tsherbok. "V sektore istorii KPSS instituta marksizman-leninizma" [In the Sector for History of the CPSU of the Institute of Marxism-Leninism], *Voprosy istorii KPSS,* no. 1 (1958), pp. 214–217.

Kliuchnik, L. I., and V. P. Nikolaeva. "Nekotorye statisticheskie svedeniia o sostoianii partiinikh organizatsii v 1918 godu" [Some Statistical Information on the Composition of Party Organizations in 1918], *Voprosy istorii KPSS,* no. 1 (1961), pp. 121–131.

Kliuchnik, L. I. "O memuarnoi literature" [Concerning Memorial Literature], *Voprosy istorii KPSS,* no. 2 (1966), pp. 150–153.

"Konferentsiia chitatelei zhurnala 'Voprosy istorii' " [Conference of

Readers of the Journal "Voprosy Istorii"], *Voprosy istorii*, no. 2 (1956), pp. 199–213.

"Konferentsiia chitatelei zhurnala 'Voprosy istorii' v Kieve" [Conference of Readers of the Journal "Voprosy Istorii" in Kiev], *Voprosy istorii*, no. 8 (1956), pp. 198–203.

"Konferentsiia chitatelei zhurnala 'Voprosy istorii' v Leningrade" [Conference of Readers of the Journal "Voprosy Istorii" in Leningrad], *Voprosy istorii*, no. 7 (1956), pp. 184–190.

Konstantinov, F., and V. Kelle. "Istoricheskii materializm — marksistskaia sotsiologiia" [Historical Materialism — Marxist Sociology], *Kommunist*, no. 1 (1965), pp. 9–23.

Kornilov, A. V., and N. S. Shevtsov. "S. P. Trapeznikov, *Istoricheskii opyt KPSS v sotsialisticheskom preobrazovanii selskogo khoziastva* (Moscow, 1959)" [S. P. Trapeznikov, *The Historical Experience of the CPSU in the Socialist Transformation of Agriculture*, Moscow: 1959], *Voprosy istorii KPSS*, no. 6 (1959), pp. 198–202.

Koroleva, N. A. "V komissii po istorii istoricheskoi nauki pri Institute istorii AN SSSR" [In the Commission on History of Historical Science under the Institute of History of the USSR Academy of Sciences], *Voprosy istorii*, no. 9 (1959), pp. 202–207.

Kostin, A. "Vazhneishii istochnik izucheniia i nauchnoi razrabotki istorii partii" [The Most Important Source for the Study and Scientific Reformulation of History of the Party], *Kommunist*, no. 18 (1958), pp. 114–119.

Kovalenko, D., A. Kotelenetz, P. Miliukov, and A. Pitersky, "Vyshe uroven nauchnoi razrabotki istorii KPSS" [A Higher Level of Scientific Study of History of the CPSU], *Kommunist*, no. 13 (1958), pp. 110–120.

Kriachko, L. "Pravda ne razediniatsia" [Truth Is Not Fragmented], *Literaturnaia rossiia*, October 28, 1966, p. 17.

Krivitsky, Aleksandr. "Fakty i legendy" [Facts and Legends], *Literaturnaia gazeta*, March 19, 1966, pp. 17–23.

Kuchkin, A., K. Gusev, and A. Konstantinov. "Kinga po istorii velikogo oktiabria" [A Book on the History of Great October], *Kommunist*, no. 12 (1963), pp. 123–125.

Kukin, D., V. Selunskaia, and N. Shatagin. "O nauchnoi razrabotke istorii KPSS" [Concerning Scientific Work on History of the CPSU], *Kommunist*, no. 16 (1960), pp. 12–25.

Kuznetsov, Anatoly. "Babi Yar" [Babi Yar], *Iunost*, no. 8 (1966), pp. 7–42; no. 9 (1966), 15–46; no. 10 (1966), pp. 23–49.

Kuznetsov, K., and R. Terekhov. "Vazhnaia vekha v zhizni leninskoi partii" [An Important Landmark in the Life of the Leninist Party], *Pravda*, May 26, 1964, p. 2.

Kuznetsov, M. "Pobedy i porazheniia Yegora Trubnikova [The Victories and Defeats of Yegor Trubnikov], *Komsomolskaia pravda*, December 12, 1964, p. 3.

Kuznetsov, V. I., and A. P. Pronshtein. "Nauchnaia rabota istorikov Rostovskogo gosudarstvennogo universiteta" [The Early Work of Historians at Rostov State University], *Voprosy istorii*, no. 8 (1958), pp. 214–216.

Lakshin, V. "Ivan Denisovich, ego druzia i nedrugi" [Ivan Denisovich, His Friends and Enemies], *Novyi mir,* no. 1 (1964), pp. 223–245.

———. "Pisatel, chitatel, kritik" [Writer, Reader, Critic], *Novyi mir,* no. 8 (1966), pp. 216–256:

Laverychev, V. Ia. "O plane nauchnoi raboty istoricheskogo fakulteta Moskovskogo gosudarstvennogo universiteta na 1959–1965 gody" [Concerning the Work Plan of the History Faculty of Moscow State University in the Years 1959–1965], *Voprosy istorii,* no. 10 (1959), pp. 172–173.

Lavrovsky, V. M. "K voprosu o predmete i methode istorii kak nauki" [On the Question of the Subject and Method of History as a Science], *Voprosy istorii,* no. 4 (1966), pp. 72–77.

"Leninskoe edinstvo partii nesokrushimo!" [The Leninist Unity of the Party Is Indestructible!], *Voprosy istorii,* no. 5 (1957), pp. 3–16.

"Leninskaia rezoliutsiia 'O edinstve partii' " [The Leninist Resolution "On Unity of the Party"], *Partiinaia zhizn,* no. 13 (1957), pp. 55–58.

"Literatura sotsialisticheskogo realizma vsegda shla ruka ob ruku s revoliutsiei" [Literature of Socialist Realism Always Goes Hand in Hand with Revolution], *Pravda,* May 12, 1963, pp. 4–5.

Lomakin, N. A. "Nastolnaia kniga partiinogo rabotnika" [A Reference Book for the Party Worker], *Voprosy istorii KPSS,* no. 3 (1958), pp. 205–207.

———. "Partiia vsogo naroda" [A Party of All the People], *Kommunist,* no. 12 (1962), pp. 12–22.

Lomidze, Georgy. "Nekotorye mysli" [Some Thoughts], *Literaturnaia rossiia,* January 18, 1963, p. 6.

Lopatkin, A. N. "Agrarnaia programma bolshevikov v velikoi oktiabrskoi sotsialisticheskoi revoliutsii" [The Agrarian Program of the Bolsheviks in the Great October Socialist Revolution], *Voprosy istorii,* no. 4 (1957), pp. 43–58.

Lukashev, A., S. Shaumian, and S. Shtseprov. "Memuarnaia literatura i istoricheskaia pravda" [Memorial Literature and Historical Truth], *Kommunist,* no. 11 (1959), pp. 107–112.

Lutsky, E. A. "O sushchnosti uravnitelnogo zemlepolzovaniia v sovetskoi rossii" [Concerning the Essence of Equalization of Land Use in Soviet Russia], *Voprosy istorii,* no. 9 (1956), pp. 59–71.

Maisky, I., M. Nechkina, A. Manfred, and L. Shkarenkov. "Istoricheskii zhurnal i sovremennost" [The Historical Journal and Contemporary Life], *Kommunist,* no. 4 (1964), pp. 87–93.

Makrushenko, Pavlo. "Liudi tridtsatikh godov" [People of the Thirties], *Izvestiia,* October 21, 1966, p. 3.

Manfred, A. Z. "I uchenyi i pisatel" [Both Scholar and Writer], *Literaturnaia gazeta,* September 12, 1961, p. 2.

Mavrodin, V. V., I. Z. Kadson, N. I. Sergeeva, and T. P. Rzhanikova. "Ob osobennostiakh krestianskikh voin v rossii" [Concerning the Peculiarities of Peasant Wars in Russia], *Voprosy istorii,* no. 2 (1956), pp. 69–79.

————, N. G. Sladkevich, and A. L. Fraiman. *"Istoricheskie zapiski"* [Historical Notes], *Voprosy istorii,* no. 10 (1956), pp. 141–151.

Mikeshin, N. P. "Iz istorii deiatelnosti kommunisticheskoi partii v period podgotovki i provedeniia oktiabrskoi revoliutsii" [From the History of the Activity of the Communist Party in the Period of Preparation and Carrying Out of the October Revolution], *Voprosy istorii,* no. 1 (1959), pp. 130–144.

Mints, I. I. "V. I. Lenin i pobeda vooruzhennogo vosstaniia v Petrograde" [V. I. Lenin and the Victory of the Armed Uprising in Petrograd], *Voprosy istorii KPSS,* no. 11 (1964), pp. 3–15.

———— "Pobeda sotsialisticheskoi revoliutsii na mestakh" [The Victory of the Socialist Revolution in the Provinces], *Istoriia SSSR,* no. 4 (1957), pp. 64–97.

———— "Stranitsy geroicheskoi borby ukrainskogo naroda za kommunizm" [Pages from the Heroic Struggle of the Ukrainian People for Communism], *Pravda,* July 25, 1962, pp. 2–3.

———— "Vtoraia revoliutsiia v Rossii" [The Second Revolution in Russia], *Pravda,* March 12, 1962, p. 4.

Mishin, M. N. "V. I. Lenin o vozmozhnosti mirnogo razvitiia revoliutsii v 1917 godu" [V. I. Lenin on the Possibility of World Development of Revolution in 1917], *Voprosy istorii,* no. 5 (1957), pp. 17–42.

"My ostavalis liudmi . . ." [We Remained People . . .], *Kazakhstanskaia pravda,* October 6, 1963, p. 4.

"Na obshchikh sobraniiakh otdelenii: V otdelenii istoricheskikh nauk" [In General Meetings of Departments: In the Departments of Historical Sciences], *Vestnik akademii nauk SSSR,* no. 12 (1961), pp. 83–85.

Naidenov, M. E. "Leninskaia periodizatsiia istorii velikoi oktiabrskoi sotsialisticheskoi revoliutsii" [The Leninist Periodization of the History of the Great October Socialist Revolution], *Istoriia SSSR,* no. 6 (1963), pp. 3–18.

———— "Sereznye nedostatki nuzhnoi knigi" [Serious Inadequacies of a New Book], *Kommunist,* no. 17 (1965), pp. 126–128.

———— "Sovetskaia istoricheskaia nauka nakanune XXII sezda KPSS" [Soviet Historical Science on the Eve of the Twenty-Second Congress of the CPSU], *Voprosy istorii,* no. 10 (1961), pp. 3–24.

———— "A. F. Tchmiga, *Ocherki po istorii kolkhoznogo dvizheniia na Ukraine (1921–1925),* Moscow, 1959," [A. F. Tchmiga, *Sketches from the History of the Kolkhoz Movement in the Ukraine (1921–1925),* Moscow, 1959] *Voprosy istorii,* no. 2 (1960), pp. 181–186.

Nechkina, M. "Monografiia: ee mesto v nauke i v izdatelskikh planakh" [Monographs: Their Place in Science and in Publishing Plans], *Kommunist,* no. 9 (1965), pp. 77–83.

————, Iu. Poliakov, and L. Cherepnin. "Nekotorye voprosy istorii sovetskoi istoricheskoi nauki" [Some Questions of History of Soviet Historical Science], *Kommunist,* no. 9 (1961), pp. 58–70.

"Nekotorye itogi raboty instituta istorii akademii nauk SSSR za 1959" [Some Work Goals of the Institute of History of the USSR Academy of Sciences for 1959], *Voprosy istorii,* no. 5 (1960), pp. 195–206.

Nemanov, I. N. "Subektivistsko-idealisticheskaia sushchnost vozzrenii T. Karleilia na istoriiu obshchestva" [The Subjectivist-Idealist Essence of T. Carlyle's Views on Social History], *Voprosy istorii*, no. 4 (1956), pp. 144–155.

Nenarokov, A. P., and A. I. Razgon. "Vsesoiuznaia sessiia istorikov v Odesse" [All-Union Session of Historians in Odessa], *Istoriia SSSR*, no. 2 (1966), pp. 233–235.

"Neopublikovannye documenty V. I. Lenina" [Unpublished Documents of V. I. Lenin], *Kommunist*, no. 9 (1956), pp. 15–26.

"Neotlozhnye zadachi istorikov KPSS" [Urgent Tasks of Historians of the CPSU], *Voprosy istorii KPSS*, no. 2 (1957), pp. 220–229.

Nikolaev, Ia. T. "O bestseremonnom obrashchenii s memuarami starykh bolshevikov" [Concerning the Unceremonious Handling of Memoirs of Old Bolsheviks], *Voprosy istorii*, no. 4 (1956), pp. 139–141.

"Novye dokumenty V. I. Lenina" [New Documents of V. I. Lenin], *Pravda*, April 22, 1956, p. 3.

"O metodologicheskikh voprosakh istoricheskoi nauki" [Concerning Methodological Questions in Historical Science], *Voprosy istorii*, no. 3 (1964), pp. 3–68.

"O profile i strukture zhurnala 'Voprosy istorii' " [Concerning the Profile and Structure of the Journal "Voprosy Istorii"], *Voprosy istorii*, no. 8 (1960), pp. 19–21.

"O sokhrannosti i obrabotke arkhivnykh dokumentov" [Concerning Preservation and Treatment of Archival Documents], *Partiinaia zhizn*, no. 15 (1966), p. 49.

"O state tov. E. Bugaeva" [Concerning the Article by Comrade E. Bugaev], *Voprosy istorii*, no. 7 (1956), pp. 215–222.

"O zhurnale 'Voprosy istorii' " [Concerning the Journal "Voprosy Istorii"], *Partiinaia zhizn*, no. 23 (1956), pp. 71–77.

"Ob izuchenii istorii istoricheskoi nauki" [Concerning the Study of the History of Historical Science], *Voprosy istorii*, no. 1 (1956), pp. 3–12.

"Ob ocherednom prieme v akademiiu obshchestvennykh nauk pri TsK KPSS" [Concerning the Regular Admission into the Academy of Social Sciences under the Central Committee of the CPSU], *Pravda*, March 21, 1964, p. 4.

"Ob uchastii starykh bolshevikov v rabote zhurnala" [Concerning Participation of Old Bolsheviks in the Work of the Journal], *Voprosy istorii KPSS*, no. 2 (1963), pp. 155–156.

"Obsuzhdenie nekotorykh voprosov istorii aviatsii" [Discussion of Several Questions on the History of Aviation], *Voprosy istorii*, no. 11 (1956), pp. 207–212.

Oskolkov, E. N., and L. A. Etenko. "Nauchnaia konferentsiia o voprosakh kollektivizatsii" [Scientific Conference on Questions of Collectivization], *Voprosy istorii KPSS*, no. 4 (1958), pp. 212–214.

"Osnovnye sily nauki — na glavnye napravleniia" [The Fundamental Strength of Science — in the Main Line], *Pravda*, July 5, 1963, p. 4.

"Ot akademii obshchestvennykh nauk pri TsK KPSS" [From the Academy of Social Sciences under the Central Committee of the CPSU], *Kommunist,* no. 1 (1956), p. 128.

"Ot redaktsii" [From the Editors], *Novyi mir,* no. 9 (1965), pp. 283–288.

"Otvetstvennost khudozhnika" [The Artist's Responsibility], *Pravda,* July 12, 1964, p. 4.

Ovsiankin, V. A., and V. V. Farsobin, "Obsuzhdenie uchebnogo posobiia 'Istoriia SSSR. Epokha sotsializma.' Leningrad, Sverdlovsk, Voronezh" [Discussion of the Textbook "History of the USSR. The Epoch of Socialism." Leningrad, Sverdlovsk, Voronezh], *Voprosy istorii,* no. 8 (1958), pp. 207–209.

Panfilova, A. A., V. Ia. Zevin, M. Ia. Pankratova, A. Ia. Velikanova, and S. P. Kiriukhin, "K voprosu o date vozvrashcheniia V. I. Lenina iz Finlandii v Petrograd oseniu 1917 g." [On the Question of the Date of the Return of V. I. Lenin from Finland to Petrograd in the Fall of 1917], *Voprosy istorii KPSS,* no. 12 (1963), pp. 70–75.

Pankratova, A. M. "K itogam X mezhdunarodnogo kongressa istorikov" [A Summary of the Tenth International Congress of Historians], *Voprosy istorii,* no. 5 (1956), pp. 3–16.

"Partorganizatsiia nauchno-issledovatelskogo instituta" [The Party Organization of the Scientific-Research Institute], *Partiinaia zhizn,* no. 16 (1963), pp. 32–39.

Paustovsky, K. "Srazhenie v tishine" [Battle in Silence], *Izvestiia,* October 28, 1962, p. 5.

Petropavlovsky, E. S. "Listovki kak istochnik dooktiabrskogo perioda istorii KPSS" [Pamphlets as Sources of the Pre-October Period of CPSU History], *Voprosy istorii KPSS,* no. 8 (1963), pp. 105–111.

Petrov, I. F. "Osveshchenie nekotorykh problem oktiabrskoi revoliutsii v istoriko-partiinoi literature" [An Interpretation of Some Problems of the October Revolution in Party History Literature], *Voprosy istorii KPSS,* no. 5 (1962), pp. 5–26.

Pikman, A. M. "O borbe kavkazskikh gortsev s tsarskimi kolonizatorami" [Concerning the Struggle of the Mountaineers of the Caucasus with Tsarist Colonizers], *Voprosy istorii,* no. 3 (1956), pp. 75–84.

"Pismo V. Smirnova" [Letter from V. Smirnov], *Pravda,* November 20, 1956, p. 2.

Pogudin, V. I. "Nekotorye voprosy istoriografii kollektivizatsii v SSSR" [Some Questions of the Historiography of Collectivization in the USSR], *Voprosy istorii,* no. 9 (1958), pp. 119–135.

——— "Problema likvidatsii kulachestva kak klassa v sovetskoi istoriografii" [The Problem of Liquidation of the Kulaks as a Class in Soviet Historiography], *Voprosy istorii,* no. 4 (1965), pp. 142–149.

Poliakov, Iu. A. "Kommunisticheskoe vospitanie i istoriia" [Communist Education and History], *Voprosy istorii,* no. 7 (1963), pp. 3–18.

Ponomarev, B. "Istoricheskuiu nauku i obrazovanie — na uroven zadach kommunisticheskogo stroitelstva" [Historical Science and Education — Abreast with the Tasks of Communist Construction], *Kommunist,* no. 1 (1963), pp. 10–35.

——— "Istoricheskii opyt KPSS — na sluzhbu kommunisticheskomu stroitelstvu" [The Historical Experience of the CPSU — in the Service of Communist Construction], *Voprosy istorii KPSS*, no. 4 (1960), pp. 11–36.

———. "Zadachi istoricheskoi nauki i podgotovka nauchnopedagogicheskikh kadrov v oblasti istorii" [The Tasks of Historical Science and Preparation of Scientific-Pedagogical Cadres in the Area of History], *Voprosy istorii*, no. 1 (1963), pp. 3–35.

Popova, E., and Iu. Sharapov. "Posle bolshogo soveta" [After the Great Council], *Izvestiia*, March 3, 1964, p. 5.

"Postanovlenie tsentralnogo komiteta KPSS: O preodolenii kulta lichnosti i ego posledstvii" [Resolution of the Central Committee of the CPSU: On Overcoming the Cult of Personality and Its Consequences], *Pravda*, July 2, 1956, pp. 1–2.

"Postanovlenie tsentralnogo komiteta partii: O zadachakh partiinoi propagandy v sovremennykh usloviiakh" [Resolution of the Central Committee of the Party: On Tasks of Party Propaganda in Contemporary Conditions], *Pravda*, January 10, 1960, pp. 1–2.

"Postanovlenie TsK KPSS 'O zadachakh partiinoi propagandy v sovremennykh usloviiakh' i istoricheskaia nauka" [Resolution of the Central Committee CPSU "On Tasks of Party Propaganda in Contemporary Conditions" and Historical Science], *Voprosy istorii*, no. 6 (1960), pp. 3–9.

"Preodolet otstavanie obshchestvennykh naukov" [Overcome the Lag in the Social Sciences], *Bakinskii rabochii*, March 28, 1956, p. 2.

"Proekt plana raboty zhurnala 'Voprosy istorii' na 1959–1965 gody" [Draft Work Plan of the Journal "Voprosy Istorii" for 1959–1965], *Voprosy istorii*, no. 8 (1959), pp. 207–213.

"Protokoly i rezoliutsii biuro TsK RSDRP (b) (mart 1917 g.)" [Protocols and Resolutions of the Bureau of the Central Committee of RSDLP (b) (March 1917)], *Voprosy istorii KPSS*, no. 3 (1962), pp. 134–157.

"Protokoly vserossiiskogo (martovskogo) soveshchaniia partiinykh rabotnikov (27 marta–2 aprelia 1917 g.)" [Protocols of the All-Russian (March) Meeting of Party Workers (27 March–2 April 1917)], *Voprosy istorii KPSS*, no. 6 (1962), pp. 130–152.

"Propagandist, narkom, istorik" [Propagandist, People's Commissar, Historian], *Izvestiia*, May 14, 1966, p. 4.

Puliakh, A. I. "Neuklonno razoblachat proiski sovremennogo revizionizma" [Unflinching Unmasking of the Intrigues of Contemporary Revisionism], *Voprosy istorii*, no. 9 (1958), pp. 195–208.

"Razvivat obshire opublikikovanie dokumentov po istorii sovetskogo obshchestva" [Develop Broader Publication of Documents on History of Soviet Society], *Istoricheskii arkhiv*, no. 1 (1956), pp. 3–8.

"Revoliutsionnaia teoriia osveshchaet nash put" [Revolutionary Theory Lights Our Path], *Pravda*, November 5, 1964, p. 2.

Romm, M. "Bolshaia tema iskusstva" [Great Theme of Art], *Pravda*, April 18, 1962, p. 6.

Rosliakov, A. A. "O metodike vyborochnogo obsledovaniia massovykh istochnikov po istorii partii" [Concerning a Method of Selective Investigation of Massive Sources on Party History], *Voprosy istorii KPSS,* no. 8 (1966), pp. 118–121.

Sarbei, V. G. "Vsesoiuznaia nauchnaia sessiia po probleme 'V. I. Lenin i istoricheskaia nauka' " [All-Union Scientific Session on the Problem "V. I. Lenin and Historical Science"], *Istoriia SSSR,* no. 6 (1965), pp. 210–214.

Sedov, K. I. "Obsuzhdenie knigi K. V. Guseva 'Krakh partii levykh eserov' " [Discussion of Book of K. V. Gusev "The Collapse of the Left Essar Party"], *Voprosy istorii,* no. 10 (1964), pp. 176–181.

Selunskaia, V. M. "Kooperativnyi plan V. I. Lenin v trudakh sovetskikh istorikov" [The Cooperative Plan of V. I. Lenin in the Works of Soviet Historians], *Voprosy istorii KPSS,* no. 9 (1964), pp. 107–116.

——— "O Kandidatskikh dissertatsiiakh po istorii kollektivizatsii selskogo khoziaistva v SSSR" [Concerning Candidates' Dissertations on the History of the Collectivization of Agriculture in the USSR], *Voprosy istorii,* no. 11 (1956), pp. 195–201.

Semenev, I. I. "Konferentsii chitatelei zhurnala 'Voprosy istorii' " [Conferences of Readers of the Journal "Voprosy Istorii"] *Voprosy istorii,* no. 7 (1959), pp. 201–207.

Semernin, P. V. "O likvidatsii kulachestva kak klassa" [Concerning the Liquidation of the Kulaks as a Class], *Voprosy istorii KPSS,* no. 4 (1958), pp. 72–85.

Sergovantsev, N. "Nesgebaemye dukhom" [The Unbending Spirit], *Oktiabr,* no. 10 (1963), pp. 212–215.

——— "Tragediia odinochestva i 'sploshnoi byt' " [The Tragedy of Loneliness and a "Routine Life"], *Oktiabr,* no. 4 (1963), pp. 198–207.

Shanshiev, G. "Velikaia vekha v istorii nashei partii" [A Great Landmark in the History of Our Party], *Partiinaia zhizn,* no. 14 (1958), pp. 24–27.

Shaumian, L. "Na rubezhe pervykh piatiletok" [At the Boundary of the First Five-Year Plan], *Pravda,* February 7, 1964, p. 2.

Sheliubsky, A. P. "Bolshevik, voin, uchenyi" [Bolshevik, Soldier, Scholar], *Voprosy istorii,* no. 3 (1966), pp. 167–170.

"Shire ispolzovat dokumentalnye bogatstva arkhivov" [Use More Widely the Documentary Riches of the Archives], *Partiinaia zhizn,* no. 4 (1965), pp. 43–46.

Shirikov, L. V. "O klassovoi sushchnosti 'legalnogo marksizma' " [Concerning the Class Nature of "Legal Marxism"], *Voprosy istorii KPSS,* no. 3 (1958), pp. 179–190.

Shitarev, G. I. "Partiia vsego naroda" [A Party of All the People], *Voprosy istorii,* no. 6 (1963), pp. 3–15.

Shkaratan, O. I. "Metodologicheskie aspekty izucheniia istorii sovetskogo rabochego klassa" [Methodological Aspects of the Study of the History of the Soviet Working Class], *Voprosy istorii,* no. 4 (1966), pp. 3–15.

Shtaerman, E. M. "O povtoriaemosti v istorii" [Concerning Repetition in History], *Voprosy istorii,* no. 7 (1965), pp. 3–20.

Shubkin, V. "O konkretnykh issledovaniiakh sotsialnykh protsessov" [Concerning Concrete Research into Social Processes], *Kommunist,* no. 3 (1965), pp. 48–57.

Shulgin, V. S. "Istoriograficheskaia konferentsiia v Moskovskom universitete" [Historiographical Conference at Moscow University], *Voprosy istorii,* no. 7 (1963), pp. 117–119.

Sidorenko, S. A. "Sborniki dokumentov po istorii borby za vlast sovetov v Sibiri" [Collections of Documents on the History of the Struggle for Soviet Power in Siberia], *Voprosy istorii,* no. 5 (1959), pp. 176–187.

Sidorov, N. K. "Konferentsiia chitatelei zhurnala˙ 'Voprosy istorii' v Leningrade" [Conference of Readers of the Journal "Voprosy Istorii" in Leningrad], *Voprosy istorii,* no. 8 (1959), pp. 183–190.

Simonov, Konstantin. "O proshlom vo imia budushchego" [Concerning the Past in the Name of the Future], *Izvestiia,* November 18, 1962, p. 5.

Sivkov, K. V., and S. V. Paparigopulo. "O vzgliadakh Fedora Krechetova" [Concerning the Views of Feodor Krechetov], *Voprosy istorii,* no. 3 (1956), pp. 121–128.

Sizov, Nikolai. "Trudnye gody" [Difficult Years], *Oktiabr,* no. 3 (1964), pp. 3–79; no. 4 (1964), pp. 33–118.

Skazkin, S. D., M. A. Barg, and V. M. Lavrovsky, "Istoriia i sovremennost" [History and Contemporary Life], *Izvestiia,* September 18, 1962, p. 3.

"Slavnaia godovshchina" [A Glorious Anniversary], *Voennii Vestnik,* no. 4 (1956), pp. 2–9.

Slutsky, Boris. "Stikhi razmykh let" [Poems of Various Years], *Literaturnaia gazeta,* November 24, 1962, p. 2.

Smirnov, A. S. "Ob otnoshenii bolshevikov k levym eseram v period podgotovki Oktiabrskoi revoliutsii [On the Relations of the Bolsheviks toward the Left Essars in the Period of Preparation for the October Revolution], *Voprosy istorii KPSS,* no. 2 (1966), pp. 12–14.

Smirnov, I. "Dostovernye fakty — osnova istoricheskogo issledovaniia" [Authenticated Facts — the Foundation of Historical Research], *Kommunist,* no. 3 (1962), pp. 75–83.

———— "Ob istochnikovedenii istorii KPSS" [On Source Work of CPSU History], *Voprosy istorii,* no. 4 (1956), pp. 194–201.

Snegov, A. V. "Neskolko stranits iz istorii partii (mart–nachalo aprelia 1917 g.)" [Several Pages from the History of the Party (March–Early April 1917)], *Voprosy istorii KPSS,* no. 2 (1963), pp. 15–30.

Sobolev, P. N. "Vopros o soiuze rabochego klassa i krestianstva v literature po istorii Oktiabrskoi revoliutsii" [The Question of the Union of the Working Class and the Peasantry in Literature on the History of the October Revolution], *Voprosy istorii,* no. 9 (1958), pp. 107–119.

Solzhenitsyn, A. "Odin den Ivana Denisovich" [One Day in the Life of Ivan Denisovich], *Novyi mir,* no. 11 (1962), pp. 8–74.

"Sovetskaia istoricheskaia nauka na novom etape razvitiia" [Soviet Historical Science at a New Stage of Development], *Voprosy istorii,* no. 8 (1960), pp. 3–18.

"Sovetskie istoriki obsuzhdaiut zadachi nauki v svete reshenii XXII sezda KPSS" [Soviet Historians Discuss the Tasks of Science in Light of the Decisions of the Twenty-Second Congress of the CPSU], *Voprosy istorii,* no. 1 (1962), pp. 3–13.

Sovokin, A. M. "O vozmozhnosti mirnogo razvitiia revoliutsii posle razgroma kornilovshchiny" [Concerning the Possibility of the Development of World Revolution after the Defeat of Kornilov], *Voprosy istorii KPSS,* no. 3 (1960), pp. 50–64.

———— "Rasshirennoe soveshchanie TsK RSDRP (b) 13–14 illulia 1917 goda" [The Enlarged Meeting of the Central Committee RSDLP (b) 13–14 July 1917], *Voprosy istorii KPSS,* no. 4 (1959), pp. 125–138.

"Spiski tem dissertatsii, zashchishchennykh v 1964 i 1965 gg. na soiskanie uchenoi stepeni kandidata istoricheskikh nauk po razdelu 'Istoriia kommunisticheskoi partii sovetskogo soiuza' " [Lists of Those Dissertations, Submitted in 1964 and 1965 in Fulfillment of the Degree of Candidate of Historical Science under the Category "History of the Communist Party of the Soviet Union"], *Voprosy istorii KPSS,* no. 4 (1966), pp. 151–158.

"Spisok tem dissertatsii na soiskani uchenoi stepeni doktora istoricheskikh nauk po razdelu 'Istoriia kommunisticheskoi partii sovetskogo soiuza,' zashchishchennykh na uchenykh sovetakh i utverzhdennykh vysshei attestatsionnoi komissiei v 1957–1966 gg" [List of Those Dissertations in Fulfillment of the Degree of Doctor of Historical Science under the Category "History of the Communist Party of the Soviet Union," Submitted to Scholarly Councils and Confirming Higher Attestation Commissions in 1957–1966], *Voprosy istorii KPSS,* no. 6 (1967), pp. 152–154.

"I. V. Stalin (k 80-letiiu so dnia rozhdeniia)" [J. V. Stalin (On the 80th Anniversary of His Birth)], *Kommunist,* no. 18 (1959), pp. 47–56.

Stishov, M. I., and D. K. Shelestov. "O nekotorykh voprosakh izuchenniia istorii borby za vlast sovetov v Sibiri v 1917–1900 gg." [Concerning Some Questions for Study of the History of the Struggle for Soviet Power in Siberia in 1917–1920], *Voprosy istorii,* no. 6 (1959), pp. 120–136.

"Strogo sobliudat leninskii printsip partiinosti istoricheskoi nauke" [Observe Strictly the Leninist Principle of Party Spirit in Historical Science], *Kommunist,* no. 4 (1957), pp. 17–29.

Struve, V., S. Okun, M. Viatkin, G. Morozov, N. Sergeeva, and Iu. Novikov, "Predmet nuzhnii vsem" [The Most Necessary Subject of All], *Izvestiia,* June 12, 1962, p. 3.

Surkov, E. "Yegor Trubnikov i ego vremia" [Yegor Trubnikov and His Times], *Izvestiia,* January 23, 1965, p. 3.

Sverdlova, K. T. "Deiatelnost Ia. M. Sverdlova v 1917" [The Activities of Ia. M. Sverdlov in 1917], *Voprosy istorii,* no. 6 (1956), pp. 3–15.

Tikhomirov, M. "Letopis nashei epokhi" [Annals of Our Time], *Izvestiia,* October 31, 1962, p. 5.

Titarenko, S. L. "O lozunge 'Vsia vlast sovetam' v period mirnogo razvitiia revoliutsii" [Concerning the Slogan "All Power to the Soviets" in the Period of the World Development of Revolution], *Voprosy istorii KPSS*, no. 3 (1958), pp. 169–178.

————— "V. I. Lenin o znachenii edinstva partii v borbe za pobedu sotsializma i kommunizma" [V. I. Lenin on the Significance of the Unity of the Party in the Struggle for Victory of Socialism and Communism], *Voprosy istorii KPSS*, no. 3 (1960), pp. 159–169.

Tretiakova, E. P. "Fevralskie sobytiia 1917 g. v. Moskve" [The February Events of 1917 in Moscow], *Voprosy istorii*, no. 3 (1957), pp. 72–84.

Trukan, G. A., and N. V. Rodin. "Sorokopiatiletie Oktiabrskogo vooruzhennogo vosstaniia" [The Forty-Fifth Anniversay of the October Armed Uprising], *Voprosy istorii KPSS*, no. 1 (1963), pp. 150–153.

Trapeznikov, S. P. "Sotsialisticheskaia kooperatsiia — leninskii put krestian k kommunizmu" [Socialist Cooperation — the Leninist Way to Communism for the Peasantry], *Voprosy istorii KPSS*, no. 1 (1962), pp. 44–62.

Turok, V. "Istorik i chitatel" [Historian and Reader], *Literaturnaia gazeta*, February 4, 1961, pp. 2–3.

Tvardovsky, A. "Po sluchaiu iubileia" [In Search of a Jubilee], *Novyi mir*, no. 1 (1965), pp. 3–18.

"Tvorit dlia naroda vo imia kommunizma" [Create for the People in the Name of Communism], *Pravda*, December 18, 1962, p. 1.

"V TsK, KPSS" [In the Central Committee, CPSU], *Voprosy istorii KPSS*, no. 1 (1963), pp. 3–5.

Vasiliev, Iu. B. "Nauchnaia sessiia po teoreticheskim probleman stroitelstva kommunizma v SSSR" [Scientific Session on the Theoretical Problems of Building Communism in the USSR], *Voprosy istorii*, no. 9 (1958), pp. 176–195.

Vasser, M. M. "Razgrom anarkho-sindikalistskogo uklona v partii" [The Defeat of the Anarchosyndicalist Deviation in the Party], *Voprosy istorii KPSS*, no. 3 (1962), pp. 62–78.

"Velikii podvig sovetskogo naroda" [Great Victory of the Soviet People], *Krasnaia zvezda*, May 9, 1956, p. 2.

Viatkin, R. V., and S. L. Tikhvinsky. "O nekotorykh voprosakh istoricheskoi nauki v KNR" [Concerning Some Questions of Historical Science in Chinese People's Republic], *Voprosy istorii*, no. 10 (1963), pp. 3–20.

Viltsan, M. A., N. A Ivnitsky, and Iu. A. Poliakov, "Nekotorye problemy istorii kollektivizatsii v. SSSR" [Some Problems of the History of Collectivization in the USSR], *Voprosy istorii*, no. 3 (1965), pp. 3–25.

"V Tsentralnom Komitete KPSS i Sovete Ministrov SSSR. O merakh po uluchsheniiu podgotovki spetsialistov i sovershenstvovaniiu rukovodstva vysshim i srednim spetsialnym obrazovaniem v strane" [In the Central Committee CPSU and USSR Council of Ministers. Concerning Measures for the Improvement of Preparation of Specialists and the Perfection of Leadership of Higher and Secondary Specialized Education in the Country], *Pravda*, September 9, 1966, pp. 1–2.

"Vo vsesoiuznom Sovete po koordinatsii nauchnoi razrabotki istorii KPSS" [In the All-Union Council for Coordination of Scientific Work on History of the CPSU], *Voprosy istorii KPSS,* no. 2 (1966), pp. 153–155.

"Voennye istoriki osuzhdaiut Stalina" [Military Historians Discuss Stalin], *Posev,* January 13, 1967, pp. 3–5.

Volin, M. S. "Vozniknovenie bolshevizma kak politicheskogo techeniia i politicheskoi partii" [The Origin of Bolshevism as a Political Tendency and as a Political Party], *Voprosy istorii,* no. 11 (1956), pp. 112–127.

Volobuiev, P. "Genialnaia programma sotsialisticheskoi revoliutsii" [The Genius Program of the Socialist Revolution], *Pravda,* April 17, 1967, pp. 2–3.

Voronovich, A. A., and D. A. Tolstykh. "Osveshchenie proletarskoi revoliutsii v Petrograde i Moskve v literature, vyshedshei k 40-letiiu sovetskoi vlasti" [The Illumination of the Proletarian Revolution in Petrograd and Moscow in Literature Published for the Fortieth Anniversary of Soviet Power], *Voprosy istorii,* no. 11 (1958), pp. 153–161.

"Vse sily nauki — stroitelstvu kommunizma" [All the Power of Science for the Building of Communism], *Pravda,* May 17, 1963, p. 2.

"Vsesoiuznoe soveshchanie istorikov" [All-Union Meeting of Historians], *Istoriia SSSR,* no. 1 (1963), pp. i–viii; no. 2 (1963), pp. 214–219.

"Vsesoiuznoe soveshchanie istorikov" [All-Union Meeting of Historians], *Pravda,* December 19, 1962, p. 4.

"Vsesoiuznoe soveshchanie istorikov" [All-Union Meeting of Historians], *Voprosy istorii,* no. 2 (1963), pp. 3–75.

"Vsesoiuznoe soveshchanie po voprosam ideologicheskoi raboty" [All-Union Meeting on the Question of Ideological Work], *Pravda,* December 26, 1961, p. 1.

Vuchetich, Yevgeny. "Vnesem iasnost" [For Clarity], *Izvestiia,* April 15, 1965, p. 3.

"Vzyskatelnost" [Exactingness], *Literaturnaia gazeta,* February 8, 1964, pp. 3–4.

Yeremenko, A. "Istoricheskaia pobeda pod Stalingradom" [The Historic Victory at Stalingrad], *Kommunist,* no. 1 (1958), pp. 26–40.

Yerikalov, E. F. "Osveshchenie Oktiabrskogo vooruzhennogo vosstaniia v Petrograde v istoriko-partinnoi literature 1956–1966 gg." [Illumination of the October Armed Uprising in Petrograd in Historical-Party Literature 1956–1966], *Voprosy istorii KPSS,* no. 5 (1966), pp. 121–127.

Yevgrafov, V. E. "Nekotorye voprosy taktiki partii v marte–nachale aprelia 1917 goda" [Some Questions of Tactics of the Party in March–Early April 1917], *Voprosy istorii KPSS,* no. 3 (1962), pp. 35–61.

——— "Ot Aprelskikh tezisov k Aprelskoi konferentsii" [From the April Theses to the April Conference], *Kommunist,* no. 7 (1957), pp. 12–26.

"Za glubokuiu nauchnuiu razrabotku istorii KPSS" [For Deep Scientific Work on History of the CPSU], *Voprosy istorii KPSS,* no. 4 (1958), pp. 3–23.

"Za leninskuiu partiinost v istoricheskoi nauke" [For Leninist Party Spirit in Historical Science], *Voprosy istorii,* no. 3 (1957), pp. 3–19.

"Za tvorcheskuiu razrabotku istorii KPSS" [For Creative Work on History of the CPSU], *Kommunist*, no. 10 (1956), pp. 14–26.

Zastenker, N. E. "Problemy istoricheskoi nauki v trudakh K. Marksa i F. Engelsa" [Problems of Historical Science in the Works of K. Marx and F. Engels], *Voprosy istorii*, no. 6 (1964), pp. 3–26.

Zemskov, A. A., and I. G. Mitrofanov. "O nekotorykh voprosakh izucheniia istorii KPSS v vyshei shkole" [Concerning Some Questions in the Study of History of the CPSU in the Higher School], *Voprosy istorii*, no. 10 (1959), pp. 137–151.

——— "O nekotorykh vorposakh nauchnoissledovatelskoi raboty v vuzakh po istorii KPSS" [Concerning Some Questions of Scientific-Research Work in Higher Educational Institutions on History of the CPSU], *Voprosy istorii KPSS*, no. 6 (1958), pp. 216–222.

Zhogin, N. V. "Ob izvrashcheniiakh vyshinskogo v teorii sovetskogo prava i praktike" [Concerning Distortions by Vyshinsky in the Theory and Practice of Soviet Law], *Sovetskoe gosudarstvo i pravo*, no. 3 (1965), pp. 22–31.

Zhukov, E. M. "XXII sezd KPSS i zadachi sovetskikh istorikov" [The Twenty-Second Congress of the CPSU and Tasks of Soviet Historians], *Voprosy istorii*, no. 12 (1961), pp. 3–13.

——— "Istoriia i sovremennost" [History and Contemporary Life], *Kommunist*, no. 11 (1959), pp. 41–51.

———, V. Trukhanovsky, and V. Shunkov. "Vysokaia otvetstvennost istorikov" [The High Responsibility of Historians], *Pravda*, January 30, 1966, p. 2.

Index

Academy of Sciences, 20, 37–38, 41, 43, 44, 45, 68, 265
and All-Union Conference (1962), 146
Department of Social Sciences, 37, 41, 113, 167
and de-Stalinization, 251
in elite structure, 52
Historical Sciences Section, 20, 37, 38, 68, 92, 114, 115, 122, 124, 134, 160
and Mints, 48
reorganization of (1963), 162
and Twenty-Second Party Congress, 122–123
volumes on collectivization, 236
Academy of Sciences Publishing House, 126, 147–148
Academy of Social Sciences, Central Committee, 41, 75
and All-Union Conference of Historians, 146
Department of History of the CPSU, 41, 207
and standards of dissertations, 85
Accuracy, 72
Activism, 2–3
among historians, 38, 134
in Lenin's historical theory, 5–6
Agitprop. See Department of Agitation and Propaganda
Agrarian policy, 22, 29, 205, 236. See also Collectivization of agriculture
"Agrarian Question in Russia at the End of the XIX Century" (Lenin), 20
Agriculture. See Collectivization of agriculture
Air Force Academy, Moscow, 48
Air Force Bulletin, 50–51
Aleksandrov, P., 237n
All-Union Conference of Historians (1962), 54, 72, 75, 145–161, 162, 188, 191, 266
affiliation of participants, 154–156
attitudes, 156–158
behavior and approach, 158–159
Bolshevik opposition to Stalin, 214
Burdzhalov's speech at, 154
concept of historian's duty, 152–153

dualism at, 147–148, 154, 159–160
group feeling at, 161
liberal-conservative polarization, 148–154
Session on History of the USSR, 154–155
sponsorship, 146
stenographic record, 148
and Stalin, 250–257
and training of party historians, 149–152
working structure, 147
All-Union Conference of Historians, Kiev (1965), 251
All-Union Conference on Measures to Improve the Training of Scientific-Pedagogical Cadres in the Historical Sciences, 146–161
All-Union Council on Coordination of Scientific Research on History of the CPSU, 40–41, 46–47
All-Union Society for the Dissemination of Political and Scientific Knowledge, 207
Aluf, I. A., 196–197
Anfilov, 256
Anikeev, V. V., 101
"Answer to Comrade Kolkhozniks, An" (Stalin), 228
Antiparty group, 86, 96–104, 132, 165
defeat of, 96, 106
denigration of, 97, 229
and intraparty opposition, 208–209, 218
in 1959 History of the CPSU, 108
and Twenty-First Party Congress, 120–121
and Twenty-Second Party Congress, 118–120, 122, 124
vilification of, 100, 103
Antiparty plot (June 1957), 96, 266
Apparat, 22, 38
April Theses, 111, 189–190
Archive Administration, Ministry of Foreign Affairs, 35, 45
Archives, CPSU, 38–41, 103
access to, 53, 76, 78, 102, 153, 198, 264–265
and All-Union Conference of Historians, 153, 154
criticism of impediments for use of, 79
publication of material, 57

Central Statistical Administration, 149
"Chairman, The," film, 164
Cheremnikh, N. A., 50–51
Chernyshevsky Institute for History, Philosophy and Literature, 47
Chief Archives Administration, 70, 71, 79
and *Sovetskii arkhiv*, 175
China, 130–131, 139. *See also* Sino-Soviet dispute
Chinese-Indian border conflict, 130–131
Civil War, 47, 48, 66, 68, 81, 217, 247
Class, 3, 5, 200
conflict, 23, 211
and the Left Essars, 203–204
Collected Works (Lenin), 19
Collective leadership. *See* Leadership
Collectivization of agriculture, 70, 143–144, 147, 165, 211, 220–238, 265. *See also* Kolkhoz
and denunciation of Stalin, 55
and kulaks, 231–234
and lower party organizations, 227, 231
and 1959 *History of the CPSU*, 107, 108, 110
rationalization of, 22
reasons for rewriting of, 235–236
rectification of errors, 106
reinterpretation of Stalin's role, 222, 224–230, 234
and revisionist historians, 81
volumes on, 236
"Colonel Starinov's Secret," 163
Cominform, 78
Commission on History of Historical Science, Institute of History of Academy of Sciences, 20
Commission on Ideology, Central Committee, 42, 46, 145
Commission on the History of the Party and the October Revolution, 39
Communist League, Yugoslavia, 101–102
Communist Party of the Soviet Union (CPSU), 14
and collectivization, 220–238 *passim*
infallibility of, 58, 63, 93, 186, 194, 268, 271

and intraparty opposition, 208–219
and Kirov murder, 24–26
and legitimation through historiography, 21, 271
as model for socialist parties, 31, 218–219
and party historian, 38–45
and prediction of changes in history, 24–26
provision for succession, 18
rationalization of policy, 22
stresses history as party science, 15
and Twentieth Congress, 62, 64, 75–76. *See also* Twentieth Party Congress
Competition, fostering of, 45, 46
Concentration camps, 22, 55, 165, 265
Consciousness, political, 8–10, 23
Conferences, professional, 72, 122–124, 146. *See also* Readers conferences
Controls, 152, 183, 185, 194
over arts, literature, etc., 96
dysfunctional aspects of, 49–58, 268–269
informal, 45–49
party, 38–45
rejection of terror as, 112
state, 23–26
Cooperatives, agricultural, 227
Correspondence divisions, 36
Council of Ministers, 35, 36, 37, 175
and archives, 78
and collectivization, 238
and degree requirements, 115–116
Criticism, literary, 162–163
Crypto-Stalinism, 162
Cuban crisis, 131
Cult of individual. *See* Personality cult
Cultural policy, 131, 136–137, 139–140
Czechoslovakia, 272, 274

Dachichev, Maior V., 177
Daniel, Iuly, 173. *See also* Siniavsky-Daniel trial
Daniels, Robert V., 212
Deborin, G. A., 176, 177
Decentralization, 183
economic, 78, 95
Decrees, official, 77, 78, 111, 115–116
Defense Ministry, 83

Degree requirements, 115–116
Demichev, P. N., 123
Denigration, 57, 68, 218
  of antiparty group, 97, 106
  of Khrushchev, 131–132, 166
  of Molotov, 229
  of Stalin, 18, 21, 54–55, 57, 61, 64–66, 83, 86, 93, 142, 145, 186, 189, 201, 227, 240, 245, 251, 264, 271
Department of Agitation and Propaganda, Party Secretariat, 14, 38, 42, 44, 55, 87, 160
  Union Republic Sector, 47, 116
Department of Culture and Science, Party Secretariat, 42–43, 44
Department of Social Sciences, Academy of Sciences, 37, 41, 45
  and reorganization of *Voprosy istorii*, 113
  Section on Historical Sciences, 20, 37, 38, 68, 92, 114, 115
Department of History of the CPSU, Academy of Social Sciences, 41, 207
Department of Social Studies of Ministry of Higher Education, Section on Party History, 36
Depersonalization, 259–260
Depolitization, 130
De-Stalinization, 52, 57, 97, 239–243.
  See also Personality cult; Stalin, J. V.
  debates concerning, 173–183 *passim*, 241–243, 250–257
  and *1959 History of the CPSU*, 105–107
  in literature, 137–138, 140
  and Nekrich affair, 253–256
  opposition to, 127–128, 130
  and provincials, 159–160
  and Stalin and the military, 246–250
  and Twenty-Second Party Congress, 122, 240
"Development of Capitalism in Russia" (Lenin), 20
Diakov, Boris, 163
Dinitas (Old Bolshevik), 216
Directorates, interlocking, 46–49
Dissertation, doctoral, 85, 126, 150, 224
"Dizzy with Success," Stalin (1930), 106, 143–144, 225, 228, 237
"Doctors' Plot," 65

Doctorates, 40, 41, 126
Documentation, 124, 126
Documents, 67, 84
  control over access to, 53–54, 58
  preservation and classification of, 38–39
  publication of archival, 70–72, 102
Donets soviet, 144
Druzhinin, N. M., 169
Dualism, historian's, 55, 72, 147–148, 154
Dvoinishnikov, M. A., 70–71
Dymshits, A., 136, 163

Eastern Europe, 86, 88, 83, 94
Economic system, 45, 185, 244–245
  determinism, 2–3
  development, 63
  reorganization, 89
Economists, 7–8, 98
Editors, 52–53
Education, 16, 30, 112
  of party historians, 41, 55–56, 134
Ehrenburg, Ilia, 136, 137, 171, 180
Eighth Party Congress, 75, 226
Ekshtein, A., 245
Eleventh International Congress of Historians, Stockholm, 114
Elites, 52–53, 185, 270, 273
Encyclopedias, 23
"Enemies" (Kazakevich), 134–135
Engels, Friedrich, 2
Erickson, John, 177
Essars (Socialist Revolutionaries), 70, 108, 109, 110, 185, 207, 271, 272
  class composition, 203
  and historians' views of Bolsheviks, 186, 197–202
Estonian Central Committee, 153
Exhibition of Works by Moscow Artists, Manezh, 139
Evolutionary socialism, 102

Facilities, research, 45, 46, 115
Fainsod, Merle, 69
"Family circles," 50–51, 268
February Revolution, 194–197
Fedoseev, P. N. 167–168, 254
Feuerbach, Ludwig, 3
Fiction, 171
Fifteenth Party Conference, 74
Fifteenth Party Congress, 209
Financial rewards, 45, 50

First Cossack Cavalry Corps, 48
First Five-Year Plan, 223, 259
Fofanova, M. V., 157, 180, 191–192
Foreign policy, 111, 112
Foreign works, 57, 73
Frantsev, Iu. P., 167–168, 199
Fringe benefits, 45

Gabay, Ilia, 273
Garmiza, V. V., 204
Georgia, 65
Germany, 6–7, 210
Gnedich, 256
Golikov, F. I., 256
Gomulka, Wladyslaw, 88
Gorodetsky, E. N., 201
Gosplan, 149
Gratification, material, 46
Great Patriotic War, 81, 107, 108.
  See also World War II
*Great Patriotic War of the Soviet
  Union, 1941–1945, A Short History,*
  252
Great Soviet Encyclopedia, 17
Grishin, V. V., 123
Gusev, K. V., 202–208
  monograph on Left Essars, 202–207
  pamphlet on non-Bolshevik parties,
  207

Haimson, Leopold, 9, 158
Handbooks, 23, 100
Hegelianism, 5
Hero, 72, 272
  military, 70, 246–250
Higher Certification Commission of
  Higher and Specialized Secondary
  Education, 115, 150n
Higher Party School, Central Com-
  mittee, 36, 47, 160
  Department of History of the USSR
  at, 48
Historians, 52, 69, 73, 77. *See also*
  Party historians
  and de-Stalinization debate, 250–257
  key issues for, 186–187
  Mikoyan's criticism of, 67–68
  tightening of policy toward, 76–92,
  94–95
  training of, 125
Historical materialism, 1–10
Historical Sciences Section, Academy

of Sciences, 20, 37, 38, 68, 92, 114,
  115, 122, 124, 134, 160
Historiography
  changes since 1956, 57
  and collectivization, 220
  of CPSU, 30–33
  debate over prose style in, 137
  didactic function, 23–24
  during Khrushchev years, 63–64, 66,
  96, 110, 120
  dysfunctional aspects of control
  system, 49–58, 268–269
  and fiction, 162–163
  formal functions of, 12–16
  future of, 270–276
  informal controls, 45–49
  informal functions of, 16–30
  and leadership, 239–260
  and Lenin's concepts of history, 13
  and Marxist-Leninist theory, 28–29
  in 1962, 130–161
  and political climate, 24–28
  as political weapon, 29–30
  -politics relationship, 76–77
  professionally oriented concerns, 116
  reemergence of, 73
  and revisionists, 80–92
  structure of, 34–58
  and Twentieth Party Congress, 63–
  76
  and Twenty-Second Party Congress,
  117–124
History
  definition of, 168–170, 173
  functions of, 12–33
  and the future, 270–276
  Lenin's view, 5–6
  Marx's view, 1–3
  official view (1956–1966), 15–16
  and the past, 263–269
  and politics, 61
  revisionism in, 76–89
  state controls, 23–26
History Institute. *See* Institute of
  History
History of Diplomacy, 48
*History of the Civil War in the
  U.S.S.R.,* 48
"History of Collectivization of Kursk
  Province Agriculture," 79
*History of the Communist Party of
  the Soviet Union,* 1959 edition, 24,
  104–111. *See also Short Course*

Journals, 37, 38, 44, 50, 72, 77, 96, 117
foundation of new (1957–1958), 76
and ideological training, 113–114
lack of, decried (1956), 69
and October Revolution, 198
July Days, 81, 105, 109, 199, 205

Kaganovich, Lazar, 65, 67, 88, 119, 153, 235
Kairov, V., 195
Kamenev, Lev B., 24, 25, 26, 99, 108, 188, 189, 252–253
and interparty opposition, 212–214
opposition to April Theses, 190
Karamzin, N. M., 73
Kasianenko, V. I., 245
Kazakevich, Em., 134–135
Kazakhstanskaia pravda, 163
Kazan University, 46
Keep, John, 194
Kerensky, Aleksandr, 29
Kharkhov, 187
Khrushchev, Nikita S., 14, 18, 21, 22, 46, 47, 93, 201, 264
abortive attempt to oust, 96
adoption of new party program, 122
and antiparty group, 96–104 *passim,* 118–122
and collective leadership, 62
and collectivization, 227, 229, 235
and Commission on Ideology, 42
concept of historiography, 63–64, 66, 96, 102, 151–152
concept of the party, 63
consolidation of power, 103–104
and CPSU history, 31–32, 105, 122, 186
and cultural policy, 131, 137, 139–141
denigration of, 131–133, 166
and de-Stalinization, 52, 64–66, 85, 137, 174, 240–241, 243
dispute over reforms, 133–134
dissemination of party line, 123
domestic policies, 111, 153
hero of 1959 *History of the CPSU,* 109, 144
and Hungarian crisis, 89, 94
and identification of party with masses, 74
image after ouster, 163–166

and investigation of Kirov murder, 24–26
and the military, 246–248
in 1962 *History of the CPSU,* 144–145
ouster, 120, 131–133, 165, 171, 202, 209, 229, 259, 271
and Pospelov, 160
and publication of Lenin Testament, 85
remonstrating Moscow youth, 89
revisions of history, 30–32, 96–97, 102, 239
revision of Stalin image, 27, 55, 83, 86, 111, 235, 239–240
and revitalization of party, 75
secret speech, 24, 52, 55, 61, 63–66, 86, 93, 96, 186, 240, 247, 264
seventieth birthday, 163
and theoretical issues, 28, 29
and Twentieth Party Congress, 61, 62–76
and Twenty-Second Party Congress, 118–119, 121, 124
and Twenty-Third Party Congress, 178, 179
and unauthorized historical revisions of 1956, 98
visits Britain, 78
Warsaw visit, 88
Khvostov, V. M., 125, 254
Kiev, 251
Special Military District, 144
University, 150
Kim, Iuli, 273
Kim, M. P., 126
Kirichenko, A. I., 108
Kirov, S. M., 24–26, 31
and 1959 *History of the CPSU,* 107
and 1962 *History of the CPSU,* 144
and Twenty-Second Party Congress, 120, 121
Kliuchevsky, V. O., 73
"Knowledge" propaganda society, 49
Kokovikhin (Old Bolshevik), 157
Kolkhoz (collective farm), 220–223, 237
and Kulaks, 232–233
and Old Bolsheviks, 230
in Ukraine, 227

Revisionists (*continued*)
and Twentieth Party Congress, 63–76
and *Voprosy istorii,* 73–74, 77, 79–80, 84–85
Revolution, and Bolsheviks, 187–197. *See also* February Revolution; 1905 Revolution; October Revolution
Right Essars, 205. *See also* Essars
Right Opportunists, 64, 224
Right Opposition, 29, 97, 208
in 1959 *History of the CPSU,* 108–109, 143, 209–212
in 1962 *History of the CPSU,* 209–212
Rodionov, P. A., his *Kollektivnost,* 257–259
Rosenberg, William G., 196n, 200
RSDLP (Russian Social Democratic Labor Party), 81, 101, 187, 192
RSFSR (Russian Soviet Federated Socialist Republic), 14, 49
Rykov, Aleksei I., 24, 25, 27, 108, 211
opposition to April Theses, 190
reexamination of, 29

Saburov, M. Z., 104
St. Petersburg, 195. *See also* Petrograd
Satiukov, P. A., 166
Savinchenko, N. V., 127
Schapiro, Leonard, 69
Scholarship, 15, 20–21, 23, 28, 91
and All-Union Conference of Historians (1962), 151–152, 162
on collectivization, 224
concern for improved (mid-fifties), 73–76
in 1960, 112, 115–117
and style, 118
and Twentieth Party Congress, 61, 68
and Twenty-Second Party Congress, 124, 129
and Twenty-Third Party Congress, 179
and *Voprosy istorii KPSS,* 142–143
Science Section, Department of Culture and Science of Party Secretariat 42–43
Scientific councils, 38
Scientific socialism, 169
Scientific-Technical Council, Ministry of Higher and Specialized Secondary Education, 36–37

Secret police administrative boards, abolition of, 78
Secretariat, CPSU, 42, 43, 109, 137
Selskaia zhizn, 230
Selunskaia, V. M., 224
Semernin, P. V., 232–233
Seventeenth Party Congress, 24–26, 29, 64, 109, 172
and collectivization, 223–224
Seventh (April) Party Conference (1917), 190, 204
Shapiro, Henry, 140
Sharapov, G. V., 237–238
Shelepin, A. N., 123
Shepilov, I. F., 50, 93
Sheverdalkin, P. R., 150–151
Sholokhov, M., 114, 178–179
Short Biography of J. V. Stalin, 225
Short Course [History of the Communist Party of the Soviet Union (Bolsheviks)], 15, 17, 20, 30, 52, 57, 63, 77, 153, 185, 264
chronicle of Kirov's murder, 24
and collectivization, 223, 225, 230
compared to 1959 *History,* 107, 112
criticism by *Voprosy istorii,* 80
and February Revolution, 194
and historians on eve of Twentieth Party Congress, 69
and intraparty opposition, 209–210
and Khrushchev, 66–67, 186
and Mensheviks and Essars, 197–198
and the military, 246
treatment of Stalin, 105–106, 251
treatment of Trotsky, 28–29, 215
Short History of the USSR, 172
Shotman, 192
Shtein, A. 215–216
Shteppa, Konstantin, 58
Shvernik, N. M., 119, 123
Sidorov, A. L., 71, 72, 154
"Silence" (Bondarev), 137
Simakov, B., 50
Simonov, Konstantin, 139
Siniavsky, Andrei, 173
Siniavsky-Daniel trial, 27, 134, 178, 179, 243, 272–273
Sino-Soviet dispute, 130–131, 134, 166, 178
Sixteenth Party Conference, 74
Sixth Party Congress, 211
Sketches of History of Historical Science in the USSR, 20

Strike of 1917, 194–195
Stuchebnikova, M. D., 71, 101, 128
Study groups, 38
Sturua, D. G., 174
Subjectivism, 244
Survey, 176, 252
Suslov, M. A., 43, 123
Sverdlov, Ia. M., 18

Teachers, 36, 53, 69, 112, 183
of party history, 149–150
Technicums (technical secondary schools), 36
Technology, 22
Telegyn, 176
Telpukhovsky, B. S., 152–153
Tenth International Congress of Historians, Rome (1955), 73
Tenth Party Congress (1921), 97
Terror, Stalinist, 49–50, 95
rejected as control, 112, 185, 268
Texts, popular, 23
Textbooks, 36, 64, 66, 67
mass-edition, 107
published in 1959, 104
Theoretical issues, 28
Third Congress of the Essars, 207
Thirteenth Party Congress, 85, 105
Tikhomirov, M., 137
Timoshenko, S. K., 247, 256
Titarenko, S. L., 117
Tomsky, Mikhail P., 24, 25, 108, 211
reexamination of, 29
Trade unions, 222
"Trade-union consciousness," 8
Tradition, history functioning as, 12–13
Training, historians, 134–135, 149–152
Transcaucasus, 84
Territory Committee of, 65
Trapeznikov, Sergei, 52
Travel abroad, party control of, 45
Trotsky, Leon, 16, 24, 27, 28, 81, 108, 239, 252
historical treatment of, 143, 215–217, 274
and intraparty opposition, 208, 209, 212, 214, 218
"Trotsky-Bukharin gang," 24, 211
Trotsky-Zinoviev opposition, 209–210
Trotskyites, 24, 26, 64, 97, 98, 211
and collectivization, 224
historical reexamination of, 28–29

Trud, 77
Trukhanovsky, V. G., 251
Tucker, Robert, 259–260
Tukhachevsky, Marshal Mikhail, 120, 247, 248
Turok, V., 118
Tvardovsky, Alexander, 138, 140, 170–171, 179
Twentieth Party Congress, 17, 28, 43, 58, 128, 132, 145, 173, 264
and antiparty group, 185–186
and collectivization, 220, 233
correction of mistakes of personality cult, 86, 119
and de-Stalinization, 240
focus on Lenin, 18, 21, 62, 64, 66, 68
Khrushchev's secret speech, 24, 52, 55, 61, 63–66, 86, 93, 96, 186, 240, 247, 264
and Lenin Testament, 85
liberalization following, 77–80, 82
Mikoyan's speech, 67–68, 240
Pankratova's speech, 68–69
and politics and historiography, 61–76
production of historiography following, 77
and publication of memoirs, 171
and rejuvenation of study of party history, 151
and sanction of criticism of Stalinist historiography, 74–75
and *Voprosy istorii*, 69–72, 73, 80
Twenty-First Party Congress, 96–104, 108, 120, 132
22 June 1941 (Nekrich), 54, 176, 177, 253
Twenty-Second Party Congress, 25, 32, 117–129, 132, 145, 154, 226
and antiparty group, 117–121
conferences following, 122–124
and de-Stalinization, 240, 247
and historians, 125
Khrushchev's remarks to, 120, 145, 166
Twenty-Third Party Congress, 14, 27, 58, 61, 133, 173–182, 273
avoidance of topic of Stalin, 133
and de-Stalinization, 242, 243
and 1966 debate on Stalin, 174–182 *passim*
and revision of *History of the CPSU*, 143–145